Swarms and Network Intelligence

Swarms and Network Intelligence

Editors

Yaniv Altshuler
Francisco Camara Pereira
Eli David

MDPI • Basel • Beijing • Wuhan • Barcelona • Belgrade • Manchester • Tokyo • Cluj • Tianjin

Editors
Yaniv Altshuler
Massachusetts Institute
of Technology
USA

Francisco Camara Pereira
Technical University of Denmark
Denmark

Eli David
Bar-Ilan University
Israel

Editorial Office
MDPI
St. Alban-Anlage 66
4052 Basel, Switzerland

This is a reprint of articles from the Special Issue published online in the open access journal *Entropy* (ISSN 1099-4300) (available at: https://www.mdpi.com/journal/entropy/special_issues/swarms_network_intelligence).

For citation purposes, cite each article independently as indicated on the article page online and as indicated below:

LastName, A.A.; LastName, B.B.; LastName, C.C. Article Title. *Journal Name* **Year**, *Volume Number*, Page Range.

ISBN 978-3-0365-7920-7 (Hbk)
ISBN 978-3-0365-7921-4 (PDF)

© 2023 by the authors. Articles in this book are Open Access and distributed under the Creative Commons Attribution (CC BY) license, which allows users to download, copy and build upon published articles, as long as the author and publisher are properly credited, which ensures maximum dissemination and a wider impact of our publications.
The book as a whole is distributed by MDPI under the terms and conditions of the Creative Commons license CC BY-NC-ND.

Contents

About the Editors vii

Yaniv Altshuler
Recent Developments in the Theory and Applicability of Swarm Search
Reprinted from: *Entropy* 2023, 25, 710, doi:10.3390/e25050710 1

Michael Amir, Noa Agmon and Alfred M. Bruckstein
A Locust-Inspired Model of Collective Marching on Rings
Reprinted from: *Entropy* 2022, 24, 918, doi:10.3390/e24070918 13

Yixiang Ren, Zhenhui Ye, Guanghua Song and Xiaohong Jiang
Space-Air-Ground Integrated Mobile Crowdsensing for Partially Observable Data Collection by Multi-Scale Convolutional Graph Reinforcement Learning
Reprinted from: *Entropy* 2022, 24, 638, doi:10.3390/e24050638 37

Christoph Manss, Isabel Kuehner and Dmitriy Shutin
Experimental Validation of Entropy-Driven Swarm Exploration under Sparsity Constraints with Sparse Bayesian Learning
Reprinted from: *Entropy* 2022, 24, 580, doi:10.3390/e24050580 57

Yining Chen, Guanghua Song, Zhenhui Ye and Xiaohong Jiang
Scalable and Transferable Reinforcement Learning for Multi-Agent Mixed Cooperative–Competitive Environments Based on Hierarchical Graph Attention
Reprinted from: *Entropy* 2022, 24, 563, doi:10.3390/e24040563 79

Itay Mosafi, Eli (Omid) David, Yaniv Altshuler and Nathan S. Netanyahu
DNN Intellectual Property Extraction Using Composite Data
Reprinted from: *Entropy* 2022, 24, 349, doi:10.3390/e24030349 95

Rafał Olszowski, Piotr Pięta, Sebastian Baran and Marcin Chmielowski
Organisational Structure and Created Values. Review of Methods of Studying Collective Intelligence in Policymaking
Reprinted from: *Entropy* 2021, 23, 1391, doi:10.3390/e23111391 113

Adi Farshteindiker and Rami Puzis
Leadership Hijacking in Docker Swarm and Its Consequences
Reprinted from: *Entropy* 2021, 23, 914, doi:10.3390/e23070914 149

Dhaval Adjodah, Yan Leng, Shi Kai Chong, P. M. Krafft, Esteban Moro and Alex Pentland
Accuracy-Risk Trade-Off Due to Social Learning in Crowd-Sourced Financial Predictions
Reprinted from: *Entropy* 2021, 23, 801, doi:10.3390/e23070801 167

Jacob Levy Abitbol and Alfredo J. Morales
Socioeconomic Patterns of Twitter User Activity
Reprinted from: *Entropy* 2021, 23, 780, doi:10.3390/e23060780 185

Anna V. Kalyuzhnaya, Nikolay O. Nikitin, Alexander Hvatov, Mikhail Maslyaev, Mikhail Yachmenkov and Alexander Boukhanovsky
Towards Generative Design of Computationally Efficient Mathematical Models with Evolutionary Learning
Reprinted from: *Entropy* 2021, 23, 28, doi:10.3390/e23010028 199

About the Editors

Yaniv Altshuler

Dr. Yaniv Altshuler is an MIT researcher, an experienced entrepreneur, and an industry-leading expert on artificial intelligence and data analysis. Altshuler's career has been dedicated to research and development in artificial intelligence. His approach is centered around the rigorous theoretical analysis of decentralized and scalable AI methods, aiming to discover new insights and opportunities for improving AI systems and their applications. Since receiving his PhD in Computer Science, Dr. Altshuler has worked with MIT Prof. Alex "Sandy" Pentland on the development of the new field of Social Physics. Yaniv has published over 70 scientific papers and filed 17 patents. His research has been covered by Harvard Business Review, the Financial Times, Communications of the ACM, IEEE Spectrum, and others. His book on Security and Privacy in Social Networks was published in 2012, followed by a second book on Swarms and Network Intelligence in 2017, and a third book on Applied Swarm Intelligence, to be published in 2023. Over the past decade, Dr. Altshuler has used his expertise to advise leading financial institutes and government agencies worldwide. He is committed to advancing the field of AI by creating systems that are ethical, robust, and accessible to all.

Francisco Camara Pereira

Francisco Camara Pereira is a Professor at the Technical University of Denmark (DTU), where he leads the Machine Learning for Smart Mobility department. His research is concerned with the methodological combination of machine learning and transport research, and some of his preferred applications generally relate to transportation research problems, demand modeling, behavior modeling, transport modeling, real-time traffic prediction, advanced data collection technologies, simulation metamodeling, and anomaly detection. He has been the Marie Curie Fellow twice (2011 and 2016) and has published over 50 articles in both the machine learning and transport research fields. Before joining DTU, he was a Senior Research Scientist with SMART/MIT (2011–2015) and Assistant Professor at the University of Coimbra (2005–2015).

Eli David

Dr. Eli David is a leading AI expert specializing in deep learning and evolutionary computation. He has published over fifty papers in leading artificial intelligence journals and conferences, mostly focusing on the applications of deep learning and genetic algorithms in various real-world domains. For the past fifteen years, he has been teaching courses on deep learning and evolutionary computation, in addition to supervising the research of graduate students in these fields. He has also served in numerous capacities, successfully designing, implementing, and leading deep-learning-based projects in real-world environments. Dr. David received the Best Paper Award in 2008 at the Genetic and Evolutionary Computation Conference, the Gold Award in the prestigious "Humies" Awards for Human-Competitive Results in 2014, and the Best Paper Award in 2016 at the International Conference on Artificial Neural Networks. He is the developer of Falcon, a grandmaster-level chess-playing program based on genetic algorithms and deep learning, which reached second place in the World Computer Chess Championship. Dr. David has co-founded several successful deep-learning-based companies, including Deep Instinct, recognized by Nvidia as the "Most Disruptive AI Startup"; DeepCube, which was acquired by Nano Dimension in early 2021; Marpai Health, which recently went public on Nasdaq; and Emporus Technologies, an AI-based fintech company. He also serves as an AI consultant to several Fortune 500 companies, and major venture capital and private equity firms. He is a frequently invited speaker to prestigious AI venues, and a member of Forbes Technology Council.

Editorial

Recent Developments in the Theory and Applicability of Swarm Search

Yaniv Altshuler

MIT Media Lab, Cambridge, MA 02139-4307, USA; yanival@media.mit.edu

Citation: Altshuler, Y. Recent Developments in the Theory and Applicability of Swarm Search. *Entropy* 2023, 25, 710. https://doi.org/10.3390/e25050710

Received: 12 March 2023
Revised: 17 April 2023
Accepted: 20 April 2023
Published: 25 April 2023

Copyright: © 2023 by the author. Licensee MDPI, Basel, Switzerland. This article is an open access article distributed under the terms and conditions of the Creative Commons Attribution (CC BY) license (https://creativecommons.org/licenses/by/4.0/).

1. Overview

Swarm intelligence (SI) is a collective behaviour exhibited by groups of simple agents, such as ants, bees, and birds, which can achieve complex tasks that would be difficult or impossible for a single individual. The collective behaviour of these organisms is characterized by decentralized decision making, self-organization, adaptive responses to environmental changes, and emergent properties that are not present in individual organisms. SI algorithms emulate these features to solve complex optimization, control, classification, clustering, routing, and prediction problems in diverse domains, such as engineering, robotics, biology, economics, social sciences, and humanities [1].

SI algorithms can be classified into two main categories: swarm-based algorithms and swarm-inspired algorithms [2]. Swarm-based algorithms involve the simulation of a population of individuals (agents) that interact with each other and their environment to achieve a collective goal. Examples of swarm-based algorithms include ant colony optimization (ACO) [3], particle swarm optimization (PSO) [4], artificial bee colony (ABC) [5], and firefly algorithm (FA) [6]. Swarm-inspired algorithms, on the other hand, extract specific mechanisms or principles from natural swarms and incorporate them into conventional optimization or machine learning algorithms. Examples of swarm-inspired algorithms include artificial immune systems (AIS) [7], bacterial foraging optimization (BFO) [8], and grey wolf optimizer (GWO) [9].

The success of SI algorithms is attributed to their ability to efficiently explore a large search space, converge to optimal or near-optimal solutions, and handle multiple objectives or constraints simultaneously. The collective intelligence of the swarm enables the sharing and exchange of information, the exploitation of promising regions, and the avoidance of suboptimal regions. Furthermore, the decentralized and distributed nature of the swarm allows for scalability, robustness, fault-tolerance, and adaptivity to dynamic or uncertain environments [10].

Despite their advantages, SI algorithms face several challenges and limitations, such as premature convergence, scalability issues, sensitivity to parameter settings, lack of theoretical guarantees, and difficulty in interpreting or explaining the obtained results. Researchers have proposed various approaches to overcome these challenges, such as hybridization with other optimization or machine learning techniques, dynamic adaptation of parameters, incorporation of domain knowledge, and rigorous analysis of convergence properties.

2. Applications

The advancement of technology has spurred a growing demand for multi-agent and swarm robotics solutions to address an ever-expanding range of complex and diverse challenges. With the emergence of distributed systems, it has become increasingly clear that relying solely on a single robot may not be the optimal approach for many application domains. Instead, teams of robots are being called upon to work in a coordinated and intelligent fashion, leveraging the power of redundancy to achieve greater efficiency and reliability.

The benefits of multi-agent systems stem from their ability to harness the collective intelligence of multiple entities, allowing them to tackle complex tasks that would be beyond the capability of a single robot. This approach provides the flexibility to scale up or down the number of robots based on the task at hand, while also providing redundancy to ensure mission success even in the face of individual robot failures. Moreover, multi-agent systems can leverage complementary skills and diverse perspectives, leading to improved problem-solving capabilities and more robust decision making.

Swarm robotics takes the concept of multi-agent systems a step further by drawing inspiration from the collective behaviour of natural swarms, such as ants, bees, and birds. Swarm robotics seeks to emulate the self-organizing and adaptive behaviour of swarms in order to create distributed systems that can operate autonomously and efficiently. By leveraging simple local interactions between agents, swarm robotics can achieve complex global behaviours, such as exploration, foraging, or assembly, without the need for centralized control or explicit communication. The emergence of swarm robotics opens up exciting new possibilities for applications in fields such as search and rescue, environmental monitoring, and precision agriculture.

In [11], a detailed description of swarm-robotics application domains is presented, demonstrating how large-scale decentralized systems of autonomous robotic agents can be significantly more effective than a single robot in many areas. However, when designing such systems it should be noted that simply increasing the number of robots assigned to a task does not necessarily improve the system's performance—multiple robots must intelligently cooperate to avoid disturbing each other's activity and achieve efficiency.

In nature, "simple-minded" animals such as ants, bees or birds cooperate to achieve common goals and exhibit amazing feats of collaborative work. It seems that these animals are "programmed" to interact locally in such a way that the desired global behaviour is likely to emerge even if some individuals of the colony die or fail to carry out their task for other reasons. A similar approach may be considered for coordinating a group of robots without a central supervisor, by using only local interactions between the robots. When this decentralized approach is used, much of the communication overhead (typical of centralized systems) is saved, the hardware of the robots can be fairly simple, and better modularity is achieved. A properly designed system should be readily scalable, achieving reliability through redundancy.

There are several key advantages to the use of such intelligent swarm robotics. First, such systems inherently enjoy the benefit of parallelism. In task-decomposable application domains, robot teams can accomplish a given task more quickly than a single robot, by dividing the task into sub-tasks and executing them concurrently. In certain cases, a single robot may simply be unable to accomplish the task on its own (e.g., to carry a large and heavy object).

Second, decentralized systems tend to be, by their very nature, much more robust than centralized systems (or systems comprised of a single but very complex unit). Generally speaking, a team of robots may provide a more robust solution by introducing redundancy, and by eliminating any single point of failure, while considering the alternative of using a single sophisticated robot, we should note that even the most complex and reliable robot may suffer an unexpected malfunction, which will prevent it from completing its task. When using a multi-agent system, on the other hand, even if a large number of the agents stop working for some reason, the entire group will often still be able to complete its task, although perhaps slower. For example, for exploring a hazardous region (such as a minefield or the surface of Mars), the benefit of redundancy and robustness offered by a multi-agent system is quite obvious, and it is in this context that Rodney Brooks wrote their famous "Fast, Cheap and Out of Control" report [12].

Another advantage of the decentralized swarm approach is the ability of dynamically reallocating sub-tasks between the swarm's units, thus adapting to unexpected changes in the environment. Furthermore, since the system is decentralized, it can respond relatively quickly to such changes, due to the benefit of locality—the ability to swiftly respond to changes without the need of notifying a hierarchical "chain of command". Note that as the swarm becomes larger, this advantage becomes increasingly important.

In addition to the ability of quick response to changes, the decentralized nature of such systems also improves their scalability. The scalability of multi-agent systems is derived from relying on the "emergence" of task completion by inherently low communication and computation overhead protocol implemented by the agents. As the tasks assigned nowadays to multi-agent-based systems become increasingly complex, so does the importance of the high scalability of the systems.

Finally, by using heterogeneous swarms, even more efficient systems could be designed, thanks to the utilization of different types of agents whose physical properties enable them to perform much more efficiently in certain special tasks.

Significant research effort has been invested during the last few years in the design and simulation of multi-agent robotics and intelligent swarm systems (see, e.g., [13–20]).

Such designs are often inspired by biology (see [21,22] for evolutionary algorithms, [23] or [24,25] for behaviour-based control models, [26–29] for flocking and dispersing models, [30–32] for predator–prey approaches and [33] for models inspired by the behaviour of cats), by physics [34–36], sociology [37–39], network theory [40–43] or by economics applications [44–54].

A swarm-based robotics system can generally be defined as a highly decentralized group of extremely simple robotic agents, with limited communication, computation and sensing abilities, designed and deployed to accomplish various tasks. Tasks that have been of particular interest to researchers in recent years include synergetic mission planning [55,56], emergency detection using decentralized sensing capabilities [57], patrolling [58–60], fault tolerance cooperation [61–63], network security [64], adversarial learning modelling [65], financial system modelling [66], crowd modelling [67], swarm control [68,69], human design of mission plans [70,71], role assignment [72–76], multi-robot path planning [59,77–81], traffic control [82–84], formation generation [85–88], formation keeping [89–91], exploration and mapping [45,92,93], target tracking [94,95], collaborative cleaning [96–99], control architecture for autonomous drones [100,101] and target search [102,103].

Unfortunately, the mathematical and geometrical theory of such multi-agent systems is far from being satisfactory, as pointed out in [104–107] and many other papers.

Our interest is focused on developing the mathematical tools necessary to design and analyse such systems. For example, in [108] it was shown that a number of agents can arrange themselves equidistantly in a row via a sequence of linear adjustments, based on a simple "local" interaction. The convergence of the configuration to the desired one is exponentially fast. A different way of cooperation between agents, inspired by the behaviour of ant colonies, is described in [109]. There it was proven that a sequence of ants engaged in deterministic chain pursuit will find the shortest (i.e., straight) path from the ant hill to the food source, using only local interactions. In [110], the behaviour of a group of agents on Z^2 was investigated, where each ant-like agent pursued their predecessor, according to a discrete biased-random-walk model of pursuit on the integer grid. The average paths of such a sequence of a(ge)nts engaged in a chain of probabilistic pursuit was shown to converge to the "straight line" between the origin and destination, and this too happens exponentially fast.

An in-depth analysis of the effect of certain geometric properties on the search efficiency of a collaborative swarm of autonomous drones appears in [111,112], whereas an example of a set of analytic complexity bounds for this problem can be found in [113,114]. A work that analysed the effect of a stochastic framework for the same problem is presented in [115].

3. Decentralized Intelligence Architectures and the Swarm Paradigm

A key principle in the notion of swarms, or multi-agent robotics, is the simplicity of the individual agent. The notion of "simplicity" here means that the agents should be significantly simpler than a "single sophisticated system", which can be constructed for the same purpose. As a result, the capabilities and the resources of such simple agents are assumed to be very limited, with respect to the following aspects:

- Memory resources—basic agents should be assumed to contain only $O(1)$ memory resources (i.e., the size of memory is independent of the size of the problem or the number of agents). This usually imposes many interesting limitations on the agents. For example, agents can remember only a limited history of their activities so far. Thus, protocols designed for agents with such limited memory resources are usually very simple and attempt to solve a given problem by relying on some (necessarily local) basic patterns arising in the environment. The task is completed by a repetition of these patterns by a large number of agents.
- Sensing capabilities—defined according to the specific nature of the problem. For example, for agents moving along a 100×100 grid, a reasonable sensing radius may be 3 or 4, but certainly not 40.
- Computational resources—although agents are assumed to employ only limited computational resources, a formal definition of this constraint is hard to define. In general, most of the time-polynomial algorithms may be used, provided that the amount of memory the agents have is sufficient.
- Communication is very limited—the issue of communication in multi-agent systems has been extensively studied in recent years. Distinctions between implicit and explicit communication are usually made, in which implicit communication occurs as a side effect of other actions, or "through the world" (see, for example [116]), whereas explicit communication is a specific act intended solely to convey information to other robots on the team. Explicit communication can be performed in several ways, such as a short-range point-to-point communication, a global broadcast, or by using some sort of distributed shared memory. Such memory is often referred to as a pheromone, used to convey small amounts of information between the agents [22,117–119]. This approach is inspired from the coordination and communication methods used by many social insects—studies on ants (e.g., [120,121]) show that the pheromone-based search strategies used by ants in foraging for food in unknown terrains tend to be very efficient. Additional information can be found in the relevant NASA survey, focusing on "intelligent swarms" comprised of multiple "stupid satellites" [122,123] or the following survey conducted by the US Naval Research Center [124]. The lack of explicit communication poses an challenge for various special configuration sets, such as symmetric environments [111].

In the spirit of designing a system which uses as simple agents as possible, we aspire that the agents will have as little communication capabilities as possible. With respect to the taxonomy of multi-agents discussed in [125], we would be interested in using agents of the types COM-NONE or if necessary COM-NEAR with respect to their communication distances, and BAND-MOTION, BAND-LOW or even BAND-NONE (if possible) with respect to their communication bandwidth. Therefore, although a certain amount of implicit communication can hardly be avoided (due to the simple fact that by changing the environment, the agents are constantly generating some kind of implicit information), explicit communication should be strongly limited or avoided altogether, in order to fit our paradigm (note that in many works in this field, this is not the case, and communication, as well as memory, resources, are often being used in order to create complex cooperative systems).

In summary, while designing intelligent swarm systems we must assume (and often even aspire for) having an available individual agents that are myopic, mute, senile and rather stupid.

4. Limitations

While SI has been applied successfully in many fields, including optimization, robotics, and networking, it also has limitations that need to be taken into account. One of the main limitations of SI is its sensitivity to initial conditions and parameter settings. Small changes in the initial configuration or the parameters of the swarm can have a significant impact on its behaviour and performance, leading to suboptimal solutions or even failure to converge. This problem is exacerbated in large-scale systems, where the number of variables and interactions increases exponentially [10].

Another limitation of SI is its vulnerability to perturbations and disturbances. Swarms are designed to be robust and resilient to individual failures or disruptions, but they can be vulnerable to systemic disturbances [126], such as environmental changes, resource depletion, or external attacks. These disturbances can destabilize the swarm beyond its self-emergent macroscopic regularities [127], leading to disintegration, divergence, or oscillations.

Real-world examples of these limitations include the behaviour of ant colonies in changing environments. Ants use SI to forage for food and build nests, but they are also susceptible to disturbances such as climate change or human intervention. In some cases, ant colonies can collapse or become maladapted to their environment due to the loss of critical resources or the disruption of communication channels.

Another limitation of SI is related to the trade-off between exploration and exploitation. Swarms can achieve impressive results by exploring a large search space and exploiting the best solutions found. However, there is a risk of getting stuck in local optima or suboptimal regions of the search space, especially if the swarm lacks diversity or adaptability [128]. In some cases, the swarm may require a balance between exploration and exploitation to achieve the best results, which can be challenging to achieve in practice [54].

A related limitation is the scalability of SI [113], while swarms can scale up to thousands or millions of agents, the computational and communication overheads can become prohibitive in large-scale systems. The swarm may require efficient algorithms for coordination, decision making, and resource allocation, which can be difficult to design and optimize. Such limitations may take form, for example, when SI is used in traffic management systems. Swarms of autonomous vehicles or drones can optimize traffic flow and reduce congestion by coordinating their movements and avoiding collisions [83]. However, these systems require efficient algorithms for path planning, decision making, and communication, as well as robust mechanisms for handling uncertainties and unexpected events.

Another example is the application of SI in social networks. Swarms of agents can learn and adapt to social dynamics by interacting with each other and with the environment [129]. However, these systems are also susceptible to biases, echo chambers, and polarization, which can affect their ability to explore new ideas and perspectives [130].

5. Swarm Search with Communication

While decentralized swarms have been the main focus of swarm-based search algorithms due to their scalability and simplicity, there are also several promising works that utilize synchronization or communication among the agents. These parallel swarms often employ communication to enhance the efficiency of the search process, such as parallel ant colony optimization, parallel particle swarm optimization, and other parallel metaheuristic approaches.

Parallel ant colony optimization (PACO) [131] is an example of a parallel swarm algorithm that utilizes communication among agents. PACO algorithms allow multiple agents to cooperate by sharing pheromone information, which helps in quickly identifying the optimal solution. For instance, PACO has been used in multi-robot coverage problems, where a group of robots are required to explore an unknown environment while avoiding collisions with each other. By sharing pheromone information, the robots can quickly converge to a solution, even in complex and large environments [22,132].

Parallel particle swarm optimization (PPSO) [133] is another example of a parallel swarm algorithm that uses communication among agents. PPSO is a variant of particle swarm optimization (PSO) that allows multiple agents to communicate with each other to improve the search process. For instance, PPSO has been used to optimize complex systems such as power grids, where the agents need to communicate to efficiently manage the distributed resources [134].

In cases where decentralized swarms may not be sufficient, parallel swarms can be beneficial. For example, in situations where the problem space is complex, the search space is vast, and the search process is time-critical, parallel swarm algorithms can offer a significant advantage over decentralized swarms. In such scenarios, communication among agents can help to identify the optimal solution more quickly and efficiently.

However, one of the main drawbacks of parallel swarm algorithms is the increased complexity of the communication mechanisms, which may require significant computational resources [135]. Additionally, communication can also lead to increased synchronization overhead, which may impact the scalability of the algorithm. Thus, in cases where the problem space is relatively simple, decentralized swarm algorithms may still be a better choice.

While decentralized swarms remain the main focus of swarm-based search algorithms, parallel swarm algorithms that utilize communication among agents have shown significant promise in enhancing the efficiency of the search process. These algorithms have been used in various applications, such as multi-robot coverage problems and power grid optimization. However, the increased complexity of communication mechanisms and synchronization overhead should also be considered when deciding on the appropriate approach for a given problem.

6. Opportunities and Future Research

SI and swarm systems have received considerable attention in recent years due to their potential for solving complex problems in various fields, such as robotics, optimization, and network design. As a result, there are numerous opportunities for future research in this area.

One promising avenue for future research is the development of more sophisticated algorithms and models for SI, while current approaches have shown promise, there is still much to be done in terms of improving the efficiency and adaptability of swarm systems [136]. Researchers may explore new ways to optimize the communication and coordination of swarm agents, or develop new approaches for dealing with the inherent uncertainty and complexity of real-world environments [137].

Another important area for future research is the application of SI to real-world problems, while there have been many successful demonstrations of swarm systems in laboratory settings, there is a need for more research on how to apply these systems to real-world problems. This may involve working with industry partners to develop practical solutions that can be deployed in the field, or collaborating with government agencies to address societal challenges such as disaster response or urban planning [138,139].

In addition to these technical challenges, there are also important ethical and social considerations to be addressed. As swarm systems become more advanced and pervasive, there may be concerns around issues such as privacy, security, and control. Researchers may need to explore new ways to address these concerns, such as developing transparent and accountable algorithms, or working with policymakers to establish appropriate regulations and standards [140].

Overall, there are numerous opportunities for future research in SI and swarm systems. By continuing to explore these systems and their potential applications, researchers can help to unlock new solutions to complex problems and contribute to the advancement of science and technology.

7. Conclusions

The study of SI has revealed that even seemingly simple organisms, such as ants, can exhibit complex and sophisticated collective behaviours when allowed to work together in a synergistic manner. This insight has led researchers to investigate the potential for applying this approach to artificial intelligence and robotics, with promising results.

In this Special Issue, a number of research studies have been presented that demonstrate the power of SI in producing complex and adaptive behaviours. By studying the ways in which ants and other social insects cooperate and communicate with one another, researchers have been able to develop algorithms and models that can be applied to a wide range of problems.

One of the key insights from these studies is that individual agents within a swarm do not necessarily need to be highly intelligent or even aware of the larger goals of the group. Rather, by following simple rules and responding to local cues, they can collectively produce intelligent and adaptive behaviours that emerge at the swarm level.

This approach has numerous potential applications, from optimizing traffic flow to coordinating the movements of swarms of robots in search and rescue operations. By harnessing the power of SI, researchers are exploring new ways to tackle complex problems that would be difficult or impossible for any individual agent to solve alone.

Overall, the research presented in this Special Issue provides compelling evidence that even the simplest organisms can exhibit remarkable intelligence and adaptability when working together in a synergistic manner. By taking inspiration from nature, researchers are opening up exciting new avenues for developing advanced technologies that can benefit society in countless ways.

In summary, let us cite a statement made by a scientist after watching an ant making his laborious way across a wind-and-wave-moulded beach [141]:

"An ant, viewed as a behaving system, is quite simple. The apparent complexity of its behavior over time is largely a reflection of the environment in which it finds itself."

Such a point of view, as well as the results of the research presented in this Special Issue, lead us to believe that even simple, ant-like beings, when allowed to synergically collaborate, can yield a complicated, adaptive and quite efficient macroscopic behaviour, in the intelligent swarm-level scope.

Funding: This research received no external funding.

Conflicts of Interest: The authors declare no conflict of interest.

References

1. Dorigo, M.; Birattari, M.; Blum, C.; Clerc, M.; Stützle, T. Swarm Intelligence. *Nature* **2019**, *406*, 39–42. [CrossRef]
2. Beni, G.; Wang, J. Swarm Intelligence in Cellular Robotic Systems. *Proc. IEEE* **2004**, *92*, 1227–1241. [CrossRef]
3. Dorigo, M.; Gambardella, L.M. Ant Colony System: A Cooperative Learning Approach to the Traveling Salesman Problem. *IEEE Trans. Evol. Comput.* **1996**, *1*, 53–66. [CrossRef]
4. Kennedy, J.; Eberhart, R. Particle Swarm Optimization. *Proc. IEEE Int. Conf. Neural Netw.* **1995**, *4*, 1942–1948. [CrossRef]
5. Karaboga, D.; Basturk, B. A Powerful and Efficient Algorithm for Numerical Function Optimization: Artificial Bee Colony (ABC) Algorithm. *J. Glob. Optim.* **2007**, *39*, 459–471. [CrossRef]
6. Yang, X.S. Firefly Algorithm, Stochastic Test Functions and Design Optimisation. *Int. J. -Bio-Inspired Comput.* **2010**, *2*, 78–84. [CrossRef]
7. Dasgupta, D.; González, F.A. Immunity-Based Systems: A Survey. *IEEE Trans. Evol. Comput.* **2002**, *6*, 252–267. [CrossRef]
8. Passino, K.M. Biomimicry of Bacterial Foraging for Distributed Optimization and Control. *IEEE Control Syst. Mag.* **2002**, *22*, 52–67. [CrossRef]
9. Mirjalili, S.; Mirjalili, S.M.; Lewis, A. Grey wolf optimizer. *Adv. Eng. Softw.* **2014**, *69*, 46–61. [CrossRef]
10. Altshuler, Y.; Pentland, A.; Bruckstein, A.M. *Swarms and Network Intelligence in Search*; Springer: Berlin/Heidelberg, Germany, 2018.
11. Dias, M.; Stentz, A. *A Market Approach to Multirobot Coordination*; Technical Report, CMU-RI - TR-01-26; Robotics Institute, Carnegie Mellon University: Pittsburgh, PA, USA, 2001.
12. Brooks, R.; Flynn, A. Fast, Cheap and out of Control, a Robot Invasion of the Solar System. *J. Br. Interplanet. Soc.* **1989**, *42*, 478–485.
13. Brambilla, M.; Ferrante, E.; Birattari, M.; Dorigo, M. Swarm robotics: A review from the swarm engineering perspective. *Swarm Intell.* **2013**, *7*, 1–41. [CrossRef]
14. Hinchey, M.G.; Sterritt, R.; Rouff, C. Swarms and swarm intelligence. *Computer* **2007**, *40*, 111–113. [CrossRef]
15. Mastellone, S.; Stipanovi, D.; Graunke, C.; Intlekofer, K.; Spong, M. Formation Control and Collision Avoidance for Multi-agent Non-holonomic Systems: Theory and Experiments. *Int. J. Robot. Res.* **2008**, *27*, 107–126. [CrossRef]

16. DeLoach, S.; Kumar, M. Chapter Multi-Agent Systems Engineering: An Overview and Case Study. In *Intelligence Integration in Distributed Knowledge Management*; Idea Group Inc. (IGI): Hershey, PA, USA, 2008; pp. 207–224.
17. Hettiarachchi, S.; Spears, W. Moving swarm formations through obstacle fields. In Proceedings of the International Conference on Artificial Intelligence, Las Vegas, NV, USA, 27–30 June 2005.
18. Chalkiadakis, G.; Markakis, E.; Boutilier, C. Coalition formation under uncertainty: Bargaining equilibria and the Bayesian core stability concept. In Proceedings of the AAMAS '07: Proceedings of the 6th International Joint Conference on Autonomous Agents and Multiagent Systems, Honolulu, HI, USA, 14–18 May 2007; ACM: New York, NY, USA, 2007; pp. 1–8.
19. Wagner, I.; Lindenbaum, M.; Bruckstein, A. Efficiently Searching a Graph by a Smell-Oriented Vertex Process. *Ann. Math. Artif. Intell.* **1998**, *24*, 211–223. [CrossRef]
20. Wagner, I.; Bruckstein, A. From Ants to A(ge)nts: A Special Issue on Ant—Robotics. *Ann. Math. Artif. Intell. Spec. Issue Ant Robot.* **2001**, *31*, 1–6. [CrossRef]
21. Klos, T.; van Ahee, G. Evolutionary dynamics for designing multi-period auctions. In Proceedings of the AAMAS '08: Proceedings of the 7th International Joint Conference on Autonomous Agents and Multiagent Systems, Estoril, Portugal, 12–16 May 2008; International Foundation for Autonomous Agents and Multiagent Systems: Richland, SC, USA, 2008; pp. 1589–1592.
22. Felner, A.; Shoshani, Y.; Altshuler, Y.; Bruckstein, A. Multi-agent Physical A* with Large Pheromones. *J. Auton. Agents Multi-Agent Syst.* **2006**, *12*, 3–34. [CrossRef]
23. Arkin, R.; Balch, T. AuRA: Principles and Practice in Review. *J. Exp. Theor. Artif. Intell.* **1997**, *9*, 175–188. [CrossRef]
24. Brooks, R. A Robust Layered Control System for a Mobile Robot. *IEEE J. Robot. Autom.* **1986**, *RA-2*, 14–23. [CrossRef]
25. Yang, X.S.; Cui, Z.; Xiao, R.; Gandomi, A.H.; Karamanoglu, M. *Swarm Intelligence and Bio-Inspired Computation: Theory and Applications*; Newnes, Elsevier: Amsterdam, The Netherlands 2013.
26. Su, H.; Wang, X.; Lin, Z. Flocking of Multi-Agents With a Virtual Leader. *IEEE Trans. Autom. Control* **2009**, *54*, 293–307. [CrossRef]
27. Ren, W.; Sorensena, N. Distributed coordination architecture for multi-robot formation control. *Robot. Auton. Syst.* **2008**, *56*, 324–333. [CrossRef]
28. Deneubourg, J.; Goss, S.; Sandini, G.; Ferrari, F.; Dario, P. Self-Organizing Collection and Transport of Objects in Unpredictable Environments. In Proceedings of the Japan-U.S.A. Symposium on Flexible Automation, Kyoto, Japan, 9–11 July 1990; pp. 1093–1098.
29. Drogoul, A.; Ferber, J. From Tom Thumb to the Dockers: Some Experiments With Foraging Robots. In Proceedings of the Second International Conference on Simulation of Adaptive Behavior, International Conference on Simulation of Adaptive Behavior, Honolulu, HI, USA, 7–11 December 1992; pp. 451–459. [Google Scholar]; pp. 451–459.
30. Weitzenfeld, A. A Prey Catching and Predator Avoidance Neural-Schema Architecture for Single and Multiple Robots. *J. Intell. Robot. Syst.* **2008**, *51*, 203–233. [CrossRef]
31. Benda, M.; Jagannathan, V.; Dodhiawalla, R. *On Optimal Cooperation of Knowledge Sources*; Technical Report BCS-G2010-28; Boeing AI Center: Arlington, VA, USA, 1985.
32. Haynes, T.; Sen, S. Evolving Behavioral Strategies in Predators and Prey. In *Adaptation and Learning in Multi-Agent Systems*; Lecture Notes in Computer Science; Springer: Berlin, Germany, 1986; Volume 1042, pp. 113–126.
33. Chu, S.C.; Tsai, P.W.; Pan, J.S. Cat swarm optimization. In Proceedings of the PRICAI 2006: Trends in Artificial Intelligence: 9th Pacific Rim International Conference on Artificial Intelligence, Guilin, China, 7–11 August 2006; Springer: Berlin/Heidelberg, Germany, 2006; Proceedings 9, pp. 854–858.
34. Hagelbäck, J.; Johansson, S. Demonstration of multi-agent potential fields in real-time strategy games. In Proceedings of the AAMAS '08: Proceedings of the 7th International Joint Conference on Autonomous Agents and Multiagent Systems, Estoril, Portugal, 12–16 May 2008; International Foundation for Autonomous Agents and Multiagent Systems: Richland, SC, USA, 2008; pp. 1687–1688.
35. Chevallier, D.; Payandeh, S. On Kinematic Geometry of Multi-Agent Manipulating System Based on the Contact Force Information. In Proceedings of the Sixth International Conference on Intelligent Autonomous Systems (IAS-6), Venice, Italy, 25–27 July 2000; pp. 188–195.
36. Kirkpatrick, S.; Schneider, J. How smart does an agent need to be? *Int. J. Mod. Phys.* **2005**, *C 16*, 139–155. [CrossRef]
37. Trajkovski, G.; Collins, S. *Handbook of Research on Agent-Based Societies: Social and Cultural Interactions*; Idea Group Inc. (IGI): Hershey, PA, USA, 2009.
38. Savarimuthu, S.; Purvis, M.; Purvis, M. *Tag Based Model for Knowledge Sharing in Agent Society*; Discussion Paper 2009/01; Department of Information Science, University of Otago: Dunedin, New Zealand, 2009.
39. Krafft, P.M.; Zheng, J.; Pan, W.; Della Penna, N.; Altshuler, Y.; Shmueli, E.; Tenenbaum, J.B.; Pentland, A. Human collective intelligence as distributed Bayesian inference. *arXiv* **2016**, arXiv:1608.01987.
40. Altshuler, Y.; Pentland, A.; Bekhor, S.; Shiftan, Y.; Bruckstein, A. Optimal Dynamic Coverage Infrastructure for Large-Scale Fleets of Reconnaissance UAVs. *arXiv* **2016**, arXiv:1611.05735.
41. Altshuler, Y.; Dolev, S.; Elovici, Y.; Aharony, N. TTLed Random Walks for Collaborative Monitoring. In Proceedings of the NetSciCom 2010 (Second International Workshop on Network Science for Communication Networks), San Diego, CA, USA, 19 March 2010.
42. Puzis, R.; Altshuler, Y.; Elovici, Y.; Bekhor, S.; Shiftan, Y.; Pentland, A. Augmented Betweenness Centrality for Environmentally-Aware Traffic Monitoring in Transportation Networks. *J. Intell. Transp. Syst.* **2013**, *17*, 91–105. [CrossRef]

43. Altshuler, Y.; Puzis, R.; Elovici, Y.; Bekhor, S.; Pentland, A.S. On the Rationality and Optimality of Transportation Networks Defense: A Network Centrality Approach. In *Securing Transportation Systems*; John Wiley & Sons, Inc.: Hoboken, NJ, USA, 2016; pp. 35–63.
44. Aknine, S.; Shehory, O. A Feasible and Practical Coalition Formation Mechanism Leveraging Compromise and Task Relationships. In Proceedings of the IEEE/WIC/ACM international conference on Intelligent Agent Technology, Hong Kong, China, 18–22 December 2006; pp. 436–439.
45. Sariel, S.; Balch, T. Real time auction based allocation of tasks for multi-robot exploration problem in dynamic environments. In Proceedings of the AAAI-05 Workshop on Integrating Planning into Scheduling, Pittsburgh, PA, USA, 9–10 July 2005; pp. 27–33.
46. Michael, N.; Zavlanos, M.; Kumar, V.; Pappas, G. Distributed multi-robot task assignment and formation control. In Proceedings of the IEEE International Conference on Robotics and Automation, 2008 (ICRA 2008), Pasadena, CA, USA, 19–23 May 2008; pp. 128–133.
47. Gerkey, B.; Mataric, M. Sold! Market Methods for Multi-Robot Control. *IEEE Trans. Robot. Autom. Spec. Issue Multi-Robot. Syst.* **2002**, *18*, 758–768. [CrossRef]
48. Liu, Y.Y.; Nacher, J.C.; Ochiai, T.; Martino, M.; Altshuler, Y. Prospect Theory for Online Financial Trading. *PLoS ONE* **2014**, *9*, e109458. [CrossRef]
49. Pan, W.; Altshuler, Y.; Pentland, A. Decoding social influence and the wisdom of the crowd in financial trading network. In Proceedings of the IEEE 2012 International Conference on Privacy, Security, Risk and Trust and 2012 International Conference on Social Computing (SocialCom), Amsterdam, The Netherlands, 3–5 September 2012; pp. 203–209.
50. Altshuler, Y.; Shmueli, E.; Zyskind, G.; Lederman, O.; Oliver, N.; Pentland, A. Campaign Optimization through Mobility Network Analysis. In *Geo-Intelligence and Visualization through Big Data Trends*; IGI Global: Hershey, PA, USA, 2015; pp. 33–74.
51. Altshuler, Y.; Shmueli, E.; Zyskind, G.; Lederman, O.; Oliver, N.; Pentland, A. Campaign Optimization Through Behavioral Modeling and Mobile Network Analysis. *IEEE Trans. Comput. Soc. Syst.* **2014**, *1*, 121–134. [CrossRef]
52. Wellman, M.; Wurman, P. Market-Aware Agents for a Multiagent World. *Robot. Auton. Syst.* **1998**, *24*, 115–125. [CrossRef]
53. Zlot, R.; Stentz, A.; Dias, M.; Thayer, S. Multi-Robot Exploration Controlled By A Market Economy. In Proceedings of the IEEE International Conference on Robotics and Automation, Washington, DC, USA, 11–15 May 2002.
54. Altshuler, Y.; Pentland, A.S.; Gordon, G. Social Behavior Bias and Knowledge Management Optimization. In *Social Computing, Behavioral-Cultural Modeling, and Prediction*; Springer: Berlin/Heidelberg, Germany, 2015; pp. 258–263.
55. Visser, U.; Ribeiro, F.; Ohashi, T.; Dellaert, F. *RoboCup 2007: Robot Soccer World Cup XI*; Lecture Notes in Computer Science; Springer: Berlin, Germany, 2008; Volume 5001.
56. Alami, R.; Fleury, S.; Herrb, M.; Ingrand, F.; Robert, F. Multi-Robot Cooperation in the Martha Project. *IEEE Robot. Autom. Mag.* **1998**, *5*, 36–47. [CrossRef]
57. Altshuler, Y.; Fire, M.; Shmueli, E.; Elovici, Y.; Bruckstein, A.; Pentland, A.S.; Lazer, D. The Social Amplifier—Reaction of Human Communities to Emergencies. *J. Stat. Phys.* **2013**, *152*, 399–418. [CrossRef]
58. Agmon, N.; Kraus, S.; Kaminka, G. Multi-robot perimeter patrol in adversarial settings. In Proceedings of the IEEE International Conference on Robotics and Automation (ICRA 2008), Pasadena, CA, USA, 19–23 May 2008; pp. 2339–2345.
59. Agmon, N.; Sadov, V.; Kaminka, G.; Kraus, S. The impact of adversarial knowledge on adversarial planning in perimeter patrol. In Proceedings of the AAMAS '08: Proceedings of the 7th International Joint Conference on Autonomous Agents and Multiagent Systems, Estoril, Portugal, 12–16 May 2008; International Foundation for Autonomous Agents and Multiagent Systems: Richland, SC, USA, 2008; pp. 55–62.
60. Altshuler, Y.; Wagner, I.; Yanovski, V.; Bruckstein, A. Multi-agent Cooperative Cleaning of Expanding Domains. *Int. J. Robot. Res.* **2010**, *30*, 1037–1071. [CrossRef]
61. Kraus, S.; Shehory, O.; Taase, G. Coalition formation with uncertain heterogeneous information. In Proceedings of the the Second International Joint Conference on Autonomous Agents and Multiagent Systems, Melbourne, Australia, 14–18 July 2003, pp. 1–8.
62. Work, H.; Chown, E.; Hermans, T.; Butterfield, J. Robust team-play in highly uncertain environments. In Proceedings of the AAMAS '08: Proceedings of the 7th international joint conference on Autonomous agents and multiagent systems, Estoril, Portugal, 12–16 May 2008; International Foundation for Autonomous Agents and Multiagent Systems: Richland, SC, USA, 2008; pp. 1199–1202.
63. Parker, L. ALLIANCE: An Architecture for Fault-Tolerant Multi-Robot Cooperation. *IEEE Trans. Robot. Autom.* **1998**, *14*, 220–240. [CrossRef]
64. Rehak, M.; Pechoucek, M.; Celeda, P.; Krmicek, V.; Grill, M.; Bartos, K. Multi-agent approach to network intrusion detection. In Proceedings of the AAMAS '08: Proceedings of the 7th International Joint Conference on Autonomous Agents and Multiagent Systems, Estoril, Portugal, 12–16 May 2008; International Foundation for Autonomous Agents and Multiagent Systems: Richland, SC, USA, 2008; pp. 1695–1696.
65. Mosafi, I.; David, E.; Altshuler, Y.; Netanyahu, N.S. DNN Intellectual Property Extraction Using Composite Data. *Entropy* **2022**, *24*, 349. [CrossRef] [PubMed]
66. Somin, S.; Altshuler, Y.; Gordon, G.; Pentland, A.; Shmueli, E. Network Dynamics of a financial ecosystem. *Sci. Rep.* **2020**, *10*, 1–10. [CrossRef]

67. Altshuler, Y.; Fire, M.; Aharony, N.; Elovici, Y.; Pentland, A. How Many Makes a Crowd? On the Correlation between Groups' Size and the Accuracy of Modeling. In Proceedings of the International Conference on Social Computing, Behavioral-Cultural Modeling and Prediction, College Park, MD, USA, 3–5 April 2012; Springer: Berlin/Heidelberg, Germany, 2012; pp. 43–52.
68. Connaughton, R.; Schermerhorn, P.; Scheutz, M. Physical parameter optimization in swarms of ultra-low complexity agents. In Proceedings of the AAMAS '08: Proceedings of the 7th international joint conference on Autonomous agents and multiagent systems, Estoril, Portugal, 12–16 May 2008; International Foundation for Autonomous Agents and Multiagent Systems: Richland, SC, USA, 2008; pp. 1631–1634.
69. Mataric, M. Interaction and Intelligent Behavior. Ph.D. Thesis, Massachusetts Institute of Technology, Cambridge, MA, USA, 1994.
70. Manisterski, E.; Lin, R.; Kraus, S. Understanding how people design trading agents over time. In Proceedings of the AAMAS '08: Proceedings of the 7th International Joint Conference on Autonomous Agents and Multiagent Systems, Estoril, Portugal, 12–16 May 2008; International Foundation for Autonomous Agents and Multiagent Systems: Richland, SC, USA, 2008; pp. 1593–1596.
71. MacKenzie, D.; Arkin, R.; Cameron, J. Multiagent Mission Specification and Execution. *Auton. Robot.* **1997**, *4*, 29–52. [CrossRef]
72. Chalkiadakis, G.; Boutilier, C. Sequential decision making in repeated coalition formation under uncertainty. In Proceedings of the 7th International Joint Conference on Autonomous Agents and Multiagent Systems, Estoril, Portugal, 12–16 May 2008; pp. 347–354.
73. Zheng, X.; Koenig, S. Reaction functions for task allocation to cooperative agents. In Proceedings of the 7th International Joint Conference on Autonomous Agents and Multiagent Systems, Estoril, Portugal, 12–16 May 2008; pp. 559–566.
74. Stone, P.; Veloso, M. Task Decomposition, Dynamic Role Assignment, and Low-Bandwidth Communication for Real-Time Strategic Teamwork. *Artif. Intell.* **1999**, *110*, 241–273. [CrossRef]
75. Candea, C.; Hu, H.; Iocchi, L.; Nardi, D.; Piaggio, M. Coordinating in Multi-Agent RoboCup Teams. *Robot. Auton. Syst.* **2001**, *36*, 67–86. [CrossRef]
76. Pagello, E.; D'Angelo, A.; Ferrari, C.; Polesel, R.; Rosati, R.; Speranzon, A. Emergent Behaviors of a Robot Team Performing Cooperative Tasks. *Adv. Robot.* **2002**, *17*, 3–19. [CrossRef]
77. Sawhney, R.; Krishna, K.; Srinathan, K.; Mohan, M. On reduced time fault tolerant paths for multiple UAVs covering a hostile terrain. In Proceedings of the AAMAS '08: Proceedings of the 7th International Joint Conference on Autonomous Agents and Multiagent Systems, Estoril, Portugal, 12–16 May 2008; International Foundation for Autonomous Agents and Multiagent Systems: Richland, SC, USA, 2008; pp. 1171–1174.
78. Svestka, P.; Overmars, M. Coordinated Path Planning for Multiple Robots. *Robot. Auton. Syst.* **1998**, *23*, 125–152. [CrossRef]
79. Lumelsky, V.; Harinarayan, K. Decentralized Motion Planning for Multiple Mobile Robots: The Cocktail Party Model. *Auton. Robot.* **1997**, *4*, 121–136. [CrossRef]
80. Ferrari, C.; Pagello, E.; Ota, J.; Arai, T. Multirobot Motion Coordination in Space and Time. *Robot. Auton. Syst.* **1998**, *25*, 219–229. [CrossRef]
81. Yamashita, A.; Fukuchi, M.; Ota, J.; Arai, T.; Asama, H. Motion Planning for Cooperative Transportation of a Large Object by Multiple Mobile Robots in a 3D Environment. In Proceedings of the IEEE International Conference on Robotics and Automation, San Francisco, CA, USA, 24–28 April 2000; pp. 3144–3151.
82. Agogino, A.; Tumer, K. Regulating air traffic flow with coupled agents. In Proceedings of the AAMAS '08: Proceedings of the 7th International Joint Conference on Autonomous Agents and Multiagent Systems, Estoril, Portugal, 12–16 May 2008; International Foundation for Autonomous Agents and Multiagent Systems: Richland, SC, USA, 2008; pp. 535–542.
83. Altshuler, T.; Altshuler, Y.; Katoshevski, R.; Shiftan, Y. Modeling and Prediction of Ride-Sharing Utilization Dynamics. *J. Adv. Transp.* **2019**, *2019*, 6125798. [CrossRef]
84. Premvuti, S.; Yuta, S. Consideration on the Cooperation of Multiple Autonomous Mobile Robots. In Proceedings of the IEEE International Workshop of Intelligent Robots and Systems, Ibaraki, Japan, 3–6 July 1990; pp. 59–63.
85. Bhatt, R.; Tang, C.; Krovi, V. Formation optimization for a fleet of wheeled mobile robots—A geometric approach. *Robot. Auton. Syst.* **2009**, *57*, 102–120. [CrossRef]
86. Arai, T.; Ogata, H.; Suzuki, T. Collision Avoidance Among Multiple Robots Using Virtual Impedance. In Proceedings of the IEEE/RSJ International Conference on Intelligent Robots and Systems, Tsukuba, Japan, 4–6 September 1989; pp. 479–485.
87. Fredslund, J.; Mataric, M. Robot Formations Using Only Local Sensing and Control. In Proceedings of the International Symposium on Computational Intelligence in Robotics and Automation (IEEE CIRA 2001), Banff, AB, Canada, 29 July–1 August 2001; pp. 308–313.
88. Gordon, N.; Wagner, I.; Bruckstein, A. Discrete Bee Dance Algorithms for Pattern Formation on a Grid. In Proceedings of the IEEE International Conference on Intelligent Agent Technology (IAT03), Halifax, NS, Canada, 13–17 October 2003; pp. 545–549.
89. Bendjilali, K.; Belkhouche, F.; Belkhouche, B. Robot formation modelling and control based on the relative kinematics equations. *Int. J. Robot. Autom.* **2009**, *24*, 79–88. [CrossRef]
90. Balch, T.; Arkin, R. Behavior-based Formation Control for Multi-robot Teams. *IEEE Trans. Robot. Autom.* **1998**, *14*, 926–939. [CrossRef]
91. Wang, P. Navigation Strategies for Multiple Autonomous Mobile Robots. In Proceedings of the IEEE/RSJ International Conference on Intelligent Robots and Systems (IROS), Ysukuba, Japan, 4–6 September 1989; pp. 486–493.
92. Pfingsthorn, M.; Slamet, B.; Visser, A. A Scalable Hybrid Multi-robot SLAM Method for Highly Detailed Maps. In *RoboCup 2007: Robot Soccer World Cup XI*; Lecture Notes in Computer Science; Springer: Berlin, Germany, 2008; Volume 5001, pp. 457–464.

93. Rekleitis, I.; Dudek, G.; Milios, E. Experiments in Free-Space Triangulation Using Cooperative Localization. In Proceedings of the IEEE/RSJ/GI International Conference on Intelligent Robots and Systems (IROS), Las Vegas, NV, USA, 27–31 October 2003.
94. Harmatia, I.; Skrzypczykb, K. Robot team coordination for target tracking using fuzzy logic controller in game theoretic framework. *Robot. Auton. Syst.* **2009**, *57*, 75–86. [CrossRef]
95. Parker, L.; Touzet, C. Multi-Robot Learning in a Cooperative Observation Task. *Distrib. Auton. Robot. Syst.* **2000**, *4*, 391–401.
96. Wagner, I.; Altshuler, Y.; Yanovski, V.; Bruckstein, A. Cooperative Cleaners: A Study in Ant Robotics. *Int. J. Robot. Res. (IJRR)* **2008**, *27*, 127–151. [CrossRef]
97. Altshuler, Y.; Bruckstein, A.; Wagner, I. Swarm Robotics for a Dynamic Cleaning Problem. In Proceedings of the IEEE Swarm Intelligence Symposium, Pasadena, CA, USA, 8–10 June 2005; pp. 209–216.
98. Altshuler, Y.; Yanovsky, V.; Wagner, I.; Bruckstein, A. Swarm intelligence—Searchers, cleaners and hunters. In *Swarm Intelligent Systems*; Springer: Berlin/Heidelberg, Germany, 2006; pp. 93–132.
99. Altshuler, Y.; Wagner, I.; Bruckstein, A. Collaborative Exploration in Grid Domains. In Proceedings of the Sixth International Conference on Informatics in Control, Automation and Robotics (ICINCO), Milan, Italy, 2–5 July 2009.
100. Altshuler, Y.; Yanovsky, V.; Wagner, I.; Bruckstein, A. The Cooperative Hunters—Efficient Cooperative Search for Smart Targets Using UAV Swarms. In Proceedings of the Second International Conference on Informatics in Control, Automation and Robotics (ICINCO), the First International Workshop on Multi-Agent Robotic Systems (MARS), Barcelona, Spain, 14–17 September 2005; pp. 165–170.
101. Altshuler, Y.; Yanovsky, V.; Bruckstein, A.; Wagner, I. Efficient Cooperative Search of Smart Targets Using UAV Swarms. *Robotica* **2008**, *26*, 551–557. [CrossRef]
102. Hollinger, G.; Singh, S.; Djugash, J.; Kehagias, A. Efficient Multi-robot Search for a Moving Target. *Int. J. Robot. Res.* **2009**, *28*, 201–219. [CrossRef]
103. LaValle, S.; Lin, D.; Guibas, L.; Latombe, J.; Motwani, R. Finding an Unpredictable Target in a Workspace with Obstacles. In Proceedings of the 1997 IEEE International Conference on Robotics and Automation (ICRA-97), Albuquerque, NM, USA, 25 April 1997; pp. 737–742.
104. Efraim, A.; Peleg, D. Distributed Algorithms for Partitioning a Swarm of Autonomous Mobile Robots. *Struct. Inf. Commun. Complexity, Lect. Notes Comput. Sci.* **2007**, *4474*, 180–194.
105. Olfati-Saber, R. Flocking for Multi-Agent Dynamic Systems: Algorithms and Theory. *IEEE Trans. Autom. Control* **2006**, *51*, 401–420. [CrossRef]
106. Bonabeau, E.; Dorigo, M.; Theraulaz, G. *Swarm Intelligence: From Natural to Artificial Systems*; Oxford University Press: New York, NY, USA, 1999.
107. Beni, G.; Wang, J. Theoretical Problems for the Realization of Distributed Robotic Systems. In Proceedings of the IEEE Internal Conference on Robotics and Automation, Sacramento, CA, USA, 9–11 April 1991; pp. 1914–1920.
108. Wagner, I.; Bruckstein, A. *Row Straightening via Local Interactions*; Technical report CIS-9406; Center for Intelligent Systems, Technion: Haifa, Israel, 1994.
109. Bruckstein, A. Why the Ant Trails Look So Straight and Nice. *Math. Intell.* **1993**, *15*, 59–62. [CrossRef]
110. Bruckstein, A.; Mallows, C.; Wagner, I. Probabilistic Pursuits on the Integer Grid. *Am. Math. Mon.* **1997**, *104*, 323–343. [CrossRef]
111. Altshuler, Y.; Wagner, I.; Bruckstein, A. On Swarm Optimality In Dynamic And Symmetric Environments. *Economics* **2008**, *7*, 11.
112. Altshuler, Y.; Wagner, I.; Bruckstein, A. Shape Factor's Effect on a Dynamic Cleaners Swarm. In Proceedings of the Third International Conference on Informatics in Control, Automation and Robotics (ICINCO), the Second International Workshop on Multi-Agent Robotic Systems (MARS), Setúbal, Portugal, 1–5 August 2006; pp. 13–21.
113. Altshuler, Y.; Bruckstein, A.M. Static and expanding grid coverage with ant robots: Complexity results. *Theor. Comput. Sci.* **2011**, *412*, 4661–4674. [CrossRef]
114. Altshuler, Y.; Bruckstein, A.M. The Complexity of Grid Coverage by Swarm Robotics. In Proceedings of the ANTS 2010, LNCS, Nancy, France, 19–23 July 2010; pp. 536–543.
115. Regev, E.; Altshuler, Y.; Bruckstein, A.M. The cooperative cleaners problem in stochastic dynamic environments. *arXiv* **2012**, arXiv:1201.6322.
116. Pagello, E.; D'Angelo, A.; Montesello, F.; Garelli, F.; Ferrari, C. Cooperative Behaviors in Multi-Robot Systems Through Implicit Communication. *Robot. Auton. Syst.* **1999**, *29*, 65–77. [CrossRef]
117. Yanovski, V.; Wagner, I.; Bruckstein, A. A distributed ant algorithm for efficiently patrolling a network. *Algorithmica* **2003**, *37*, 165–186. [CrossRef]
118. Wagner, I.; Bruckstein, A. ANTS: Agents, networks, trees and subgraphs. *Future Gener. Comput. Syst. J.* **2000**, *16*, 915–926. [CrossRef]
119. Yanovski, V.; Wagner, I.; Bruckstein, A. Vertex-ants-walk: A robust method for efficient exploration of faulty graphs. *Ann. Math. Artif. Intell.* **2001**, *31*, 99–112. [CrossRef]
120. Adler, F.; Gordon, D. Information collection and spread by networks of partolling agents. *Am. Nat.* **1992**, *140*, 373–400. [CrossRef]
121. Gordon, D. The expandable network of ant exploration. *Anim. Behav.* **1995**, *50*, 372–378. [CrossRef]
122. Rouff, C.A.; Truszkowski, W.F.; Rash, J.; Hinchey, M. *A Survey of Formal Methods for Intelligent Swarms*; NASA Goddard Space Flight Center: Greenbelt, MD, USA, 2005.

123. Rouff, C.; Truszkowski, W.; Rash, J.; Hinchey, M. Formal approaches to intelligent swarms. In Proceedings of the 28th Annual NASA Goddard Software Engineering Workshop, Greenbelt, MD, USA, 3–4 December 2003; pp. 51–57.
124. Schultz, A.C.; Parker, L.E. *Multi-Robot Systems: From Swarms to Intelligent Automata: Proceedings from the 2002 NRL Workshop on Multi-robot Systems*; Springer Science & Business Media: Berlin/Heidelberg, Germany, 2013.
125. Dudek, G.; Jenkin, M.; Milios, E.; Wilkes, D. A taxonomy for multi-agent robotics. *Auton. Robot. J.* **1996**, *3*, 375–397. [CrossRef]
126. Somin, S.; Altshuler, Y.; 'Sandy'Pentland, A.; Shmueli, E. Beyond preferential attachment: Falling of stars and survival of superstars. *R. Soc. Open Sci.* **2022**, *9*, 220899. [CrossRef] [PubMed]
127. Somin, S.; Altshuler, Y.; Shmueli, E. Remaining popular: Power-law regularities in network dynamics. *EPJ Data Sci.* **2022**, *11*, 61. [CrossRef]
128. Lazer, D.; Friedman, A. The network structure of exploration and exploitation. *Adm. Sci. Q.* **2007**, *52*, 667–694. [CrossRef]
129. Altshuler, Y.; Elovici, Y.; Cremers, A.B.; Aharony, N.; Pentland, A. *Security and Privacy in Social Networks*; Springer Science & Business Media: Berlin/Heidelberg, Germany, 2012.
130. Somin, S.; Gordon, G.; Altshuler, Y. Social Signals in the Ethereum Trading Network. *arXiv* **2018**, arXiv:1805.12097.
131. Pedemonte, M.; Nesmachnow, S.; Cancela, H. A survey on parallel ant colony optimization. *Appl. Soft Comput.* **2011**, *11*, 5181–5197. [CrossRef]
132. Felner, A.; Stern, R.; Ben-Yair, A.; Kraus, S.; Netanyahu, N. PHA*: Finding the Shortest Path with A* in Unknown Physical Environments. *J. Artif. Intell. Res.* **2004**, *21*, 631–679. [CrossRef]
133. Lalwani, S.; Sharma, H.; Satapathy, S.C.; Deep, K.; Bansal, J.C. A survey on parallel particle swarm optimization algorithms. *Arab. J. Sci. Eng.* **2019**, *44*, 2899–2923. [CrossRef]
134. Gies, D.; Rahmat-Samii, Y. Reconfigurable array design using parallel particle swarm optimization. In Proceedings of the IEEE Antennas and Propagation Society International Symposium. Digest. Held in conjunction with: USNC/CNC/URSI North American Radio Sci. Meeting (Cat. No. 03CH37450), Columbus, OH, USA, 22–27 June 2003; Volume 1, pp. 177–180.
135. Chu, S.C.; Roddick, J.F.; Pan, J.S. A parallel particle swarm optimization algorithm with communication strategies. *J. Inf. Sci. Eng* **2005**, *21*, 809–818.
136. Dorigo, M.; Theraulaz, G.; Trianni, V. Swarm robotics: Past, present, and future [point of view]. *Proc. IEEE* **2021**, *109*, 1152–1165. [CrossRef]
137. Dorigo, M.; Theraulaz, G.; Trianni, V. Reflections on the future of swarm robotics. *Sci. Robot.* **2020**, *5*, eabe4385. [CrossRef] [PubMed]
138. Winfield, A.F.; Blum, C.; Liu, W. Towards an ethical robot: Internal models, consequences and ethical action selection. In Proceedings of the Advances in Autonomous Robotics Systems: 15th Annual Conference, TAROS 2014, Birmingham, UK, 1–3 September 2014; Springer: Berlin/Heidelberg, Germany, 2014; Proceedings 15, pp. 85–96.
139. Yang, G.Z.; Bellingham, J.; Dupont, P.E.; Fischer, P.; Floridi, L.; Full, R.; Jacobstein, N.; Kumar, V.; McNutt, M.; Merrifield, R.; et al. The grand challenges of science robotics. *Sci. Robot.* **2018**, *3*, eaar7650. [CrossRef]
140. Decker, M. Caregiving robots and ethical reflection: The perspective of interdisciplinary technology assessment. *AI Soc.* **2008**, *22*, 315–330. [CrossRef]
141. Simon, H. *The Sciences of the Artificial*, 2nd ed.; MIT Press: Cambridge, MA, USA, 1981.

Disclaimer/Publisher's Note: The statements, opinions and data contained in all publications are solely those of the individual author(s) and contributor(s) and not of MDPI and/or the editor(s). MDPI and/or the editor(s) disclaim responsibility for any injury to people or property resulting from any ideas, methods, instructions or products referred to in the content.

Article

A Locust-Inspired Model of Collective Marching on Rings

Michael Amir [1,*], Noa Agmon [2] and Alfred M. Bruckstein [1]

[1] Department of Computer Science, Technion—Israel Institute of Technology, Haifa 3200003, Israel; freddy@technion.ac.il
[2] Department of Computer Science, Bar-Ilan University, Ramat Gan 5290002, Israel; agmon@cs.biu.ac.il
* Correspondence: ammicha3@technion.ac.il

Abstract: We study the collective motion of autonomous mobile agents in a ringlike environment. The agents' dynamics are inspired by known laboratory experiments on the dynamics of locust swarms. In these experiments, locusts placed at arbitrary locations and initial orientations on a ring-shaped arena are observed to eventually all march in the same direction. In this work we ask whether, and how fast, a similar phenomenon occurs in a stochastic swarm of simple locust-inspired agents. The agents are randomly initiated as marching either clockwise or counterclockwise on a discretized, wide ring-shaped region, which we subdivide into k concentric tracks of length n. Collisions cause agents to change their direction of motion. To avoid this, agents may decide to switch tracks to merge with platoons of agents marching in their direction. We prove that such agents must eventually converge to a local consensus about their direction of motion, meaning that all agents on each narrow track must eventually march in the same direction. We give asymptotic bounds for the expected time it takes for such convergence or "stabilization" to occur, which depends on the number of agents, the length of the tracks, and the number of tracks. We show that when agents also have a small probability of "erratic", random track-jumping behavior, a global consensus on the direction of motion across all tracks will eventually be reached. Finally, we verify our theoretical findings in numerical simulations.

Keywords: mobile robotics; swarms; crowd dynamics; natural algorithms; locusts

1. Introduction

Birds, locusts, human crowds, and swarm-robotic systems exhibit interesting collective motion patterns. The underlying autonomous agent behaviors from which these patterns emerge have attracted a great deal of academic interest over the last several decades [1–6]. In particular, the formal analysis of models of swarm dynamics has led to varied and deep mathematical results [7–10]. Rigorous mathematical results are necessary for understanding swarms and for designing predictable and provably effective swarm-robotic systems. However, multi-agent swarms have a uniquely complex and "mesoscopic" nature [11], and relatively few standard techniques for the analysis of such systems have been established. Consequently, the analysis of new models of swarm dynamics is important for advancing our understanding of the subject.

In this work, we study the dynamics of "locust-like" agents moving on a discrete ringlike surface. The model we study is inspired by the following well-documented experiment [12]. Place many locusts on a ringlike arena at random positions and orientations. They start to move around and bump into the arena's walls and into each other, and as they do, remarkably, over time, they begin to collectively march in the same direction—either clockwise or counterclockwise (see Figure 1). Inspired by observing these experiments, we asked the following question: What are simple and reasonable myopic rules of behavior that might lead to this phenomenon? Our goal is to study this question from an *algorithmic* perspective by considering a swarm of autonomous and identical discretized mobile agents that act according to a local algorithm. The precise mechanisms underlying locusts' behaviors are very complex and subject to intense ongoing research, e.g., [3,12–15]. Consequently, as with much of the literature on swarm dynamics [7,16,17], our goal is

not to study an exact mathematical model of locusts in particular, but to study the kinds of algorithmic local interactions that lead to collective marching and related phenomena. The resulting model is idealized and simple to describe, but the patterns of motion that emerge while the locusts progress toward a "stabilized" state of collective marching are surprisingly complex.

Figure 1. Image from locust experiments, courtesy of Amir Ayali. The collective clockwise marching of locusts in a ring arena is shown. Locusts were initiated at random positions and orientations in the arena but converged to clockwise marching over time.

The starting point for this work is the following postulated "rationalization" of what a locust-like agent wants to do. It wants to keep moving in the same direction of motion (clockwise or counterclockwise) for as long as possible. We can therefore consider a model of locust-like agents that never change their heading unless they collide head-on with agents marching in the opposite direction and are forced to do so due to the pressure which is exerted on them. When possible, these agents prefer to bypass agents that are headed toward them rather than collide with those agents. This is accomplished by changing lanes, moving in an orthogonal manner between concentric narrow *tracks* which partition the ringlike arena. The formal description of this "rationalized" model is given in Section 3, and will be our subject of study.

Contribution

We describe and study a stochastic model of locust-inspired agents in a 2D discretized ringlike arena which is subdivided into k tracks, each consisting of n locations. We show that our agents eventually reach a "local consensus" about the direction of marching, meaning that all agents on the same track will march in the same direction. We give asymptotic bounds for the time this takes based on the number of agents and the physical dimensions of the arena. Due to the idealized deterministic nature of our model, a global consensus where *all* locusts walk in the same direction is not guaranteed, since locusts in different tracks might never meet. However, we show that when a small probability of "erratic", random behavior is added to the model, such a global consensus must occur. We verify our claims via simulations and make further empirical observations that may inspire future investigations into the model.

Despite being simple to describe, analyzing the model proved tricky in several respects. Our analysis strategy is to show that the model oscillates between two phases: one in which it is "chaotic", and locusts are moving about without a discernible pattern; and one in which it is "orderly", and all locusts are stuck in dense deadlock situations where collisions are frequent. We derive our asymptotic bounds from studying orderly phases while bounding the amount of time the locusts can spend in the chaotic phases.

Previous works in the literature (e.g., [18,19]) have explained collective marching by appealing to a principle of local averaging, wherein each agent attempts to average its direction of motion with its neighbors'. It is interesting to note that our model attains collective marching from nearly the opposite set of assumptions. Our agents' primary motivation is to *avoid* changing their direction of motion, and any change to it is thus the result of an unavoidable conflict. We refer the reader to the Related Work section below for further discussion.

2. Related Work

Some of our results were presented at DARS2021 [20]. Here we extend our work by improving the time bounds for reaching consensus (Theorem 2) by substantially expanding and restructuring the technical analysis to include the full details which were omitted in [20] and by adding new simulation results, technical figures, and references.

The locust experiments inspiring our work are discussed in [3,12–14,18,19]. The phenomenon was originally studied by Buhl et al. [18]. They show that above a certain critical density, a rapid transition occurs from disordered movements of locust nymphs to highly aligned collective motion. Buhl et al., and subsequently Yates et al. [19], hypothesize that a main cause of this behavior is the locusts' tendency to change their direction to align with neighbors within a local interaction range (a common modeling assumption in multi-agent dynamics [9]) and that individual behavior does not change in relation to group density. In this work, we show how collective marching might emerge from almost the opposite set of assumptions; the locust-like agents we describe try to *avoid* changing their direction of motion for as long as possible, going as far as actively avoiding locusts that are headed in the opposite direction However, consensus eventually occurs as a result of unavoidable conflicts where locusts bump into each other. The assumption that locusts want to maintain their direction of motion is critical for enabling collective marching in our model, since it characterizes the stable states of the system. Bazazi et al. [21] hypothesize collective marching occurs due to a model of cannibalistic pursuit wherein locusts attempt to pursue locusts in front of them and evade locusts behind them to bite and avoid being bitten. Our model includes an element of evasion, too, but it is motivated by the locusts' desire to avoid changing their direction of motion. All previous models assume local interactions between locusts, i.e., locusts are only affected by neighboring locusts. Interactions in our model consist of conflicts between adjacent locusts and track changes that occur as a result of trying to avoid said conflicts. Conflicts are by definition local. Track-changing rules can be assumed either local or global, and our analysis applies in both cases.

Notably, in [18,19], it is observed that at intermediate densities swarms of locusts exhibit periodic directional switching, and at low densities the directions of motion are random. Our model does not replicate these phenomena; we show that our locust-like agents converge to local consensus at every density (or global consensus, assuming noise). Interestingly, we note that if we assume each locust has a small probability $r > 0$ of randomly flipping their heading at the beginning of a time step, such directional switching becomes possible. The probability of directional switching under such a postulate is inversely proportional to the density, thus likelier at low and intermediate densities than at high densities. We emphasize, however, that unlike works such as Buhl et al., replicating all features of locust swarms is not the goal of this work. Whereas the works we discussed seek to model actual locusts, our work can be characterized as trying to find a minimalistic locust-*inspired* set of assumptions that provably attains collective marching and to study it analytically for the sake of deepening our understanding of multi-agent systems.

More generally, the mathematical modeling of the collective motion of natural organisms, such as birds, locusts, and ants, and the convergence of such systems of agents to stable formations, has been discussed in numerous works including [5,9,10,22]. The most relevant to us among these are works within the field of *natural algorithms*, which assert that the behavior of natural organisms can be understood using concepts from the theory of robotics and computer science [11,16,17], such as complexity analysis, look-compute-move phases, and decision-making based on discrete internal states. Natural algorithms open up interplay between biology and computer science, allowing us to study nature via the language of algorithms and vice versa, allowing us to translate principles, algorithms, and mechanisms gleaned from nature to the design of systems that are meant to service or interact with humans, such as autonomous vehicles and warehouse robots.

The central focus of this work regards consensus. Do the agents eventually converge to the same direction of motion, and how long does it take? These questions bear mathematical and conceptual resemblance to questions in the field of opinion dynamics [23–25]. If the agents' direction of motion (clockwise or counterclockwise) is considered an "opinion", and the agents' interactions that cause changes in the direction of motion are considered social pressure, we can ask how long it takes for the agents to arrive at a consensus of opinions. Building on this analogy, we note that when there are no empty locations in the environment, our agent model is distinctly similar to the *voter model* on a ring network with two opinions. The voter model is a classical model in opinion dynamics explored in numerous works (we refer the reader to the survey [26]).

The comparison to the voter model breaks when we introduce empty locations and multiple ringlike tracks at which point we must take into account the agents' dynamically changing positions. Unlike the voter model, where only an agent's static neighborhood can influence its opinion, in our model, an agent's current location determines which agents can influence it. Several works have explored models of opinion dynamics in a ring environment where the agents' physical location is taken into account [27,28]. Our model is distinct from these in several respects. First, in our model, an agent's internal state—its direction of motion—plays an active part in the algorithm that determines which locations an agent may move to. Second, we partition our ring topology into several narrow rings ("tracks") that agents may switch between, and an agent's decision to switch tracks is influenced by the presence of platoons of agents moving in its direction in the track that it wants to switch to. In other words, we model agents that actively attempt to "swarm" together with agents moving in their direction of motion. We believe our work is unique in that we study, in a single model, both how an agent's physical location affects its opinion (via conflicts with nearby agents), and how an agent's opinion affects its physical location (via the desire to swarm with agents of the same opinion or equivalently, evade those of a different opinion).

Protocols for achieving consensus about a value, location, or the collective direction of motion have also been investigated in swarm robotics and distributed algorithms [29–32]. The purpose of these protocols is typically to be as efficient as possible in terms of parameters such as time, computational load, and distance traveled. However, in this work, we are not searching for a protocol that is designed to efficiently bring about consensus; we are investigating a protocol that is inspired by natural phenomena and want to see *whether* it leads to consensus and how long this process is expected to take.

Broadly speaking, some mathematical similarities may be drawn between our model and interacting particle systems such as the simple exclusion process, which has been used to understand biological transport and traffic phenomena [33,34]. Such particle systems have been studied on rings [35]. In these discrete models, as in our model, agents possess a physical dimension, which constrains the locations they might move to in their environment. These are not typically multi-agent models where agents have an internal state (such as a persistent direction of motion), but rather models of particle motion and diffusion, and the research focus is quite different. The main point of similarity to our model is in the way that a given discrete location can only be occupied by a single agent and in the random occurrence of "traffic shocks" where agents line up one after the other and are prevented from moving for a long time.

3. Model and Definitions

We postulate a locust-inspired model of marching in a wide 2D ringlike arena which is discretized into k narrow concentric rings, each consisting of n locations. Each narrow concentric ring is called a *track*. This discretized environment is *topologically* equivalent to the surface of a discretized cylinder of height k partitioned into k narrow rings of length n which are layered on top of each other. For example, the environment of Figure 2 corresponds to $k = 3, n = 8$ (3 tracks of length 8). The coordinate (x, y) refers to the xth location on the yth track (which can also be seen as the xth location of a ring of length n wrapped around the cylinder at height y). We define $\forall x, (x + n, y) \equiv (x, y)$.

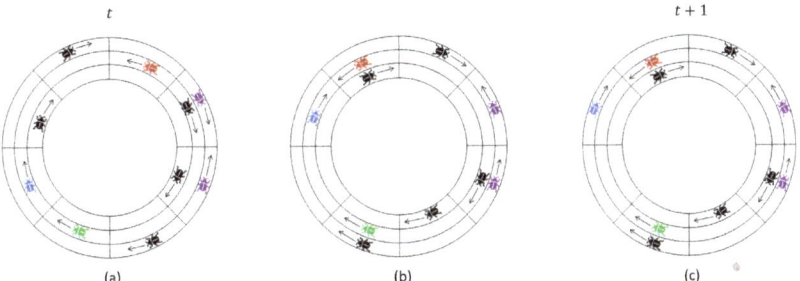

Figure 2. One step of the locust model with $k = 3, n = 8$ split into horizontal and vertical movements: (**a**) shows the initial configuration at the beginning of the current time step t; (**b**) illustrates changes to the configuration after conflicts and horizontal movements; and (**c**) is the configuration at the beginning of time $t + 1$ (or equivalently the end of time t) after vertical movements. The *front* and *back* of the blue locust are the red and green locusts, respectively. The purple locusts conflict with each other. Since conditions (1)–(3) are fulfilled, the blue locust may switch tracks, and it does so in the illustration.

A swarm of m identical agents, or "locusts", which we label $A_1, \ldots, A_m$, are dispersed at arbitrary locations and move autonomously at discrete time steps $t = 0, 1, \ldots$. A given location (x, y) can contain at most one locust. Each locust A_i is initiated with either a "clockwise" or "counterclockwise" *heading*, which determines their present direction of motion. We define $b(A_i) = 1$ when A_i has clockwise heading, and $b(A_i) = -1$ when A_i has a counterclockwise heading.

The locusts move synchronously at discrete time steps $t = 0, 1, \ldots$. At every time step, locusts try to take a step in their direction of motion. If locust A is at (x, y), it will attempt to move to $(x + b(A), y)$. A clockwise movement corresponds to adding 1 to x, and a counterclockwise movement corresponds to subtracting 1. The locusts have physical dimension, so if the location a locust attempts to move to already contains another locust at the beginning of the time step, the locust instead stays put. If A_i and A_j are both attempting to move to the same location, one of them is chosen uniformly at random to move to the location, and the other stays put.

Locusts that are adjacent exert pressure on each other to change their heading. If A_i has a clockwise heading and A_j has a counterclockwise heading, and they lie on the coordinates (x, y) and $(x + 1, y)$, respectively, then at the end of the current time step, one locust (chosen uniformly at random) will flip its heading to the other locust's heading. An equivalent way to model these dynamics is as follows: at the start of a conflict, each of the two locusts uniformly samples a random number $r_i, r_j \in (0, 1)$ called 'pressure'. The locust with lower pressure "loses" the conflict and changes its heading (noting that the probability of $r_i = r_j$ is 0). Such an event is called a **conflict** between A_i and A_j. A conflict is "won" by the locust that successfully converts the other locust to their heading.

Let A be a locust at (x, y). If the locust A has a clockwise heading, then the *front* of A is the first locust after A in the clockwise direction, and the *back* of A is the first locust in the counterclockwise direction. The reverse is true when A has a counterclockwise heading. Formally, let $i > 0$ be the smallest positive integer such that $(x + b(A)i, y)$ contains a locust, and let $j > 0$ be the smallest positive integer such that $(x - b(A)j, y)$ contains a locust. The *front* of A is the locust in $(x + b(A)i, y)$, and the *back* of A is the locust in $(x - b(A)j, y)$. The locusts in the front and back of A are denoted $A^\rightarrow$ and $A^\leftarrow$, respectively, and are called A's *neighbors*; these are the locusts that are directly in front of and behind A. Note that when a track has two or less locusts, $A^\rightarrow = A^\leftarrow$. When a track has one locust, $i = j = n$, and $A = A^\rightarrow = A^\leftarrow$.

At any given time step, besides moving in the direction of their heading within their track, locust A at (x, y) can switch tracks, moving vertically from (x, y) to $(x, y + 1)$ or $(x, y - 1)$ unless this would cause it to go above track k or below track 1. Such vertical movements occur *after* the horizontal movements of locusts along the tracks but on the same time step where those horizontal movements took place. Locusts are incentivized to move vertically when this enables them to avoid changing their heading ("inertia"). Specifically, A may move to the location $E = (x, y \pm 1)$ at time t when:

1. At the beginning of time t, A and $A^\rightarrow$ are not adjacent to each other and $b(A) \neq b(A^\rightarrow)$.
2. Once A moves to E, the updated $A^\leftarrow$ and $A^\rightarrow$ in the new track will have heading $b(A)$.
3. No locust will attempt to move horizontally to E at time $t + 1$.

Condition (1) states that there is an imminent conflict between A and $A^\rightarrow$ which is bound to occur. Condition (2) guarantees that, by changing tracks to avoid this conflict, A is not immediately advancing toward another collision; A's new neighbor will have the same heading as A. Condition (3) guarantees that the location A wants to move to on the new track is not being contested by another locust already on that track. Together, these conditions mean that locusts only change tracks if this results in avoiding collisions and in "swarming" together with other locusts marching in the same direction of motion. If a locust cannot sense that all three conditions (1)–(3) are fulfilled, it does not switch tracks.

Besides these conditions, we make no assumptions about *when* locusts move vertically. In other words, locusts do not always need to change tracks when they are allowed to by rules (1)–(3); they may do so arbitrarily, say with some probability q or according to any internal scheduler or algorithm, and we may impose visibility range constraints on the locusts such that they only switch tracks when they can *see* that rules (1)–(3) are fulfilled. We do not determine in any sense the times when locusts move between tracks, but only determine the preconditions required for such movements. Our results in the following sections remain true regardless. This makes our results general in the sense that they hold for many different track-switching "swarming" rules, as long as those rules do not break the conditions (1)–(3).

Figure 2 illustrates one time step of the model, split into horizontal and vertical movement phases.

To slightly simplify our analysis of the model, we assume that every track has at least two locusts at all times, although our results remain true without this assumption.

Although we work in a discrete time model where movement is instantaneous, it is helpful for the sake of formal analysis to define *the beginning* of a time step as the configuration of the swarm at that time step before any locusts moved, and *the end* of a time step as the configuration at that time step after all locust movements are complete. Somewhat idiosyncratically, the end of time t is precisely the beginning of time $t + 1$—both terms refer to the same thing. By default and unless stated otherwise, the words "time step t" refer to the beginning of that time step.

4. Stabilization Analysis

We will mainly be interested in studying the stability of the headings of the locusts over time. Does the model reach a point where the locusts stabilize and stop changing their heading? If so, are their headings all identical? How long does it take?

In the case of a single track ($k = 1$), we shall see that the locusts all eventually stabilize with identical heading and bound the expected time for this to happen in terms of m and n. In the multi-track case, we shall see that the locusts stabilize and agree on a heading *locally* (i.e., all locusts *on the same track* eventually have the identical heading and thereafter never change their heading) and bound the expected time to stabilization in terms of m, n, k. In the multi-track case, we further show that adding a small probability of "erratic" track-switching behavior to the model induces *global* consensus: all locusts across all tracks eventually have the identical heading.

4.1. Locusts on Narrow Ringlike Arenas (k = 1)

We start by studying the case $k = 1$; that is, we study a swarm of m locusts marching on a single track of length n. Throughout this section, we assume this is the case, except in Definition 1, which is also used in later sections.

For the rest of this section, let us call the swarm *non-stable* at time t if there are two locusts A_i and A_j such that $b(A_i) \neq b(A_j)$; otherwise, the swarm is *stable*. A swarm which is stable at time t remains stable thereafter. We wish to bound the number of time steps it takes for the system to become stable, which we denote T_{stable}. Our goal is to prove Theorem 1, which tells us that the expected time to stabilization grows quadratically in the number of locusts m and linearly in the track length n.

Theorem 1. *For any configuration of m locusts on a ring with a single track, $\mathbb{E}[T_{stable}] \leq m^2 + 2(n - m)$. This bound is asymptotically tight; there are initial locust configurations for which $\mathbb{E}[T_{stable}] = \Omega(m^2 + n - m)$.*

Theorem 1 tells us that all locusts must have identical bias within a finite expected time. This fact in isolation (without the time bounds in the statement of the theorem) is relatively straightforward to prove by noting that the evolution of the locusts' headings and locations can be modeled as a finite Markov chain, and the only absorbing classes in this Markov chain are ones in which all locusts have the same heading (see [36]).

Next we define *segments*: sets of consecutive locusts on the same track which all have the same heading. This allows us to partition the swarm into segments such that every locust belongs to a unique segment (see Figure 3). Although this section focuses on the case of a single track (and claims in this section are made under the assumption that there is only a single track), the definition is general, and we will use it in subsequent sections.

Definition 1. *Let A be a locust for which $b(A^{\leftarrow}) \neq b(A)$ at time t, and consider the sequence of locusts $B_0 = A$, $B_{i+1} = B_i^{\rightarrow}$. Let B_q be the first locust in this sequence for which $b(B_q) \neq b(B_0)$. The set $\{B_0, B_1, \ldots B_{q-1}\}$ is called the **segment** of the locusts $B_0, \ldots B_{q-1}$ at time t. The locust B_{q-1} is called the **segment head**, and A is called the **segment tail** of this segment.*

Figure 3. A locust configuration with $n = 8, k = 3$. Locusts are colored based based on the segment they belong to (Definition 1). There are 8 segments in total.

Only locusts which are segment heads at the beginning of a time step can change their heading by the end of that time step. When the heads of two segments are adjacent to each other, the resulting conflict causes one to change its heading, leave its previous segment, and instead become part of the other segment. If the head of a segment is also the tail of a segment, the segment is eliminated when it changes heading. Two segments separated by a segment of opposite heading merge if the opposite-heading segment is eliminated, which decreases the number of segments by two. No other action by a locust can change the segments. Hence, the number of segments and segment tails can only decrease.

Since our model is stochastic, different sequences of events may occur and result in different segments. However, by the above argument, we can conclude that in any such sequence of events, there must always exist at least one locust which remains a segment tail at all times $t < T_{stable}$ and never changes its heading (since at least one segment must exist as long as $t < T_{stable}$). Arbitrarily, we denote one such segment tail "A_W".

Definition 2. *The segment of A_W at the beginning of time t is called the **winning segment** at time t and is denoted $SW(t)$. The head of $SW(t)$ is labelled $H_W(t)$. For convenience, if at time t_0 the swarm is stable (i.e., $t_0 \geq T_{stable}$), then we define $SW(t_0)$ as the set that contains all m locusts.*

Lemma 1. *The expected number of time steps $t < T_{stable}$ in which $|SW(t)|$ changes is bounded by m^2.*

Proof. Let C_m denote the number of changes to the size of $SW(t)$ that occurs before time T_{stable}. Note that T_{stable} is the first time step where $|SW(t)| = m$. $|SW(t)|$ can only decrease, by one locust at a time, if $H_W(t)$ conflicts with another locust and loses. $|SW(t)|$ can increase in several ways, for example, when it merges with other segments. In particular, $|SW(t)|$ increases by at least one whenever $H_W(t)$ conflicts with a locust and wins, which happens with probability at least $\frac{1}{2}$. Hence, whenever $SW(t)$ changes in size, it is more likely to grow than to shrink. We can bound $E[C_m]$ by comparing the growth of $|SW(t)|$ to a random walk with absorbing boundaries at 0 and m:

Consider a random walk on the integers which starts at $|SW(0)|$. At any time step t, the walker takes a step left with probability $\frac{1}{2}$, otherwise it takes a step right. If the walker reaches either 0 or m, the walk ends. Denote by C_m^* the time it takes the walk to end. Using *coupling* (cf. [37]), we see that $\mathbb{E}[C_m] \leq \mathbb{E}[C_m^*|\text{the walker never reaches 0}]$, since per the previous paragraph, $|SW(t)|$ clearly grows at least as fast as the position of the random walker (note that $|SW(t)| > 0$ is always true, which is analogous to the walker never reaching 0).

Let us show how to bound $\mathbb{E}[C_m^*|\text{the walker never reaches 0}]$. Since the walk is memoryless, we can think of this quantity as the number of steps the random walker takes to get to m, assuming it must move right when it is at 0, and assuming the step count restarts whenever it moves from 0 to 1. If we count the steps without resetting the count, we realize that this is simply the expected number of steps it takes a random walker walled at 0 to reach position m, which is at most m^2 (cf. [38]). Hence $\mathbb{E}[C_m^*|\text{the walker never reaches 0}] \leq m^2$. □

Lemma 2. *The expected number of time steps $t < T_{stable}$ in which $|SW(t)|$ does not change is bounded by $2(n - m)$.*

Lemma 2 will require other lemmas and some new definitions to prove.

Definition 3. *Let A and B be two locusts or two locations which lie on the same track. The clockwise distance from A to B at time t is the number of clockwise steps required to get from A's location to B's location and is denoted $dist^c(A, B)$. The counterclockwise distance from A to B is denoted $dist^{cc}(A, B)$ and equals $dist^c(B, A)$.*

For the rest of this section, let us assume without loss of generality that the winning segment's tail A_W has a clockwise heading. Label the empty locations in the ring at time $t = 0$ (i.e., the locations not containing locusts at time $t = 0$) as $E_1, E_2, \ldots E_{n-m}$, sorted by their counterclockwise distance to A_W at time $t = 0$, such that E_1 minimizes $dist^{cc}(E_i, A_W)$, E_2 has the second smallest distance, and so on. We will treat these empty locations as having persistent identities. Whenever a locust A moves from its current location to E_i, we will instead say that A and E_i swapped, and so E_i's new location is A's old location.

We say a location E_i is *inside* the segment $SW(t)$ at time t if the two locusts which have the smallest clockwise and counterclockwise distance to E_i, respectively, are both in $SW(t)$. Otherwise, we say that E_i is *outside* $SW(t)$. A locust or location A is said to be *between* E_i and E_j, $j > i$, if $dist^c(E_i, A) < dist^c(E_i, E_j)$.

Definition 4. *All empty locations are initially **blocked**. A location E_i becomes **unblocked** at time $t + 1$ if all empty locations E_j such that $j < i$ are unblocked at time t, and a locust from $SW(t)$ swapped locations with E_i at time t. Once a location becomes **unblocked**, it remains that way forever.*

Lemma 3. *There is some time step $t^* \leq n - m$ such that:*

1. *Every blocked empty location E is outside $SW(t^*)$ (if any exist)*
2. *At least t^* empty locations are unblocked.*

Proof. If E_1 is outside $SW(0)$, then the same must be true for all other empty locations, so $t^* = 0$ and we are finished. Otherwise, E_1 becomes unblocked at time $t = 1$. If E_i becomes unblocked at time t, then at time t, it cannot be adjacent to E_{i+1}, since the locust that swapped with E_i in the previous time step is now between E_i and E_{i+1}. By definition, there are no empty locations E_j between E_i and E_{i+1}. Consequently, if E_{i+1} is inside $SW(t)$ at time t, it will swap with a locust of $SW(t)$ at time t, and become unblocked at time $t + 1$. If E_{i+1} is outside the segment at time t, it will become unblocked at the first time step $t' > t$ that begins with E_{i+1} inside $SW(t')$. Hence, if E_i becomes unblocked at time t, then E_{i+1} becomes unblocked at time $t + 1$ or E_{i+1} is outside $SW(t + 1)$ at time $t + 1$.

Let t^* be the smallest time where there are no blocked empty locations inside $SW(t^*)$. By the above, at every time step $t \leq t^*$ an empty location becomes unblocked; hence there are at least t^* unblocked empty locations at time t^*. Moreover, since there are $n - m$ empty locations, this implies $t^* \leq n - m$. □

Lemma 4. *There is no time $t < T_{stable}$ where an unblocked location is clockwise-adjacent to $H_W(t)$ (i.e., there is no time t where an unblocked empty location E is located one step clockwise from $H_W(t)$).*

Proof. First consider what happens when E_1 becomes unblocked: it swaps its location with a locust in $SW(t)$, and since E_1 is the clockwise-closest empty location to A_W, the entire counterclockwise path from E_1 to A_W consists only of locusts from $SW(t)$. Hence E_1 will move counterclockwise at every time step until it swaps with A_W. Once it swaps with A_W, E_1 will not swap with another locust at all times $t < T_{stable}$, since for that to occur we must have that $b(A_W^\leftarrow) = b(A_W)$, which is impossible since by definition A_W remains a segment tail until $t = T_{stable}$. E_1 does not swap with $H_W(t)$ while E_1 moves counterclockwise toward A_W nor after E_1 and A_W swap as long as the swarm is unstable; hence there is no time step $t < T_{stable}$ when E_1 is unblocked and swaps with $H_W(t)$.

Now consider E_2. E_2 becomes unblocked at least one time step after E_1, and there is at least one locust in $SW(t)$ which is between E_1 and E_2 at the time step E_1 that becomes unblocked (in particular, the locust in $SW(t)$ that swapped with E_1 must be between E_1 and E_2 at that time). Since E_1 subsequently moves toward A_W at every time step until they swap, E_2 cannot become adjacent to E_1 until they both swap with A_W. Hence the location one step counterclockwise to E_2 must always be a locust until E_2 swaps with A_W, meaning that similar to E_1, E_2 also moves counterclockwise toward A_W at every time step after E_2 becomes unblocked until they swap locations. Consequently, just like E_1, there is no time step $t < T_{stable}$ when E_2 is unblocked and swaps with $H_W(t)$.

More generally, by a straightforward inductive argument, the exact same thing is true of E_i: once it becomes unblocked, it moves counterclockwise toward A_W at every time step until it swaps with A_W. Thus, upon becoming unblocked, E_i does not swap with $H_W(t)$ as long as $t < T_{stable}$. □

Using Lemmas 3 and 4, let us prove Lemma 2.

Proof. If, at the beginning of time step t, $H_W(t)$ is adjacent to a locust from a different segment, then $|SW(t)|$ will change at the end of this time step due to the locusts' conflict. Hence, to prove Lemma 2, it suffices to show that out of all the time steps before time T_{stable}, $H_W(t)$ is not adjacent to the head of a different segment in at most $2(n-m)$ different steps in expectation.

If all empty locations are unblocked at time $n-m$, then by Lemma 4, $H_W(t)$ conflicts with the head of another segment at all times $t \geq n-m$. Therefore, $|SW(t)|$ will change at every time step $n-m < t < T_{stable}$, which is what we wanted to prove.

If there is a blocked location at time $n-m$, then by Lemma 2, there must be some time $t^* \leq n-m$ where at least t^* empty locations are unblocked and all blocked empty locations are outside $SW(t^*)$. Let E_j be the minimal-index blocked location which is outside $SW(t^*)$ at time t^*. Since there are no blocked empty locations inside $SW(t^*)$, all locations E_i with $i < j$ are unblocked. Hence, E_j will become unblocked as soon as it swaps with the head of the winning segment. Since (by the clockwise sorting order of $E_1, E_2, \ldots$) E_{j+1} cannot swap with the winning segment head before E_j is unblocked, E_{j+1} will also become unblocked after the first time step where it swaps the winning segment head. The same is true for $E_{j+2}, \ldots E_{n-m}$. Hence, every empty location that $H_W(t)$ swaps with after time t^* becomes unblocked in the subsequent time step. By Lemma 2, the total swaps $H_W(t)$ could have made before time T_{stable} is thus most $t^* + (n-m-j) \leq n-m$. Whenever an empty location is one step clockwise from $H_W(t)$, they will swap with probability at least 0.5 (the swap is not guaranteed, since it is possible the location is also adjacent to the head of another segment, and hence a tiebreaker will occur in regards to which segment head occupies the empty location in the next time step). Consequently, the expected number of time steps $H_W(t)$ is not adjacent to the head of another segment is bounded by $2(n-m)$. □

The proof of Theorem 1 now follows.

Proof. Lemma 2 tells us that before time T_{stable}, $|SW(t)|$ does not change in at most $2(n-m)$ time steps in expectation, whereas Lemma 1 tells us that the expected number of changes to $|SW(t)|$ before time T_{stable} is at most m^2. Hence, for any configuration of m locusts on a ring of track length n, $\mathbb{E}[T_{stable}] \leq m^2 + 2(n-m)$.

Let us now show a locust configuration for which $\mathbb{E}[T_{stable}] = \Omega(m^2 + n)$, so as to asymptotically match the upper bound we found. Consider a ring with $k = 1$, m divisible by 2, and an initial locust configuration where locusts are found at coordinates $(0,1), (1,1), \ldots (m/2, 1)$ with a clockwise heading and at $(-1,1), (-2,1), \ldots (-m/2-1, 1)$ with a counterclockwise heading, and the rest of the ring is empty. This is a ring with exactly two segments, each of size $m/2$. Since after every conflict, the segment sizes are offset by one in either direction, the expected number of conflicts between the heads of the segments that is necessary for stabilization is equal to the expected number of steps a random walk with absorbing boundaries at $m/2$ and $-m/2$ takes to end, which is $m^2/4$ (see [39]). Since the heads of the segments start at distance $n-m$ from each other, it takes $\Omega(n-m)$ steps for them to reach each other. Hence the expected time for this ring to stabilize is $\Omega(m^2 + n - m)$. □

4.2. Locusts on Wide Ringlike Arenas ($k > 1$)

Let us now investigate the case where m locusts are marching on $k > 1$ tracks of length n. The first question we should ask is whether, just as in the case of the $k = 1$ setting, there exists some time T where all locusts have identical heading. The answer is "not necessarily": consider for example the case $k = 2$ where on the $k = 1$ track, all locusts march clockwise, and on the $k = 2$ track, all locusts march counterclockwise. According to the track-switching conditions (Section 3), no locust will ever switch tracks in this configuration; hence the locusts will perpetually have opposing headings. As we shall prove in this section, swarms stabilize *locally*–meaning that eventually, all locusts *on the same track* have identical heading, but this heading may be different between tracks.

Let us say that the yth track is stable if all locusts whose location is $(\cdot, y)$ have the identical heading. Note that once a track becomes stable, it remains this way forever, as by the model, the only locusts that may move into the track must have the same heading as its locusts. Let T_{stable} be the first time when all the k tracks are stable. Our goal will be to prove the following asymptotic bounds on T_{stable}:

Theorem 2. $\mathbb{E}[T_{stable}] = \mathcal{O}(\min(\log(k)n^2, mn))$.

Recalling Definition 1, each locust in the system belongs to some segment. Each track has its own segments. Locusts leave and join segments due to conflicts or when they pass from their current segment to a track on a different segment. In this section, we will treat segments as having persistent identities similar to SW in the previous section. We introduce the following notation:

Definition 5. *Let S be a segment whose tail is A at some time t_0. We define $S(t)$ to be the segment whose tail is A at the beginning of time t. If A is not a segment tail at time t, then we will say $S(t) = \emptyset$ (this can happen once A changes its heading or moves to another track, or due to another segment merging with $S(t)$ which might cause $b(A^{\leftarrow})$ to equal $b(A)$, thus making A no longer the tail).*
Furthermore, define S_1 to be the segment tail of S and $S_{i+1} = S_i^{\rightarrow}$.

Let us give a few examples of the notation in Definition 5. Suppose at time t_1 we have some segment S. Then the tail of S is S_1, and the head is $S_{|S|}$. $S(t)$ is the segment whose tail is S_1 at time t; hence $S(t_1) = S$. Finally, $S(t)_{|S(t)|}$ is the head of the segment $S(t)$.

In the $k > 1$ setting, locusts can frequently move between tracks, which complicates our study of T_{stable}. Crucially, however, the number of segments on any individual track is non-increasing. This is because, first, as shown in the previous section, locusts moving and conflicting on the same track can never create new segments. Second, by the locust model, locusts can only move into another track when this places them between two locusts that already belong to some (clockwise or counterclockwise) segment.

That being said, locusts moving in and out of a given track make the technique we used in the previous section unfeasible. In the following definitions of *compact* and *deadlocked* locust sets, our goal is to identify configurations of locusts on a given track which locusts cannot enter from another track. Such configurations can be studied locally, focusing only on the track they are in. In the next several lemmas, we will bound the amount of time that can pass without either the number of segments decreasing or all segments entering into deadlock.

Definition 6. *We call a sequence of locusts $X_1, X_2, \ldots$ **compact** if $X_{i+1} = X_i^{\rightarrow}$ and either:*
1. *every locust in X has a clockwise heading and for every $i < |X|$, $dist^c(X_i, X_{i+1}) \leq 2$, or*
2. *every locust in X has a counterclockwise heading and for every $i < |X|$, $dist^{cc}(X_i, X_{i+1}) \leq 2$.*

An unordered set of locusts is called compact if there exists an ordering of all its locusts that forms a compact sequence.

Definition 7. *Let $X = \{X_1, X_2, \ldots X_j\}$ and $Y = \{Y_1, Y_2, \ldots Y_k\}$ be two compact sets, such that the locusts of X have a clockwise heading and the locusts of Y have a counterclockwise heading. X and Y are **in deadlock** if $dist^c(X_j, Y_k) = 1$. (See Figure 4).*

A compact set of locusts X is essentially a platoon of locusts all on the same track which are heading in one direction and are all jammed together with at most one empty space between each consecutive pair. As long as X remains compact, no new locusts can enter the track between any two locusts of X because the model states that locusts do not move vertically into empty locations to which a locust is attempting to move horizontally, and the locusts in a compact set are always attempting to move horizontally to the empty location in front of them.

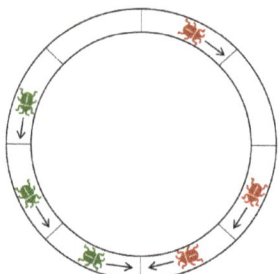

Figure 4. Two segments in deadlock, colored green and red (Definition 7).

Definition 8. *A maximal compact set is a set X such that for any locust $A \notin X$, $X \cup A$ is not compact.*

A straightforward observation is that locusts can only belong to one maximal compact set:

Observation 1. *Let A be a locust. If X and Y are maximal compact sets containing A, then $X = Y$.*

Lemma 5. *Let X and Y be two sets of locusts in deadlock at the beginning of time t. Then at every subsequent time step, the locusts in $X \cup Y$ can be separated into sets X' and Y' that are in deadlock, or the locusts in $X \cup Y$ all have identical heading.*

Proof. Let $X = \{X_1, X_2, \ldots X_j\}$ and $Y = \{Y_1, Y_2, \ldots Y_k\}$ be compact sets such that $X_{i+1} = X_i^{\rightarrow}$, $Y_{i+1} = Y_i^{\rightarrow}$. It suffices to show that if X and Y are in deadlock at time t, they will remain that way at time $t + 1$, unless $X \cup Y$'s locusts all have identical heading. Let us assume without loss of generality ("w.l.o.g.") that X has a clockwise heading, and therefore Y has a counterclockwise heading. By the definition of deadlock, at time t, X_j and Y_k conflict, and the locust that loses joins the other set. Suppose w.l.o.g. that X_j is the locust that lost. If $|X| = 1$, then the locusts all have an identical heading, and we are finished. Otherwise, set $X' = \{X_1, \ldots X_{j-1}\}$ and $Y' = \{Y_1, Y_2, \ldots Y_k, X_j\}$. Note that since X and Y are compact at time t, no locust could have moved vertically into the empty spaces between pairs of locusts in $X \cup Y$. Furthermore the locusts of X and Y all march toward X_j and Y_k, respectively; hence the distance between any consecutive pair X_i, X_{i+1} or Y_i, Y_{i+1} could not have increased. Thus X' and Y' are compact.

To show that X' and Y' are deadlocked at time $t + 1$, we just need to show that $dist^c(X_{j-1}, X_j)$ is 1 at time $t + 1$. Since the distances do not increase, if $dist^c(X_{j-1}, X_j)$ was 1 at time t, we are finished. Otherwise $dist^c(X_{j-1}, X_j) = 2$ at time t, and since X_j did not move (it was in a conflict with Y_k), X_{j-1} decreased the distance in the last time step, hence it is now 1. □

Lemma 6. *Suppose P and Q are the only segments on track K at time t_0, and P's locusts have a clockwise heading. Let $d = dist^c(P_1, Q_1)$. After at most 3d time steps, $P(t_0 + 3d)$ and $Q(t_0 + 3d)$ are in deadlock, or the track is stable.*

Proof. The track K consists of locations of the form (x, y) for some fixed y and $1 \leq x \leq n$. For brevity, in this proof we will denote the location (x, y) simply by its horizontal coordinate, i.e., x, by writing $(x) = (x, y)$.

We may assume w.l.o.g. that $t_0 = 0$ and that P_1 is initially at (0). Note that this means Q_1 is at (d) at time 0. If at any time $t \leq 3d$ the track is stable, then we are finished, so we assume for contradiction that this is not the case. This means that P_1 and Q_1 do not change their headings before time $3d$. This being the case, we get that $dist^c(P_1, Q_1)$ is non-increasing before time $3d$. Since the segments $P(t)$ and $Q(t)$ move toward each other at every time step $t \leq 3d$, we may focus only on the interval of locations $[0, d]$, i.e., the locations $(0), (1), \ldots (d)$. We then define the distance $dist(\cdot, \cdot)$ between two locusts in this interval whose x-coordinates are x_1 and x_2 as $|x_1 - x_2|$.

At any time $t \leq 3d$, we may partition the locusts in $[0, d]$ into maximal compact sets of locusts. This partition is unique, by Observation 1. Let us label the maximal compact sets of locusts that belong to $P(t)$ as $\mathcal{C}_1^t, \mathcal{C}_2^t, \ldots \mathcal{C}_{c_t}^t$, where the segments are indexed from 1 to c_t, sorted by increasing x coordinates, such that $\mathcal{C}_1^t$ contains the locusts closest to (0). Analogously, we label the maximal compact sets that belong to $Q(t)$ as $\mathcal{W}_1^t, \mathcal{W}_2^t, \ldots \mathcal{W}_{w_t}^t$, with indices running from 1 to w_t, sorted by decreasing x-coordinates such that $\mathcal{W}_1^t$ contains the locusts that are closest to (d) (see Figure 5). In this proof, the distance between two sets of locusts X, Y, denoted $dist(X, Y)$, is defined simply as the minimal distance between two locusts $A \in X, B \in Y$. Our proof will utilize the functions:

$$L_1(t) = \sum_{i=1}^{c_t-1} dist(\mathcal{C}_i^t, \mathcal{C}_{i+1}^t), \quad L_2(t) = \sum_{i=1}^{w_t-1} dist(\mathcal{W}_i^t, \mathcal{W}_{i+1}^t) \quad (1)$$
$$L_3(t) = dist(\mathcal{C}_{c_t}^t, \mathcal{W}_{w_t}^t), \quad L(t) = L_1(t) + L_2(t) + L_3(t)$$

$L_1(t)$ is the sum of distances between consecutive clockwise-facing sets in the partition at time t. $L_2(t)$ is the sum of distances between the counterclockwise sets. $L_3(t)$ is the distance between the two closest clockwise and counterclockwise facing sets. The function $L(t)$ is the sum of distances between consecutive compact sets in the partition. When $L(t) = 1$, there are necessarily only one clockwise and one counterclockwise facing sets in the partition, which must equal $P(t)$ and $Q(t)$, respectively. Furthermore, $L(t) = 1$ implies that the distance between $P(t)$ and $Q(t)$ is 1. Hence, when $L(t) = 1$, $P(t)$ and $Q(t)$ are both in deadlock. The converse is true as well; hence $L(t) = 1$ if and only if $P(t), Q(t)$ are in deadlock. We will use $L(t)$ as a potential or "Lyapunov" function [40] and show it must decrease to 1 within $3d$ time steps. By Lemma 5, once P and Q are in deadlock they will remain in deadlock until one of them is eliminated, which completes the proof.

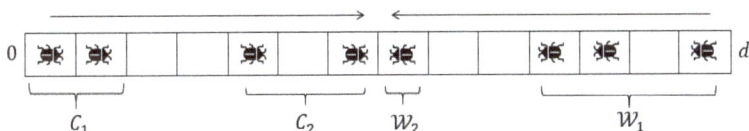

Figure 5. A partition into maximal compact subsets as in our construction. In this configuration, $L_1(t) = 3, L_2(t) = 3, L_3(t) = 1$, and $L(t) = 7$. Note that although $\mathcal{C}_1, \mathcal{C}_2$ are compact, $P(t) = \mathcal{C}_1 \cup \mathcal{C}_2$ is not compact, and similarly $Q(t)$ is not compact; thus $P(t)$ and $Q(t)$ are not in deadlock, and $L(t) \neq 1$.

Let us denote by $max(X)$ the locust with maximum x-coordinate in X, and by $min(X)$ the locust with minimal x-coordinate. We may also use $max(X)$ and $min(X)$ to denote the x coordinate of said locust. Note that $dist(\mathcal{C}_i^t, \mathcal{C}_{i+1}^t)$ is the distance between $max(\mathcal{C}_i^t)$ and $min(\mathcal{C}_{i+1}^t)$.

Recall that in the locust model, every time step is divided into a phase where locusts move horizontally (on their respective tracks), and a phase where they move vertically. First, let us show that the sum of distances $L_1(t)$ does not increase due to changes in either the horizontal or vertical phase. Since $L_1(t)$ is the sum of distances between compact partition sets whose locusts move clockwise, and for all $\mathcal{C}_i^t$ except perhaps $\mathcal{C}_{c_t}^t$, $max(\mathcal{C}_i^t)$ always moves clockwise, the distance $dist(\mathcal{C}_i^t, \mathcal{C}_{i+1}^t)$ does not increase as a result of locust movements (note that clockwise movements of $max(\mathcal{C}_i^t)$ do not result in a new compact set because the rest of the locusts in $\mathcal{C}_i^t$ follow it). Furthermore, since conflicts cannot result in a new maximal compact set in the partition, conflicts do not increase $L_1(t)$. Hence, $L_1(t)$

does not increase in the horizontal phase. In the vertical phase, clockwise-heading locusts entering the track either create a new set in the partition, which does not affect the sum of distances (as they then merely form a "mid-point" between two other maximal compact sets), or they join an existing compact set, which can never increase $L_1(t)$. By the locust model, the only locusts that can move tracks are $max(\mathcal{C}_{c_t}^t)$ and $min(\mathcal{W}_{w_t}^t)$, since these are the only locusts for which the condition $b(A) \neq b(A^\rightarrow)$ is true, so locusts moving tracks cannot increase $L_1(t)$ either. In conclusion, $L_1(t)$ is non-increasing at any time step. By analogy, $L_2(t)$ is non-increasing.

Similar to L_1 and L_2, the distance $L_3(t)$ cannot increase as a result of locusts entering the track. It can increase as a result of a locust conflict which eliminates either $\mathcal{W}_{w_t}^t$ or $\mathcal{C}_{c_t}^t$, but such an increase is compensated for by a comparable decrease in either $L_1(t)$ or $L_2(t)$. It is also simple to check that, since $P(t)$ and $Q(t)$ are always moving toward each other when they are not in deadlock (i.e., when $L(t) > 1$), there will be at least two compact sets in the partition that decrease their distance to each other; hence L_1, L_2 or L_3 must decrease by at least one in the horizontal phase.

To conclude: $L_1(t)$ and $L_2(t)$ are non-increasing. $L_3(t)$ is non-increasing during the horizontal phase and as a result of new locusts entering $\mathcal{K}$. If $L(t) > 1$, $L(t)$ decreases during each horizontal phase. Hence, $L(t)$ decreases in every time step where $L(t) > 1$, and no locusts in $\mathcal{K}$ move to another track.

What happens when locusts in $\mathcal{K}$ do move to another track? As proven, $L_1(t)$ and $L_2(t)$ do not increase. However, the distance $L_3(t)$ will increase, since the only locusts that can move tracks are $max(\mathcal{C}_{w_t}^t)$ and $min(\mathcal{W}_{c_t}^t)$. It is straightforward to check that when $\mathcal{C}_{c_t}^t$ contains more than one locust, $L_3(t)$ will increase by at most two as a result of $max(\mathcal{C}_{w_t}^t)$ moving tracks. When $\mathcal{C}_{c_t}^t$ contains exactly one locust, $L_3(t)$ can increase significantly (as $L_3(t)$ then becomes the distance between $\mathcal{C}_{c_t-1}^t$ and W_{w_t}), but any increase is matched by the decrease in $L_1(t)$ as a result of $\mathcal{C}_{c_t}^t$ being eliminated. Analogous statement hold for $\mathcal{W}_{w_t}^t$, and hence $L_3(t)$ can increase by at most two as a result of one locust moving out of the track. We need to bound, then, the number of locusts in $\mathcal{K}$ that move tracks before time $3d$. We define the potential function $F(t)$:

$$F(t) = \sum_{i=1}^{c_t-1}(dist(\mathcal{C}_i^t, \mathcal{C}_{i+1}^t) - 1) + \sum_{i=1}^{w_t-1}(dist(\mathcal{W}_i^t, \mathcal{W}_{i+1}^t) - 1) + |P(t) \cup Q(t)|$$
$$= L_1(t) + L_2(t) - c_t - w_t + |P(t) \cup Q(t)| \quad (2)$$

$F(t)$ is the sum of the empty locations between consecutive compact sets in the partition whose locusts have the same heading plus the number of locusts in $\mathcal{K}$. Note that $F(t) \geq 0$ at all times t. We will show $F(t)$ is non-increasing and that it decreases whenever a locust leaves the track. Hence, at most $F(0)$ locusts can leave the track.

Let us show that $F(t)$ is non-increasing. We already know L_1 and L_2 are non-increasing. In the horizontal phase, $|P(t) \cup Q(t)|$ is of course unaffected. Then c_t and w_t can decrease as a result of maximal compact sets merging, hence increasing F, but this can only happen when the distance between two such sets has decreased; hence the resulting increase to F is undone by a decrease in L_1 and L_2. Hence, $F(t)$ does not increase because of locusts' actions during the horizontal phase.

Likewise, locusts leaving $\mathcal{K}$ can decrease c_t or w_t when they cause a maximal compact set to be eliminated, but this is matched by a comparable decrease in L_1 or L_2 which means that F does not increase due to locusts moving out of the track. Furthermore, $|P(t) \cup Q(t)|$ decreases when this happens. Hence, a locust moving out of the track decreases $F(t)$ by at least one. Finally, let us show that locusts entering the track does not increase $F(t)$.

At time t, locusts can only enter the track at empty locations that are found in intervals of the form $[max(\mathcal{W}_i^t), min(\mathcal{W}_{i+1}^t)]$ or $[max(\mathcal{C}_{i+1}^t), min(\mathcal{C}_i^t)]$ for some i. In particular, locusts cannot enter empty locations that are between two locusts belonging to the same compact set (because a locust in that set will always be attempting to move to that location in the next time step, and the model disallows vertical movements to such locations), nor can they enter the track on the empty locations between $min(C_{c_t}^t)$ and $max(W_{w_t}^t)$. Thus, locusts entering the track at time t decrease the amount of empty locations between two clockwise or counterclockwise compact partition sets (and perhaps cause the sets between which they enter to merge into a single compact set). This will always decrease $L_1(t) + L_2(t) - c_t - w_t$ by at least one and increase $|P(t) \cup Q(t)|$ by 1. On net, we see that new locusts entering $\mathcal{K}$ either decrease or do not affect F.

In conclusion, $F(t)$ is non-increasing, and any time a locust moves to another track, $F(t)$ decreases by one. Thus, at most $F(0)$ locusts can move from $\mathcal{K}$ to another track. Recall that locusts moving out of the track can increase $L(t)$ by at most two. Hence after at most $L(0) + 2F(0) \leq d + 2d = 3d$ time steps, $L(t) = 1$. □

Lemma 7. *Let $seg(t)$ denote the set of segments in all tracks at time t. At time $t + 3n$, either every segment is in deadlock with some other segment, or $|seg(t + 3n)| < |seg(t)|$.*

Proof. Consider some track $\mathcal{K}$ and a segment P which is in that track at time t. Let us assume that $|seg(t + 3n)| = |seg(t)|$, and show that $P(t + 3n)$ must be in deadlock with another segment. At any time $t' \geq t$, as long as the number of segments on $\mathcal{K}$ does not decrease, the locusts of $P(t')$ will be marching toward locusts of another segment, which we will label $Q(t')$. They cannot collide or conflict with locusts belonging to any segment other than $Q(t')$. Hence, other segments in $\mathcal{K}$ do not affect the evolution of $P(t)$ and $Q(t)$ before time $t + 3n$, and we can assume w.l.o.g. that $P(t)$ and $Q(t)$ are the only segments in $\mathcal{K}$ at time t. Let d be as in the statement of Lemma 6. Since $n \geq d$, Lemma 6 tells us that at some time $t \leq t^* \leq t + 3n$, $P(t^*)$ and $Q(t^*)$ must be in deadlock. Since by Lemma 5, P and Q must remain in deadlock until one of them is eliminated, we see that at time $t + 3n$ they must still be in deadlock, since we assumed $|seg(t)| = |seg(t + 3n)|$. □

Theorem 3. $\mathbb{E}[T_{stable}] = \mathcal{O}(mn)$.

Proof. Let $|seg(t)|$ denote the number of segments at time t. $\mathbb{E}[T_{stable}]$ can be computed as the sum of times $\mathbb{E}[T_2 + T_4 + \ldots + T_{|seg(0)|}]$, where T_i is the expected time until the number of segments drops below i, if it is currently i (we increment the index by two since segments are necessarily eliminated in pairs).

Let us estimate $E[T_{2i}]$. Suppose that at time t, the number of segments is $2i$. Then after $3n$ steps at most, either the number of segments has decreased, or all segments are in deadlock. There are in total i pairs of segments in deadlock, and as there are m locusts, there must be a pair P, Q that contains at most $\min(m/i, n)$ locusts at time $t + 3n$. By Lemma 5, P, Q remain in deadlock until either P or Q is eliminated. We can compute how long this takes in expectation, since at every time step after time $t + 3n$, the heads of P and Q conflict, resulting in one of the segments increasing in size and the other decreasing. Hence, the expected time it takes P or Q to be eliminated is precisely the expected time it takes a symmetric random walk starting at 0 to reach either $|P|$ or $-|Q|$, which is $|P| \cdot |Q| \leq \min((\frac{m}{2i})^2, (\frac{n}{2})^2)$. Hence, $E[T_{2i}] \leq 3n + \min((\frac{m}{2i})^2, (\frac{n}{2})^2)$.

Let us first assume $m \geq n$. Using the fact that $\min((\frac{m}{2i})^2, (\frac{n}{2})^2) = (\frac{n}{2})^2$ for $i \leq \lfloor m/n \rfloor$, we have:

$$\mathbb{E}[T_2 + T_4 + \ldots + T_{|seg(0)|}] \leq 3n \cdot \frac{|seg(0)|}{2} + \lfloor m/n \rfloor (\frac{n}{2})^2 + \sum_{i=\lceil m/n \rceil}^{\infty} (\frac{m}{2i})^2$$

$$\leq \frac{3}{2}mn + \frac{1}{4}mn + \frac{1}{4}m^2 \sum_{i=0}^{\infty} (\frac{1}{m/n + i})^2 \quad (3)$$

$$\leq \frac{7}{4}mn + \frac{1}{4}m^2(\frac{n^2}{m^2} + \frac{n}{m}) \leq \frac{9}{4}mn$$

where we used the inequalities $\sum_{i=0}^{\infty}(\frac{1}{m/n+i})^2 \leq \frac{n^2}{m^2} + \int_{i=0}^{\infty}(\frac{1}{m/n+i})^2 = \frac{n^2}{m^2} + \frac{n}{m}$ and $|seg(0)| \leq m$. If $m < n$, by using the identity $\sum_{i=1}^{\infty}(\frac{1}{i})^2 = \frac{\pi^2}{6}$ we obtain:

$$\mathbb{E}[T_2 + T_4 + \ldots + T_{|seg(0)|}] \leq 3n \cdot \frac{|seg(0)|}{2} + \sum_{i=1}^{m}(\frac{m}{2i})^2 \leq \frac{3}{2}mn + \frac{\pi^2}{24}m^2 \leq (\frac{3}{2} + \frac{\pi^2}{24})mn \quad (4)$$

So we see that $\mathbb{E}[T_{stable}] = \mathcal{O}(mn)$. □

Next we wish to show that $E[T_{stable}] = \mathcal{O}(\log(k)n^2)$. For this, we require the following result:

Lemma 8. *Consider k independent random walks with absorbing barriers at 0 and $2n$, i.e., random walks that end once they reach 0 or $2n$. The expected time until **all** k walks end is $\mathcal{O}(n^2 \log(k))$.*

Proof. First, let us set $k = 1$ and estimate the probability that the one walk has not ended by time t. Let P be the transition probability matrix of the random walk, and let $\mathbf{v}$ be the vector describing the initial probability distribution of the location of the random walker. Then $\mathbf{v}P^t$ is the probability distribution of its location after t time steps [41]. The evolution of $\mathbf{v}P^t$ is well-studied and relates to "the discrete heat equation" [42]. The probability that the walk has not ended at time t is the sum $\sum_{i=1}^{2n-1} \mathbf{v}(i)$. Asymptotically, this sum is bounded by $\mathcal{O}(\lambda^t)$, where $\lambda = \cos(\frac{\pi}{2n})$ is the second largest eigenvalue of P (cf. [42]).

Returning to general k, let $\mathcal{T}_k$ be a random variable denoting the time when all k walks end. By looking at the series expansion of $\cos(1/x)$, we may verify that for $n > 1$, $\cos(\frac{\pi}{2n}) < 1 - \frac{1}{n^2}$. From the previous paragraph, and because the walks are independent, we therefore see that

$$Pr(\mathcal{T}_k \geq t) = 1 - Pr(\mathcal{T}_1 < t)^k = 1 - (1 - \mathcal{O}(\lambda^t))^k = 1 - (1 - \mathcal{O}((1 - \frac{1}{n^2})^t))^k \quad (5)$$

Consequently, for $t \gg n^2$, the following asymptotics hold for some constant C:

$$Pr(\mathcal{T}_k \geq t) < 1 - (1 - Ce^{-t/n^2})^k \quad (6)$$

where we used the fact that $(1 + x/n)^n \to e^x$ as $n \to \infty$. Note that $Pr(\mathcal{T}_k \geq t + n^2 \log(C)) < 1 - (1 - e^{-t/n^2})^k$. Hence:

$$\begin{aligned}\mathbb{E}[\mathcal{T}_k] &= \int_0^{\infty} Pr(\mathcal{T}_k > t)dt \leq n^2 \log(C) + \int_0^{\infty} 1 - (1 - e^{-t/n^2})^k dt \\ &= n^2 \log(C) + \int_0^{\infty} 1 - \sum_{j=0}^{k} \binom{k}{j}(-1)^j e^{-tj/n^2} dt \\ &= n^2 \log(C) + - \sum_{j=1}^{k} \binom{k}{j}(-1)^j \int_0^{\infty} e^{-tj/n^2} dt \\ &= n^2 \log(C) + -n^2 \sum_{j=1}^{k} \binom{k}{j}\frac{(-1)^j}{j} = \mathcal{O}(n^2 \log(k))\end{aligned} \quad (7)$$

where we used the equality $\sum_{j=1}^{k} \binom{k}{j}\frac{(-1)^j}{j} = -\sum_{j=1}^{k} \frac{1}{j} \approx \log(k)$. □

Theorem 4. $\mathbb{E}[T_{stable}] = \mathcal{O}(\log(k) \cdot n^2)$.

Proof. Let $seg_i(t)$ denote the number of segments in track i at time t, and define $\mathcal{M}_t = \max_{1 \leq i \leq k} seg_i(t)$. Let us bound the expected time it takes for $\mathcal{M}_t$ to decrease. Define the set $K(t)$ to be all tracks that have $|\mathcal{M}_t|$ segments at time t. Then $\mathcal{M}_t$ decreases at the first time $t' > t$ when all tracks in $K(t)$ have had their number of segments decrease. We may bound this with the following argument: slightly generalizing Lemma 7 to hold for subsets of tracks (Lemma 7 holds not just for the set $seg(t)$ but for the segments in a given subset of tracks, with the proof being virtually identical. Here we apply the Lemma to the subset $K(t+3n)$.), if $\mathcal{M}_t$ does not decrease after $3n$ time steps (i.e., $\mathcal{M}_t = \mathcal{M}_{t+3n}$), all tracks in $K(t+3n)$ now have all their segments in deadlock. The number of deadlocked segment pairs at every track in $K(t+3n)$ is $\mathcal{M}_t/2$, so in every such track there is such a pair with at most $2n/\mathcal{M}_t$ locusts. By Lemma 8, using a similar argument as Theorem 3, these pairs of deadlocked segments resolve into a single segment after at most $c \cdot \log(k) \left(\frac{2n}{\mathcal{M}_t}\right)^2$ expected time for some constant c. Hence, the number of expected time steps for $\mathcal{M}_t$ to decrease is bounded above by $3n + c \log(k) \left(\frac{2n}{\mathcal{M}_t}\right)^2$.

T_{stable} is the first time when $\mathcal{M}_t = 0$. Let us assume n is even for simplicity (the computation will hold regardless, up to rounding). We have that $\mathcal{M}_0 \leq n$, and $\mathcal{M}_t$ decreases in leaps of two or more (since segments can only be eliminated in pairs). Hence, T_{stable} is bounded by the amount of time it takes $\mathcal{M}_t$ to decrease at most $n/2$ times. By linearity of expectation, this time can be bounded by summing $3n + c \log(k) \left(\frac{2n}{\mathcal{M}_t}\right)^2$ over $\mathcal{M}_t = n, n-2, n-4, \ldots 2$:

$$\mathbb{E}[T_{stable}] \leq \frac{n}{2} \cdot 3n + c \log(k) \left(\frac{2n}{n}\right)^2 + c \log(k) \left(\frac{2n}{n-2}\right)^2 + \ldots + c \log(k) \left(\frac{2n}{2}\right)^2$$
$$\leq \frac{3}{2}n^2 + 4c \log(k) n^2 \sum_{i=1}^{\infty} \left(\frac{1}{2i}\right)^2 = \frac{3}{2}n^2 + \frac{\pi^2}{6} c \log(k) n^2 = \mathcal{O}(\log(k) n^2) \quad (8)$$

as claimed. □

The proof of Theorem 2 follows immediately from Theorems 3 and 4 by taking the minimum.

Erratic Track Switching and Global Consensus

Theorem 2 shows that, after finite expected time, all locusts on a track have an identical heading. This is a stable *local* consensus, in the sense that two different tracks may have locusts marching in opposite directions forever. We might ask what modifications to the model would force a *global* consensus, i.e., make it so that stabilization occurs only when all locusts across *all* tracks have the identical heading. There is in fact a simple change that would force this to occur. Let us assume that at time step t any locust has some probability of acting "erratically" in either the vertical or horizontal phases:

1. With probability r, a locust might behave erratically in the horizontal phase, staying in place instead of attempting to move according to its heading.
2. With probability p, a locust may behave erratically in the vertical phase, meaning that even if the vertical movement conditions (1)–(3) of the model (see Section 3) are not fulfilled, the locust attempts to move vertically to an adjacent empty space on the track above or below them (if such empty space exists).

These behaviors are independent, and so a locust may behave erratically in both the vertical and horizontal phases, in just one of them, or in neither.

The next theorem shows that the existence of erratic behavior forces a global consensus of locust headings. The goal is to prove that there is some finite time after which all locusts must have the same heading. Note that the bound we find for this time is crude and is not intended to approximate T_{stable}. We study the question of how p affects T_{stable} empirically in the next section.

Theorem 5. *Assuming there is at least one empty space (i.e., $m < nk$), and the probability of erratic track switching is $0 < r, p < 1$, the locusts all have identical heading in finite expected time.*

Proof. Our goal is to show that all locusts must have identical heading in finite expected time. We will find a crude upper bound for this time. It suffices to show that as long as there are two locusts with different headings in the system (perhaps not on the same track), there is a bounded-above-zero probability q that within a some constant, finite number of time steps C (and shall show $C = \mathcal{O}(\log(k)n^2 + nk)$), the number of locusts with a clockwise heading will increase. This amounts to showing that there is a sequence of events, each individual event happening with non-zero probability, that culminates in a conflict between two locusts occurring (since any conflict has probability 0.5 of increasing the number of clockwise locusts). Since $q > 0$, the only stable state of locust headings is the state where all locusts have the identical heading, as otherwise there is always some probability that all locusts will have a clockwise heading after $m \cdot C$ time steps. This completes the proof.

Let us show such a sequence of events. First let us consider the case where there is a track in which two locusts have non-identical headings. In this case, assuming no locusts behave erratically for $\mathcal{O}(\log(k)n^2)$ steps (which occurs with a tiny but bounded-above-zero probability since $p, r > 0$), Theorem 2 tells us that in expected $\mathcal{O}(\log(k)n^2)$ steps, locusts on the same track will have the identical heading. Hence, there is a sequence of events that happens with non-zero probability which leads to local consensus in the tracks.

If any conflict occurs during this sequence, we are finished. Otherwise, we need to show a sequence of events that leads to a conflict, assuming all tracks are stable. The only thing that causes locusts in local consensus to move tracks is erratic behavior. If two adjacent tracks have locusts with non-identical heading, and there is at least one empty space in one of them, then (since $r > 0$) with some probability within at most n time steps an empty space in one track will be vertically adjacent to a locust in the other track. At this point, with probability p, that locust will move from one track to the other. This creates a situation where in one track there are locusts of different headings again. If the erratic locust moves tracks at the right time, upon moving it will be adjacent to another locust in its new track, whose heading is different. Hence, the erratic locust will enter a conflict in the next time step, which will increase the number of clockwise locusts with probability 0.5.

Now let us consider a pair of two adjacent tracks with locusts of different headings such that there no empty space in one of them. We note that since there is at least one empty location in *some* track, erratic behavior can cause that empty location to move vertically in an arbitrary fashion until, after at most k movements, it enters a track from the pair. With non-zero probability, this can take at most nk time steps, after which we are reduced to the situation in the previous paragraph.

A pair of adjacent tracks that have locusts with different headings must exist unless there is global consensus. Hence, in every $\mathcal{O}(\log(k)n^2 + nk)$ time steps where there is no global consensus, there is a some probability $q > 0$ that the number of clockwise-heading locusts will increase. □

5. Simulation and Empirical Evaluation

Let us explore some questions about the expected value of T_{stable} through numerical simulations. Certain aspects of the locusts' dynamics were not studied in our formal analysis, the most interesting of which is the helpful effects of track switching on T_{stable}. Recall that our model allows locusts to switch tracks if this would enable them to avoid a conflict and join a track where *locally*, locusts are marching in their same direction. At least in principle, this seems like it should help our locusts achieve local stability faster, hence decrease T_{stable}. However, recall also that we do not specify *when* locusts switch tracks, which means that some locusts might never switch tracks, or they might choose to do so in the worst possible moments. Hence, the positive effect track-switching usually has on T_{stable} cannot be reflected in the bounds we found for $\mathbb{E}[T_{stable}]$, since these bounds must reflect all possible locust behaviors. Under ordinary circumstances, however, it seems as though frequent track switching should noticeably decrease the time to local stabilization. As we shall see numerically, this is indeed the case. This justifies the track-switching behavior as a mechanism that, despite being highly local, enables the locusts to achieve local consensus about the direction of motion sooner.

In Figure 6a,b, we measure T_{stable} as it varies with n and k, assuming the probabilities of erratic behavior are 0 (i.e., $r = p = 0$). We simulate two different locust configurations: a "dense" configuration and a "sparse" configuration. In the dense configuration, 50% of locations are initiated with a locust, with the locations chosen at random. In the sparse configuration, 10% of locations are initiated with a locust (or slightly more, to guarantee all tracks start with two locusts). The locusts are initiated with random heading. We measure the effect of track switching on T_{stable}; the opaque lines measure T_{stable} when locusts switch tracks as often as they can (while still obeying the rules of the model), and the dotted lines measure T_{stable} when locusts never switch tracks. For every value of n, k, we ran the simulation 2000 times and averaged T_{stable} over all simulations.

As we can see, in the sparse configuration, track-switching has a significantly positive effect on time to stabilization. For example, with $k = 30$, $n = 30$, T_{stable} is approximately 13.5 when locusts switch tracks as soon as they can and approximately 25 when they never switch tracks—nearly double. In the dense configuration, we see that enabling locusts to move tracks has little to no effect, since the locust model rarely allows them to do so due to the tracks being overcrowded.

In column (c) of Figure 6, we measure how a non-zero probability p of erratic behavior affects T_{stable}. We set $r = 0$. As we proved in the previous section, whenever $p > 0$, stabilization requires *global* rather than local consensus. Hence, we cannot directly compare the T_{stable} of these graphs with columns (a) and (b), where T_{stable} measures the time to local consensus. We note that the expectation and variance of T_{stable} approach ∞ as p goes to 0, since when $p = 0$, global stability can never occur in some initial configurations. $\mathbb{E}[T_{stable}]$ decreases sharply as p goes to some critical point around 0.1, and decreases at a slower rate afterwards. It is interesting to note that low probability of erratic behavior affects $\mathbb{E}[T_{stable}]$ significantly more in the *sparse* configuration, where for $p = 0.02$, if locusts also switch tracks whenever the model allows them, $\mathbb{E}[T_{stable}]$ was measured as being approximately 1974, as opposed to 669 in the dense configuration. One of the core reasons for this seems to be that in the sparse configuration, when a locust erratically moves to a track with a lot of locusts not sharing its heading, it will often be able to *non-erratically* move back to its former track, thus preventing locust interactions between tracks of different headings. When we disabled the locusts' ability to switch tracks non-erratically, T_{stable} was significantly smaller in the sparse configuration ($\mathbb{E}[T_{stable}] \approx 232$ for $p = 0.02$).

Based on the above, we make the curious observation that, while non-erratic track switching accelerates local consensus, for some track-switching behaviors it will in fact decelerate the attainment of global consensus. This is seen by the fact that frequent non-erratic track-switching was helpful in Columns (a) and (b) of Figure 6 but increased time to stabilization in Column (c). This is perhaps a very natural observation because agents that aggressively switch tracks will attempt to avoid conflict as often as possible, whereas conflict is necessary to create global consensus.

To finish this section, we also verify the bounds of Theorem 1 by numerical simulation, by fixing $k = 1$ and measuring T_{stable} as n goes from 1 to 100—see Figure 7. We again measure both sparse and dense configurations (i.e., $m \approx 0.1n$ and $m \approx 0.5n$, respectively). The average expected time appears asymptotically bounded by m^2, as expected. We also simulated the asymptotic worst-case locust configuration in the proof of Theorem 1 (not illustrated in Figure 7) and confirmed its stabilization time is asymptotically $\Omega(m^2 + n - m)$, verifying that the bounds of Theorem 1 are asymptotically tight.

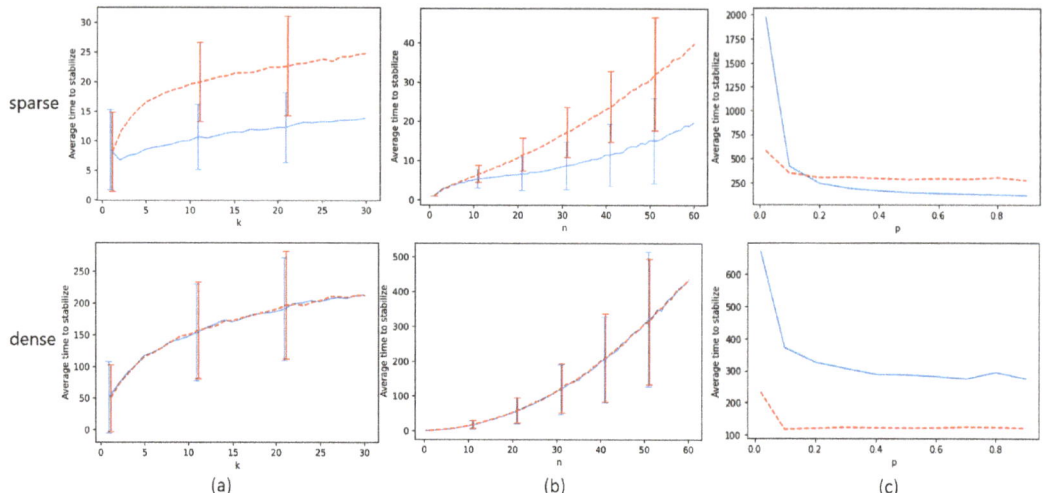

Figure 6. Simulations of the locust model. The y axis is T_{stable}. Column (**a**) measures T_{stable} for $k = 1 \ldots 30$, with n fixed at 30. Column (**b**) measures T_{stable} for $n = 1 \ldots 60$, with k fixed at 5. Column (**c**) measures T_{stable} with $n = 30, k = 5$, and p (the probability of erratic behavior) going from 0 to 1. The top row measures T_{stable} in sparse locust configurations ($m \approx 0.1n$), while the bottom row does so for dense configurations ($m \approx 0.5n$). The dashed red line estimates T_{stable} when locusts never switch tracks (except while behaving erratically in column (**c**)); the blue line estimates T_{stable} when locusts switch tracks as often as the model rules allow. Error bars show the standard deviations.

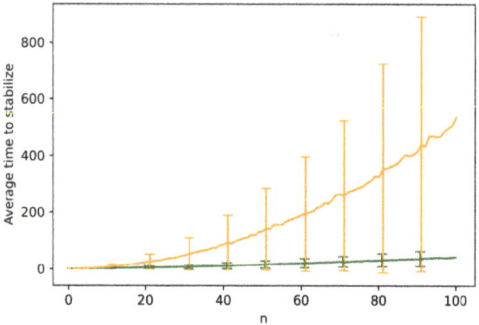

Figure 7. Simulations of the locust model fixing $k = 1$ and letting n run from 1 to 100. The y axis is T_{stable}. The orange line denotes dense locust configurations ($m \approx 0.5n$), and the green line denotes sparse configurations ($m \approx 0.1n$). Error bars show the standard deviations.

6. Concluding Remarks

We studied collective motion in a model of discrete locust-inspired swarms, and bounded the expected time to stabilization in terms of the number of agents m, the number of tracks k, and the length of the tracks n. We showed that when the swarm stabilizes, there must be a local consensus about the direction of motion. We also showed that, when the model is extended to allow a small probability of erratic behavior to perturb the system, global consensus eventually occurs.

A direct continuation of our work would be to find upper bounds on time to stabilization when there is some probability of erratic behavior. Furthermore, our empirical simulations suggest several curious phenomena related to erratic behavior. First, there seems to be a clash between "erratic" and non-erratic, "rational" track-switching, as when locusts switch tracks non-erratically to avoid collisions. This seems to accelerate the attainment of local consensus but mostly hinder the attainment of global consensus. Second, increasing the probability of erratic track-switching p behavior was helpful in accelerating global consensus up to a point, but in simulations, its impact seemed to fall off past a small critical value of p. In future work, it would be interesting to investigate these "phase transition" aspects of the model.

As discussed in the Related Work section, in [18,19] it is observed that at intermediate densities, swarms of locusts exhibit periodic directional switching, and at low densities the directions of motion are random. Although this phenomenon does not occur in our model, if we assume each locust has a small probability $r > 0$ of randomly flipping their heading at the beginning of a time step, such directional switching becomes possible, with probability inversely proportional to the density (or so we expect). This extension of our model, of course, does not have stable states, thus cannot be studied by the same methods we used in this work. Nevertheless, we would be interested in studying it in terms of the *expected time* the swarm spends in consensus or near-consensus about the direction of motion before directional switching occurs.

For the sake of mathematical theory, the authors would be very interested in rigorous results established over a fully asynchronous version of this model where locust wake-up times are determined independently. In such a model, the winner of a conflict between two locusts can be determined as the locust that wakes up first (thus exerts pressure on the other locust first), which is perhaps more elegant. We speculate that most of the conclusions will not be majorly affected by transitioning to an asynchronous model.

Although our agent marching model is inspired by experiments on locusts, it can be understood in more abstract terms as a model that describes a situation where many agents that wish to maintain a direction of motion are confined to a small space where they exert pressure on each other. It is natural to ask what kinds of collective dynamics, if any, we should expect when this small space has a different topology; rather than a ringlike arena, we might consider, e.g., a square arena. We believe that rich models of swarm dynamics can be discovered through observing natural organisms exert pressure on each other in such environments. In the introduction, we mentioned points of similarity between our model and models of opinion dynamics. We suspect that these points of similarity will remain in settings with non-ringlike arenas and might provide a starting point for formally modeling and analyzing them.

Author Contributions: Conceptualization, M.A., N.A. and A.M.B.; Formal analysis, M.A.; Writing—original draft, M.A.; Writing—review & editing, N.A. and A.M.B. All authors have read and agreed to the published version of the manuscript.

Funding: This research was partially supported by the Israeli Science Foundation grant no. 2306/18, and partially by the Israeli Smart Transportation Research Center (ISTRC).

Data Availability Statement: Not applicable.

Acknowledgments: This research was partially supported by the Israeli Science Foundation grant no. 2306/18, and partially by the Israeli Smart Transportation Research Center (ISTRC). The authors would like to thank Amir Ayali (Tel Aviv University) for bringing our attention to the locust experiments and for graciously letting us use the image in Figure 1, and Ofer Zeitouni (Weizmann Institute of Science) for helpful discussions. We are grateful to the anonymous referees for their insightful feedback, and for bringing our attention to several important references.

Conflicts of Interest: The authors declare no conflict of interest.

References

1. Altshuler, Y.; Pentland, A.; Bruckstein, A.M. Introduction to Swarm Search. In *Swarms and Network Intelligence in Search*; Springer: Berlin/Heidelberg, Germany, 2018; pp. 1–14.
2. Wagner, I.A.; Altshuler, Y.; Yanovski, V.; Bruckstein, A.M. Cooperative cleaners: A study in ant robotics. *Int. J. Robot. Res.* **2008**, *27*, 127–151. [CrossRef]
3. Ariel, G.; Ayali, A. Locust Collective Motion and Its Modeling. *PLoS Comput. Biol.* **2015**, *11*, e1004522. [CrossRef] [PubMed]
4. Fridman, N.; Kaminka, G.A. Modeling pedestrian crowd behavior based on a cognitive model of social comparison theory. *Comput. Math. Organ. Theory* **2010**, *16*, 348–372. [CrossRef]
5. Garnier, S.; Combe, M.; Jost, C.; Theraulaz, G. Do Ants Need to Estimate the Geometrical Properties of Trail Bifurcations to Find an Efficient Route? A Swarm Robotics Test Bed. *PLoS Comput. Biol.* **2013**, *9*, e1002903. [CrossRef] [PubMed]
6. Altshuler, Y.; Yanovsky, V.; Wagner, I.A.; Bruckstein, A.M. Efficient cooperative search of smart targets using UAV Swarms1. *Robotica* **2008**, *26*, 551–557. [CrossRef]
7. Bruckstein, A.M. Why the ant trails look so straight and nice. *Math. Intell.* **1993**, *15*, 59–62. [CrossRef]
8. Chaté, H.; Ginelli, F.; Grégoire, G.; Peruani, F.; Raynaud, F. Modeling collective motion: Variations on the Vicsek model. *Eur. Phys. J. B* **2008**, *64*, 451–456. [CrossRef]
9. Czirók, A.; Vicsek, M.; Vicsek, T. Collective motion of organisms in three dimensions. *Phys. A Stat. Mech. Its Appl.* **1999**, *264*, 299–304. [CrossRef]
10. Ried, K.; Müller, T.; Briegel, H.J. modeling collective motion based on the principle of agency: General framework and the case of marching locusts. *PLoS ONE* **2019**, *14*, e0212044. [CrossRef]
11. Chazelle, B. Toward a theory of Markov influence systems and their renormalization. *arXiv* **2018**, arXiv:1802.01208.
12. Amichay, G.; Ariel, G.; Ayali, A. The effect of changing topography on the coordinated marching of locust nymphs. *PeerJ* **2016**, *4*, e2742. [CrossRef] [PubMed]
13. Ariel, G.; Ophir, Y.; Levi, S.; Ben-Jacob, E.; Ayali, A. Individual pause-and-go motion is instrumental to the formation and maintenance of swarms of marching locust nymphs. *PLoS ONE* **2014**, *9*, e101636. [CrossRef] [PubMed]
14. Knebel, D.; Sha-Ked, C.; Agmon, N.; Ariel, G.; Ayali, A. Collective motion as a distinct behavioral state of the individual. *Iscience* **2021**, *24*, 102299. [CrossRef] [PubMed]
15. Knebel, D.; Ayali, A.; Guershon, M.; Ariel, G. Intra-versus intergroup variance in collective behavior. *Sci. Adv.* **2019**, *5*, eaav0695. [CrossRef]
16. Chazelle, B. Natural algorithms and influence systems. *Commun. ACM* **2012**, *55*, 101–110. [CrossRef]
17. Amir, M.; Bruckstein, A.M. Probabilistic pursuits on graphs. *Theor. Comput. Sci.* **2019**, *795*, 459–477. [CrossRef]
18. Buhl, J.; Sumpter, D.J.; Couzin, I.D.; Hale, J.J.; Despland, E.; Miller, E.R.; Simpson, S.J. From disorder to order in marching locusts. *Science* **2006**, *312*, 1402–1406. [CrossRef]
19. Yates, C.A.; Erban, R.; Escudero, C.; Couzin, I.D.; Buhl, J.; Kevrekidis, I.G.; Maini, P.K.; Sumpter, D.J. Inherent noise can facilitate coherence in collective swarm motion. *Proc. Natl. Acad. Sci. USA* **2009**, *106*, 5464–5469. [CrossRef]
20. Amir, M.; Agmon, N.; Bruckstein, A.M. A Discrete Model of Collective Marching on Rings. In *International Symposium Distributed Autonomous Robotic Systems*; Springer: Cham, Switzerland, 2021; pp. 320–334.
21. Bazazi, S.; Buhl, J.; Hale, J.J.; Anstey, M.L.; Sword, G.A.; Simpson, S.J.; Couzin, I.D. Collective motion and cannibalism in locust migratory bands. *Curr. Biol.* **2008**, *18*, 735–739. [CrossRef]
22. Shiraishi, M.; Aizawa, Y. Collective patterns of swarm dynamics and the Lyapunov analysis of individual behaviors. *J. Phys. Soc. Jpn.* **2015**, *84*, 054002. [CrossRef]
23. Altshuler, Y.; Pan, W.; Pentland, A.S. Trends prediction using social diffusion models. In Proceedings of the International Conference on Social Computing, Behavioral-Cultural Modeling, and Prediction, College Park, MD, USA, 3–5 April 2012; Springer: Berlin/Heidelberg, Germany, 2012; pp. 97–104.
24. Yildiz, E.; Ozdaglar, A.; Acemoglu, D.; Saberi, A.; Scaglione, A. Binary opinion dynamics with stubborn agents. *ACM Trans. Econ. Comput. (TEAC)* **2013**, *1*, 1–30. [CrossRef]
25. Xia, H.; Wang, H.; Xuan, Z. Opinion dynamics: A multidisciplinary review and perspective on future research. *Int. J. Knowl. Syst. Sci. (IJKSS)* **2011**, *2*, 72–91. [CrossRef]
26. Dong, Y.; Zhan, M.; Kou, G.; Ding, Z.; Liang, H. A survey on the fusion process in opinion dynamics. *Inf. Fusion* **2018**, *43*, 57–65. [CrossRef]
27. Chandra, A.K.; Basu, A. Diffusion controlled model of opinion dynamics. *Rep. Adv. Phys. Sci.* **2017**, *1*, 1740008. [CrossRef]
28. Hegarty, P.; Martinsson, A.; Wedin, E. The Hegselmann-Krause dynamics on the circle converge. *J. Differ. Equ. Appl.* **2016**, *22*, 1720–1731. [CrossRef]
29. Barel, A.; Manor, R.; Bruckstein, A.M. Come together: Multi-agent geometric consensus. *arXiv* **2017**, arXiv:1902.01455.
30. Cortés, J. Distributed algorithms for reaching consensus on general functions. *Automatica* **2008**, *44*, 726–737. [CrossRef]
31. Manor, R.; Bruckstein, A.M. Chase your farthest neighbour. In *Distributed Autonomous Robotic Systems*; Springer: Berlin/Heidelberg, Germany, 2018; pp. 103–116.
32. Olfati-Saber, R.; Fax, J.A.; Murray, R.M. Consensus and cooperation in networked multi-agent systems. *Proc. IEEE* **2007**, *95*, 215–233. [CrossRef]

33. Chou, T.; Mallick, K.; Zia, R. Non-equilibrium statistical mechanics: From a paradigmatic model to biological transport. *Rep. Prog. Phys.* **2011**, *74*, 116601. [CrossRef]
34. Amir, M.; Bruckstein, A.M. Fast uniform dispersion of a crash-prone swarm. *arXiv* **2019**, arXiv:1907.00956.
35. Kriecherbauer, T.; Krug, J. A pedestrian's view on interacting particle systems, KPZ universality and random matrices. *J. Phys. A Math. Theor.* **2010**, *43*, 403001. [CrossRef]
36. Grinstead, C.M.; Snell, J.L. *Introduction to Probability*; American Mathematical Society: Providence, RI, USA, 2012.
37. Lindvall, T. *Lectures on the Coupling Method*; Courier Corporation: North Chelmsford, MA, USA, 2002.
38. Aldous, D.; Fill, J. Reversible Markov chains and random walks on graphs. *J. Theor. Prob.* **1999**, *2*, 91–100. [CrossRef]
39. Epstein, R.A. *The Theory of Gambling and Statistical Logic*; Academic Press: Cambridge, MA, USA, 2012.
40. La Salle, J.; Lefschetz, S. *Stability by Liapunov's Direct Method with Applications*; Elsevier: Amsterdam, The Netherlands, 2012.
41. Levin, D.A.; Peres, Y.; Wilmer, E.L. *Markov Chains and Mixing Times*; American Mathematical Society: Providence, RI, USA, 2009.
42. Lawler, G.F. *Random Walk and the Heat Equation*; American Mathematical Society: Providence, RI, USA, 2010; Volume 55.

Article

Space-Air-Ground Integrated Mobile Crowdsensing for Partially Observable Data Collection by Multi-Scale Convolutional Graph Reinforcement Learning

Yixiang Ren [1,†], Zhenhui Ye [2,†], Guanghua Song [1,*] and Xiaohong Jiang [2]

1. School of Aeronautics and Astronautics, Zhejiang University, Hangzhou 310027, China; yixiangren@zju.edu.cn
2. College of Computer Science and Technology, Zhejiang University, Hangzhou 310027, China; zhenhuiye@zju.edu.cn (Z.Y.); jiangxh@zju.edu.cn (X.J.)
* Correspondence: ghsong@zju.edu.cn
† These authors contributed equally to this work.

Abstract: Mobile crowdsensing (MCS) is attracting considerable attention in the past few years as a new paradigm for large-scale information sensing. Unmanned aerial vehicles (UAVs) have played a significant role in MCS tasks and served as crucial nodes in the newly-proposed space-air-ground integrated network (SAGIN). In this paper, we incorporate SAGIN into MCS task and present a *Space-Air-Ground integrated Mobile CrowdSensing* (SAG-MCS) problem. Based on multi-source observations from embedded sensors and satellites, an aerial UAV swarm is required to carry out energy-efficient data collection and recharging tasks. Up to date, few studies have explored such multi-task MCS problem with the cooperation of UAV swarm and satellites. To address this multi-agent problem, we propose a novel deep reinforcement learning (DRL) based method called *Multi-Scale Soft Deep Recurrent Graph Network* (ms-SDRGN). Our ms-SDRGN approach incorporates a multi-scale convolutional encoder to process multi-source raw observations for better feature exploitation. We also use a graph attention mechanism to model inter-UAV communications and aggregate extra neighboring information, and utilize a gated recurrent unit for long-term performance. In addition, a stochastic policy can be learned through a maximum-entropy method with an adjustable temperature parameter. Specifically, we design a heuristic reward function to encourage the agents to achieve global cooperation under partial observability. We train the model to convergence and conduct a series of case studies. Evaluation results show statistical significance and that ms-SDRGN outperforms three state-of-the-art DRL baselines in SAG-MCS. Compared with the best-performing baseline, ms-SDRGN improves 29.0% reward and 3.8% CFE score. We also investigate the scalability and robustness of ms-SDRGN towards DRL environments with diverse observation scales or demanding communication conditions.

Keywords: mobile crowdsensing; deep reinforcement learning; UAV control; graph network; maximum-entropy learning

1. Introduction

In the past few years, Mobile Crowdsensing (MCS [1,2]) has rapidly become a popular research paradigm for large-scale information gathering and data sensing, which is an essential solution for the construction of smart cities or the Internet of Things [3]. In general, an MCS task consists of several stages: mobile sensing, crowd data collection, and crowdsourced data processing [4]. The traditional human-centric MCS paradigm relies on the perception capabilities of a large crowd of citizens' mobile devices, such as mobile phones, wearable devices or portable sensors. Compared with ordinary sensing networks, a human-centric MCS system makes full use of human intelligence for large-scale sensing purposes. However, the major challenge to traditional MCS lies that, users may be reluctant to participate in the MCS system for privacy and security concerns.

With the help of high-precision embedded sensors and path planning algorithms [5], smart unmanned vehicles, including automated guided vehicles (AGVs) and unmanned aerial vehicles (UAVs), are gradually taking the place of human participants for data collection. A swarm of intelligent unmanned vehicles can perform collaborative sensing tasks round-the-clock [6,7], or even cooperate with humans [8]. Among all kinds of unmanned vehicles, UAVs have better maneuverability and versatility compared to ground vehicles. Hence, UAV-based MCS technology can achieve large-scale, high-quality, long-term, and in-depth data collection in diverse real-world scenarios, such as efficient area coverage [9,10], smart city traffic monitoring [11,12], field search and rescue [13], post-disaster relief [14], communication support [15,16], reconnaissance in future wars [17], etc.

As the rapid developments and applications of modern network technologies [18,19], several studies have dug deep into heterogeneous networking and proposed an architecture called Space-Air-Ground Integrated Network (SAGIN [20,21]). SAGIN interconnects space, air, and ground network segments using different networking protocols. Satellite-based networks in space could provide global yet fuzzy observations of large-scale areas, but have some propagation delay due to the operating orbits and long communication ranges. Aerial networks, such as Flying Ad-Hoc Network (FANET [22]), have high mobility and self-organizing ability, but their performance are commonly constrained by unstable connections or dynamic network topology [23]. Ground networks have low transmission latency and efficient power supply, while they cannot maintain network coverage in certain remote areas.

In this paper, we employ the concept of SAGIN into the data collection task, and present a new MCS framework with a collection of UAVs, ground nodes and satellites, namely *Space-Air-Ground integrated Mobile CrowdSensing (SAG-MCS)*. In SAG-MCS scenario, a UAV swarm is used to cooperate autonomously and fly above an area with multiple Points of Interest (PoIs) for coverage and sensing. As illustrated in Figure 1, UAV agents can partially observe ground information using embedded sensors within a fixed observation range. They also have access to fuzzy global information periodically from remote sensing satellites in space, which contains ambiguous locations of PoIs and other agents. As the coverage range is set smaller than the observation radius, UAVs should get close enough to the observed PoIs for valid data collection. Based on the FANET, UAV pairs that within maximum communication range can interconnect together and share current states and observations using Wi-Fi, Bluetooth or LoRa. We consider communication dropout would occur inevitably during such aerial ad-hoc network connections. As for energy consumption, due to the limitations of the rotor power efficiency and the onboard battery capacity, we set all UAVs with limited battery attributes as energy constraints. Several charging stations and barriers are deployed in the SAG-MCS simulation scenario as well. The UAV swarm is required to avoid collision with obstacles when performing data collection and flight path planning tasks, and makes proper decisions to go for charging before their batteries run out. On arrival at the charging stations, UAVs can transfer the data collected and batteries will be replaced.

On the whole, this paper endeavours to propose a decision-making model for UAVs, which are powered by limited onboard batteries and distributed charging stations, to energy-efficiently and persistently sense and collect PoIs on the ground. The multi-UAV swarm shall perform actions according to local airborne observations and global observations from satellites. The overall optimization objective of the UAV swarm is to maximize the data coverage and geographical fairness among all PoIs, and minimize the power consumed during flying or battery charging.

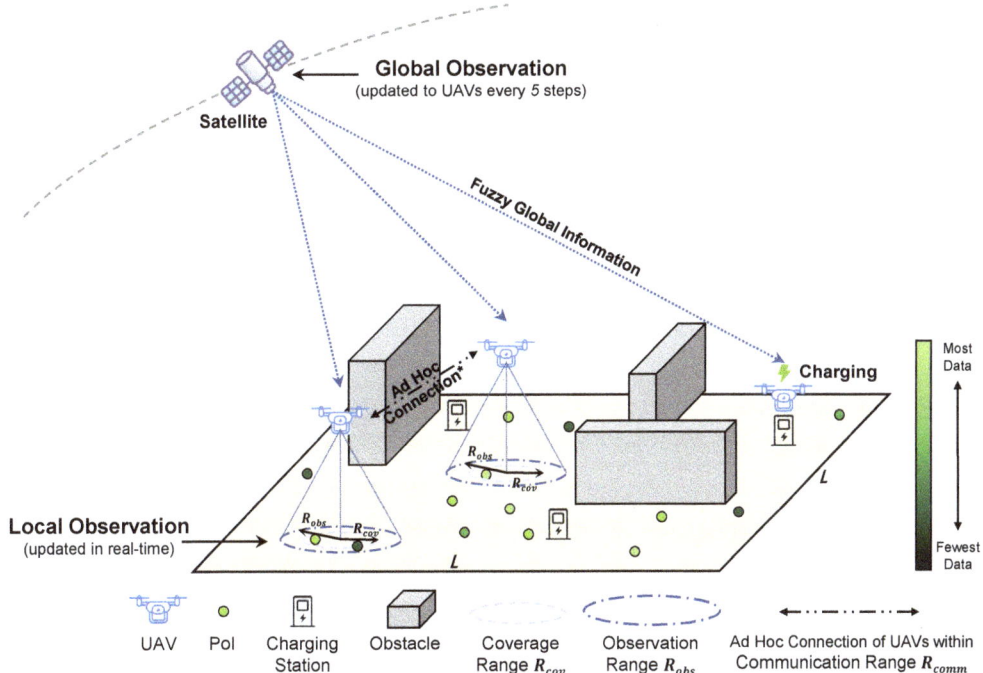

Figure 1. Proposed SAG-MCS Scenario Schematic.

For such an MCS task that has multiple complex objectives, existing approaches that modeling MCS as an optimization problem is no longer effective. However, recently well-explored Deep Reinforcement Learning (DRL) could be a feasible solution. It has achieved great performances in several game-playing tasks [24] or path planning problems [25]. Based on powerful deep neural networks, DRL models can extract more complicated features of higher dimensions from environmental states, thereby can optimize action policies to achieve different objectives. For multi-agent systems such as our SAG-MCS, typical methods that take the whole system as a single agent cannot guarantee promising results, while recent studies on Multi-Agent Deep Reinforcement Learning (MADRL) focus on controlling multiple agents in a fully distributed manner. The action strategy of each agent in MADRL depends on not only the interaction with the environment, but also other agents' actions, observations, etc.

Contributions

To this end, this paper formulates the problem as a Partially Observable Markov Decision Process (POMDP) and proposes a stochastic MADRL algorithm in SAG-MCS environment, to perform data collection and task allocation simultaneously. The main contributions of this article are summarized as follows:

1. We design a realistic SAG-MCS environment with obstacles and charging stations for simulation. To further enhance exploration of the global area, the UAV swarm can acquire multi-source observation inputs from embedded sensors and satellites.
2. We propose a DRL algorithm based on graph attention mechanism, namely *Multi-Scale Soft Deep Recurrent Graph Network (ms-SDRGN)*. It integrates a multi-scale convolutional encoder to process different sizes of observations. This method also utilizes

graph attention network (GAT [26]), gated recurrent unit (GRU [27]), as well as a maximum entropy method.
3. Although UAV swarm can receive parts of global observations from satellites, SAG-MCS is formulated as a practical partially-observed problem, and UAVs cannot have access to the overall system states during training. Therefore, we propose a heuristic reward function that only utilizes local observed information, but manages to train the UAV swarm to properly act for optimizing several global metrics.
4. We have designed and conducted several simulation case studies to verify the effectiveness of our stochastic MADRL method and reward function. Additionally, we validate the robustness of the trained model and the multi-scale CNN encoder under different communication conditions and at different environment scales.

The remaining part of this paper proceeds as follows: Section 2 reviews the related research efforts about MCS and DRL approaches. Section 3 introduces the SAG-MCS problem definition and the 2D simulation environment in detail. Section 4 presents the proposed solution ms-SDRGN for SAG-MCS problem. We introduce simulation settings and present the experimental results and analysis in Section 5. Then, Section 6 discusses the practical implementation issues and limitation of the proposed approach. Finally, conclusions are made in Section 7.

2. Related Works

In this section, we review the literature related to mobile crowdsensing problem, DRL approaches for multi-agent systems, and the joint studies of these two topics.

Threat to validity [28,29]: For this review, we have used multiple strings to search and identify relevant literature in recent decade, such as 'UAV swarm and mobile crowdsensing', 'multi-task allocation and mobile crowdsensing' and 'multi-agent deep reinforcement learning'. Google Scholar is used for forward searches and most of the related works are retrieved from five databases: IEEE Xplore, SpringerLink, Web of Science, ScienceDirect and Arxiv.

2.1. Multi-Task Allocation for Mobile Crowdsensing

MCS scenarios usually have multiple constraints and objectives. One of the key issues is how to perform task allocation, or how to choose appropriate action strategies for different tasks. The main tasks of SAG-MCS are data collection by covering PoIs and energy management by keeping batteries charged. UAVs need to automatically select action strategies to meet the data collection requirements under the energy-efficiency constraint. Solving such multi-agent task allocation is an NP-hard problem, and the related research is still in a relatively early stage. Feng et al. [30] utilized dynamic programming for path planning in UAV-aided MCS and used Gale-Shapley-based matching algorithm to allocate different tasks for agents. Wang et al. [31] modeled multi-task allocation as a dynamic matching problem, then proposed a multiple-waitlist based task assignment (MWTA) algorithm. In addition, several surveys of task allocation have demonstrated the effectiveness of heuristic algorithms. Hayat et al. [13] proposed a genetic algorithm approach to get the minimum task completion time for UAV path planning. Similarly, Xu et al. [32] formulated this problem as a specific mathematical model, and tried to minimize incentive cost under the constraint of sensing quality based on greedy algorithms and genetic algorithms.

2.2. Deep Reinforcement Learning (DRL) for Multi-Agent Systems

In multi-agent systems, Reinforcement Learning (RL) generally targets at problems of agents sequentially interacting with local environment. At timestep t, the environment is at state s_t and agent i obtains a observation o_t^i. Then, agent i selects and executes an action a_t^i based on o_t^i, and then gets a reward r_t^i from the environment. In POMDP, agents cannot directly perceive the underlying states and o_t^i is not equal to s_t. The objective of RL is to learn a policy $\pi_i(a_i \mid o_i)$ for agent i. The policy is expected to maximize the discounted reward $\mathbb{E}[R_t] = \mathbb{E}\left[\sum_{k=0}^{\infty} \gamma^k r_k^i\right]$, with a discounted factor $\gamma \in [0, 1]$.

Currently, DRL methods have achieved state-of-the-art performance in various RL tasks [24,25], and can be categorized into value-based or policy-based ones. In this paper, we adopted the value-based method. Deep Q-learning (DQN [24]) is one of the most vital value-based DRL approaches. Based on Q-learning, DQN uses deep neural networks to learn a Q-value function $Q(o, a)$, which could estimate the expected reward return $\mathbb{E}[R_t]$ and be recursively updated. DQN regards the action with biggest Q-value as the most optimal policy $\pi'(s) = \arg\max Q^{\pi}(o, a)$, and selects it to interact with the environment. In addition, DQN integrates fixed target network and experience replay methods to make the training process more efficient and stable [33]. Specifically, the Q-value function $Q(o, a)$ is updated through minimizing the Q-loss function as:

$$Q_{loss} = \left(r_t + \max_{a_{t+1}} Q'(o_{t+1}, a_{t+1}) - Q(o_t, a_t)\right)^2. \tag{1}$$

where Q is the learned network and Q' is the target network. Note that the policies learned by DQN are deterministic, therefore DQN should be trained with action policies such as $\epsilon - greedy$ to enhance exploration.

Compared with classical heuristic algorithms, agents can learn a strategy more efficiently and independently through DRL algorithms, so as to achieve multiple objectives in the sensing area simultaneously.

2.3. DRL Methods for UAV Mobile Crowdsensing

To date, several studies have investigated the application of DRL algorithms in the UAV Mobile Base Station (MBS) scenario, which is a sub-topic of MCS. In the UAV MBS scenario, a swarm of UAV serve as mobile base stations to provide long-term communication services for ground users. Liu et al. [15] proposed a DRL model based on Deep Deterministic Policy Gradient (DDPG [34]) to provide the long-term communications coverage in the MBS scenario. Further, Liu et al. [16] implemented DDPG in a fully distributed manner.

Different from policy gradient methods, Dai et al. [35] applied Graph Convolutional Reinforcement Learning (DGN [36]) in MBS. They modeled the UAV swarm as a graph, and used Graph Attention Network (GAT [26]) as a convolution kernel to extract adjacent information between neighboring UAVs. To further explore the potential of graph networks, Ye et al. [37] designed a FANET based on GAT, named GAT-FANET, allowing two adjacent UAV agents within the communication range to communicate and exchange information at low costs. This work also applied Gated Recurrent Unit (GRU) as a memory unit to record and process long-term temporal information from the graph network.

On the basis of MBS, Liu et al. [38,39] took practical factors such as obstacles and charging stations into consideration in the UAV MCS scenario. Based on the actor-critic network of DDPG, their DRL models used CNN to extract observed spatial information, and deployed a distributed experience replay buffer to store previous training information. Piao et al. [40], Dai et al. [41] and Liu et al. [38] utilized the concept of the Long Short-term Memory (LSTM [42]) network to store sequential temporal information of previous interaction episodes. As a specific application of MCS, Dai et al. [41] designed an approach for mobile crowdsensing, where mobile agents are required to retrieve data and refresh the sensors distributed in the city, with limited storage capacities of the sensors. Wang et al. [43] proposed a more practical and challenging 3D MCS scene for disaster response simulation, where the UAVs' action space had been expanded to three dimensions.

Compared with the UAV MBS and MCS works mentioned above, this paper proposes a more complicated and promising SAG-MCS scenario, which incorporates global and local observations from space and air, respectively, and encourages UAVs to interact with charging stations as ground nodes. While [38–41] proposed multi-UAV MCS scenarios and used policy-based DRL methods as solutions which utilized LSTM to store temporal information of MCS systems, our approach selects the value-based method based on DQN and uses GRU as the memory unit, which performs similarly to LSTM but is more computationally efficient [44]. Furthermore, when most MADRL studies about MCS solved the problem with deterministic policies, our method learns a stochastic policy following Ye et al. [37] to improve robustness.

3. System Model and Problem Statement

In this section, we design a partially observable space-air-ground integrated MCS system, with space-based remote sensing satellites and an aerial UAV swarm jointly performing the MCS task. We define the problem and present the 2D simulation system model specifically. Then, we describe the design of evaluation metrics.

3.1. System Model

As illustrated in Figure 1, the SAG-MCS scenario is simplified to a 2-dimensional continuous square area with the size of $L \times L$ pixels. The simulation area has fixed borders and multiple obstacles that UAVs cannot fly over. We assume that there are a set $\mathcal{K} \triangleq \{k \mid k = 1, 2, \ldots, K\}$ of PoIs, and each PoI is assigned a certain data amount $d(k), \forall k$. Note that PoIs are regarded as persistent information nodes and are not going to disappear after coverage. Additionally, we consider a set $\mathcal{C} \triangleq \{c \mid c = 1, 2, \ldots, C\}$ of charging stations and a set $\mathcal{B} \triangleq \{b \mid b = 1, 2, \ldots, B\}$ of round and rectangular obstacles. At the beginning of each simulation episode, the locations of all the PoIs, charging stations, and obstacles are randomly distributed in the 2D map. Each PoI's data amount $d(k), \forall k$ is randomly assigned in a certain range as well, but the total data volume $\Sigma_k d(k)$ of different episodes remains consistent.

Let $\mathcal{U} \triangleq \{u \mid u = 1, 2, \ldots, U\}$ be U UAV agents deployed in the simulation area, where the UAVs can perform continuous and horizontal flying movements at a fixed altitude. We define R_{obs} as the observation range, and R_{cov} as the coverage range or sensing range of each UAV. Arbitrary UAV can observe the local map within the radius R_{obs} in real-time and receive $L_{sat} \times L_{sat}$ fuzzy global map captured by satellites every some timesteps. Any PoI k within a UAV's R_{cov} is recognized as covered and all its data $d(k)$ is collected once at each timestep t. Note that R_{cov} is smaller than R_{obs}, as UAVs can only collect data when approaching to PoIs, but they can observe a wider range of area in general. Moreover, we consider the UAV swarm can autonomously form the ad-hoc network, and each pair of agents can be interconnected within communication range R_{comm} and exchange observed information for joint decision making. Considering the delays and packet losses in real-world ad-hoc networking, we set a communication dropout probability p between adjacent UAV nodes in training and evaluation. As for the energy consumption, we set the onboard battery status $\phi(u) \in [0, 100\%], \forall u$.

For each simulation episode, the data collection task in SAG-MCS scenario will last for T timesteps in total. Each UAV's position is randomly assigned and their batteries are fully-charged in the beginning. At each timestep t, UAV u can obtain local observation from embedded sensors; while every few timesteps, it can obtain fuzzy global observation from the satellite. Using the multi-scale observations $\{\mathbf{o}_t^u\}_{u \in \mathcal{U}}$, UAV u performs an action $\{\mathbf{a}_t^u\}_{u \in \mathcal{U}}$. We set the battery $\phi(u)$ consumed at timestep t as $\{e_t^u\}_{u \in \mathcal{U}}$, which is determined by the current flying speed $\{v_t^u\}_{u \in \mathcal{U}}$ and will be introduced in Section 3.4. When flying close to charging stations, their batteries will be fully charged in next timestep, simulating the real-world battery replacement process on the ground.

3.2. Observation Space

In SAG-MCS, each UAV agent u can obtain the multi-scale observation $\{\mathbf{o}_t^u\}_{u \in \mathcal{U}}$ at timestep t from different sources, as introduced in Section 3.1. In Figure 2, we formulate the observation space with three elements: $\mathcal{O} \triangleq \{\mathbf{o}_t^u = (\mathcal{O}_{local}^u, \mathcal{O}_{global}^u, \mathcal{O}_{self}^u)\}_{\forall u \in \mathcal{U}}$.

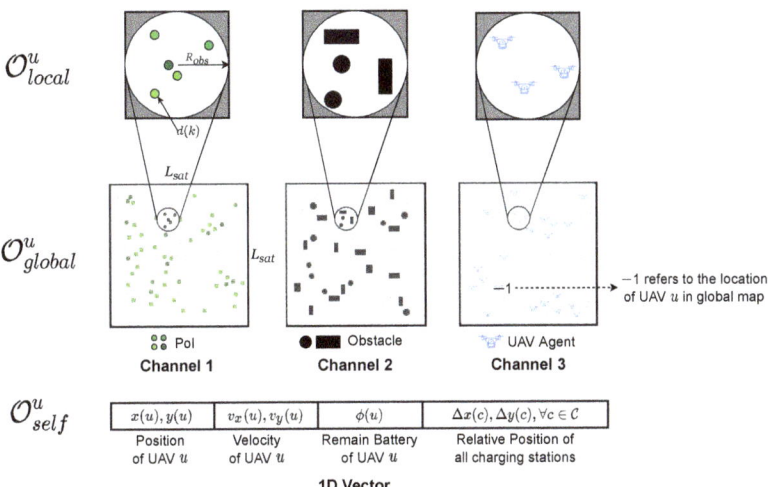

Figure 2. The observation space of UAV u in SAG-MCS.

(1) Local observation $\mathcal{O}_{local}$ from embedded sensors: UAV can observe local information within a circle of radius R_{obs} in real-time, centering on itself. Let $\mathcal{O}_{local} \triangleq \{\mathbf{o}_l^u = (\mathcal{O}_{local}^{u,1}, \mathcal{O}_{local}^{u,2}, \mathcal{O}_{local}^{u,3})\}_{\forall u \in \mathcal{U}}$ denotes local observation space, which consists of three 2D vector channels. The first channel contains the data amounts and distribution of surrounding PoIs. We set the data value $d(k)$ as the corresponding pixel value if it refers to PoI k, otherwise 0. The second channel contains the locations of obstacles relative to the UAV, where we set pixel value 1 for coordinates of obstacles, otherwise 0. The third channel includes the locations of other UAVs within R_{obs}. In addition, we define pixel value 1 for coordinates of UAV agents as well, otherwise 0.

(2) Global observation $\mathcal{O}_{global}^u$ from satellites: Every n timesteps, satellites will capture fuzzy global observation and transmit the information to all UAVs. As shown in Figure 2, $\mathcal{O}_{global}^u$ consists of three 2D channels with reduced size of $L_{sat} \times L_{sat}(L_{sat} < L)$, which cannot provide precise locations of the environment elements globally. We define $\mathcal{O}_{global} \triangleq \{\mathbf{o}_g^u = (\mathcal{O}_{global}^{u,1}, \mathcal{O}_{global}^{u,2}, \mathcal{O}_{global}^{u,3})\}_{\forall u \in \mathcal{U}}$ in absolute positioning coordinates. The encoding method for global observation is nearly the same as local observation, except in the third channel of UAV locations, we set -1 as the corresponding pixel value if it refers to the absolute location of UAV u in global map.

(3) Auxiliary observation $\mathcal{O}_{self}^u$: Then we utilize information from onboard flight control computer to assist UAV to learn optimal policy. Specifically, we define $\mathcal{O}_{self} \triangleq \{\mathbf{o}_s^u = \text{concatenate}(x(u), y(u), v_x(u), v_y(u), \phi(u), \{\Delta x(c), \Delta y(c)\}_{\forall c \in \mathcal{C}})\}_{\forall u \in \mathcal{U}}$. For UAV u, $\mathbf{o}_s^u$ includes its absolute position, velocity and current remaining battery, and the relative locations of all charging stations towards UAV u.

3.3. Action Space

The rotor UAVs are capable of applying different *thrust* at all directions responsively. We choose to discretize the entire 2-dimensional continuous space into eight directions for simplicity, and UAV agents can apply *maximum-thrust* (denoted as 1.0 unit), *half-thrust* (0.5 unit), or *zero-thrust* (0 unit) at any direction. Note that zero-thrust represents hovering in place. Therefore, the action space in SAG-MCS is defined as:

$$\mathcal{A} \triangleq \left\{ \mathbf{a}_t^u = (\theta_t^u, f_t^u) \mid \theta_t^u \in \{\frac{k\pi}{4} \mid k = 0, 1, \ldots, 7\}, f_t^u \in \{0, 0.5, 1.0\} \right\}. \quad (2)$$

where θ_t^u denotes the thrust angle and f_t^u is the thrust magnitude. The action space $\mathcal{A}$ consists of 17 actions in total. Since the timestep interval in the simulation is quite short, we assume the physical model is a uniform acceleration process. UAV can adjust the magnitude and direction of velocity using certain actions.

3.4. Evaluation Metrics

As stated in Section 3.1, the UAV swarm is aimed at collecting maximum information over PoIs as long as possible. UAVs should avoid collisions with obstacles and borders during movement, and recharge in time when power is low. Following Ye et al. [37] and Liu et al. [45], we propose three global evaluation metrics to evaluate the effectiveness of the joint cooperation of the UAV swarm in this SAG-MCS task. These metrics are ultimately used to evaluate the DRL policy we have trained.

The first metric is *Data Coverage Index*, which describes the average data amounts collected by the whole UAV swarm per timestep, as:

$$c_t = \frac{\sum_{k=1}^{K} w_t(k) d(k)}{Kt}, \quad t = 1, \ldots, T. \tag{3}$$

where $w_t(k)$ denotes the number of timesteps when PoI k was successfully collected from timestep 1 till t. $d(k)$ denotes the data amount carried by PoI k and K is the number of PoIs.

We noticed that in some cases, isolated PoIs in rural areas may not be covered even when the data coverage index is quite high; however, isolated or sparse PoIs in remote areas can carry valuable information in certain scenarios such as disaster relief. Considering the comprehensiveness of the data collection task, we propose the second global metric *Geographical Fairness Index* to evaluate the exploration ability of the UAV team, as:

$$f_t = \frac{\left(\sum_{k=1}^{K} w_t(k) d(k)\right)^2}{K \sum_{k=1}^{K} (w_t(k) d(k))^2}, \quad t = 1, \ldots, T. \tag{4}$$

where $w_t(k)$ and $d(k)$ are defined the same as Equation (3). When all PoIs are evenly covered, Equation (4) gives $f_t = 1$.

In addition, the third metric *Energy Consumption Index* is used to indicate the energy-saving status of the UAV swarm. In order to further simulate the energy consumed by multi-rotor UAV in reality, we adopt an equation of power on the flight speed [46], as:

$$P_T = \frac{1}{2} C_D A \rho v^3 + \frac{W^2}{\rho b^2 v}, \tag{5}$$

where C_D is the aerodynamic drag coefficient, ρ is the density of air and v is the current flying speed. Parameter A, W, b denote UAV's front facing area, total weight, and width, respectively. For simplicity, we adopt a general UAV model and specific values are omitted in this paper. In timestep t, we assume the consumed energy e_t^u by UAV u is linear to its battery power, as:

$$e_t^u = e_0 + \eta_e P_{T_t}^u, \tag{6}$$

where e_0 represents hovering energy consumption and η_e is an energy coefficient. $P_{T_t}^u$ refers to the output power of UAV u in timestep t. Equations (5) and (6) reveal that UAV's battery is more efficient at an optimal cruising flight speed, while hovering or flying at maximum speed will consume more power. Note that energy consumed during flight is mainly from rotors and embedded sensors, and we ignore the communication budgets in the ad-hoc network. Therefore, we define the energy consumption index by taking the average of all U UAVs in T timesteps:

$$e_t = \frac{1}{t \times U} \sum_{\tau=1}^{t} \sum_{u=1}^{U} e_\tau^u, \quad t = 1, \ldots, T. \tag{7}$$

After a complete simulation episode, we calculate the metrics mentioned above as *final global metrics*, denoted as $\{c_T, f_T, e_T\} = \{c_t, f_t, e_t\}_{t=T}$. We hope to maximize the coverage and fairness index for sensing data adequately, while minimize the energy consumption index for energy-saving. Therefore, following Ye et al. [37], we define the overall objective *coverage-fairness-energy score* (CFE score) by a DRL policy π:

$$CFE_t(\pi) = \frac{c_t \times f_t}{e_t}, \quad t = 1, \ldots, T. \tag{8}$$

Obviously, our objective is to optimize the policy π to maximize $CFE_T(\pi)$ of the whole episode. As our SAG-MCS is a practical partially observable scenario, UAV agents cannot be aware of these global metrics of the whole swarm. They can only make actions according to the decentralized policy $\pi_u, \forall u \in \mathcal{U}$ and self-owned information. Therefore, we propose a heuristic reward function to train the optimal policy π, which will be further introduced in Section 4.4.

4. Proposed ms-SDRGN Solution For SAG-MCS

Due to the multi-scale observation space and complicated SAG-MCS task, we propose a heuristic DRL method named *Multi-Scale Soft Deep Recurrent Graph Network (ms-SDRGN)*. As illustrated in Figure 3, we first utilize a Multi-scale Convolutional Encoder to integrate local and global observed information for better feature extraction from observation space. Based on the concept of DRGN [37], we use graph attention mechanism (GAT [26]) to aggregate neighboring information through ad-hoc connections, and adopt gated recurrent unit (GRU [27]) as a memory unit for better long-term performance. In addition, we utilize a maximum-entropy method to learn stochastic policies via a configurable action entropy objective, and control each UAV agent in a distributed manner. Furthermore, a customized heuristic reward function is proposed for decentralized training.

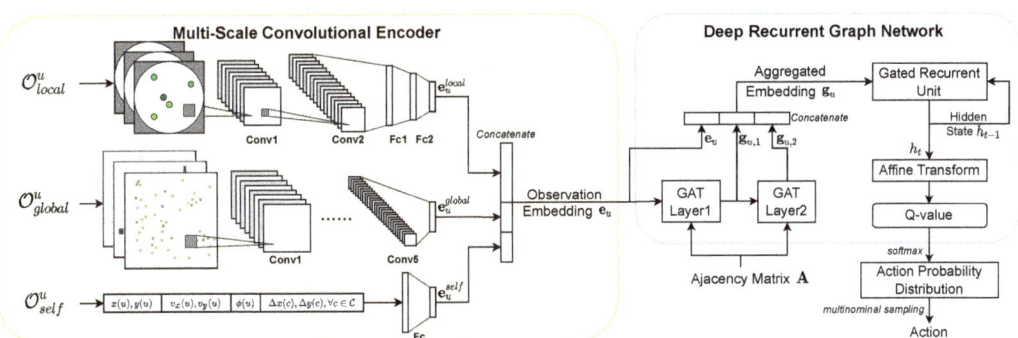

Figure 3. ms-SDRGN Model Architecture.

4.1. Multi-Scale Convolutional Encoder

Exploiting observations properly is essential for agents to perceive the current state of RL systems and make corresponding actions. Previous DRL methods (e.g., DQN, DGN, MAAC) apply multi-layer perceptron (MLP) as linear encoders to process raw observations, which is preferred for scenarios with smaller observation dimensions or less information, such as Cooperative Navigation [47]. However, in our SAG-MCS task, observations and environment states are more complicated and their input sizes are relatively larger.

Our intuition lies that compared with MLP, convolutional neural network (CNN) is more capable of processing data that has spatial information and large receptive fields, such as images. CNN can integrate information from different input channels as well. So we treat the local observation $\mathcal{O}_{local}$ and satellites' fuzzy global observation $\mathcal{O}_{global}$ as simplified real images, and design two CNN to extract spatial feature representations of local and global input states separately. Specifically, we construct the local CNN with two convolutional layers and two fully connected layers, which outputs local embedding e_u^{local}. The global CNN has a larger input scale, and we use five convolutional layers, which yields global embedding e_u^{global}. As for the auxiliary information in $\mathcal{O}_{self}$, we simply use a fully connected layer and take e_u^{self} as output from UAV self-owned information. Finally, we use concatenation operation to combine them as a multi-scale observation embedding e_u for UAV u:

$$e_u = \text{concatenate}(e_u^{local} \mid e_u^{global} \mid e_u^{self}), \ \forall u \in \mathcal{U}. \tag{9}$$

Such multi-scale features can help UAVs better select actions, by taking full account of: (a) the relative position between current UAV and surrounding PoIs, obstacles or other agents; (b) the correlation of current UAV's remaining battery and the distance to the closest charging station; (c) the distribution of PoIs in the fuzzy global map for better exploration and coverage.

4.2. Aggregate Adjacent Information with Graph Attention Mechanism

For the purpose of multi-agents exchanging information through ad-hoc connections in SAG-MCS, we model the UAV swarm as a graph network, where each node is represented as a UAV, and the edges are the communication links of neighboring UAV pairs. For each node i, we denote e_i extracted from observation space as its node embedding. Let all UAVs networked with UAV node i as a set G_i. This is implemented by an adjacency mask $\mathbf{A}$, which is a $U \times U$ symmetric matrix and satisfies $\mathbf{A}(i,j) = 1$ if UAV node i is interconnected with UAV node j. For all UAV node $j \in G_i$, we utilize GAT to determine the weight of UAV node i towards its different neighbors j as α_{ij}. Building on the concept of self-attention [48], an attention coefficient between node i and its neighboring node j is defined as $e_{ij} = a(\mathbf{W}e_i, \mathbf{W}e_j)$, where $a()$ is a shared attentional mechanism. Then, we calculate the attention weight α_{ij} by normalizing e_{ij} across all possible node j using softmax function:

$$\alpha_{ij} = \text{softmax}_j(e_{ij}) = \frac{\exp\left((W_K e_j)^T \cdot W_Q e_i\right)}{\sum_{k \in G_i} \exp\left((W_K e_k)^T \cdot W_Q e_i\right)}, \tag{10}$$

Then GAT aggregates information from all adjacent nodes j by weighted summation, which is given by:

$$g_i = \sum_{j \in G_i} \alpha_{ij}^k \cdot W_V e_j. \tag{11}$$

where we denote g_i as the aggregated output embedding of UAV j after one GAT layer. In addition, $W_Q, W_K, W_V \in \mathbf{W}$ are learnable weight matrices related with query, key, and value vector.

As shown in Figure 3, we utilize two GAT layers to aggregate information from neighboring UAV agents within a two-hop communication range, which could further expand the perception range and enhance cooperation of the UAV swarm. For better convergence, we then use skip connections [49] by concatenating the input observation embedding e_i, the outputs of the first GAT layer $g_{i,1}$ and the second GAT layer $g_{i,2}$, as $g_i = \text{concatenate}(e_i \mid g_{i,1} \mid g_{i,2})$.

Additionally, to make full use of temporal information during the interaction with RL environments and improve long-term performance, we integrate a gated recurrent unit (GRU) to memorize temporal features as:

$$h_t = \text{GRU}(g_i \mid h_{t-1}). \tag{12}$$

where we take g_i as input and h_t is the hidden state of timestep t stored in the memory unit. After adjacent information aggregation and GRU, we apply an affine transformation layer to h_t for calculating Q-value $Q(\mathcal{O}_t, a_t)$.

4.3. Learn Stochastic Policies with Adjustable Action Entropy

Based on the Q-value produced by DRGN, we can learn a deterministic policy, where each Q-value represents a fixed probability of the corresponding action. However, deterministic policies can easily jump into local optimum and lack for exploration in complex, real-world scenarios. Inspired by the maximum entropy RL framework [50,51], we utilize soft Q-loss to learn a stochastic policy in SAG-MCS, with the objective of maximizing expected reward and optimizing the action entropy towards a certain target. A flow chart of the training process is presented in Figure 4.

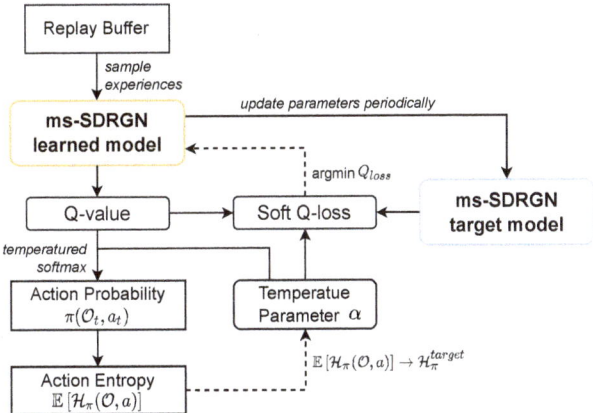

Figure 4. The training process of ms-SDRGN. In the flow chart, solid lines indicate feed forward propagation, and dashed lines denote updating parameters by backpropagation.

Firstly, we sample previous interaction experiences from the replay buffer as training inputs. The ms-SDRGN learned model infers a set of Q-value from the experiences. Then, we apply temperatured softmax operation to Q-value for getting the action probability:

$$\pi(\mathcal{O}_t, a_t) = \text{softmax}_{a_t}\left(\frac{Q(\mathcal{O}_t, a_t)}{\alpha}\right) = \exp\left(\frac{Q(\mathcal{O}_t, a_t)}{\alpha} - \log \Sigma_{a_t} \exp\left(\frac{Q(\mathcal{O}_t, a_t)}{\alpha}\right)\right), \quad (13)$$

where α is an adjustable temperature parameter, and Q-value $Q(\mathcal{O}_t, a_t)$ is produced by the learned model when receiving $\mathcal{O}_t$ and a_t as inputs. Specific action during simulation is sampled from the action probability. Then, we use Equation (13) to estimate the action entropy by calculating the information entropy expectation from sampled experiences:

$$\mathbb{E}[\mathcal{H}_\pi(\mathcal{O}, a)] = \mathbb{E}[-\Sigma_{a_t \sim \pi} \pi(\mathcal{O}_t, a_t) \cdot \log \pi(\mathcal{O}_t, a_t)], \quad (14)$$

The action entropy represents the action uncertainty of policy π, which can be adjusted by the temperature parameter α. Therefore, we preset a target action entropy as $\mathcal{H}_\pi^{target} = p_\alpha \cdot \max \mathcal{H}_\pi$, where the maximum action entropy is determined by action space as $\max \mathcal{H}_\pi = \log(\dim \mathcal{A})$, and p_α is a hyper-parameter named target entropy factor. Note that different RL tasks require different levels of exploration, so p_α shall be modified according to specific scenarios. More concretely, our goal is to let the action entropy $\mathbb{E}[\mathcal{H}_\pi(\mathcal{O}, a)]$ approach the pre-defined target action entropy $\mathcal{H}_\pi^{target}$, by updating the temperature parameter α through gradient descent:

$$\nabla_\alpha = f\left(\mathcal{H}_\pi^{target} - \mathbb{E}[\mathcal{H}_\pi(\mathcal{O}, a)]\right). \quad (15)$$

where f is a customized activation function and $\mathcal{H}_\pi^{target}$ denotes the target action entropy. The configurable action entropy mentioned above guarantees the balance between interaction stability and exploration capability of the policy.

Following Soft Q-learning [50], we also include the temperature parameter α to help define a V-value function for the target model. Finally, we use the mean squared error calculated by Q-value function and V-value function as Q_{loss}:

$$V(\mathcal{O}_t) = \alpha \cdot \log \Sigma_{a_t} \exp\left(\frac{Q(\mathcal{O}_t, a_t)}{\alpha}\right), \tag{16}$$

$$Q_{loss} = \frac{1}{S}\Sigma(r_t + V(\mathcal{O}_{t+1}) - Q(\mathcal{O}_t, a_t))^2. \tag{17}$$

where r_t is the reward earned in timestep t, $V(\mathcal{O}_t)$ denotes the V-value function and S is the batch size. The Q-value function $Q(o, a)$ of the learned model is updated through minimizing the Q_{loss} in Equation (17). In the learning process, ms-SDRGN target model will be updated periodically by duplicating the parameters of the learned model directly.

4.4. Heuristic Reward Function

In this section, we design a heuristic reward function to evaluate the result when the UAV swarm conducted action $\mathbf{a}_t$ based on respective observation $\mathbf{o}_t$. Since each UAV agent in SAG-MCS is only exposed to local information and acts in a decentralized manner, we expect the reward function can help agents to achieve a better CFE score, while not directly aiming at optimizing the global metrics mentioned in Section 3.4. Therefore, the reward function considers the impact of data collection, battery charging, energy consumption and collision with boundaries.

Firstly, we encourage the UAV swarm to collect data as much as possible. Note that PoIs that within UAV's coverage range R_{cov} are referred as 'covered'. For UAV u, we design an individual coverage term r_u^{self} and a swarm coverage term r_u^{swarm}:

$$r_u^{self} = \begin{cases} \eta_1 \cdot \Sigma_p d(p), & \text{if PoI } p \text{ is covered only by UAV } u \\ -1, & \text{if none PoI is covered by UAV } u \end{cases} \tag{18}$$

$$r_u^{swarm} = \begin{cases} \frac{\eta_2}{n_u} \cdot \Sigma_q d(q), & \text{if PoI } q \text{ is covered by other UAVs in } G_u \\ 0, & \text{if UAV } u \text{ is not networking with others} \end{cases} \tag{19}$$

where r_u^{self} counts the data amounts collected individually by UAV u, and r_u^{swarm} counts the data amounts covered by agents that network with UAV u in one-hop connection. They are expected to improve the data coverage index through both individual exploration and swarm cooperation. Let n_u denote the number of UAV u's one-hop neighboring nodes. In addition, we set balance coefficients $\eta_1 = 0.4$, $\eta_2 = 0.04$.

Secondly, in order to guide UAVs to charging stations when their batteries are low, we propose a charge term r_u^{charge} as:

$$r_u^{charge} = -\min \theta_c^u, \quad \forall c \in \mathcal{C}, \tag{20}$$

where $\theta_c^u \in [0, 1]$ is normalized euclidean distance between UAV u and charging station c. The charge term r_u^{charge} will increase as UAV moving closer to its nearby charging station. We deem the UAV is in charging state when the relative distance meets $\theta_c^u \leq 2.0$, then an extra reward of 2.0 points will be added to r_u^{charge}.

Other factors such as energy consumption and collisions are considered as well. According to Equation (6), we simply define an energy term as $r_u^{energy} = 1/e_t^u$. UAVs that consume less energy are expected to gain higher rewards. Then, we define a penalty term $p_u = 1$ when UAV u collides with the fixed boundary in our scenario, otherwise put $p_u = 0$.

We integrate local evaluation terms and define the heuristic reward function as:

$$r_u = \frac{\left(r_u^{self} + r_u^{swarm}\right) \times \epsilon + r_u^{charge} \times (1 - \epsilon)}{r_u^{energy}} + p_u, \quad \text{if } \phi(u) > 0, \tag{21}$$

where the weight parameter ϵ refers to the remaining battery percentage, denoted as $\epsilon = \phi(u)/100\%$. Equation (21) only functions when battery is not empty, otherwise the reward function is defined as:

$$r_u = r_u^{energy}, \quad \text{if } \phi(u) \leq 0. \tag{22}$$

For training simplicity, UAV can still operate when its battery has drained, but it cannot get reward from data collection and will get an extra punishment.

5. Experiments

In this section, we introduce the setup of experiments and performance metrics. Then, we compare our approach with three state-of-the-art DRL baselines. Case studies are performed to analyze the effectiveness, expansibility and robustness of ms-SDRGN.

5.1. Experimental Settings

In this section, we use Pytorch 1.9.0 to perform experiments on Ubuntu 20.04 servers with two NVIDIA 3080 GPUs and an A100 GPU. In the SAG-MCS simulation environment, we set the 2D continuous target area of 200 × 200 pixels, where 120 PoIs, 3 charging stations, and 50 obstacles (20 round obstacles and 30 rectangular obstacles) are randomly initialized. PoIs are scattered around 3 major points from Gaussian distribution, each PoI is randomly assigned associated data within [1, 5]. We deploy 20 UAVs in the training stage with a parameter-shared model for action inference. We define their coverage range $R_{cov} = 10$, the observation range $R_{cov} = 13$, and the communication range $R_{comm} = 18$ with the probability $p = 0.5$ of communication dropout. The fuzzy global observation with the size of 40 × 40 pixels is updated from satellites to UAVs every 5 timesteps. Each UAV's battery is initially fully charged to 100% and the consumed energy at each timestep is calculated after every movement, according to Equations (5) and (6).

In our implementation, the target entropy factor is set to $p_\alpha = 0.3$ and the discounted factor γ is 0.99. We use Adam for optimization with the learning rate of 1×10^{-4}, and ReLU as the activation function for all hidden layers. The experience replay buffer is initialized with the size of 2.5×10^4 for storing interaction histories, and the batch size is set to 256. As for the exploration strategy, we apply $\epsilon - multinomial$ for stochastic policies such as ms-SDRGN, letting ϵ start with 0.9 and exponentially decay to 0 in the end. For deterministic policies, we use $\epsilon - greedy$ strategy and set ϵ to exponentially decay to 0.05 at 30,000 training episodes.

One simulation episode lasts for 100 timesteps, and each DRL model interacts with the simulation environment for 50,000 episodes in total. Interaction experiences will be pushed to the replay buffer concurrently. After each simulation episode, the learned network is trained for 4 times using the experiences sampled from the replay buffer, while the target network is updated every 5 episodes by directly copying the parameters from the learned network. After training, we test the converged models for 1000 episodes to reduce randomness.

As introduced in Section 3.4, we use the following metrics to evaluate the performance.
- *Episodic Reward*: calculates the accumulated reward of the whole evaluation episode. It generally evaluates the SAG-MCS task achievements by the UAV swarm, considering data collection, battery management and collisions.
- *Data Coverage Index* (c_T): describes the average data amount collected from PoIs.
- *Geographical Fairness Index* (f_T): shows how evenly the PoIs are covered by all UAVs geographically and represents the UAV swarm's exploration level.

- *Energy Consumption Index* (e_T): calculates the average energy consumed by the UAV swarm, according to the flight speed and hovering status.
- *CFE Score* (CFE_T): represents the overall performance by combining c_T, f_T and e_T as Equation (8). We expect CFE score to be as large as possible.

5.2. Analysis of Training Convergence and Heuristic Reward Function

To validate the feasibility and effectiveness of our SAG-MCS environment design and the heuristic reward function, we first present the learning curves of episodic reward and the global metrics over time. During the training phase, we evaluate the model for 20 episodes after every 100 training episodes, and calculate the average global metrics and accumulated reward, as illustrated in Figure 5.

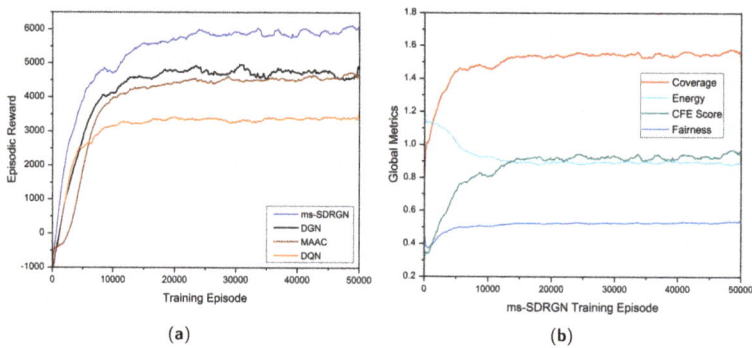

Figure 5. (a) The episodic reward learning curves of DRL algorithms. (b) The global metrics learning curves of ms-SDRGN.

In Figure 5a, we observe the average episodic reward of ms-SDRGN improves very quickly at the beginning, and gradually converges at around 20,000 episodes. Figure 5b presents the changes of four global metrics during the training progress of ms-SDRGN. The final energy index gradually drops and stabilizes to 0.9 at 20,000 episodes, indicating that UAVs have learned to operate at an optimal cruising speed. In addition, the final coverage and fairness index quickly grow and converge at around 10,000 episodes. Correspondingly, the overall CFE score has a similar growth trend and reaches convergence rapidly. Therefore, it can be proved that ms-SDRGN has learned the policy to fulfill the overall objective of maximizing the CFE score. After convergence, the UAV swarm can continuously collect PoIs maximumly using energy-efficient flying speed. The training results have suggested the effectiveness of the heuristic reward function.

Through visualization, we can observe that UAVs have learned to appropriately assign tasks at different remaining batteries. When its battery drops to around 25~40%, the UAV will proceed to the closest charging stations for battery exchange. In each simulation episode with 100 timesteps, the whole swarm rarely runs out of power, as such a charging process will happen two times for each UAV.

5.3. Comparing with DRL Baselines

We then compare our approach ms-SDRGN with three DRL baselines, including DGN [36], DQN [24] and MAAC [52]. DQN is a simple and efficient single-agent DRL approach, but it is still applicable for multi-agent tasks. Based on DQN, DGN uses GAT for modeling and exploiting the communication between agents. MAAC integrates self-attention mechanism with MADDPG [47], and provides agents with fully observable information to learn decentralized stochastic policy using a centralized critic. Thus, we compare ms-SDRGN with DGN to show the effectiveness of the multi-scale encoder and memory unit. Then, we compare with MAAC to validate the necessity of communication for the multi-agent swarm, especially in a partially observable environment.

We have evaluated the converged methods for 1000 episodes, and taken the mean value and standard deviation of all metrics, as shown in Table 1. Note that for a fair comparison, we also provide fuzzy global observations for the baselines, to ensure the raw observation inputs are the same.

Table 1. Comparison of DRL Baselines.

Algorithm	Reward	CFE Score	Coverage	Fairness	Energy
ms-SDRGN	**6025.82 ± 911.13**	**0.8911 ± 0.1699**	**1.5345 ± 0.1509**	0.5205 ± 0.0423	0.9067 ± 0.0347
DGN	4730.38 ± 840.32	0.8104 ± 0.1802	1.4636 ± 0.1600	0.5032 ± 0.0514	0.9226 ± 0.0514
MAAC	4670.71 ± 783.61	0.8587 ± 0.1799	1.4496 ± 0.1519	**0.5255 ± 0.0484**	**0.8992 ± 0.0373**
DQN	3291.03 ± 631.22	0.6273 ± 0.1367	1.3332 ± 0.1554	0.5027 ± 0.0521	1.0819 ± 0.0227

The evaluation results are presented in Table 1. Then, we conduct a independent T-test between our approach and other three DRL baselines on every evaluation metric. It can be concluded that ms-SDRGN has a significant difference comparing to the baselines ($p < 0.05$). We can obtain the following observations from Table 1:

Firstly, the proposed approach ms-SDRGN outperforms all other baselines in terms of reward and coverage index significantly. It demonstrates that with the help of multi-scale convolutional encoder and graph-based communication, ms-SDRGN achieves better data collection and energy management efficiency in SAG-MCS scenario. Compared with DQN and DGN, ms-SDRGN can better sense the surrounding environment from previous experiences in the memory unit, and make decisions more efficiently between seeking for more PoIs or returning for charging.

Secondly, from the perspective of fairness and energy, MAAC improves 0.005 fairness and 0.0075 energy index than ms-SDRGN. As a fully observable algorithm, we believe that MAAC can achieve similar cooperative exploration as ms-SDRGN using the observation embeddings from the whole UAV swarm. Regardless of extracting features from neighboring UAV nodes or from the memory unit, MAAC has a simpler objective to reduce its energy consumption for getting a higher reward.

Furthermore, the reward standard deviation of ms-SDRGN is higher than other methods, which may be attributed to randomness generated by the complex MADRL framework.

5.4. Analysis of Communication Dropout

In practical wireless networking applications, communication losses commonly occur in forms of delay, congestion or packet losses. To better cope with such real-world demanding communication conditions, we assume a $p = 0.5$ probability of communication dropout between interconnected UAVs during the training phase. Theoretically, this setting can improve the robustness of our model when implemented in different conditions. Therefore, we have trained two ms-SDRGN models in environments with and without communication dropout, respectively. Then, we test them in SAG-MCS, where the random communication dropout rate p varies in $[0, 1]$, with an interval of 0.1. The evaluation result is shown in Figure 6.

From Figure 6a, it is observed that as the dropout rate grows in evaluation environment, the reward of the model trained w/o dropout continuously decreases. While the model trained w/ dropout achieves more stable evaluated reward and outperforms the other when the dropout rate p is larger than 0.4. In terms of the major metric CFE score in Figure 6b, ms-SDRGN trained w/ dropout continuously surpasses ms-SDRGN trained w/o dropout. When the evaluating communication dropout rate changes from 0 to 1.0, the CFE score of ms-SDRGN trained w/ dropout drops around 0.05 point. By contrast, ms-SDRGN trained w/ dropout gets 0.19 point of degradation on CFE score.

Random communication dropout can affect the stability of timing correlation in GRU memory unit. However, after trained in environment with 50% probability of communication losses, our ms-SDRGN is proved to be more robust, and will not result in significant performance loss even under unreliable communication conditions.

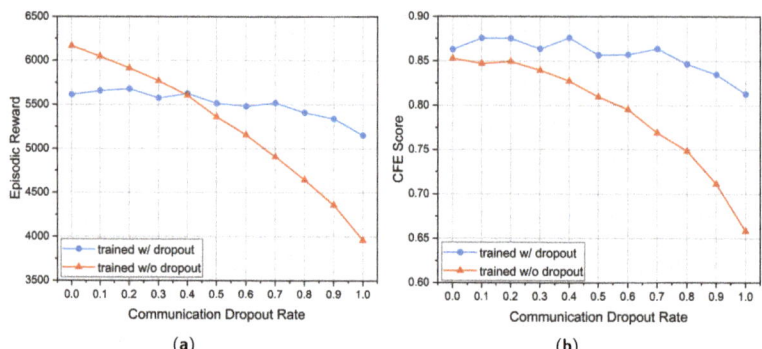

Figure 6. The evaluation results in environments with different communication dropout rate: (a) mean episodic reward and (b) CFE score.

5.5. Impact of Simulation Environment Scale Setting

Next, we proceed to verify the performance of the multi-scale convolutional encoder. In actual MCS tasks, UAVs could encounter various densities of overground PoIs. For regions with dense PoI distributions such as modern cities, we hope to perform finer-grained observations for higher feature resolution. While we can perform coarse-grained or lightsized observations for areas with sparse PoIs. In order to handle tasks of different observation scales and enhance robustness, we implement CNNs as the multi-scale encoder, which technically is more applicable than linear encoders for large-scale observations. Therefore, we expect to compare the front-end multi-scale convolutional encoder with original linear encoder using different local observation scales.

In this experiment, we simulate different sizes of observation inputs by proportionally scaling the whole map, which could maintain the distribution of all elements and ensure comparison fairness. Specifically, we set the original environment setting introduced in Section 5.1 as scale 1.0 unit, and adjust the scale factor from 0.5 to 2.0 with the interval of 0.5 unit. The major settings of different scale factors are listed in Table 2.

Table 2. Simulation Environment Scale Experiment Settings.

Environment Scale Factor	0.5	1.0	1.5	2.0
Environment Size in Pixels	100×100	200×200	300×300	400×400
Coverage Range R_{cov}	5	10	15	20
Observation Range R_{obs}	7	13	20	26
Communication Range R_{comm}	9	18	27	36

The evaluation results of four environment scales are presented in Figure 7. As size of local observation space varying with observation range R_{obs}, we can observe that CNN encoder outperforms linear encoder consistently on episodic reward. As for CFE score, ms-SDRGN with local CNN encoder achieves better CFE score than linear encoder when the scale factor is greater than or equal to 1.0, while linear encoder exceeds CNN encoder by 0.04 points at scale 0.5. The above result demonstrates that linear encoder can efficiently extract features from small-size input. In addition, the local CNN used in our multi-scale convolutional encoder has better representational capacity for large observation space. This finding demonstrates the expansibility of ms-SDRGN towards various scales of raw observations.

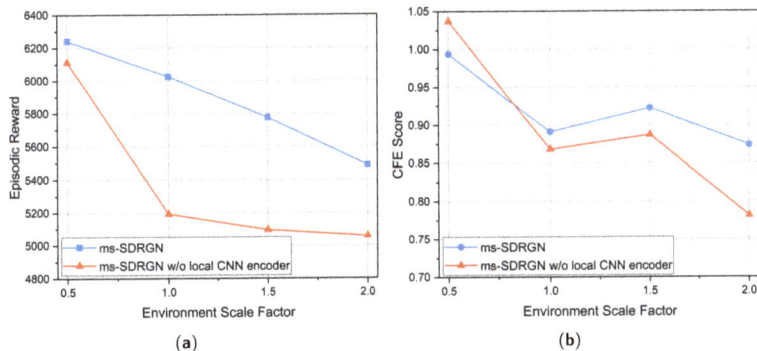

Figure 7. The evaluation results in environments with different scale factors: (**a**) mean episodic reward and (**b**) CFE score. ('w/o local CNN encoder' denotes using linear encoder to process local observations).

5.6. Ablation Study

Finally, we conduct an ablation study by separately removing components of ms-SDRGN, including multi-scale encoder, GAT layers, and GRU. We evaluate each case for 1000 episodes and the average results are listed in Table 3.

Table 3. Ablation study of ms-SDRGN method.

Algorithm	Reward	CFE Score
ms-SDRGN	6025.82 ± 911.13	0.8911 ± 0.1699
ms-SDRGN-ms	5198.48 ± 877.04	0.8674 ± 0.1985
ms-SDRGN-Soft	5337.79 ± 814.41	0.8592 ± 0.1791
ms-SDRGN-1GAT	5523.05 ± 905.01	0.8102 ± 0.1762
ms-SDRGN-2GAT	4984.57 ± 837.96	0.7956 ± 0.1729
ms-SDRGN-GRU	4318.14 ± 815.62	0.8017 ± 0.1878

'-ms' means removing local CNN encoder. '-Soft' means training a deterministic policy instead of a stochastic policy. '-1GAT' and '-2GAT' denotes disabling one GAT layer and two GAT layers separately. '-GRU' means disabling GRU memory unit.

It can be observed in Table 3 that when removing any components, our ms-SDRGN will generally result in performance degradation. Firstly, removing local CNN encoder in case '-ms' will reduce average CFE score and reward, which demonstrates the validity of CNN encoder, as discussed in Section 5.5. Secondly, case '-Soft' demonstrates the stochastic policy outperforms the deterministic policy by improving exploration and coverage efficiency. Thirdly, case '-1GAT' disables one GAT layer and limits the ad-hoc communication to one-hop range, which decreases 0.08 points on CFE score and 530 points on reward. Case '-2GAT' disables both two GAT layers, which completely cuts off the communication of the UAV swarm and causes further performance loss. This finding suggests the necessity of GAT mechanism for modeling the communication between agents. Moreover, case '-GRU' removes the memory unit and significantly reduces the average reward and CFE score. For complex MARL tasks such as SAG-MCS in this paper, the memory unit can help agents recall long-term experiences, especially when the positions of PoIs and obstacles are fixed.

6. Discussion

In this section, we discuss two limitations of our method and explore future directions for practical implementation.

Firstly, the computational complexity is crucial for practical applications. The proposed MADRL approach functions in a decentralized manner. Each UAV agent infers its action using on-board processor and executes the action subsequently. In addition, the multi-scale convolutional encoder introduced in Section 4.1 becomes the major computational burden for embedded processors. Therefore, future works will focus on introducing more computationally efficient spatial feature extractors.

Secondly, hand-crafted reward function limits the scalability. The heuristic reward function designed in Section 4.4 is customized for SAG-MCS simulation environment. When migrated to other application scenarios, the reward function requires modification case to case. Inverse reinforcement learning can be a solution for agents to infer reward functions from expert trajectories [53].

7. Conclusions

This paper introduced a partially observable MCS scenario named SAG-MCS, with an aerial UAV swarm jointly performing data collection task under energy limits. We proposed a value-based MADRL model named ms-SDRGN to address this multi-agent problem. Conclusively, ms-SDRGN applied a multi-scale convolutional encoder to handle the multi-scale observations, and utilized GAT and GRU for modeling communications and providing long-term memories. Effectively, a maximum-entropy method with configurable action entropy was employed to learn a stochastic policy. Experiments were conducted to demonstrate the superiority of our model compared with other DRL baselines, and validate the necessity of major components in ms-SDRGN. In addition, we analyzed the effectiveness of the communication dropout setting and the front-end CNN encoder. Future works will be focused on implementing fully continuous action space and exploring multi-stage multi-agent scenarios.

Author Contributions: Conceptualization, Y.R. and Z.Y.; methodology, Z.Y.; software, Y.R.; validation, Y.R., Z.Y. and G.S.; formal analysis, Y.R.; investigation, Y.R.; resources, X.J.; data curation, Z.Y.; writing—original draft preparation, Y.R.; writing—review and editing, Y.R., Z.Y. and G.S.; visualization, Y.R.; supervision, G.S.; project administration, G.S.; funding acquisition, X.J. All authors have read and agreed to the published version of the manuscript.

Funding: This research was funded by the National key R & D program of China sub project "Emergent behavior recognition, training and interpretation techniques" grant number No. 2018AAA0102302.

Institutional Review Board Statement: Not applicable.

Informed Consent Statement: Not applicable.

Data Availability Statement: Not applicable.

Acknowledgments: We gratefully acknowledge the reviewers for their comments and suggestions.

Conflicts of Interest: The authors declare no conflict of interest.

Abbreviations

The following abbreviations are used in this manuscript:

MCS	Mobile Crowdsensing
SAG-MCS	Space-Air-Ground integrated Mobile CrowdSensing
DRL	Deep Reinforcement Learning
MADRL	Multi-Agent Deep Reinforcement Learning
UAV	Unmanned Aerial Vehicle
PoI	Point of Interest
POMDP	Partially Observable Markov Decision Process
ms-SDRGN	Multi-Scale Soft Deep Recurrent Graph Network
GAT	Graph Attention Network
GRU	Gated Recurrent Unit
CFE	Coverage-Fairness-Energy Score
CNN	Convolutional Neural Network
MLP	Multi-Layer Perceptron

References

1. Capponi, A.; Fiandrino, C.; Kantarci, B.; Foschini, L.; Kliazovich, D.; Bouvry, P. A Survey on Mobile Crowdsensing Systems: Challenges, Solutions, and Opportunities. *IEEE Commun. Surv. Tutor.* **2019**, *21*, 2419–2465. [CrossRef]
2. Ganti, R.; Ye, F.; Lei, H. Mobile Crowdsensing: Current State and Future Challenges. *IEEE Commun. Mag.* **2011**, *49*, 32–39. [CrossRef]
3. Shaukat, K.; Alam, T.M.; Hameed, I.A.; Khan, W.A.; Abbas, N.; Luo, S. A Review on Security Challenges in Internet of Things (IoT). In Proceedings of the 2021 26th International Conference on Automation and Computing (ICAC), Portsmouth, UK, 2–4 September 2021; pp. 1–6. [CrossRef]
4. Guo, B.; Wang, Z.; Yu, Z.; Wang, Y.; Yen, N.; Huang, R.; Zhou, X. Mobile Crowd Sensing and Computing: The Review of an Emerging Human-Powered Sensing Paradigm. *ACM Comput. Surv.* **2015**, *48*, 1–31. [CrossRef]
5. Radmanesh, M.; Kumar, M.; Guentert, P.; Sarim, M. Overview of Path Planning and Obstacle Avoidance Algorithms for UAVs: A Comparative Study. *Unmanned Syst.* **2018**, *6*, 1–24. [CrossRef]
6. Altshuler, Y.; Pentland, A.; Bruckstein, A.M. (Eds.) Introduction to Swarm Search. In *Swarms and Network Intelligence in Search*; Studies in Computational Intelligence; Springer International Publishing: Cham, Switzerland, 2018; pp. 1–14. [CrossRef]
7. Altshuler, Y.; Bruckstein, A.M. Static and Expanding Grid Coverage with Ant Robots: Complexity Results. *Theor. Comput. Sci.* **2011**, *412*, 4661–4674. [CrossRef]
8. Rosenfeld, A.; Agmon, N.; Maksimov, O.; Kraus, S. Intelligent Agent Supporting Human–Multi-Robot Team Collaboration. *Artif. Intell.* **2017**, *252*, 211–231. [CrossRef]
9. Altshuler, Y.; Yanovsky, V.; Wagner, I.A.; Bruckstein, A.M. Efficient Cooperative Search of Smart Targets Using UAV Swarms1. *Robotica* **2008**, *26*, 551–557. [CrossRef]
10. Paull, L.; Thibault, C.; Nagaty, A.; Seto, M.; Li, H. Sensor-Driven Area Coverage for an Autonomous Fixed-Wing Unmanned Aerial Vehicle. *IEEE Trans. Cybern.* **2014**, *44*, 1605–1618. [CrossRef]
11. Menouar, H.; Guvenc, I.; Akkaya, K.; Uluagac, A.S.; Kadri, A.; Tuncer, A. UAV-Enabled Intelligent Transportation Systems for the Smart City: Applications and Challenges. *IEEE Commun. Mag.* **2017**, *55*, 22–28. [CrossRef]
12. Altshuler, Y.; Pentland, A.; Bruckstein, A.M. Optimal Dynamic Coverage Infrastructure for Large-Scale Fleets of Reconnaissance UAVs. In *Swarms and Network Intelligence in Search*; Altshuler, Y., Pentland, A., Bruckstein, A.M., Eds.; Studies in Computational Intelligence; Springer International Publishing: Cham, Switzerland, 2018; pp. 207–238. [CrossRef]
13. Hayat, S.; Yanmaz, E.; Brown, T.X.; Bettstetter, C. Multi-Objective UAV Path Planning for Search and Rescue. In Proceedings of the 2017 IEEE International Conference on Robotics and Automation (ICRA), Singapore, 29 May–3 June 2017; pp. 5569–5574. [CrossRef]
14. ur Rahman, S.; Kim, G.H.; Cho, Y.Z.; Khan, A. Positioning of UAVs for Throughput Maximization in Software-Defined Disaster Area UAV Communication Networks. *J. Commun. Netw.* **2018**, *20*, 452–463. [CrossRef]
15. Liu, C.H.; Chen, Z.; Tang, J.; Xu, J.; Piao, C. Energy-Efficient UAV Control for Effective and Fair Communication Coverage: A Deep Reinforcement Learning Approach. *IEEE J. Sel. Areas Commun.* **2018**, *36*, 2059–2070. [CrossRef]
16. Liu, C.H.; Ma, X.; Gao, X.; Tang, J. Distributed Energy-Efficient Multi-UAV Navigation for Long-Term Communication Coverage by Deep Reinforcement Learning. *IEEE Trans. Mob. Comput.* **2019**, *19*, 1274–1285. [CrossRef]
17. Li, P.; Duan, H. A Potential Game Approach to Multiple UAV Cooperative Search and Surveillance. *Aerosp. Sci. Technol.* **2017**, *68*, 403–415. [CrossRef]
18. Shaukat, K.; Shaukat, U. Comment Extraction Using Declarative Crowdsourcing(CoEx Deco). In Proceedings of the 2016 International Conference on Computing, Electronic and Electrical Engineering (ICE Cube), Quetta, Pakistan, 11–12 April 2016; pp. 74–78. [CrossRef]
19. Javed, I.; Tang, X.; Shaukat, K.; Sarwar, M.U.; Alam, T.M.; Hameed, I.A.; Saleem, M.A. V2X-Based Mobile Localization in 3D Wireless Sensor Network. *Secur. Commun. Netw.* **2021**, *2021*, 6677896. [CrossRef]
20. Liu, J.; Shi, Y.; Fadlullah, Z.M.; Kato, N. Space-Air-Ground Integrated Network: A Survey. *IEEE Commun. Surv. Tutor.* **2018**, *20*, 2714–2741. [CrossRef]
21. Wang, Y.; Wang, M.; Meng, L.; Zhang, Q.; Tong, X.; Cai, Z. New Crowd Sensing Computing in Space-Air-Ground Integrated Networks. 2021. Available online: https://www.researchgate.net/publication/355709897_New_Crowd_Sensing_Computing_in_Space-Air-Ground_Integrated_Networks (accessed on 22 March 2022).
22. Bekmezci, İ.; Sahingoz, O.K.; Temel, Ş. Flying Ad-Hoc Networks (FANETs): A Survey. *Ad. Hoc. Netw.* **2013**, *11*, 1254–1270. [CrossRef]
23. Hassan, M.U.; Shahzaib, M.; Shaukat, K.; Hussain, S.N.; Mubashir, M.; Karim, S.; Shabir, M.A. DEAR-2: An Energy-Aware Routing Protocol with Guaranteed Delivery in Wireless Ad-hoc Networks. In *Recent Trends and Advances in Wireless and IoT-enabled Networks*; Jan, M.A., Khan, F., Alam, M., Eds.; Springer International Publishing: Cham, Switzerland, 2019; pp. 215–224. [CrossRef]
24. Mnih, V.; Kavukcuoglu, K.; Silver, D.; Graves, A.; Antonoglou, I.; Wierstra, D.; Riedmiller, M. Playing Atari with Deep Reinforcement Learning. *arXiv* **2013**, arXiv:1312.5602.
25. Walker, O.; Vanegas, F.; Gonzalez, F.; Koenig, S. A Deep Reinforcement Learning Framework for UAV Navigation in Indoor Environments. In Proceedings of the 2019 IEEE Aerospace Conference, Big Sky, MT, USA, 2–9 March 2019; pp. 1–14. [CrossRef]
26. Veličković, P.; Cucurull, G.; Casanova, A.; Romero, A.; Liò, P.; Bengio, Y. Graph Attention Networks. *arXiv* **2018**, arXiv:1710.10903.

27. Cho, K.; van Merrienboer, B.; Bahdanau, D.; Bengio, Y. On the Properties of Neural Machine Translation: Encoder-Decoder Approaches. *arXiv* **2014**, arXiv:1409.1259.
28. Shaukat, K.; Luo, S.; Varadharajan, V.; Hameed, I.A.; Xu, M. A Survey on Machine Learning Techniques for Cyber Security in the Last Decade. *IEEE Access* **2020**, *8*, 222310–222354. [CrossRef]
29. Shaukat, K.; Luo, S.; Varadharajan, V.; Hameed, I.A.; Chen, S.; Liu, D.; Li, J. Performance Comparison and Current Challenges of Using Machine Learning Techniques in Cybersecurity. *Energies* **2020**, *13*, 2509. [CrossRef]
30. Feng, J.; Gu, B.; Ai, B.; Mumtaz, S.; Rodriguez, J.; Guizani, M. When Mobile Crowd Sensing Meets UAV: Energy-Efficient Task Assignment and Route Planning. *IEEE Trans. Commun.* **2018**, *66*, 5526–5538. [CrossRef]
31. Wang, B.; Sun, Y.; Liu, D.; Nguyen, H.M.; Duong, T.Q. Social-Aware UAV-Assisted Mobile Crowd Sensing in Stochastic and Dynamic Environments for Disaster Relief Networks. *IEEE Trans. Veh. Technol.* **2020**, *69*, 1070–1074. [CrossRef]
32. Xu, S.; Zhang, J.; Meng, S.; Xu, J. Task Allocation for Unmanned Aerial Vehicles in Mobile Crowdsensing. *Wirel. Netw.* **2021**, 1–13. [CrossRef]
33. Francois-Lavet, V.; Henderson, P.; Islam, R.; Bellemare, M.G.; Pineau, J. An Introduction to Deep Reinforcement Learning. *Found. Trends Mach. Learn.* **2018**, *11*, 219–354. [CrossRef]
34. Lillicrap, T.P.; Hunt, J.J.; Pritzel, A.; Heess, N.; Erez, T.; Tassa, Y.; Silver, D.; Wierstra, D. Continuous Control with Deep Reinforcement Learning. *arXiv* **2019**, arXiv:1509.02971.
35. Dai, A.; Li, R.; Zhao, Z.; Zhang, H. Graph Convolutional Multi-Agent Reinforcement Learning for UAV Coverage Control. In Proceedings of the 2020 International Conference on Wireless Communications and Signal Processing (WCSP), Nanjing, China, 21–23 October 2020; pp. 1106–1111. [CrossRef]
36. Jiang, J.; Dun, C.; Huang, T.; Lu, Z. Graph Convolutional Reinforcement Learning. *arXiv* **2020**, arXiv:1810.09202.
37. Ye, Z.; Wang, K.; Chen, Y.; Jiang, X.; Song, G. Multi-UAV Navigation for Partially Observable Communication Coverage by Graph Reinforcement Learning. *IEEE Trans. Mob. Comput.* **2022**. [CrossRef]
38. Liu, C.H.; Dai, Z.; Zhao, Y.; Crowcroft, J.; Wu, D.; Leung, K.K. Distributed and Energy-Efficient Mobile Crowdsensing with Charging Stations by Deep Reinforcement Learning. *IEEE Trans. Mob. Comput.* **2019**, *20*, 130–146. [CrossRef]
39. Liu, C.H.; Chen, Z.; Zhan, Y. Energy-Efficient Distributed Mobile Crowd Sensing: A Deep Learning Approach. *IEEE J. Sel. Areas Commun.* **2019**, *37*, 1262–1276. [CrossRef]
40. Piao, C.; Liu, C.H. Energy-Efficient Mobile Crowdsensing by Unmanned Vehicles: A Sequential Deep Reinforcement Learning Approach. *IEEE Internet Things J.* **2019**, *7*, 6312–6324. [CrossRef]
41. Dai, Z.; Wang, H.; Liu, C.H.; Han, R.; Tang, J.; Wang, G. Mobile Crowdsensing for Data Freshness: A Deep Reinforcement Learning Approach. In Proceedings of the IEEE INFOCOM 2021—IEEE Conference on Computer Communications, Vancouver, BC, Canada, 10–13 May 2021; pp. 1–10. [CrossRef]
42. Hochreiter, S.; Schmidhuber, J. Long Short-Term Memory. *Neural Comput.* **1997**, *9*, 1735–1780. [CrossRef] [PubMed]
43. Wang, H.; Liu, C.H.; Dai, Z.; Tang, J.; Wang, G. Energy-Efficient 3D Vehicular Crowdsourcing for Disaster Response by Distributed Deep Reinforcement Learning. In Proceedings of the 27th ACM SIGKDD Conference on Knowledge Discovery & Data Mining, Virtual Event, 14–18 August 2021; pp. 3679–3687. [CrossRef]
44. Chung, J.; Gulcehre, C.; Cho, K.; Bengio, Y. Empirical Evaluation of Gated Recurrent Neural Networks on Sequence Modeling. *arXiv* **2014**, arXiv:1412.3555.
45. Liu, C.H.; Dai, Z.; Yang, H.; Tang, J. Multi-Task-Oriented Vehicular Crowdsensing: A Deep Learning Approach. In Proceedings of the IEEE INFOCOM 2020—IEEE Conference on Computer Communications, Nanjing, China, 25–27 June 2020; pp. 1123–1132. [CrossRef]
46. Thibbotuwawa, A.; Nielsen, P.; Zbigniew, B.; Bocewicz, G. Energy Consumption in Unmanned Aerial Vehicles: A Review of Energy Consumption Models and Their Relation to the UAV Routing. In *Information Systems Architecture and Technology: Proceedings of 39th International Conference on Information Systems Architecture and Technology – ISAT 2018*; Świątek, J.; Borzemski, L.; Wilimowska, Z., Eds.; Springer International Publishing: Cham, Switzerland, 2019; Volume 853, pp. 173–184. [CrossRef]
47. Lowe, R.; Wu, Y.; Tamar, A.; Harb, J.; Abbeel, P.; Mordatch, I. Multi-Agent Actor-Critic for Mixed Cooperative-Competitive Environments. *arXiv* **2020**, arXiv:1706.02275.
48. Vaswani, A.; Shazeer, N.; Parmar, N.; Uszkoreit, J.; Jones, L.; Gomez, A.N.; Kaiser, Ł.; Polosukhin, I. Attention Is All You Need. In *Advances in Neural Information Processing Systems*; Curran Associates, Inc.: New York, NY, USA, 2017; Volume 30.
49. He, K.; Zhang, X.; Ren, S.; Sun, J. Deep Residual Learning for Image Recognition. In Proceedings of the 2016 IEEE Conference on Computer Vision and Pattern Recognition (CVPR), Las Vegas, NV, USA, 26 June–1 July 2016; pp. 770–778. [CrossRef]
50. Haarnoja, T.; Tang, H.; Abbeel, P.; Levine, S. Reinforcement Learning with Deep Energy-Based Policies. In Proceedings of the 34th International Conference on Machine Learning, Sydney, Australia, 6–11 August 2017; pp. 1352–1361.
51. Haarnoja, T.; Zhou, A.; Abbeel, P.; Levine, S. Soft Actor-Critic: Off-Policy Maximum Entropy Deep Reinforcement Learning with a Stochastic Actor. *arXiv* **2018**, arXiv:1801.01290.
52. Iqbal, S.; Sha, F. Actor-Attention-Critic for Multi-Agent Reinforcement Learning. *arXiv* **2019**, arXiv:1810.02912.
53. Ng, A.Y.; Russell, S.J. Algorithms for Inverse Reinforcement Learning. In Proceedings of the Seventeenth International Conference on Machine Learning, San Francisco, CA, USA, 29 June–2 July 2000; pp. 663–670.

Article

Experimental Validation of Entropy-Driven Swarm Exploration under Sparsity Constraints with Sparse Bayesian Learning

Christoph Manss [1,2,*], Isabel Kuehner [2] and Dmitriy Shutin [2]

1. German Research Center on Artifical Intelligence, Marie-Curie-Straße 1, 26129 Oldenburg, Germany
2. German Aerospace Center, Münchener Straße 22, 82234 Wessling, Germany; isabel.kuehner@dlr.de (I.K.); dmitriy.shutin@dlr.de (D.S.)
* Correspondence: christoph.manss@dfki.de

Abstract: Increasing the autonomy of multi-agent systems or swarms for exploration missions requires tools for efficient information gathering. This work studies this problem from theoretical and experimental perspectives and evaluates an exploration system for multiple ground robots that cooperatively explore a stationary spatial process. For the distributed model, two conceptually different distribution paradigms are considered. The exploration is based on fusing distributively gathered information using Sparse Bayesian Learning (SBL), which permits representing the spatial process in a compressed manner and thus reduces the model complexity and communication load required for the exploration. An entropy-based exploration criterion is formulated to guide the agents. This criterion uses an estimation of a covariance matrix of the model parameters, which is then quantitatively characterized using a D-optimality criterion. The new sampling locations for the agents are then selected to minimize this criterion. To this end, a distributed optimization of the D-optimality criterion is derived. The proposed entropy-driven exploration is then presented from a system perspective and validated in laboratory experiments with two ground robots. The experiments show that SBL together with the distributed entropy-driven exploration is real-time capable and leads to a better performance with respect to time and accuracy compared with similar state-of-the-art algorithms.

Keywords: distributed estimation; Sparse Bayesian Learning; exploration; swarm; multi-agent systems; consensus; D-optimal design

1. Introduction

For exploration tasks that rely on multi-agent systems, with complex, unstructured terrains, autonomy plays a key role to lower potential threats or tedious work for human operators, be it space exploration, disaster relief, or routine industrial facility inspections. The main objective here is to give a human operator more detailed information about the explored area, e.g., in terms of a map, and to support further decision making. While multiple agents do provide an increased sensing aperture and can potentially collect information more efficiently than a single-agent system, they have to rely more heavily on autonomy to compensate, e.g., possible large (or unreliable) communication delays [1] or the complexity of teleoperating multiple agents.

One of the approaches to increase the autonomy of multi-agent systems consists of using in situ analysis of the collected data with the agents' own computing resources to decide on future actions. In the context of mapping, such an approach is also known as active information gathering [2,3] or exploration. Note that mapping is generally not restricted to sensing with imaging sensors, such as cameras. The exploration of gas sources [4] or of the magnetic field [5] also falls in this category.

An approach for active information gathering lies in the focus of the presented work. In the following, we provide an overview of work related to the approach discussed in this paper, the arising challenges, and a proposed solution.

1.1. Related Work

The objective of active information gathering is to utilize the collected data, represented in terms of a parameterized model, to compute information content as a function of space. This can be done using heuristic approaches, as in [6,7], where the authors modify the random walk strategy by adjusting the movement steps of each robot such as to collect more information. Alternatively, information–theoretic approaches can be used. In [8], the authors use a probabilistic description of the model to steer cameras mounted on multiple unmanned aerial vehicles (UAVs). In this case, the information metric can be computed directly based on statistics of the pixels. The resulting quantity is then used to autonomously coordinate UAVs in an optimal configuration. In [9], the authors propose an *exploration driven by uncertainty* by minimizing the determinant of the covariance matrix for an optimal camera placement for a 3D image. This approach essentially implements an optimal experiment design [10], which in turn relates the determinant of the covariance matrix of the model parameters to the Shannon entropy of Gaussian random variables. This connection has been further explored in [11], where the authors compare criteria for optimal experiment design with mutual information for Gaussian processes regression and sensor placement. This leads to a greedy algorithm that uses mutual information for finding optimal sensor placements. An extension of [11] for multiple agents and a decentralized estimation of the mutual information is presented in [2,12]. In the latter, the authors also considered robotic aspects, such as optimal trajectory planning along with information gathering: an approach that has been further investigated in [13].

One of the key elements in experiment design-based information gathering is the ability to compute the covariance structure of the model parameters as a function of space and evaluate it in a distributed fashion. In [14], the authors studied the information-gathering approach for sparsity constrained models, i.e., under assumption that the model parameters are sparse. This required implementing non-smooth ℓ_1 constraints in the optimization problem, which in turn made the exact computation of the parameter covariance impossible. Instead, the covariance structure was approximated by locally smoothing the curvature of the objective function. In [14], the method was applied to generalized linear models with sparsity constraints for a distributed computation with two versions of data splitting over agents: homogeneous splitting, also called splitting-over-examples (SOE), and heterogeneous splitting, also called splitting-over-features (SOF). However, despite the method yielding in simulations a better performance as compared to systematic or random exploration approaches, the used approximation has been derived with purely empirical arguments.

1.2. Paper Contribution

To address this, the exploration problem with sparsity constraints has been cast into a probabilistic framework, where the parameter covariance can be computed exactly. In [15], we formulated a Bayesian approach toward cooperative sparse parameter estimation for SOF, and in [16] for SOE data splitting. However, the distributed computation of the covariance matrix and information-driven exploration has not been considered so far. With this contribution, we close this gap and study an information-driven exploration strategy that is based on a Bayesian approach toward distributed sparse regression. Specifically,

- We consider a distributed computation of the corresponding parameter covariance matrices for information-seeking exploration using a Bayesian formulation of the model, and
- Validate the algorithm's performance both in simulations as well as in an experiment with two robots exploring the magnetic field variations on a laboratory floor.

The rest of the paper is structured as follows. We begin with a model formulation and model learning in Section 2. In Section 3, we discuss a distributed computation of the exploration criterion for the considered regression problem. Afterwards, we outline the experimental setting, the collection of ground truth data, and the sensor calibration in

Section 4, as well as the overall system design in Section 5. The experimental results are summarized in Section 6, and Section 7 concludes this work.

2. Distributed Sparse Bayesian Learning

2.1. Model Definition

We make use of a classical basis function regression [17] to express an unknown scalar physical process $p(x) \in \mathbb{R}$, with $x \in \mathbb{R}^d$ and $d \in \mathbb{N}$. Typically, the process is d-dimensional, with $d \in \{2,3\}$. To represent the process $p(x)$, a set of $N \in \mathbb{N}$ basis functions $\phi_n(x, \pi_n) \in \mathbb{R}$, $n = 1, \ldots, N$ are used, where $\pi_n \in \mathbb{R}^s$ is dependent on the used basis function and s is a number of parameters per basis function.

Each basis function is parameterized with π_n, $n = 1, \ldots, N$, which can represent centers of corresponding basis functions, their width, etc. More formally, we assume that

$$p(x) = \sum_{n=1}^{N} \phi_n(x, \pi_n) w_n, \quad (1)$$

where $w_n \in \mathbb{R}$ are generally unknown weights in the representation.

To estimate w_n, $n = 1, \ldots, N$, we make M observations of the process $p(x)$ at locations $X = [x_1, \ldots, x_M]^T \in \mathbb{R}^{M \times d}$. The corresponding m-th measurement is then represented as

$$y(x_m) = p(x_m) + \eta(x_m) = \sum_{n=1}^{N} \phi_n(x_m, \pi_n) w_n + \eta(x_m), \quad (2)$$

where $\eta(x_m) \propto \mathcal{N}(0, \lambda^{-1})$ is an additive sample of white Gaussian noise with a known precision $\lambda \in \mathbb{R}_+$. By collecting M measurements in a vector $y(X) = [y(x_1), \ldots, y(x_M)]^T \in \mathbb{R}^M$, we can reformulate (2) in a vector-matrix notation. To this end, we define

$$\Pi \triangleq [\pi_1, \ldots, \pi_N]^T \in \mathbb{R}^{N \times s}, \quad (3)$$

$$\phi_n(X, \pi_n) \triangleq [\phi_n(x_1, \pi_n), \ldots, \phi_n(x_M, \pi_n)]^T \in \mathbb{R}^M, \quad (4)$$

$$\Phi(X, \Pi) \triangleq [\phi_1(X, \pi_1), \ldots, \phi_N(X, \pi_N)] \in \mathbb{R}^{M \times N}, \quad (5)$$

$$\text{and} \quad w \triangleq [w_1, \ldots, w_N]^T \in \mathbb{R}^N, \quad (6)$$

which allows us to formulate the measurement model in a vectorized form

$$y(X) = \Phi(X, \Pi) w + \eta(X), \quad (7)$$

with $\eta(X) \triangleq [\eta(x_1), \ldots, \eta(x_M)]^T \in \mathbb{R}^M$.

Based on (7), we define the likelihood of the parameters w as follows

$$p(y(X)|w) \propto \exp\left\{-\frac{\lambda}{2} \|y(X) - \Phi(X, \Pi) w\|^2 \right\}. \quad (8)$$

Often, the representation (1) is selected such that $N \gg M$, i.e., it is underdetermined. This implies that there is an infinite number of possible solutions for w. A popular approach to restrict a set of solutions consists of introducing sparsity constraints on parameters. Within the Bayesian framework, this can be achieved by defining a prior over the parameter weights w. This leads to a class of probabilistic approaches referred to as Sparse Bayesian Learning (SBL).

The basic idea of SBL is to assign an appropriate prior to the N-dimensional vector w such that the resulting maximum a posteriori (MAP) estimate $\hat{w}$ is sparse, i.e., many of its entries are zero. Typically, SBL specifies a hierarchical factorable prior $p(w|\gamma)p(\gamma) = \prod_{n=1}^{N} p(w_n|\gamma_n) p(\gamma_n)$, where $p(w_n|\gamma_n) = \mathcal{N}(w_n|0, \gamma_n)$, $n \in \{1, \ldots, N\}$ [18–20]. For each $n \in \{1, \ldots, N\}$, the hyperparameter γ_n, also called sparsity parameter, regulates the width of $p(w_n|\gamma_n)$; the product $p(w_n|\gamma_n)p(\gamma_n)$ defines a Gaussian scale mixture (the authors in work [21] extend this framework by generalizing $p(w_n|\gamma_n)$ to be the probability density function (PDF) of a power exponential distribution, which makes the hierarchical prior a power exponential scale mixture distribution). Bayesian inference on a linear model with such a hierarchical prior is commonly realized via two types of techniques: MAP estimation of w (Type I estimation; note that many traditional "non-Bayesian" methods for learning sparse representations such as basis pursuit de-noising or re-weighted ℓ_p-norm regressions [22–24] can be interpreted as Type I estimation within the above Bayesian framework [21]) or MAP estimation of γ (Type II estimation, also called maximum evidence estimation, or empirical Bayes method). Type II estimation has proven (both theoretically and empirically) to perform consistently better than Type I estimation in the present application context. One reason is that the objective function of a Type II estimator typically exhibits significantly fewer local minima than that of the corresponding Type I estimator and promotes greater sparsity [25]. The hyperprior $p(\gamma_n)$, $n \in \{1,\ldots,N\}$, is usually selected to be non-informative, i.e., $p(\gamma_n) \propto \gamma_n^{-1}$ [26–28]. The motivation for this choice is twofold. First, the resulting inference schemes typically demonstrate superior (or similar) performance as compared to schemes derived based on other hyperprior selections [21]. Second, very efficient inference algorithms can be constructed and studied [26–30].

In the following, we consider only SBL Type II optimization as it leads to usually sparser parameter vectors w [21], and we drop explicit dependencies on measurements X and basis function parameters Π to simplify notation. The marginalized likelihood for SBL Type II optimization is therefore

$$p(y|\gamma) = \int_{-\infty}^{\infty} p(y|w)p(w|\gamma)dw \propto |\Sigma|^{-\frac{1}{2}}\exp\left\{-\frac{1}{2}y^T\Sigma^{-1}y\right\}, \tag{9}$$

where $\Sigma = \lambda^{-1}I + \Phi\Gamma\Phi^T$, $\Gamma = \text{diag}\{\gamma\}$, and I being the identity. Taking the negative logarithm of (9), we obtain the objective function for SBL Type II optimization in the following form

$$\mathcal{L}(\gamma) = -\log p(y|\gamma) = \log(|\Sigma|) + y^T\Sigma^{-1}y. \tag{10}$$

An estimate of hyperparameters γ is then found as

$$\widehat{\gamma} = \arg\min_{\gamma} \mathcal{L}(\gamma). \tag{11}$$

Once the estimate $\widehat{\gamma}$ is obtained, the posterior probability density function (PDF) of the the parameter weights w can be easily computed: it is known to be Gaussian $p(w|y,\widehat{\gamma}) = \mathcal{N}(\widehat{w},\Sigma_w)$ with the moments given as

$$\widehat{w} = \lambda\Sigma_w\Phi^Ty, \qquad \Sigma_w = \left(\lambda\Phi^T\Phi + \widehat{\Gamma}^{-1}\right)^{-1}, \tag{12}$$

where $\widehat{\Gamma} = \text{diag}\{\widehat{\gamma}\}$ (see also [18]).

2.2. Sparse Bayesian Learning with the Automatic Relevance Determination

The key to a sparse estimate of w is a solution to (11). There are a number of efficient schemes [26–28] to solve this problem. The method that we use in this paper is based on [26]. In the following, we shortly outline this algorithm.

In [26], the authors introduced the reformulated automatic relevance determination (R-ARD) by using an auxiliary function that upper bounds the objective function $\mathcal{L}(\gamma)$ in (10). Specifically, using the concavity of the log-determinant in (10) with respect to γ, the former can be represented using a Fenchel conjugate as

$$\log|\Sigma| = \min_{z} z^T\gamma - h^*(z), \tag{13}$$

where $z \in \mathbb{R}^N$ is a dual variable and $h^*(z)$ is the dual (or conjugate) function (see also [31] (Chapter 5) or [32]).

Using (13), we can now upper-bound (10) as follows

$$\mathcal{L}(\gamma, z) \triangleq z^T \gamma - h^*(z) + y^T \Sigma^{-1} y \geq \mathcal{L}(\gamma). \tag{14}$$

Note that for any γ, the bound becomes tight when minimized over z. This fact is utilized for the numerical estimation of γ, which is the essence of the R-ARD algorithm.

R-ARD alternates between estimating z, which can be found in closed form as [26,31]

$$\hat{z} = \arg\min_z \mathcal{L}(\hat{\gamma}, z) = \frac{\partial}{\partial \gamma} \log |\Sigma| \bigg|_{\gamma = \hat{\gamma}} = \operatorname{diag}\{\Phi^T \Sigma^{-1} \Phi\}, \tag{15}$$

and estimating $\hat{\gamma}$ as a solution to a convex optimization problem

$$\hat{\gamma} = \arg\min_\gamma \mathcal{L}(\gamma, \hat{z}) = \arg\min_\gamma \hat{z}^T \gamma + y^T \Sigma^{-1} y. \tag{16}$$

In order to solve (16), the authors in [26] proposed to use yet another upper bound on $\mathcal{L}(\gamma, z)$. Specifically, by noting that

$$y^T \Sigma^{-1} y = \min_w \lambda \|y - \Phi w\|^2 + \sum_{l=1}^N \frac{w_l^2}{\gamma_l} \tag{17}$$

the cost function in (16) can be bounded with

$$\mathcal{L}(w, \gamma, \hat{z}) \triangleq \lambda \|y - \Phi w\|^2 + \sum_{l=1}^N \left(\hat{z}_l \gamma_l + \frac{w_l^2}{\gamma_l} \right) \geq \mathcal{L}(\gamma, \hat{z}). \tag{18}$$

The right-hand side of (18) is convex both in w and γ. As such, for any fixed w, the optimal solution for γ can be easily found as $\gamma_l = \hat{z}_l^{-\frac{1}{2}} |w_l|, l = 1, \ldots, N$. By inserting the latter in (18), we find the solution for w that minimizes the upper-bound $\mathcal{L}(w, \gamma, \hat{z})$ as

$$\hat{w} = \arg\min_w \mathcal{L}(w, \hat{\gamma}, \hat{z}) = \arg\min_w \lambda \|y - \Phi w\|^2 + 2 \sum_{l=1}^N \hat{z}_l^{\frac{1}{2}} |w_l|, \tag{19}$$

which can be recognized as a weighted least absolute shrinkage and selection operator (LASSO) cost function. Expression (19) builds a basis for a distributed estimation learning of SBL parameters, since there exist techniques to optimize a LASSO function over a network, which are presented in the following section.

2.3. The Distributed Automated Relevance Determination Algorithm for SOF Data Splitting

The derivation of the distributed R-ARD (D-R-ARD) for SOF is shown in [14]. Here, we would like to show the main aspects of the distribution paradigm and the resulting algorithm. The main aspect of heterogeneous data splitting is that each agent has its own model. Therefore, the parameter weights w are distributed among $K \in \mathbb{N}$ agents as $w = [w_1^T, \ldots, w_K^T]^T$ and each agent has its part $w_k \in \mathbb{R}^{N_k}$, where $N = \sum_{k=1}^K N_k$. Likewise, the matrix Φ is partitioned among K agents as $\Phi = [\Phi_1, \ldots, \Phi_K]$ where $\Phi_k \in \mathbb{R}^{M \times N_k}$. The SOF model is then formulated as

$$y = [\Phi_1 \quad \cdots \quad \Phi_K] \begin{bmatrix} w_1 \\ \vdots \\ w_K \end{bmatrix} + \eta = \sum_{k=1}^K \Phi_k w_k + \eta. \tag{20}$$

Similarly, the hyper-parameters γ are also partitioned as $\gamma = [\gamma_1^T, \ldots, \gamma_K^T]^T$.

The solution to cooperative SOF inference then amounts to computing z from (15) and optimizing the upper bound (18) over a network of K agents.

Unfortunately, in the case of the SOF model, the dual variable $z = [z_1^T, \ldots, z_K^T]^T$ in (15) cannot be computed exactly. Instead it is upper-bounded [14] as $z_k \leq \tilde{z}_k$, where $\tilde{z}_k$ is computed for each agent:

$$\tilde{z}_k = \text{diag}\left\{ \mathbf{\Phi}_k^T \mathbf{\Lambda} \mathbf{\Phi}_k - \mathbf{\Phi}_k^T \mathbf{\Lambda} \mathbf{\Phi}_k \mathbf{\Sigma}_{w,k} \mathbf{\Phi}_k^T \mathbf{\Lambda} \mathbf{\Phi}_k \right\}, \tag{21}$$

with $\mathbf{\Sigma}_{w,k} = (\mathbf{\Phi}_k^T \mathbf{\Lambda} \mathbf{\Phi}_k + \mathbf{\Gamma}_k^{-1})^{-1}$ and $\mathbf{\Lambda} = \lambda \mathbf{I}$. This approximation preserves the upper bound in (18). Consequently, (19) can be reformulated to fit for SOF as

$$\hat{w}_k = \arg\min_{w_k} \mathcal{L}(w, \tilde{z}) = \arg\min_{w_k} \lambda \left\| \sum_{k=1}^K y - \mathbf{\Phi}_k w_k \right\|^2 + 2 \sum_{l=1}^{N_k} \tilde{z}_{k,l}^{\frac{1}{2}} |w_{k,l}|, \tag{22}$$

which can be solved distributively via the alternating direction method of multipliers (ADMM) algorithm [33] (Section 8.3). The D-R-ARD algorithm for SOF is summarized in Algorithm 1. When using ADMM to solve for $\hat{w}_k$, the only communication between the agents takes place inside of the ADMM algorithm. The communication load of the ADMM algorithm for SOF is discussed in [33] (Chapter 8).

Algorithm 1 D-R-ARD for SOF

1: $\tilde{z}_k \leftarrow \text{diag}\{\mathbf{\Phi}_k^T \mathbf{\Lambda} \mathbf{\Phi}_k\}$
2: **while** not converged **do**
3: $\quad \hat{w} \leftarrow \arg\min_w \mathcal{L}(w, \tilde{z})$ ▷ See (22); is solved distributively using ADMM [33] (Section 8.3)
4: $\quad \hat{\gamma}_k \leftarrow \frac{|\hat{w}_{k,n}|}{\sqrt{\tilde{z}_{k,n}}}, \forall n = 1, \ldots, N_k$
5: $\quad \tilde{z}_k \leftarrow$ (21)
6: $\hat{w} = [\hat{w}_1^T, \ldots, \hat{w}_K^T]^T, \hat{\gamma} = [\hat{\gamma}_1^T, \ldots, \hat{\gamma}_K^T]^T$

2.4. The Distributed Automated Relevance Determination Algorithm for SOE Data Splitting

For SOE, we will assume that measurements y at locations X are partitioned into K disjoint subsets $\{y_k(X_k), X_k\}_{k=1}^K$, each associated with the corresponding agent in the network. Hence, each agent k makes M_k observations $y_k(X_k) = [y_{k,1}(x_{k,1}), \ldots, y_{k,M_k}(x_{k,M_k})]$ at locations $X_k = [x_{k,1}, \ldots, x_{k,M_k}]^T$, such that $M = \sum_{k=1}^K M_k$, $y = [y_1^T, \ldots, y_K^T]^T$, $X = [X_1^T, \ldots, X_K^T]^T$, $\mathbf{\Phi} = [\mathbf{\Phi}_1^T, \ldots, \mathbf{\Phi}_K^T]^T$, and $\eta = [\eta_1^T, \ldots, \eta_K^T]^T$. This allows us to rewrite (7) in an equivalent form as

$$y = \begin{bmatrix} y_1 \\ \vdots \\ y_K \end{bmatrix} = \begin{bmatrix} \mathbf{\Phi}_1 \\ \vdots \\ \mathbf{\Phi}_K \end{bmatrix} w + \begin{bmatrix} \eta_1 \\ \vdots \\ \eta_K \end{bmatrix}, \tag{23}$$

where we assumed that perturbations $\eta_k, k = 1, \ldots, K$, are independent between agents, i.e.,

$$E\{\eta_k \eta_m^T\} = \begin{cases} 0\mathbf{I} & k \neq m \\ \lambda_k^{-1} \mathbf{I} & k = m. \end{cases}$$

To cast R-ARD in a distributed setting, we need to be able to solve (19) and compute $\hat{z}$ in (15) over a network of agents. To this end, let us define

$$D \triangleq \mathbf{\Phi}^T \mathbf{\Lambda} \mathbf{\Phi} = \sum_{k=1}^{K} \mathbf{\Phi}_k^T \lambda_k \mathbf{\Phi}_k = K \times \underbrace{\frac{1}{K} \sum_{k=1}^{K} \mathbf{\Phi}_k^T \lambda_k \mathbf{\Phi}_k}_{\text{averaged consensus}}. \quad (24)$$

where $\mathbf{\Lambda} = \text{diag}\,[\lambda_1 \mathbf{I}_1, \ldots, \lambda_K \mathbf{I}_K]$, and $\mathbf{I}_k$ is an identity matrix of size $M_k \times M_k$, $k = 1, \ldots, K$. We point out that D, or rather the last factor in (24), can be computed over a network of agents using an averaged consensus algorithm [34,35].

Next, we apply the Woodbury identity to $\mathbf{\Sigma}^{-1}$ to obtain

$$\mathbf{\Sigma}^{-1} = \left(\mathbf{\Lambda}^{-1} + \mathbf{\Phi}\mathbf{\Gamma}\mathbf{\Phi}^T\right)^{-1} = \mathbf{\Lambda} - \mathbf{\Lambda}\mathbf{\Phi}\mathbf{\Sigma}_w \mathbf{\Phi}^T \mathbf{\Lambda}, \quad (25)$$

where $\mathbf{\Sigma}_w = (\mathbf{\Phi}^T \mathbf{\Lambda} \mathbf{\Phi} + \mathbf{\Gamma}^{-1})^{-1}$. Inserting (25) and (24) into (15), we get

$$\hat{z} = \text{diag}\{\mathbf{\Phi}^T \mathbf{\Lambda} \mathbf{\Phi} - \mathbf{\Phi}^T \mathbf{\Lambda} \mathbf{\Phi} \mathbf{\Sigma}_w \mathbf{\Phi}^T \mathbf{\Lambda} \mathbf{\Phi}\} = \text{diag}\{D - D \mathbf{\Sigma}_w D\}, \quad (26)$$

where $\mathbf{\Sigma}_w = (D + \mathbf{\Gamma}^{-1})^{-1}$. Thus, once D becomes available, $\hat{z}$ can be found distributively using expression (26).

To solve (19) distributively, we first note that for the model (23) the likelihood (8) can be equivalently rewritten as

$$p(y|w) \propto \exp\left\{-\frac{1}{2}\sum_{k=1}^{K} \lambda_k \|y_k - \mathbf{\Phi}_k w\|^2\right\}. \quad (27)$$

It is then straightforward to show that the upper bound (18) will take the form

$$\mathcal{L}(w, \gamma, \hat{z}) \triangleq \frac{1}{2} \sum_{k=1}^{K} \lambda_k \|y_k - \mathbf{\Phi}_k w\|^2 + \sum_{l=1}^{M} \left(\hat{z}_l \gamma_l + \frac{w_l^2}{\gamma_l}\right) \geq \mathcal{L}(\gamma, \hat{z}). \quad (28)$$

Similarly to (18), for any w_l, $l = 1, \ldots, M$, the bound is minimized with respect to γ_l at $\gamma_l = |w_l|/\sqrt{\hat{z}_l}$, $l = 1, \ldots, M$. Inserting the latter in (28), we obtain an objective function for estimating w_l

$$\hat{w} = \arg\min_{w} \frac{1}{2} \sum_{k=1}^{K} \lambda_k \|\mathbf{\Phi}_k w - y_k\|_2^2 + 2 \sum_{l=1}^{M} \sqrt{\hat{z}_l} |w_l|. \quad (29)$$

Expression (29) can be readily solved distributively using an ADMM algorithm (see e.g., [33] (Chapter 8) and [36]). Once $\hat{w}$ is found, optimal parameter values $\hat{\gamma}$ are found as $\hat{\gamma}_l = \hat{z}_l^{-\frac{1}{2}} |\hat{w}_l|$, $l = 1, \ldots, N$.

In Algorithm 2, we now summarize the key steps of the resulting D-R-ARD algorithm for SOE. As we can see from Algorithm 2, D-R-ARD includes two optimizing loops. The inner optimization loop is an ADMM algorithm, which is guaranteed to converge to a solution [33]. The convergence of the outer loop is basically the convergence of the R-ARD algorithm presented in [26].

Algorithm 2 D-R-ARD for SOE
─────────────────────────────────────
1: $\hat{z}_n \leftarrow 1, \forall n = 1, \ldots, N$
2: Compute D using averaged consensus over $\Phi_k^T \Lambda \Phi_k$ as in (24)
3: **while** not converged **do**
4: $\quad \hat{w} \leftarrow \arg\min_w \mathcal{L}(w, \gamma, \hat{z})$ ▷ See (29); is solved distributively using ADMM [33,36]
5: $\quad \hat{\gamma} \leftarrow \frac{|\hat{w}_n|}{\sqrt{\hat{z}_n}}, \forall n = 1, \ldots, N$
6: $\quad \Sigma_w \leftarrow (D + \Gamma^{-1})^{-1}$
7: $\quad \hat{z} \leftarrow$ (26)
─────────────────────────────────────

Communication Load of D-R-ARD

In the D-R-ARD algorithm, two communication steps are required. The first communication step involves the computation of the matrix D, where we leverage an average consensus algorithm. There, each of the $A \in \mathbb{N}$ consensus steps requires the transmission of $N(N+1)/2$ floats due to the symmetry of D. Note that the number A of averaged consensus iterations can vary depending on the connectivity of the network.

The second communication step involves the iterative estimation of the model parameters. Assuming that the update loop of D-R-ARD requires $I \in \mathbb{N}$ iterations, the distributed estimation of parameters $\hat{w}$ with $R \in \mathbb{N}$ ADMM iterations then scales up as $\mathcal{O}(I \times ARN)$. Thus, the total communication load of D-R-ARD algorithm behaves as $AN(N+1)/2 + \mathcal{O}(I \times ARN)$. Please note also that for this estimation of the communication load, the network structure remains unchanged.

3. Distributed Entropy-Driven Exploration for Sparse Bayesian Learning

The learning algorithm described in the previous section estimates the parameters of the model w and γ given the measurements y and X. In the following, we focus on the question of how a new measurement is acquired in an optimal fashion. As we will show, the main criterion for this purpose is the information or, more specifically, the entropy change as a function of a possible sampling location.

3.1. D-Optimality

One possible strategy to optimally select a new measurement location $\tilde{x}$ is provided by the theory of optimal experiment design. Optimal experiment design aims at optimizing the variance of an estimator through a number of optimality criteria. One of these criteria is a so-called D-optimality: it measures the "size" of an estimator covariance matrix by computing the volume of the corresponding uncertainty ellipsoid. More specifically, a determinant (or rather the logarithm of a determinant) of the covariance matrix is computed. The latter can then be optimized with respect to the experiment parameter. In our case, the covariance matrix Σ_w of the model parameters w is readily given in (12) as a second central moment of $p(w|y)$. Thus, the D-optimality criterion can be formulated as

$$\min \log|\Sigma_w(X, \Pi)|, \qquad (30)$$

where the dependency of Σ_w on measurement locations X has been made explicit. Note that due to the normality of the posterior pdf $p(w|y)$, the term $\log|\Sigma_w(X, \Pi)|$ is proportional to the entropy of w; thus, minimization of the criterion (30) would imply a reduction of the entropy of the parameter estimates. Note that in contrast to [14], the covariance matrix is not approximated here, but it is computed exactly based on the resulting probabilistic inference model. Our intention is now to evaluate and optimize (30) as a function of the new possible sampling location $\tilde{x}$.

Let us consider a modification of the model (7) as a function of the location $\tilde{x}$. The incorporation of $\tilde{x}$ into (7) would imply that the design matrix Φ would be extended as

$$\widetilde{\Phi}([X^T, \tilde{x}]^T, [\Pi^T, \tilde{\pi}]^T) = \begin{bmatrix} \Phi(X, \Pi) & \phi(X, \tilde{\pi}) \\ \phi^T(\tilde{x}, \Pi) & \phi(\tilde{x}, \tilde{\pi}) \end{bmatrix}, \quad (31)$$

where $\tilde{\pi}$ is a new parameterization of a function ϕ based on the new location $\tilde{x}$—a new regression feature. Let us stress that in general, the potential measurement at $\tilde{x}$ does not have to lead to a new column in (31)—columns, i.e., basis functions in Φ can be fixed from the initial design of the problem. In the latter case, Φ would be extended only by a row vector $\phi^T(\tilde{x}, \Pi) = [\phi(\tilde{x}, \pi_1), \ldots, \phi(\tilde{x}, \pi_N)]$. However, a basis function with a currently zero parameter weight estimate might be useful for explaining the new measurement value at $\tilde{x}$ and, thus, might be activated. Our next step is to consider how

1. The D-optimality criterion can be evaluated efficiently for the "grown" design matrix $\widetilde{\Phi}$ in (31),
2. And how the criterion can be evaluated in a distributed fashion.

3.1.1. Measurement Only-Update of the D-Optimality Criterion

We will begin with considering the update of the D-optimality criterion with respect to a new measurement location $\tilde{x}$ assuming that only the number of rows in Φ grows, while the number of features stays constant. In this case, (31) can be represented as

$$\widetilde{\Phi}([X^T, \tilde{x}]^T, \Pi) = \begin{bmatrix} \Phi(X, \Pi) \\ \phi^T(\tilde{x}, \Pi) \end{bmatrix}. \quad (32)$$

Based on (32), the new covariance matrix $\widetilde{\Sigma}_w$ that accounts for the new measurement location $\tilde{x}$ can be computed as

$$\widetilde{\Sigma}_w(X, \Pi, \tilde{x}) = \left(\widetilde{\Phi}([X^T, \tilde{x}]^T, \Pi) \widetilde{\Lambda} \widetilde{\Phi}([X^T, \tilde{x}]^T, \Pi) + \hat{\Gamma}^{-1} \right)^{-1}, \quad (33)$$

where $\widetilde{\Lambda} = \text{diag}\{\Lambda, \tilde{\lambda}\} \in \mathbb{R}^{M+1 \times M+1}$ and $\tilde{\lambda}$ is the assumed noise precision at the potential measurement location. It is worth noting that we assume every measurement to be independent white Gaussian noise.

By combining terms that depend on $\tilde{x}$, we can represent (33) as

$$\widetilde{\Sigma}_w(X, \Pi, \tilde{x})^{-1} = [\Phi^T \Lambda \Phi + \hat{\Gamma}^{-1}] + \tilde{\lambda} \phi(\tilde{x}, \Pi) \phi(\tilde{x}, \Pi)^T$$
$$= \Sigma_w^{-1} + \tilde{\lambda} \phi(\tilde{x}, \Pi) \phi(\tilde{x}, \Pi)^T. \quad (34)$$

As we see from (34), an addition of a new measurement row causes a rank-1 perturbation of the information matrix Σ_w^{-1}. Using matrix determinant lemma [37], we can thus compute

$$\log |\widetilde{\Sigma}_w(X, \Pi, \tilde{x})| = -\log |\Sigma_w^{-1} + \tilde{\lambda} \phi(\tilde{x}, \Pi) \phi(\tilde{x}, \Pi)^T| \quad (35)$$
$$= \log |\Sigma_w| - \log \left| 1 + \tilde{\lambda} \phi(\tilde{x}, \Pi)^T \Sigma_w \phi(\tilde{x}, \Pi) \right| \quad (36)$$

Note that Σ_w is independent of $\tilde{x}$, and thus, only the second term on the right-hand side of (36) is relevant for the estimation.

Finally, the D-optimality criterion with respect to a location $\tilde{x}$ can be formulated as

$$\arg\min_{\tilde{x}} \log |\widetilde{\Sigma}_w| \equiv \arg\max_{\tilde{x}} \log \left| 1 + \tilde{\lambda} \phi(\tilde{x}, \Pi)^T \Sigma_w \phi(\tilde{x}, \Pi) \right| = \arg\max_{\tilde{x}} \log \left| f(\tilde{x}, \tilde{\lambda}) \right|, \quad (37)$$

where we have exchanged minimization with a maximization by changing the sign of the cost function.

3.1.2. Computation of the D-Optimality Criterion with Addition of a New Feature

The computation of the D-optimality criterion becomes more involved when a measurement at a location $\tilde{x}$ is associated with a new feature $\tilde{\pi}$. This can happen if, e.g., $\tilde{\pi}$ is a center or location of a new basis function.

Then, based on (31), the new covariance matrix $\tilde{\Sigma}_w$ that accounts for $\tilde{x}$ and $\tilde{\pi}$ is formulated as

$$\tilde{\Sigma}_w(X, \Pi, \tilde{x}, \tilde{\pi}) = \left(\tilde{\Phi}^T([X^T, \tilde{x}]^T, [\Pi^T, \tilde{\pi}]^T) \tilde{\Lambda} \tilde{\Phi}([X^T, \tilde{x}]^T, [\Pi^T, \tilde{\pi}]^T) + \begin{bmatrix} \hat{\Gamma}^{-1} & 0 \\ 0 & \tilde{\gamma}^{-1} \end{bmatrix} \right)^{-1}, \tag{38}$$

where $\tilde{\gamma}$ is a sparsity parameter associated with a new column $[\phi^T(X, \tilde{\pi}), \phi(\tilde{x}, \tilde{\pi})]^T$. By combining terms that depend on $\tilde{x}$, we can represent (38) as

$$\tilde{\Sigma}_w(X, \Pi, \tilde{x}, \tilde{\pi})^{-1} = \begin{bmatrix} \Phi^T \Lambda \Phi + \hat{\Gamma}^{-1} & \Phi^T \Lambda \phi(X, \tilde{\pi}) \\ \phi^T(X, \tilde{\pi}) \Lambda \Phi & \phi^T(X, \tilde{\pi}) \Lambda \phi(X, \tilde{\pi}) + \tilde{\gamma}^{-1} \end{bmatrix}$$
$$+ \tilde{\lambda} \begin{bmatrix} \phi(\tilde{x}, \Pi) \\ \phi(\tilde{x}, \tilde{\pi}) \end{bmatrix} \begin{bmatrix} \phi(\tilde{x}, \Pi) \\ \phi(\tilde{x}, \tilde{\pi}) \end{bmatrix}^T. \tag{39}$$

To simplify the notation, let us define

$$c(\tilde{\pi}) \triangleq \Phi^T \Lambda \phi(X, \tilde{\pi}), \quad b(\tilde{\pi}) \triangleq \phi^T(X, \tilde{\pi}) \Lambda \phi(X, \tilde{\pi}) + \tilde{\gamma}^{-1}, \tag{40}$$

which can be inserted into (39), leading to

$$\tilde{\Sigma}_w(X, \Pi, \tilde{x}, \tilde{\pi})^{-1} = \begin{bmatrix} \Sigma_w^{-1} & c(\tilde{\pi}) \\ c^T(\tilde{\pi}) & b(\tilde{\pi}) \end{bmatrix} + \tilde{\lambda} \begin{bmatrix} \phi(\tilde{x}, \Pi) \\ \phi(\tilde{x}, \tilde{\pi}) \end{bmatrix} [\phi^T(\tilde{x}, \Pi) \quad \phi(\tilde{x}, \tilde{\pi})]. \tag{41}$$

The first term in (41) describes how much the new feature column contributes to the covariance matrix, while the second term represents the contribution of a measurement at location $\tilde{x}$. Let us now insert (41) into the D-optimality criterion in (30). By applying the matrix determinant lemma [37] to the resulting expression, we compute

$$\log |\tilde{\Sigma}_w(X, \Pi_N, \tilde{x}, \tilde{\pi})| = -\log \begin{vmatrix} \Sigma_w^{-1} & c(\tilde{\pi}) \\ c(\tilde{\pi})^T & b(\tilde{\pi}) \end{vmatrix}$$
$$- \log \left| 1 + \tilde{\lambda} \begin{bmatrix} \phi(\tilde{x}, \Pi) \\ \phi(\tilde{x}, \tilde{\pi}) \end{bmatrix}^T \begin{bmatrix} \Sigma_w^{-1} & c(\tilde{\pi}) \\ c(\tilde{\pi})^T & b(\tilde{\pi}) \end{bmatrix}^{-1} \begin{bmatrix} \phi(\tilde{x}, \Pi) \\ \phi(\tilde{x}, \tilde{\pi}) \end{bmatrix} \right|. \tag{42}$$

Now, consider separately the contribution of the two terms in the right-hand side of (42) to the D-optimality criterion. For the first term, we can use the Schur complement [38] $q(\tilde{\pi}) = b(\tilde{\pi}) - c^T(\tilde{\pi}) \Sigma_w c(\tilde{\pi})$ such that the first logarithmic term can be reformulated as

$$\log \begin{vmatrix} \Sigma_w^{-1} & c(\tilde{\pi}) \\ c(\tilde{\pi})^T & b(\tilde{\pi}) \end{vmatrix} = -\log |\Sigma_w| + \log q(\tilde{\pi}). \tag{43}$$

Note that Σ_w is independent of $\tilde{x}$ and of $\tilde{\pi}$, which is a fact that will become useful later.

To simplify the second term in the right-hand side of (42), we first apply inversion rules for structured matrices [39], which allows us to write

$$\begin{bmatrix} \Sigma_w^{-1} & c(\tilde{\pi}) \\ c(\tilde{\pi})^T & b(\tilde{\pi}) \end{bmatrix}^{-1} = \begin{bmatrix} \Sigma_w - \Sigma_w c(\tilde{\pi}) q(\tilde{\pi})^{-1} c(\tilde{\pi})^T \Sigma_w & -\Sigma_w c(\tilde{\pi})/q(\tilde{\pi}) \\ -c(\tilde{\pi})^T \Sigma_w / q(\tilde{\pi}) & 1/q(\tilde{\pi}) \end{bmatrix} \tag{44}$$

and thus

$$\log\left|1 + \begin{bmatrix}\boldsymbol{\phi}(\widetilde{x},\Pi)\\\boldsymbol{\phi}(\widetilde{x},\widetilde{\pi})\end{bmatrix}^T \begin{bmatrix}\Sigma_w^{-1} & c(\widetilde{\pi})\\c(\widetilde{\pi})^T & b(\widetilde{\pi})\end{bmatrix}^{-1} \begin{bmatrix}\boldsymbol{\phi}(\widetilde{x},\Pi)\\\boldsymbol{\phi}(\widetilde{x},\widetilde{\pi})\end{bmatrix}\right|$$

$$= \log\left(1 + \widetilde{\lambda}\boldsymbol{\phi}^T(\widetilde{x},\Pi)\Sigma_w\boldsymbol{\phi}(\widetilde{x},\Pi) + \widetilde{\lambda}\left(\boldsymbol{\phi}(\widetilde{x},\widetilde{\pi}) - c(\widetilde{\pi})^T\Sigma_w\boldsymbol{\phi}(\widetilde{x},\Pi)\right)^2/q(\widetilde{\pi})\right)$$

$$= \log\left(f(\widetilde{x},\widetilde{\lambda}) + \widetilde{\lambda}\left(\boldsymbol{\phi}(\widetilde{x},\widetilde{\pi}) - c(\widetilde{\pi})^T\Sigma_w\boldsymbol{\phi}(\widetilde{x},\Pi)\right)^2/q(\widetilde{\pi})\right). \tag{45}$$

Finally, after inserting (43) and (45) into (42), the D-optimality criterion with respect to a location $\widetilde{x}$ can be formulated as

$$\arg\min_{\widetilde{x}} \log|\widetilde{\Sigma}_w(X,\Pi,\widetilde{x},\widetilde{\pi})| \equiv \tag{46}$$

$$\arg\max_{\widetilde{x}} \log\left[q(\widetilde{\pi})f(\widetilde{x},\widetilde{\lambda}) + \widetilde{\lambda}\left(\boldsymbol{\phi}(\widetilde{x},\widetilde{\pi}) - c(\widetilde{\pi})^T\Sigma_w\boldsymbol{\phi}(\widetilde{x},\Pi)\right)^2\right],$$

where we have exchanged minimization with a maximization by changing the sign of the cost function, and we dropped $\log|\Sigma_w|$ as it is independent of $\widetilde{x}$ and $\widetilde{\pi}$.

3.1.3. Distributed Computation of the D-Optimality Criterion for SOE

Let us begin first with evaluating the D-optimality criterion for the SOE case. Evaluating (37) for this data splitting is easier as compared with SOF.

Since Π is known to each agent, the vector $\boldsymbol{\phi}(\widetilde{x},\Pi)$ can be evaluated without any cooperation between the agents. The covariance Σ_w can then be evaluated distributively using averaged consensus as $\Sigma_w = (D + \widehat{\Gamma}^{-1})^{-1}$, where D is computed using network-wide averaging. To compute (46), a few more steps are needed. Specifically, in addition to Σ_w, we also need to compute the quantities $c(\widetilde{\pi})$ and $b(\widetilde{\pi})$ in (40) to evaluate the criterion. These can already be computed using averaged consensus as

$$c(\widetilde{\pi}) = \boldsymbol{\Phi}^T \boldsymbol{\Lambda} \boldsymbol{\phi}(X,\widetilde{\pi}) = K \times \frac{1}{K}\sum_{k=1}^K \boldsymbol{\Phi}_k^T \boldsymbol{\Lambda} \boldsymbol{\phi}(X_k,\widetilde{\pi}), \tag{47}$$

$$b(\widetilde{\pi}) = \boldsymbol{\phi}(X,\widetilde{\pi})^T \boldsymbol{\Lambda} \boldsymbol{\phi}(X,\widetilde{\pi}) + \widetilde{\gamma}^{-1} = K \times \frac{1}{K}\sum_{k=1}^K \boldsymbol{\phi}(X_k,\widetilde{\pi})^T \boldsymbol{\Lambda} \boldsymbol{\phi}(X_k,\widetilde{\pi}) + \widetilde{\gamma}^{-1}. \tag{48}$$

Then, using (47) and (48) as well as Σ_w computed distributively, the criterion (46) can be easily evaluated by each agent.

It is worth noting that the choice of $\widetilde{\gamma}^{-1}$ in (48) is the only parameter that can be set manually in this exploration criterion. Basically, it controls how much we know about the potential measurement location. If $\widetilde{\gamma}^{-1}$ is large, the criterion would yield that the potential measurement location is not informative. On the other side, if $\widetilde{\gamma}^{-1} \to 0$, the criterion yields that the considered measurement location is potentially informative. We set $\widetilde{\gamma}^{-1} = 0$ for all considered measurement locations, such that the current information in the model determines how informative a measurement location could be.

3.1.4. Distributed Computation of the D-Optimality Criterion for SOF

For SOF, (37) is unsuited for a distributed computation such that some changes have to be made. First, we define the following terms to facilitate the distributed formulation

$$H \triangleq \boldsymbol{\Phi}\widehat{\boldsymbol{\Gamma}}\boldsymbol{\Phi}^T = K \times \frac{1}{K}\sum_{k=1}^{K} \boldsymbol{\Phi}_k \widehat{\boldsymbol{\Gamma}}_k \boldsymbol{\Phi}_k^T, \tag{49}$$

$$d \triangleq \boldsymbol{\Phi}\widehat{\boldsymbol{\Gamma}}\boldsymbol{\phi}(\widetilde{x}, \Pi) = K \times \frac{1}{K}\sum_{k=1}^{K} \boldsymbol{\Phi}_k \widehat{\boldsymbol{\Gamma}}_k \boldsymbol{\phi}(\widetilde{x}, \Pi_k), \tag{50}$$

$$v \triangleq \boldsymbol{\phi}^T(\widetilde{x}, \Pi)\widehat{\boldsymbol{\Gamma}}\boldsymbol{\phi}(\widetilde{x}, \Pi) = K \times \frac{1}{K}\sum_{k=1}^{K} \boldsymbol{\phi}_k^T(\widetilde{x}, \Pi_k)\widehat{\boldsymbol{\Gamma}}_k \boldsymbol{\phi}(\widetilde{x}, \Pi_k), \tag{51}$$

where $\Pi_k = [\pi_1, \ldots, \pi_{N_k}]^T \in \mathbb{R}^{N_k \times s}$ and $\widehat{\boldsymbol{\Gamma}}_k = [\widehat{\gamma}_1, \ldots, \widehat{\gamma}_{N_k}]^T$. All terms in (49)–(51) can then be computed by means of an averaged consensus [40,41]. Next, we reformulate Σ_w with the help of the matrix-inversion-lemma as

$$\Sigma_w = \widehat{\boldsymbol{\Gamma}} - \widehat{\boldsymbol{\Gamma}}\boldsymbol{\Phi}^T(\Lambda^{-1} + \boldsymbol{\Phi}\widehat{\boldsymbol{\Gamma}}\boldsymbol{\Phi}^T)^{-1}\boldsymbol{\Phi}\widehat{\boldsymbol{\Gamma}} = \widehat{\boldsymbol{\Gamma}} - \widehat{\boldsymbol{\Gamma}}\boldsymbol{\Phi}^T(\Lambda^{-1} + H)^{-1}\boldsymbol{\Phi}\widehat{\boldsymbol{\Gamma}}. \tag{52}$$

Now, (37) can be reformulated in a distributed setting for SOF as

$$\begin{aligned} f(\widetilde{x}, \widetilde{\lambda}) &= 1 + \widetilde{\lambda}\boldsymbol{\phi}^T(\widetilde{x}, \Pi)\Sigma_w \boldsymbol{\phi}(\widetilde{x}, \Pi) \\ &= 1 + \widetilde{\lambda}\boldsymbol{\phi}^T(\widetilde{x}, \Pi)\left(\widehat{\boldsymbol{\Gamma}} - \widehat{\boldsymbol{\Gamma}}\boldsymbol{\Phi}^T(\Lambda^{-1} + H)^{-1}\boldsymbol{\Phi}\widehat{\boldsymbol{\Gamma}}\right)\boldsymbol{\phi}(\widetilde{x}, \Pi) \\ &= 1 + \widetilde{\lambda}\boldsymbol{\phi}^T(\widetilde{x}, \Pi)\widehat{\boldsymbol{\Gamma}}\boldsymbol{\phi}(\widetilde{x}, \Pi) - \widetilde{\lambda}\boldsymbol{\phi}^T(\widetilde{x}, \Pi)\widehat{\boldsymbol{\Gamma}}\boldsymbol{\Phi}^T(\Lambda^{-1} + H)^{-1}\boldsymbol{\Phi}\widehat{\boldsymbol{\Gamma}}\boldsymbol{\phi}(\widetilde{x}, \Pi) \\ &= 1 + \widetilde{\lambda}v - \widetilde{\lambda}d^T(\Lambda^{-1} + H)^{-1}d. \end{aligned} \tag{53}$$

For the case when the criterion (46) is used for evaluaton of the D-optimality, the variable $q(\widetilde{\pi})$ in (46) and the second additive term there have to be reformulated in a form suitable for SOF data splitting. For the former, we utilize the definitions in (49)–(51), together with (52) such that

$$\begin{aligned} q(\widetilde{\pi}) &= \gamma^{-1} + \boldsymbol{\phi}^T(X, \widetilde{\pi})\Lambda \boldsymbol{\phi}(X, \widetilde{\pi}) - \boldsymbol{\phi}^T(X, \widetilde{\pi})\Lambda \boldsymbol{\Phi}\Sigma_w \boldsymbol{\Phi}^T \Lambda \boldsymbol{\phi}(X, \widetilde{\pi}) \\ &= \gamma^{-1} + \boldsymbol{\phi}^T(X, \widetilde{\pi})\Lambda \boldsymbol{\phi}(X, \widetilde{\pi}) - \boldsymbol{\phi}^T(X, \widetilde{\pi})\Lambda(H - H(\Lambda^{-1} + H)^{-1}H)\Lambda \boldsymbol{\phi}(X, \widetilde{\pi}) \\ &= \gamma^{-1} + \boldsymbol{\phi}^T(X, \widetilde{\pi})\Lambda \boldsymbol{\phi}(X, \widetilde{\pi}) - \boldsymbol{\phi}^T(X, \widetilde{\pi})\Lambda(\Lambda + H^{-1})^{-1}\Lambda \boldsymbol{\phi}(X, \widetilde{\pi}) \\ &= \gamma^{-1} + \boldsymbol{\phi}^T(X, \widetilde{\pi})(\Lambda - \Lambda(\Lambda + H^{-1})^{-1}\Lambda)\Lambda \boldsymbol{\phi}(X, \widetilde{\pi})\boldsymbol{\phi}(X, \widetilde{\pi}) \\ &= \gamma^{-1} + \boldsymbol{\phi}^T(X, \widetilde{\pi})(\Lambda^{-1} + H)^{-1}\boldsymbol{\phi}(X, \widetilde{\pi}). \end{aligned} \tag{54}$$

The other term in (46) is then reformulated similarly using the results (49)–(52) as

$$\begin{aligned} c^T(\widetilde{\pi})\Sigma_w \boldsymbol{\phi}(\widetilde{x}, \Pi) &= \boldsymbol{\phi}^T(X, \widetilde{\pi})\Lambda \boldsymbol{\Phi}(\widehat{\boldsymbol{\Gamma}} - \widehat{\boldsymbol{\Gamma}}\boldsymbol{\Phi}^T(\Lambda^{-1} + H)^{-1}\boldsymbol{\Phi}\widehat{\boldsymbol{\Gamma}})\boldsymbol{\phi}(\widetilde{x}, \Pi) \\ &= \boldsymbol{\phi}^T(X, \widetilde{\pi})\Lambda(\boldsymbol{\Phi}\widehat{\boldsymbol{\Gamma}}\boldsymbol{\phi}(\widetilde{x}, \Pi) - \boldsymbol{\Phi}\widehat{\boldsymbol{\Gamma}}\boldsymbol{\Phi}^T(\Lambda^{-1} + H)^{-1}\boldsymbol{\Phi}\widehat{\boldsymbol{\Gamma}}\boldsymbol{\phi}(\widetilde{x}, \Pi)) \\ &= \boldsymbol{\phi}^T(X, \widetilde{\pi})\Lambda(d - H(\Lambda^{-1} + H)^{-1})d) \\ &= \boldsymbol{\phi}^T(X, \widetilde{\pi})\Lambda(I - H(\Lambda^{-1} + H)^{-1})d. \end{aligned} \tag{55}$$

As a result, the exploration criterion can be re-formulated for SOF in the following form

$$\arg\min_{\widetilde{x}} \log|\widetilde{\Sigma}_w(X, \Pi, \widetilde{x}, \widetilde{\pi})| \equiv \tag{56}$$

$$\arg\max_{\widetilde{x}} \log\left[q(\widetilde{\pi})f(\widetilde{x}, \widetilde{\lambda}) + \widetilde{\lambda}\left(\boldsymbol{\phi}(\widetilde{x}, \widetilde{\pi}) - \boldsymbol{\phi}^T(X, \widetilde{\pi})\Lambda(I - H(\Lambda^{-1} + H)^{-1})d\right)^2\right],$$

with $q(\widetilde{\pi})$ defined in (54) and $f(\widetilde{x}, \widetilde{\lambda})$ given in (53).

4. Experimental Setup

This section describes definition of the experimental setup, calibration of the sensors, and collection of ground-truth data for performance evaluation.

4.1. Map Construction

The following describes our experimental setup. We conducted the experiments indoor in our laboratory with two paper boxes as obstacles displayed in Figure 1a. Red lines in the figure represent the borders of the experimental area. We use two Commonplace Robotics (https://cpr-robots.com, accessed on 19 March 2022) ground-based robots with mecanum wheels; further in the text, we will refer to the robots as sliders due to their ability to move holonomically. To position the slider within the environment, the laboratory is equipped with 16 VICON (https://www.vicon.com/, accessed on 19 March 2022) Bonita cameras. For the experiment itself, we assume that the map is a priori known to the system. Thus, we need to record the map before the experiment. So, a single slider is equipped with a light detection and ranging (LIDAR) sensor. We use a Velodyne (https://velodynelidar.com/, accessed on 19 March 2022) *VLP-16* LIDAR and the corresponding robot operating system (ROS) package, which can be downloaded from the ROS repository. We construct the map while sending waypoints to the slider manually. The steering of the slider is done with the help of ROS' *navigation stack* [42] together with the *Teb Local Planner* [43]. The sensor output of the LIDAR and the slider position estimated by the VICON system are then used to generate a map with the *Octomap* [44] ROS package. Because we use the VICON position of the slider, which is accurate, this mapping procedure is simpler compared to simultaneous localization and mapping (SLAM) algorithms [45,46]. Figure 1b shows the constructed map, which is afterwards used in the experiment.

(a)   (b)

Figure 1. (**a**) The experimental setting with obstacles. The red line indicates the experimental area, where the slider can navigate. (**b**) The constructed map.

4.2. Sensor Calibration

Each slider is equipped with a XSens MTw inertial measurement unit (IMU). The sensor comprises a three-axis magneto-resistive magnetometer, an accelerometer, gyroscopes, and a barometer. For the following experiment, we only use the magnetometer. The sensor is attached to a wooden stick to reduce the influence of the metal wheels on the measurement. Although the sliders are equipped with sensors from the same product line of the same manufacturer, their absolute perception differs. Additionally, the sensors can still perceive the metal in the wheels of the robots. Therefore, we need to calibrate the sensors relatively to each other to perceive the environment equally using the approach proposed in [47].

The authors in [47] assume that the sensor readings of one sensor can be expressed as another sensor's reading through an affine transformation. To estimate the rotation and translation, multiple sensor readings of all sensors have to be acquired. These readings are then exploited to estimate the rotation and translation relative to one specific sensor by means of a least squares method. In this experiment, each magnetic field sensor reads at a position x_m one measurement of the magnetic field per Euclidean axis. During the estimation, absolute values of these measurements are used. Figure 2a shows the absolute values of the sensor readings for multiple measurement locations of two sensors. The error of the sensor readings before and after calibration are presented in Figure 2b. The correction thus reduces the bias and the standard deviation of the error between both sensors.

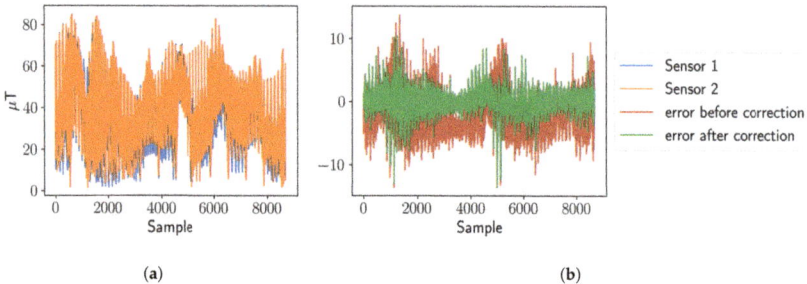

Figure 2. (**a**) Absolute values of the magnetic field samples of two sensors. It is assumed that each sensor measured at the same locations. (**b**) Error of the absolute values of the magnetic field samples before and after the corrections. The calibrated sensor has now the same mean as the reference sensor, and the standard deviation of the error is reduced.

However, this calibration is only useful if the orientation of both sensors is constant during the experiment. As the sensors always measure in the same orientation, this assumption is fulfilled for our experiments. For further information on intrinsic calibration of inertial and magnetic sensors, the reader is referred to [48].

4.3. Collecting Ground Truth Data

In order to evaluate the performance of the distributed exploration, we also need to know the actual magnetic field in the laboratory—a ground truth data. For collecting the ground truth data, one slider measures the area of the Holodeck in a systematic fashion, where the distance between each measurement was set to be 5 cm such that in total, 8699 measurement points were collected. On each measurement position, multiple sensor readings are taken and averaged. The resulting ground truth is displayed in Figure 3.

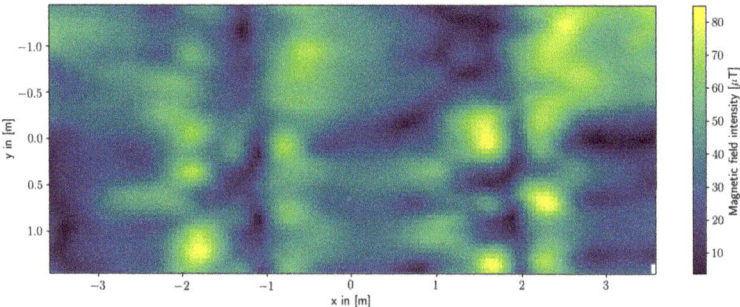

Figure 3. Magnetic field intensity of the Holodeck collected for the experiment with real sensors. The measurements were made in 5 cm steps.

5. Experimental System Design

Our setup relies on ROS (https://www.ros.org/, accessed on 19 March 2022), which manages the communication between all software modules called *nodes*. On each slider, several ROS nodes are running such as the motor controller, which translates the measurement locations into velocity commands for each wheel, the path-planner, and the sensor.

As a path-planner, we use the popular A* [49,50]. We implemented the A* algorithm as a global and as a local planner, which is utilized for collision avoidance. Therefore, each slider does not only consider the global map but also a local map around its current position.

After receiving a new waypoint, the global path planner estimates a path in the global map from the current position to the goal avoiding the obstacles. If there is no other robotic system in its path, the goal is reached. However, if another slider enters the local frame while the robot is on its way toward the goal, the robot stops, and the path within the local frame is re-planned to avoid collisions. If the planner is not able to find a solution in the local frame within a given time, the global path planning is re-initiated, taking the current slider as an obstacle into account.

The whole system design for this experiment is shown in Figure 4. The distributed exploration criterion uses the computed map excluding the locations of the obstacles. In addition, the map information is used by the path-planner to find an obstacle-free path to the estimated measurement location $\hat{x}$. Figure 4 also describes the process-flow of the whole system.

For comparison, we will use non-Bayesian SOF and SOE formulations as discussed in [14]. As in these formulations, the ADMM algorithm [33] was used for estimation, we will refer to them as ADMM for SOF and ADMM for SOE, respectively. For the Bayesian learning and algorithms discussed in this paper, we will refer to them as D-R-ARD for SOF and the D-R-ARD for SOE (see also Table 1).

Table 1. The algorithms that are used in this experiment and where they are introduced.

	Algorithm Introduced in	Exploration Introduced in
ADMM for SOE	[33]	[14]
ADMM for SOF	[33]	[14]
D-R-ARD for SOE	Section 2.4	Section 3.1.3
D-R-ARD for SOF	[15]	Section 3.1.4

In the experiments, we will set the number of basis functions to $N = 560$, which also determines the size of the vector w. The basis functions are distributed in a regular grid. We consider Gaussian basis functions with a width set to $\sigma_n = 0.25$ such that

$$\phi_n(x, \pi_n) = \exp\left\{-\frac{\|x - \pi_n\|^2}{2\sigma_n^2}\right\}, \tag{57}$$

where $\pi_n \in \mathbb{R}^s$ and $s = d$.

After initialization of the system, every agent takes a first measurement and incorporates it in its local measurement model to calculate the first estimate of the regression. Then, each algorithm requires that the intermediate estimated parameter weights are distributed to the neighbors (following Figure 4) to do an average consensus [40,41]. Consequently, each agent can proceed to estimate with the regression using the averaged intermediate parameter weights. When the distributed regression converged, the agents use the estimated covariance matrix in the distributed exploration step. In this step, the agents propose candidate positions to their neighbors and receive information to compute the D-optimality criterion locally. When the best next measurement locations are chosen, they are passed to the coordination part [51] to verify that all agents go to different positions. If the measurement location is considered as valid, an agent locally plans its path on the global frame to reach the goal. While approaching the goal, the agent checks if other agents entered into the local frame to avoid collisions. When all agents reached their goal, the agents take measurements and the process flow continues.

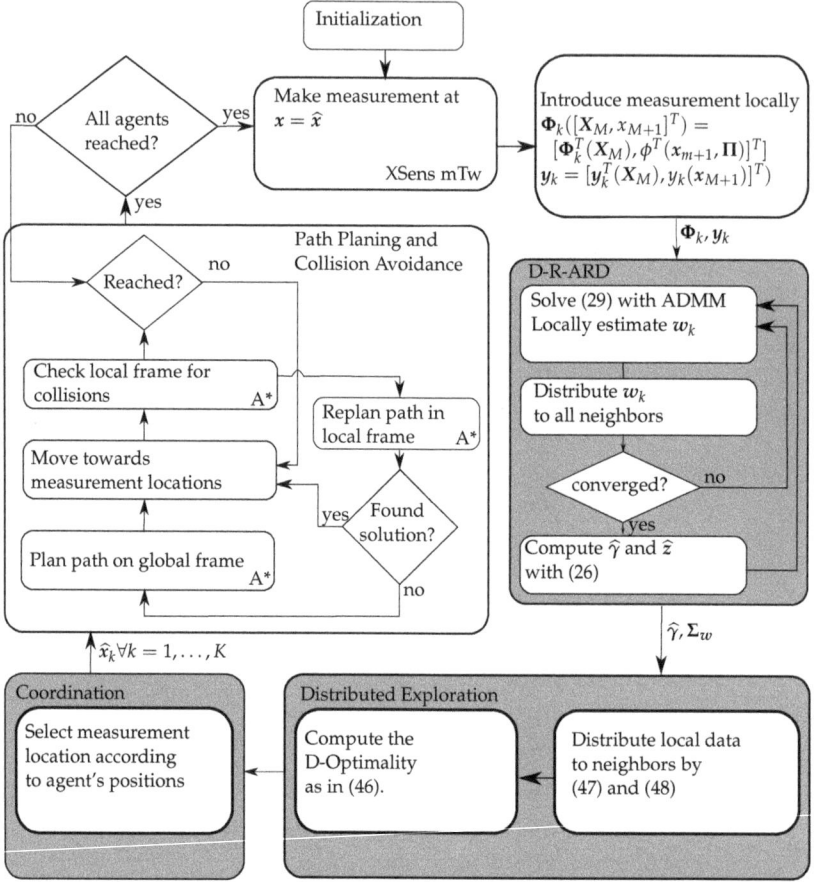

Figure 4. System design with additional path planner and map constraints. Each gray box represents interaction between other agents. In some boxes, the lower right indicates where this process belongs. This software setup is representative for the SOE distribution paradigm.

As evaluation metric, we chose the normalized mean square error (NMSE), which can be defined as

$$e \triangleq \frac{\|y_{\text{true}}(X_T) - \Phi(X_T, \Pi)\hat{w}\|}{\|y_{\text{true}}(X_T)\|}, \tag{58}$$

where $y_{\text{true}}(X_T) \in \mathbb{R}^T$ is the ground truth measured at $T \in \mathbb{N}$ positions $X_T \in \mathbb{R}^{T \times d}$. Here, we set $T = 560$, and these locations are equal to the center positions of the Gaussian basis functions.

6. Experimental Validation

Figure 5 shows the NMSE of all conducted experiments with respect to time (top plot) and to the number of measurements (bottom plot). Each experimental run has a different duration, and the ROS system uses asynchronous interprocess communication resulting in asynchronous time-steps. Thus, all runs of one particular algorithm are visualized as a scatter plot. The number of measurements varies because the computation time for each measurement could be different. As a consequence, an averaging along multiple experimental runs along the time axis is not reasonable. For both ADMM algorithms, we conducted four experiments, whereas for each D-R-ARD algorithm, we conducted two experiments. The corresponding results are summarized in Figure 5.

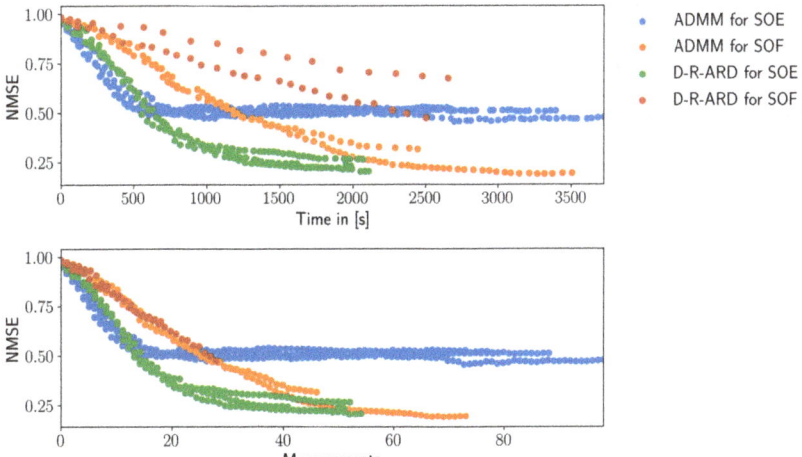

Figure 5. The NMSE of the conducted experiments with respect to time and with respect to the number of measurements.

When looking at the top plot in Figure 5, the D-R-ARD for SOE has the best performance because the NMSE is reduced faster compared to the other methods.

Regarding the ADMM algorithms, the SOE paradigm has a brief benefit until the 1200 s until SOF paradigm outperforms the SOE paradigm. The weak performance of D-R-ARD for SOF might result from the distributed structure of the algorithm, which requires the algorithm to compute a matrix inversion in each iteration together with the computational complex estimation of parameter weights and variances. In contrast to that, the corresponding algorithm with the SOE distribution paradigm is able to cache the matrix inversion, which drastically increases the performance. Yet, the D-R-ARD algorithms have generally a higher computational complexity compared to the ADMM algorithms. This is due to the fact that the Bayesian methods require the covariance to be computed in each iteration. The ADMM algorithm, in contrast, does not require this.

The plot at the bottom of Figure 5 displays the NMSE with respect to the number of obtained measurements. There, the D-R-ARD for SOF and ADMM for SOF have almost the same performance. However, the ADMM for SOF is able to achieve substantially more measurements because it is computationally less complex. Consequently, the ADMM for SOF achieves not only more measurements but is on a par with the D-R-ARD for SOF when it comes to efficiency per measurement.

For the SOE distribution paradigm, on the contrary, it is beneficial to use the Bayesian methodology. In the experiments we present here, the D-R-ARD for SOE achieves a lower NMSE with fewer measurements compared to ADMM for SOE algorithm. This could be due to the fact that D-R-ARD for SOE computes the entropy of the parameter weights and does not approximate it. The computed entropy seems then to be better for the D-optimality criterion than the approximated version for the ADMM for SOE.

To support the claim that the Bayesian framework estimates a better covariance of the parameter weights when the SOE paradigm is applied, Figure 6a,b present the estimated magnetic field and the estimated covariance at different timesteps. In both figures, the left most plots display the beginning of the experiment and the most right plots show the end result of the experiment. At the beginning of the experiments, both algorithms—ADMM and D-R-ARD for SOE—estimate a sparse covariance with not much difference. As the measurements increase, the approximated covariance becomes smoother, and the covariance estimated in the Bayesian framework stays sparse. This effect might result from the approximation of a covariance as introdcued in [14], where a penalty parameter needs to be chosen as a compromise between sparsity and a reasonably well approximated covariance.

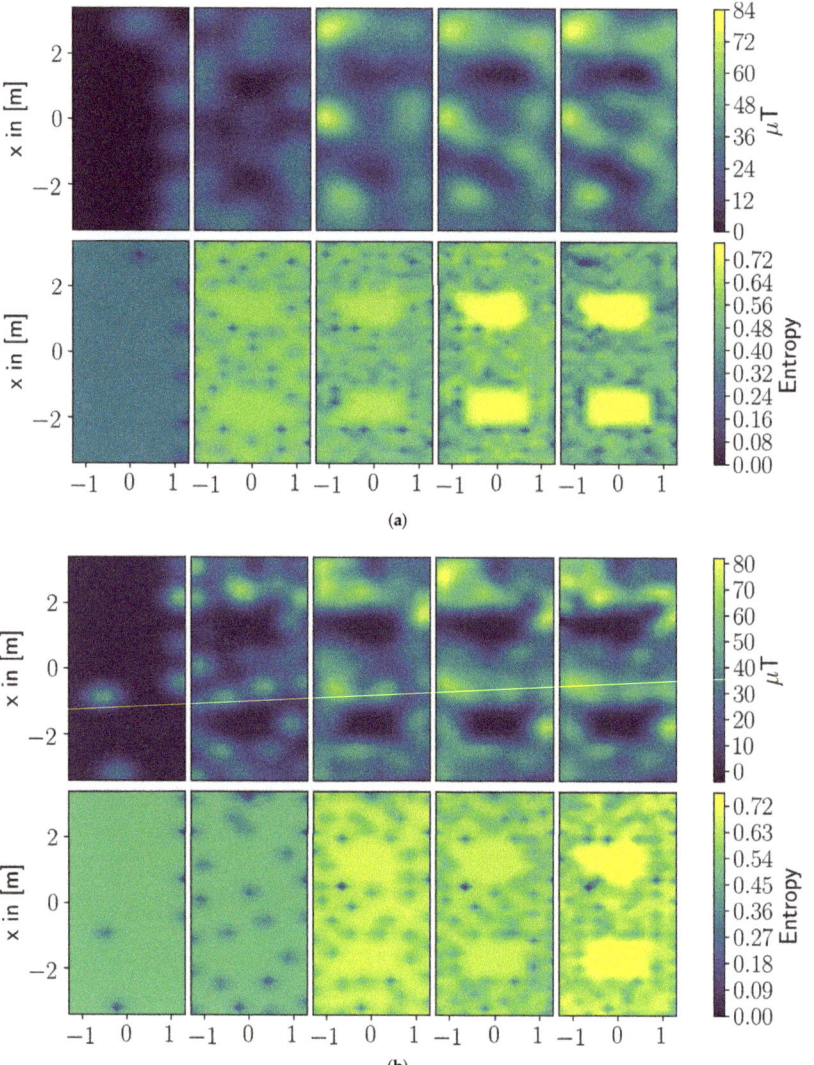

Figure 6. (**a**) SOE with a classic framework. (**b**) SOE with a Bayesian framework. In both figures, the upper row displays the estimates at different time steps and the lower row shows the entropy at the same time steps.

As a second remark, the ADMM algorithms involve a thresholding operator, which sets all not used basis functions to zero such that these basis functions can not be considered by the exploration step. This is controlled by a manually set penalty parameter and might be sub-optimal. The D-R-ARD for SOE, on the other side, estimates a hyper-parameter for each basis function based on the current data. Therefore, the influence of each basis function is addressed more individually and, hence, leads to a better covariance estimate.

The way basis functions and parameter weights are introduced in the SOF paradigm makes this effect eventually not observable between the Bayesian and the Frequentist framework.

7. Conclusions

The presented paper proposes and validates a method for spatial regression using Sparse Bayesian Learning (SBL) and exploration, which are both implemented over a network of interconnected mobile agents. The spatial process of interest is described as a linear combination of parameterized basis functions; by constraining the weights of these functions in the final representation using a sparsifying prior, we find a model with only a few, relevant functions contributing to the model. The learning is implemented in a distributed fashion, such that no centralized processing unit is necessary. We also considered two conceptually different distribution paradigms splitting-over-features (SOF) and splitting-over-examples (SOE). To this end, a numerical algorithm based on alternating direction method of multipliers is used.

The learned representation is used to devise an information-driven optimal data collection approach. Specifically, the perturbation of the parameter covariance matrix with respect to a new measurement location is derived. This perturbation allows us to choose new measurement locations for agents such that the size of the resulting joint parameter uncertainty, as measured by the log-determinant of the covariance, is minimized. We show also how this criterion can be evaluated in a distributed fashion for both distribution paradigms in an SBL framework.

The resulting scheme thus includes two key steps: (i) cooperative sparse models that fit data collected by agents, and (ii) the cooperative identification of new measurement locations that optimizes the D-optimality criterion. To validate the performance of the scheme, we set up an experiment involving two mobile robots that navigated in an environment with obstacles. The robots were tasked with reconstructing the magnetic field which was measured on the floor of the laboratory by a magnetometer sensor. We tested the proposed scheme against a non-Bayesian sparse regression method and a similar exploration criterion.

The experimental results show that the Bayesian methods explore more efficiently than the benchmark algorithms. Efficiency is measured as the reduction of error over the number of measurements or the reduction of error over time. The reason is that the used Bayesian method directly computes the covariance matrix from the data and has fewer parameters that have to be manually adjusted. The exploration with these methods is therefore simpler to set up as compared with non-Bayesian inference approaches studied before. Yet, for the SOF distribution paradigm, the Bayesian method is computationally too demanding such that significantly fewer measurements can be collected in the same amount of time as compared with the non-Bayesian learning method.

Author Contributions: Conceptualization, C.M.; Data curation, C.M.; Formal analysis, C.M. and D.S.; Investigation, C.M. and I.K.; Methodology, C.M. and D.S.; Software, C.M. and I.K.; Supervision, C.M. All authors have read and agreed to the published version of the manuscript.

Funding: This research received no external funding.

Conflicts of Interest: The authors declare no conflict of interest.

Abbreviations

The following abbreviations are used in this manuscript:

ADMM	alternating direction method of multipliers
ROS	robot operating system
SBL	Sparse Bayesian Learning
PDF	probability density function
SOF	splitting-over-features
SOE	splitting-over-examples

NMSE	normalized mean square error
D-R-ARD	distributed R-ARD
R-ARD	reformulated automatic relevance determination
IMU	inertial measurement unit
LIDAR	light detection and ranging
SLAM	simultaneous localization and mapping
UAV	unmanned aerial vehicle
LASSO	least absolute shrinkage and selection operator
MAP	maximum a posteriori

References

1. Truszkowski, W.; Hinchey, M.; Rash, J.; Rouff, C. Autonomous and Autonomic Systems: A Paradigm for Future Space Exploration Missions. *IEEE Trans. Syst. Man Cybern. Part C Appl. Rev.* **2006**, *36*, 279–291. [CrossRef]
2. Patten, T.; Fitch, R. Large-Scale Near-Optimal Decentralised Information Gathering with Multiple Mobile Robots. In Proceedings of the Australasian Conference on Robotics and Automation, Sydney, Australia, 2–4 December 2013; p. 9.
3. Zhou, X.; Wang, W.; Wang, T.; Li, M.; Zhong, F. Online Planning for Multiagent Situational Information Gathering in the Markov Environment. *IEEE Syst. J.* **2019**, *14*, 1798–1809. [CrossRef]
4. Wiedemann, T.; Manss, C.; Shutin, D.; Lilienthal, A.J.; Karolj, V.; Viseras, A. Probabilistic Modeling of Gas Diffusion with Partial Differential Equations for Multi-Robot Exploration and Gas Source Localization. In Proceedings of the 2017 European Conference on Mobile Robots (ECMR), Paris, France, 6–8 September 2017; pp. 1–7. [CrossRef]
5. Olsen, N. Exploring Earth's Magnetic Field—Three Make a Swarm. *Spatium* **2019**, *2019*, 3–15.
6. Pang, B.; Song, Y.; Zhang, C.; Wang, H.; Yang, R. A Swarm Robotic Exploration Strategy Based on an Improved Random Walk Method. *J. Robot.* **2019**, *2019*, 1–9. [CrossRef]
7. Pang, B.; Song, Y.; Zhang, C.; Yang, R. Effect of Random Walk Methods on Searching Efficiency in Swarm Robots for Area Exploration. *Appl. Intell.* **2021**, *51*, 5189–5199. [CrossRef]
8. Schwager, M.; Julian, B.J.; Angermann, M.; Rus, D. Eyes in the Sky: Decentralized Control for the Deployment of Robotic Camera Networks. *Proc. IEEE* **2011**, *9*, 1541–1561. [CrossRef]
9. Whaite, P.; Ferrie, F.P. Autonomous Exploration: Driven by Uncertainty. *IEEE Trans. Pattern Anal. Mach. Intell.* **1997**, *19*, 13. [CrossRef]
10. Fedorov, V.V. *Theory of Optimal Experiments*; Academic Press: Cambridge, MA, USA, 1972.
11. Krause, A.; Singh, A.; Guestrin, C. Near-Optimal Sensor Placements in Gaussian Processes: Theory, Efficient Algorithms and Empirical Studies. *J. Mach. Learn. Res.* **2008**, *9*, 235–284.
12. Cho, D.H.; Ha, J.S.; Lee, S.; Moon, S.; Choi, H.L. Informative Path Planning and Mapping with Multiple UAVs in Wind Fields. In *Distributed Autonomous Robotic Systems: The 13th International Symposium*; Springer: Cham, Switzerland, 2018; pp. 269–283.
13. Viseras, A.; Shutin, D.; Merino, L. Robotic Active Information Gathering for Spatial Field Reconstruction with Rapidly-Exploring Random Trees and Online Learning of Gaussian Processes. *Sensors* **2019**, *19*, 1016. [CrossRef]
14. Manss, C.; Shutin, D. Global-Entropy Driven Exploration with Distributed Models under Sparsity Constraints. *Appl. Sci.* **2018**, *8*, 21. [CrossRef]
15. Manss, C.; Shutin, D.; Leus, G. Distributed Splitting-Over-Features Sparse Bayesian Learning with Alternating Direction Method of Multipliers. In Proceedings of the 2018 IEEE International Conference on Acoustics, Speech and Signal Processing (ICASSP), Calgary, AB, Canada, 15–20 April 2018; pp. 3654–3658. [CrossRef]
16. Manss, C.; Shutin, D.; Leus, G. Consensus Based Distributed Sparse Bayesian Learning By Fast Marginal Likelihood Maximization. *IEEE Signal Process. Lett.* **2020**, *27*, 2119–2123. [CrossRef]
17. Bishop, C. *Pattern Recognition and Machine Learning*; Information Science and Statistics; Springer: New York, NY, USA, 2006.
18. Tipping, M.E. Sparse Bayesian Learning and the Relevance Vector Machine. *J. Mach. Learn. Res.* **2001**, *1*, 211–244.
19. Wipf, D.; Rao, B. Sparse Bayesian Learning for Basis Selection. *IEEE Trans. Signal Process.* **2004**, *52*, 2153–2164. [CrossRef]
20. Tzikas, D.G.; Likas, A.C.; Galatsanos, N.P. The Variational Approximation for Bayesian Inference. *IEEE Signal Process. Mag.* **2008**, *25*, 131–146. [CrossRef]
21. Giri, R.; Rao, B. Type I and Type II Bayesian Methods for Sparse Signal Recovery Using Scale Mixtures. *IEEE Trans. Signal Process.* **2016**, *64*, 3418–3428. [CrossRef]
22. Candes, E.; Wakin, M. An Introduction To Compressive Sampling. *IEEE Signal Process. Mag.* **2008**, *25*, 21–30. [CrossRef]
23. Chartrand, R.; Yin, W. Iteratively reweighted algorithms for compressive sensing. In Proceedings of the 2008 IEEE International Conference on Acoustics, Speech and Signal Processing, Las Vegas, NV, USA, 30 March–4 April 2008; pp. 3869–3872. [CrossRef]
24. Rao, B.D.; Kreutz-Delgado, K. An affine scaling methodology for best basis selection. *IEEE Trans. Signal Process.* **1999**, *47*, 187–200. [CrossRef]
25. Wipf, D.; Rao, B.; Nagarajan, S. Latent Variable Bayesian Models for Promoting Sparsity. *IEEE Trans. Inf. Theory* **2011**, *57*, 6236–6255. [CrossRef]
26. Wipf, D.P.; Nagarajan, S.S. A New View of Automatic Relevance Determination. In *Advances in Neural Information Processing Systems 20*; Platt, J.C., Koller, D., Singer, Y., Roweis, S.T., Eds.; Curran Associates, Inc.: Red Hook, NY, USA, 2008; pp. 1625–1632.

27. Shutin, D.; Kulkarni, S.R.; Poor, H.V. Incremental Reformulated Automatic Relevance Determination. *IEEE Trans. Signal Process.* **2012**, *60*, 4977–4981. [CrossRef]
28. Tipping, M.E.; Faul, A.C. Fast Marginal Likelihood Maximisation for Sparse Bayesian Models. In Proceedings of the Ninth International Workshop on Artificial Intelligence and Statistics, Key West, FL, USA, 3–6 January 2003; p. 14.
29. Shutin, D.; Buchgraber, T.; Kulkarni, S.R.; Poor, H.V. Fast Variational Sparse Bayesian Learning With Automatic Relevance Determination for Superimposed Signals. *IEEE Trans. Signal Process.* **2011**, *59*, 6257–6261. [CrossRef]
30. Hansen, T.L.; Fleury, B.H.; Rao, B.D. Superfast Line Spectral Estimation. *IEEE Trans. Signal Process.* **2018**, *66*, 2511–2526. [CrossRef]
31. Boyd, S.; Vandenberghe, L. *Convex Optimization*; Cambridge University Press: Cambridge, UK, 2004.
32. Moon, T.; Stirling, W.C. *Mathematical Methods and Algorithms for Signal Processing*; Number 621.39: 51 MON; Prentice Hall: Upper Saddle River, NJ, USA, 2000.
33. Boyd, S. Distributed Optimization and Statistical Learning via the Alternating Direction Method of Multipliers. *Found. Trends Mach. Learn.* **2010**, *3*, 1–122. [CrossRef]
34. Dimakis, A.G.; Kar, S.; Moura, J.M.F.; Rabbat, M.G.; Scaglione, A. Gossip Algorithms for Distributed Signal Processing. *Proc. IEEE* **2010**, *98*, 1847–1864. [CrossRef]
35. Nedic, A.; Ozdaglar, A.; Parrilo, P. Constrained Consensus and Optimization in Multi-Agent Networks. *IEEE Trans. Autom. Control* **2010**, *55*, 922–938. [CrossRef]
36. Mateos, G.; Bazerque, J.A.; Giannakis, G.B. Distributed Sparse Linear Regression. *IEEE Trans. Signal Process.* **2010**, *58*, 5262–5276. [CrossRef]
37. Ding, J.; Zhou, A. Eigenvalues of Rank-One Updated Matrices with Some Applications. *Appl. Math. Lett.* **2007**, *20*, 1223–1226. [CrossRef]
38. Brezinski, C. Schur Complements and Applications in Numerical Analysis. In *The Schur Complement and Its Applications*; Zhang, F., Ed.; Numerical Methods and Algorithms; Springer: Boston, MA, USA, 2005; pp. 227–258. [CrossRef]
39. Tylavsky, D.; Sohie, G. Generalization of the Matrix Inversion Lemma. *Proc. IEEE* **1986**, *74*, 1050–1052. [CrossRef]
40. Aysal, T.C.; Yildiz, M.E.; Sarwate, A.D.; Scaglione, A. Broadcast Gossip Algorithms for Consensus. *IEEE Trans. Signal Process.* **2009**, *57*, 2748–2761. [CrossRef]
41. Nedić, A.; Olshevsky, A.; Rabbat, M.G. Network Topology and Communication-Computation Tradeoffs in Decentralized Optimization. *Proc. IEEE* **2018**, *106*, 953–976. [CrossRef]
42. Marder-Eppstein, E.; Berger, E.; Foote, T.; Gerkey, B.; Konolige, K. The Office Marathon: Robust Navigation in an Indoor Office Environment. In Proceedings of the 2010 IEEE International Conference on Robotics and Automation, Anchorage, Alaska, 3–7 May 2010; pp. 300–307. [CrossRef]
43. Rösmann, C.; Hoffmann, F.; Bertram, T. Planning of Multiple Robot Trajectories in Distinctive Topologies. In Proceedings of the 2015 European Conference on Mobile Robots (ECMR), Lincoln, UK, 2–4 September 2015; pp. 1–6. [CrossRef]
44. Hornung, A.; Wurm, K.M.; Bennewitz, M.; Stachniss, C.; Burgard, W. OctoMap: An Efficient Probabilistic 3D Mapping Framework Based on Octrees. *Auton. Robot.* **2013**, *34*, 189–206. [CrossRef]
45. Dubé, R.; Gawel, A.; Sommer, H.; Nieto, J.; Siegwart, R.; Cadena, C. An Online Multi-Robot SLAM System for 3D LiDARs. In Proceedings of the 2017 IEEE/RSJ International Conference on Intelligent Robots and Systems (IROS), Vancouver, BC, Canada, 24–28 September 2017; pp. 1004–1011. [CrossRef]
46. Vallvé, J.; Andrade-Cetto, J. Mobile Robot Exploration with Potential Information Fields. In Proceedings of the 2013 European Conference on Mobile Robots, Barcelona, Spain, 25–27 September 2013; pp. 222–227. [CrossRef]
47. Siebler, B.; Sand, S.; Hanebeck, U.D. Localization with Magnetic Field Distortions and Simultaneous Magnetometer Calibration. *IEEE Sens. J.* **2020**, *21*, 3388–3397. [CrossRef]
48. Bonnet, S.; Bassompierre, C.; Godin, C.; Lesecq, S.; Barraud, A. Calibration Methods for Inertial and Magnetic Sensors. *Sens. Actuators A Phys.* **2009**, *156*, 302–311. [CrossRef]
49. Zeng, W.; Church, R.L. Finding Shortest Paths on Real Road Networks: The Case for A. *Int. J. Geogr. Inf. Sci.* **2009**, *23*, 531–543. [CrossRef]
50. Renton, P.; Greenspan, M.; ElMaraghy, H.A.; Zghal, H. Plan-N-Scan: A Robotic System for Collision-Free Autonomous Exploration and Workspace Mapping. *J. Intell. Robot. Syst.* **1999**, *24*, 207–234. [CrossRef]
51. Manss, C.; Shutin, D.; Leus, G. Coordination Methods for Entropy-Based Multi-Agent Exploration under Sparsity Constraints. In Proceedings of the 2019 IEEE 8th International Workshop on Computational Advances in Multi-Sensor Adaptive Processing (CAMSAP), Le Gosier, Guadeloupe, 15–18 December 2019.

Article

Scalable and Transferable Reinforcement Learning for Multi-Agent Mixed Cooperative–Competitive Environments Based on Hierarchical Graph Attention

Yining Chen [1], Guanghua Song [1,*], Zhenhui Ye [2] and Xiaohong Jiang [2]

[1] School of Aeronautics and Astronautics, Zhejiang University, Hangzhou 310027, China; ch19930611@zju.edu.cn
[2] College of Computer Science and Technology, Zhejiang University, Hangzhou 310027, China; zhenhuiye@zju.edu.cn (Z.Y.); jiangxh@zju.edu.cn (X.J.)
* Correspondence: ghsong@zju.edu.cn

Abstract: Most previous studies on multi-agent systems aim to coordinate agents to achieve a common goal, but the lack of scalability and transferability prevents them from being applied to large-scale multi-agent tasks. To deal with these limitations, we propose a deep reinforcement learning (DRL) based multi-agent coordination control method for mixed cooperative–competitive environments. To improve scalability and transferability when applying in large-scale multi-agent systems, we construct inter-agent communication and use hierarchical graph attention networks (HGAT) to process the local observations of agents and received messages from neighbors. We also adopt the gated recurrent units (GRU) to address the partial observability issue by recording historical information. The simulation results based on a cooperative task and a competitive task not only show the superiority of our method, but also indicate the scalability and transferability of our method in various scale tasks.

Keywords: multi-agent; deep reinforcement learning; partial observability

1. Introduction

The last few years witnessed the rapid development of the multi-agent system. Due to its ability to solve complex computing or coordinating problems [1], it has been widely used in different fields, such as computer networks [2,3], robotics [4,5], etc. In the multi-agent system, agents try to learn their policies and execute tasks collaboratively, in either cooperative or competitive environments, by making autonomous decisions. However, in large-scale multi-agent systems, partial observability, scalability, and transferability are three important issues to be addressed for developing efficient and effective multi-agent coordination methods. Firstly, it is impossible for agents to learn their policies from the global state of the environment, as it contains massive information about a large number of agents. Therefore, they need to communicate with other agents in some ways, to reach consensus on decision making. Secondly, the previous methods either learn a policy to control all agents [6] or train their policies individually [7], which is difficult to be extended for large-scale agents. Thirdly, in existing deep-learning-based methods, the policies are trained and tested under the same number of agents, making them untransferable to different scales.

In this paper, we propose a scalable and transferable multi-agent coordination control method, based on deep reinforcement learning (DRL) and hierarchical graph attention networks (HGAT) [8], for mixed cooperative-competitive environments. By regarding the whole system as a graph, HGAT helps agents extract the relationships among different groups of entities in their observations and learn to selectively pay attention to them, which brings high scalability when applying in large-scale multi-agent systems. We enforce inter-agent communication to share agents' local observations with their neighbors and process the received messages through HGAT; therefore, agents can reach consensus by learning from their local observations and information aggregated from the neighbors. Moreover, we introduce the gated recurrent unit (GRU) [9] into our method to record the historical information of agents and utilize it when determining actions, which optimizes the policies under partial observability. We also apply parameter sharing to make our method transferable. Compared with previous works, our method achieves a better performance in mixed cooperative–competitive environments while acquiring high scalability and transferability.

The rest of this paper is organized as follows. In Section 2, we review the related works. We describe some background knowledge of multi-agent reinforcement learning and hierarchical graph attention networks in Section 3. In Section 4, we describe a cooperative scenario, UAV recon and a competitive scenario, predator-prey. We present the mechanism of our method in Section 5. The simulation results are shown in Section 6. We discuss advantages of our method in Section 7 and draw the conclusion in Section 8. The list of abbreviations is shown in Abbreviations.

2. Related Work

Multi-agent coordination has been studied extensively in recent years and implemented in various frameworks, including heuristic algorithms and reinforcement learning (RL) algorithms. In [10], the authors presented a solution to the mission planning problems in multi-agent systems. They encoded the assignments of tasks as alleles and applied the genetic algorithm (GA) for optimization. The authors of [11] designed a control method for the multi-UAV cooperative search-attack mission. UAVs employ ant colony optimization (ACO) to perceive surrounding pheromones and plan flyable paths to search and attack fixed threats. The authors of [12] focused on the dynamic cooperative cleaners problem [13], and presented a decentralized algorithm named "sweep" to coordinate several agents to cover an expanding region of grids. It was also used to navigate myopic robots who cannot communicate with each other [14]. In [15], the authors designed a randomized search heuristic (RSH) algorithm to solve the coverage path planning problem in multi-UAV search and rescue tasks, where the search area is transformed into a graph. The authors of [16] proposed a centralized method to navigate UAVs for crowd surveillance. They regarded the multi-agent system as a single agent and improved its Quality of Service (QoS) by using an on-policy RL algorithm state-action-reward-state-action (SARSA) [17]. Ref. [18] proposed a distributed task allocation method based on Q-learning [19] for cooperative spectrum sharing in robot networks, where each robot maximizes the total utility of the system by updating its local Q-table.

However, as the scale of multi-agent systems increases, the environment becomes more complex while the action space of the whole system expands exponentially. It is difficult for heuristic algorithms and the original RL methods to coordinate agents since they need more time and storage space to optimize their policies. Combining deep neural networks (DNNs) and RL algorithms, deep reinforcement learning (DRL) is widely used for multi-agent coordination in cooperative or competitive environments. It extracts features from the environment state with DNN and uses them to determine actions for agents, which brings better performance. Moreover, since the environment is affected by the action of all agents in multi-agent systems, it is hard for adversarial deep RL [20] to train another policy to generate possible disturbances from all agents. Semi-supervised RL [21] also fails to apply in multi-agent systems, as it cannot learn to evaluate the contribution of each agent from the global state and their actions. DRL can either control the whole multi-agent system by a centralized policy (such as [6]) or control agents individually in a distributed framework called multi-agent reinforcement learning (MARL). In a large-scale environment, MARL is more robust and reliable than the centralized methods because each agent can train its policies to focus on its local observation instead of learning from the global state.

The goal of MARL is to derive decentralized policies for agents and impose a consensus to conduct a collaborative task. To achieve this, the multi-agent deep deterministic policy gradient (MADDPG) [22] and counterfactual multi-agent (COMA) [23] construct a centralized critic to train decentralized actors by augmenting it with extra information about other agents, such as observations and actions. Compared with independent learning [24], which only uses local information, MADDPG and COMA can derive better policies in a non-stationary environment. However, it is difficult for these approaches to be applied in a large-scale multi-agent system, as they directly use the global state or all observations when training. Multi-actor-attention-critic (MAAC) [25] applies the attention mechanism to improve scalability by quantifying the importance of each agent through the attention weights. Deep graph network (DGN) [26] regards the multi-agent system as a graph and employs a graph convolutional network (GCN) with shared weight to process information from neighboring nodes, which also brings high scalability. Ref. [8] proposed a scalable and transferable model, named the hierarchical graph attention-based multi-agent actor-critic (HAMA). It clusters all agents into different groups according to prior knowledge and constructs HGAT to extract the inter-agent relationships in each group of agents and inter-group relationships among groups, aggregating them into high-dimensional vectors. By using MADDPG with shared parameters to process those vectors and determine actions, HAMA can coordinate agents better than the original MADDPG and MAAC when executing cooperative and competitive tasks.

Various MARL-based methods have recently been proposed for multi-agent coordination. Ref. [27] designed a distributed method to provide long-term communication coverage by navigating several UAV mobile base stations (UAV-MBSs) through MADDPG. Ref. [7] presented a MADDPG-based approach that jointly optimizes the trajectory of UAVs to achieve secure communications, which also enhanced the critic with the attention mechanism, such as [25]. The authors of [28] adopted GCN to solve the problem for large-scale multi-robot control. Ref. [29] separated the search problem in indoor environments into high-level planning and low-level action. It applied trust region policy optimization (TRPO) [30] as the global and local planners to handle the control at different levels. In our previous work, we proposed the deep recurrent graph network (DRGN) [31], a novel method that is designed for navigation in a large-scale multi-agent system. It constructs inter-agent communication based on a graph attention network (GAT) [32] and applies GRU to recall the long-term historical information of agents. By utilizing extra information from neighbors and memories, DRGN performs better than DQN and MAAC when navigating a large-scale UAV-MBS swarm to provide communication services for targets that are randomly distributed on the ground.

The difference between our method and the previous works are summarized as follows. DRGN represents the observation as a pixel map of the observable area and processes it by DNN. Our method regards the global state as a graph where the nodes represent the entities in the environment and employs HGAT to process the observation. It is more effective for our method to learn relationships between agents and entities through HGAT. Moreover, our method spends less space to store the observation than DRGN, as the scale of the observation in our method is independent of the observation range. In HAMA, each agent observes up to K nearest neighboring entities per type, where K is a constant. Our method considers that agents can observe all entities inside the observation range and uses an adjacency matrix to denote the relationships of the observation, which can describe the actual observation of agents more accurately than HAMA. In addition, our method introduces GRU and HGAT-based inter-agent communication to provide extra information for agents, so they can optimize policies for coordination by learning from historical information and neighbors.

3. Background

3.1. Multi-Agent Reinforcement Learning (MARL)

The process of MARL is regarded as a decentralized partially observable Markov decision process (Dec-POMDP) [33]. In MARL, each agent i observes the environment state s and obtains a local observation o_i. Then, it selects an action according to its policy π_i. The environment executes the joint actions $\boldsymbol{a} = (a_1, \cdots, a_N)$ and transforms s to the next state

s'. After execution, each agent acquires a reward $r_i = \mathcal{R}_i(s, \boldsymbol{a})$ and a next observation o'_i from the environment. Each agent aims to optimize its policy to maximize its total expected return $R_i = \sum_{t=0}^{T} \gamma^t r_i(t)$, where T is a final timeslot, and $\gamma \in [0, 1]$ is the discount factor.

Q-learning [19] and policy gradient [34] are two popular RL methods. The idea of Q-learning is to estimate an state-action value function $Q(s, a) = \mathbb{E}[R]$ and select the optimal action to maximize $Q(\cdot)$. Deep Q-network (DQN) [35], a Q-learning-based algorithm, uses a DNN as a function approximator and trains it by minimizing the loss:

$$\mathcal{L}(\theta) = \mathbb{E}_{s,a,r,s'}[(y - Q(s, a|\theta))^2] \tag{1}$$

where θ is the parameter of the DNN. The target value y is defined as $y = r + \gamma \max_{a'} Q'(s', a')$ [35], where Q' is the target network, whose parameters are periodically updated from θ. DQN also applies a replay buffer to stabilize learning.

Policy gradient directly optimizes the policy π to maximize $\mathcal{J}(\theta^\pi) = \mathbb{E}[R]$ and updates parameters based on the gradient [34]:

$$\nabla_{\theta^\pi} \mathcal{J}(\theta^\pi) = \mathbb{E}_{s \sim p^\pi, a \sim \pi}[\nabla_{\theta^\pi} \log \pi(a|s, \theta^\pi) Q(s, a)] \tag{2}$$

where p^π is the state distribution. $Q(s, a)$ can be estimated by samples [36] or a function approximator, such as DQN, which leads to the actor–critic algorithm [37].

3.2. Hierarchical Graph Attention Network (HGAT)

HGAT is an effective method for processing hierarchically structured data represented as a graph and introduced into MARL to extract the relationships among agents. By stacking multiple GATs hierarchically, HGAT firstly aggregates embedding vectors e^l_{ij} from neighboring agents in each group l into e'^l_i and subsequently aggregates e'^l_i from all groups into e'_i. The aggregated embedding vector e'_i represents the hierarchical relationships among different groups of neighbors.

4. System Model and Problem Statement

In this section, we describe the settings of a multi-agent cooperative scenario, UAV recon and a competitive scenario, predator-prey.

4.1. UAV Recon

As shown in Figure 1a, we deploy N UAVs into a hot-spot area to scout n point-of-interests (PoIs) for T timeslots, where PoIs are randomly distributed. As we consider our UAVs to move at the same altitude, the area of our mission is two-dimensional. Each UAV has a circled recon area whose radius is considered as a recon range. If the Euclidean distance between a UAV and a PoI is less than the recon range, we consider the PoI to be covered.

In the beginning, each UAV is deployed in a random position. At each timeslot t, each UAV i determines its acceleration $acc_i \in \{(acc, 0), (-acc, 0), (0, acc), (0, -acc), (0, 0)\}$ as its action. The action space of i is discrete. The energy consumption of i is defined as:

$$E_i = E_h + \frac{v_i}{v_{max}} E_m \tag{3}$$

where v_i is the velocity of i and v_{max} is the maximum velocity of UAVs. E_h and E_m are the energy consumption for hovering and movement, respectively.

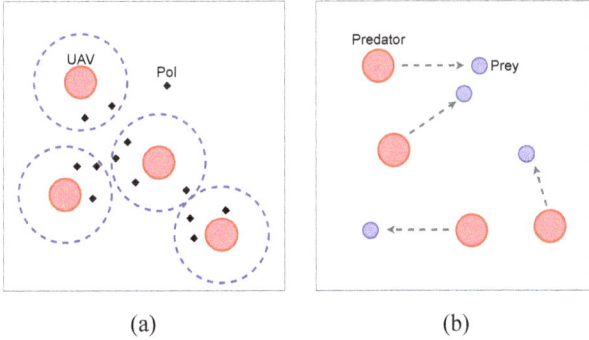

Figure 1. Illustrations of (**a**) *UAV Recon* and (**b**) *Predator-Prey*.

In our scenario, our goals of UAVs are to cover more PoIs more fairly with less energy consumption. To evaluate the quality of tasks, we consider three metrics: coverage C, fairness F, and energy consumption E. The score of C denotes the proportion of covered PoIs, which is defined as:

$$C = \frac{n_C(t)}{n} \qquad (4)$$

where $n_C(t)$ is the number of covered PoIs at timeslot t.

The score of fairness denotes how fair all PoIs are covered. Here, we use Jain's fairness index [38] to define the score of F as:

$$F = \frac{(\sum_{j=1}^{n} c_j)^2}{n \sum_{j=1}^{n} c_j^2} \qquad (5)$$

while c_j is the coverage time of PoI j.

Finally, UAVs need to control energy consumption in tasks. We define the score of E as:

$$E = \frac{1}{N} \sum_{i=1}^{N} E_i \qquad (6)$$

When executing recon missions, each UAV needs to observe local states of other UAVs and PoIs to determine its action. The local state of UAV i is defined as $s_i = (P_i, v_i)$, where P_i and v_i are the position and the velocity of i, respectively. Each PoI j's local state $s_j = (P_j)$. If a PoI is in UAV i's observation range, we consider the PoI is observed by i. If another UAV j is in i's communication range, we consider i can communicate with j. To train UAV's policy, we define a heuristic reward r_i as:

$$r_i = \frac{\eta_1 \times r_{indv} + \eta_2 \times r_{shared}}{E_i} - p_i \qquad (7)$$

where p_i is a penalty factor. When UAV i flies across the border, it is penalized by p_i. $r_{indv} = -1$ if no PoIs is covered by i individually, otherwise $r_{indv} = n_{indv}$, where n_{indv} means the number of PoIs that are only covered by i. $r_{shared} = 0$ if i does not share PoIs with others, otherwise $r_{shared} = \frac{n_{shared}}{N_{share}}$, where n_{shared} denotes the number of PoIs which are covered by N_{share} neighboring UAVs. η_1 and η_2 are the importance factor of $r_{individual}$ and r_{shared}, respectively. We empirically set $\eta_1 \gg \eta_2$ to encourage UAVs to cover more PoIs and avoid overlapping with others.

4.2. Predator-Prey

As shown in Figure 1b, we deploy $N_{predator}$ predators to eliminate N_{prey} prey.

Both of them are controlled by a DRL-based method. If the distance between a predator and a prey is less than predators' attack range, we consider the prey to be eliminated. The goal of the predators is to eliminate all prey, while the goal of the prey is to escape from the predators. The speed of the predators is slower than the prey speed, so they need to cooperate with each other when chasing prey.

The action space of the predators and the prey is the same as the UAVs in the UAV recon scenario. The local state of each predator or prey is defined as $s_i = (P_i, v_i)$, where P_i and v_i are the position and the velocity of a predator or prey, respectively. We consider that each predator and prey can observe the local state of adversaries inside its observation range, while it can communicate with companions inside its communication range. The eliminated preys can neither be observed nor communicate with others. To evaluate the performance of predators and prey, we define the score as:

$$S = \frac{T - T_{eliminate}}{T} \quad (8)$$

where T is the total timeslots of an episode, while $T_{eliminate}$ is the timeslot when all prey are eliminated.

When predator i eliminates prey j, i will obtain a positive reward, while j will obtain a negative reward. When all prey are eliminated, the predators will get an additional reward.

5. HGAT-Based Multi-Agent Coordination Control Method

To achieve the goals of two scenarios described in Section IV, we present a multi-agent coordination control method based on HGAT for mixed cooperative–competitive environments. In our method, the global state of the environment is regarded as a graph, containing the local state of agents and the relationship among them. Each agent summarizes the information from the environment by HGAT and subsequently computes the Q-value and action in a value-based or actor–critic framework.

5.1. HGAT-Based Observation Aggregation and Inter-Agent Communication

In the multi-agent system, the environment involves multiple kinds of entities, including agents, PoIs, etc. As they are heterogeneous, agents need to treat their local states and model their relationships separately. Thus, we categorize all entities into different groups at the first step of execution in cooperative or competitive scenarios. As shown in Figure 2, M entities (containing N agents) are clustered into K groups and represent the environment's state as graphs. The agents construct an observation graph $G^\mathcal{O}$ and a communication graph $G^\mathcal{C}$ respectively based on their observation ranges $\mathcal{O}_1, \cdots, \mathcal{O}_N$ and communication ranges $\mathcal{C}_1, \cdots, \mathcal{C}_N$. The edges of $G^\mathcal{O}$ represent that the entities can be observed by agents, while the edges of $G^\mathcal{C}$ represent that two of the agents can communicate with each other. The adjacency matrix of $G^\mathcal{O}$ and $G^\mathcal{C}$ are $\mathbf{A}^\mathcal{O}$ and $\mathbf{A}^\mathcal{C}$, respectively. i's observation is defined as $o_i = \{s_j | j \in \mathcal{O}_i\}$. Its received messages from the others is $m_i = \{m_{ji} | j \in \mathcal{C}_i\}$, where s_j is agent j's local state and m_{ji} is the message that j sends to i.

At each timeslot, the agents use the network shown in Figure 3 to determine their actions according to s, $\mathbf{A}^\mathcal{O}$, and $\mathbf{A}^\mathcal{C}$ received from the environment, where $s = (s_1,, \cdots, s_M)$. The parameters of the network are shared among the agents in the same group. The network contains three components, a set of encoders, two stacked HGAT layers, and a recurrent unit, which consists of a gated recurrent unit (GRU) layer and a fully connected layer. GRU is a variant of the recurrent neural network (RNN). To summarize the information in each agent i's observation o_i, the first HGAT layer processes o_i into a high-dimensional aggregated embedding vector e'_i as shown in Figure 4. Firstly, the encoder which consists of a fully connected layer transforms the local states from each group l into embedding vectors as $e_j = f_e^l(s_j)$, where f_e^l means the encoder for group l. e_j is the embedding vector for entity j in group l. Then, it aggregates e_j as $e'^l_i = \sum_j \alpha_{ij} \mathbf{W}_v^l e_j$ [32], where $\mathbf{W}_v^l$ is a matrix that transforms

e_j into a "value". The attention weight α_{ij} represents the importance of the embedding vector e_j from j to i, which is calculated by softmax as $\alpha_{ij} \propto \exp(e_j^T \mathbf{W}_k^{l\,T} \mathbf{W}_q e_i)$ [32] if $a_{i,j}^\mathcal{O}$ in $\mathbf{A}^\mathcal{O}$ is 1, otherwise $\alpha_{ij} = 0$. $\mathbf{W}_k$ and $\mathbf{W}_q$ transform a embedding vector into a "key" and a "query", respectively. $\mathbf{A}^\mathcal{O}$ is used for selection so that only the local states from $\mathcal{O}_i$ are summarized. To improve the performance, we use the multiple attention heads here. Finally, e'^{l}_i from all groups are aggregated into e'_i by a fully connected layer f_G, as:

$$e'_i = f_G(\|_{l=1}^{K} e'^{l}_i) \tag{9}$$

where $\|$ represents the concatenation operation. We do not apply another GAT for aggregating, such as HAMA, as our approach has less computing overhead.

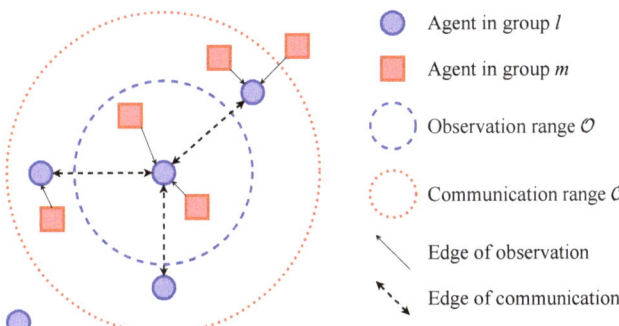

Figure 2. The clustering of agents and their topology.

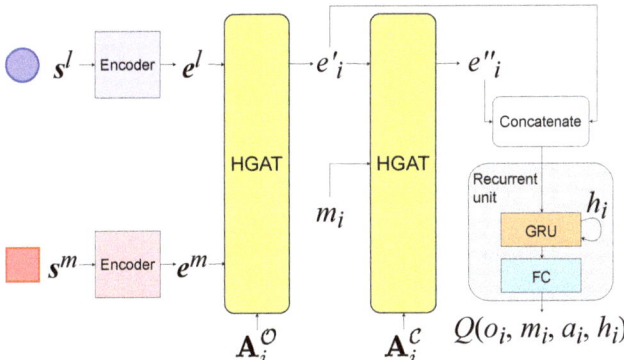

Figure 3. The overall structure of the network. $\mathbf{s}^l$ and e^l represent the local states and embedding vectors of agents in group l. $\mathbf{A}_i$ denotes the ith row of $\mathbf{A}$.

After calculating e'_i, agent i sends it as a message m_{ij} to each neighboring agent j in $\mathcal{C}(i)$. Inter-agent communication helps agents to share their observations with neighbors, which brings a better performance in coordination. To summarize each agent i's received messages m_i, the second HGAT layer processes m_i and aggregates it into another embedding vector e''_i by the same means as shown in Figure 4. The adjacency matrix used here is $\mathbf{A}^\mathcal{C}$ instead of $\mathbf{A}^\mathcal{O}$. Our method is capable of inner-group and inter-group communication and can easily extend to a multi-hop by stacking new HGAT layers.

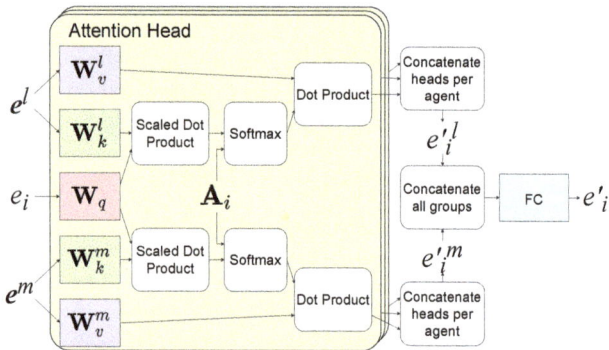

Figure 4. The architecture of an HGAT layer.

5.2. Implementation in a Value-Based Framework

This implement is based on DQN. Each agent i maintains hidden states h_i for the recurrent unit and calculates its Q-values by a Q-network, as shown in Figure 3. Similar to DQN, our method also employs a target network with the same structure.

We introduce the skip-connection strategy by concatenating e'_i and e''_i as an input of the recurrent unit when computing the Q-value, so agents can use the information both from their observation and others'. The Q-value is calculated as:

$$Q^l(o_i, m_i, a_i, h_i) \approx f_R^l(e'_i, e''_i, h_i) \tag{10}$$

where Q^l represents the Q-network of group l where i belongs, f_R^l means the recurrent unit in Q^l, and a_i is the action determined by i according to Q-values. We apply ϵ-greedy policy [35] to balance the exploitation and exploration as:

$$a_i = \begin{cases} \arg\max_{a \in \mathcal{A}_i} Q^l(o_i, m_i, a, h_i), & \text{with probability } 1 - \epsilon \\ random(\mathcal{A}_i), & \text{with probability } \epsilon \end{cases} \tag{11}$$

where $\mathcal{A}_i$ is the action space of i.

After executing the joint actions $\mathbf{a} = (a_1, \cdots, a_N)$, the environment transforms the current state to the next and sends the next local states s', the next adjacency matrix $\mathbf{A}'^{\mathcal{O}}$ and $\mathbf{A}'^{\mathcal{C}}$, and the reward r_i to each agent i. The experience $(s, \mathbf{A}^{\mathcal{O}}, \mathbf{A}^{\mathcal{C}}, \mathbf{a}, \mathbf{r}, s', \mathbf{A}'^{\mathcal{O}}, \mathbf{A}'^{\mathcal{C}}, \mathbf{h}, \mathbf{h}')$ is stored in a shared replay buffer B, where $\mathbf{r} = (r_1, \cdots, r_N)$, $\mathbf{h} = (h_1, \cdots, h_N)$, and $\mathbf{h}' = (h'_1, \cdots, h'_N)$. h'_i is the next hidden state that the Q-network outputs when agent i calculates Q-values. h_i is initialized to zero at the beginning of an episode.

To training the Q-network of each group, we sample H experiences from B as a minibatch and minimize the loss:

$$\mathcal{L}(\theta_l^Q) = \frac{1}{N_l} \sum_{i=1}^{N_l} \mathbb{E}[(y_i - Q^l(o_i, m_i, a_i, h_i | \theta_l^Q))^2] \tag{12}$$

where N_l means the number of agents in group l and θ_l^Q denote the parameters of Q^l. y_i is the target value that calculated by the target network Q'^l, as:

$$y_i = r_i + \gamma \max_{a' \in \mathcal{A}_i} Q'^l(o'_i, m'_i, a', h'_i | \theta_l^{Q'}) \tag{13}$$

where o'_i and m'_i are i's next observation and next received messages, respectively. $\theta_l^{Q'}$ denote the parameters of Q'^l, which are periodically updated from θ_l^Q.

5.3. Implementation in an Actor–Critic Framework

Our method can also be implemented on the actor–critic framework. In this implementation, each agent i has an actor network and a critic network, maintaining hidden states h_i^π and h_i^Q. After obtaining s, $\mathbf{A}^\mathcal{O}$ and $\mathbf{A}^\mathcal{C}$, agent i in group l computes the probability of actions as:

$$\pi^l(o_i, m_i, h_i^\pi) \approx f_R^{\pi^l}(e'^\pi_i, e''^\pi_i, h_i^\pi) \tag{14}$$

where π^l represents the actor network of group l and $f_R^{\pi^l}$ represents the recurrent unit in π^l. We employ the ϵ-categorical policy here. Agent i determines an action based on $\pi^l(o_i, m_i, h_i^\pi)$ with probability $1 - \epsilon$ and makes a random choice with probability ϵ. The critic network Q^l subsequently calculates Q-values, such as the value-based framework. The hidden states h_i^π and h_i^Q and the next hidden states h'^π_i and h'^Q_i are stored in the replay buffer, where h'^π_i and h'^Q_i are the outputs of π^l and Q^l, respectively.

The critic network of each group is trained by minimizing the loss $\mathcal{L}(\theta_l^Q)$, which is computed as (13). As the actor–critic framework selects actions according to $\pi^l(o_i, m_i, h_i^\pi)$ instead of the maximum Q-value, we use the expectation of the next state's Q-value to calculate the target value y_i as:

$$y_i = r_i + \gamma \sum_{a' \in \mathcal{A}_i} \pi'^l(a'|o'_i, m'_i, h'^\pi_i, \theta_l^{\pi'}) Q'^l(o'_i, m'_i, a', h'^Q_i|\theta_l^{Q'}) \tag{15}$$

where $\theta_l^{\pi'}$ and $\theta_l^{Q'}$ are the parameters of target network π'^l and Q'^l, respectively.

The actor network of each group is trained according to the gradient:

$$\nabla_{\theta_l^\pi}(\mathcal{J}(\theta_l^\pi)) = \frac{1}{N_l} \sum_{i=1}^{N_l} \mathbb{E}[\log \pi^l(a_i|o_i, m_i, h_i^\pi, \theta_l^\pi)(Q^l(o_i, m_i, a_i, h_i^Q|\theta_l^Q) - b_i)] \tag{16}$$

where the baseline b_i is designed to reduce variance and stabilize training [39], which is defined as:

$$b_i = \sum_{a \in \mathcal{A}_i} \pi^l(a|o_i, m_i, h_i^\pi, \theta_l^\pi) Q^l(o_i, m_i, a, h_i^Q|\theta_l^Q) \tag{17}$$

After training, $\theta_l^{\pi'}$ and $\theta_l^{Q'}$ are updated as $\theta_l^{\pi'} \leftarrow \tau \theta_l^\pi + (1 - \tau) \theta_l^{\pi'}$, and $\theta_l^{Q'} \leftarrow \tau \theta_l^Q + (1 - \tau) \theta_l^{Q'}$, respectively [40].

Our method can be extended to continuous action space by estimating the expectation of b_i with Monte Carlo samples or a learnable state value function $V(o_i, m_i)$ [23].

6. Simulation

6.1. Set Up

To evaluate the performance of our method, we conduct a series of simulations on an Ubuntu 18.04 server with 2 NVIDIA RTX 3080 GPUs. We implement a value-based (VB) version and an actor–critic (AC) version of our method in PyTorch. Each fully connected layer and GRU layer contains 256 units. The activation functions in encoders and HGAT layers are ReLU [41]. The number of attention heads is 4. Empirically, we set the learning rate of the optimizer to 0.001, and the discount factor γ to 0.95. The replay buffer size is 50 K and the size of a minibatch is 128. ϵ is set to 0.3. For the value-based version, The target networks are updated every five training steps. For the actor–critic version, we set τ to 0.01. The networks are trained every 100 timeslots and update their parameters four times in a training step.

We compare our method with four MARL baselines, including DGN, DQN, HAMA, and MADDPG. For non-HGAT-based approaches, each agent concatenates all local states in its observation into a vector, while padding 0 for unobserved entities. The parameters of networks are shared among agents in all baselines except MADDPG. We use the Gumbel-Softmax reparameterization trick [42] in HAMA and MADDPG to make them trainable in discrete action spaces. DGN is based on our proposed algorithm [31], which applies a GAT layer for inter-agent communication. We train our method and each baseline for 100 K episodes and test them for 10 K episodes.

6.2. UAV Recon

As summarized in Table 1, we deploy several UAVs in a 200 × 200 area where 120 PoIs are distributed. The penalty factor p in (7) is set to 1. We evaluate the performance of our method in the test stage under different number of UAVs and compare it with baselines.

Table 1. Experiment parameters of UAV recon.

Parameters	Settings
Target Area	200 × 200
Number of PoIs	120
Recon Range	10
Observation Range	15
Communication Range	30
Maximum Speed	10/s
Energy Consumption for Hovering	0.5
Energy Consumption for Movement	0.5
Penalty Factor p	1
Importance Factor η_1	1
Importance Factor η_2	0.1
Timeslots of Each Episode	100

Figure 5 shows the performance of each method in terms of coverage, fairness, and energy consumption under different numbers of UAVs. Note that both two versions of our method are trained with 20 UAVs and transferred to a different scale of UAV swarms. From Figure 5a,b, we observe that our method outperforms all baselines in terms of coverage and fairness. Compared with DGN and DQN, our method employs HGAT to extract features from observation, which is more effective than processing raw observation vectors directly. Therefore, our method helps UAVs to search PoIs and better optimize their flight trajectories. Although HAMA also applies HGAT, UAVs cannot cooperate as effectively as our method, owing to the lack of communication. In our method, the UAVs communicate with others and process received messages by another HGAT layer. Furthermore, the recurrent unit helps UAVs to learn from the hidden states, which induces a better performance. In MADDPG, each UAV trains an individual network and concatenates observations and actions of all agents into a high-dimensional vector as an input of the critic. As the networks in MADDPG expands exponentially to the scale of the agents, it is hard to be trained effectively and efficiently in large-scale multi-agent systems. As a consequence, the MADDPG consumes more time to train but obtains the lowest score.

Figure 5c indicates that our method consumes less energy than DGN and DQN. As their flight trajectories are better, UAVs can cover more PoIs fairly while consuming less energy. The energy consumption of HAMA is considerable with our method in low-scale environments and increases when the number of UAVs is up to 40. MADDPG fails to improve coverage and fairness, so it tends to save on energy to maximize its reward.

To test the capability of transferred learning, we compare the transferred policies with those trained under the same settings of testing. As shown in Figure 6, the performance does not deteriorate when the policy is transferred to execute with 10, 30, or 40 UAVs, which indicates that our method is highly transferable under various numbers of UAVs.

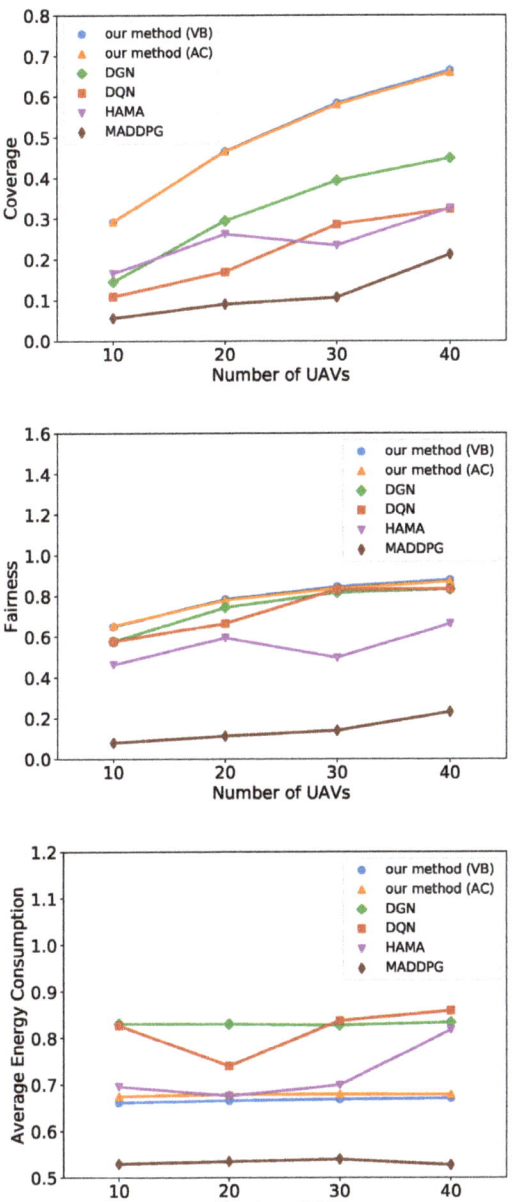

Figure 5. Simulation results of all methods on coverage, fairness, and energy consumption under different number of UAVs.

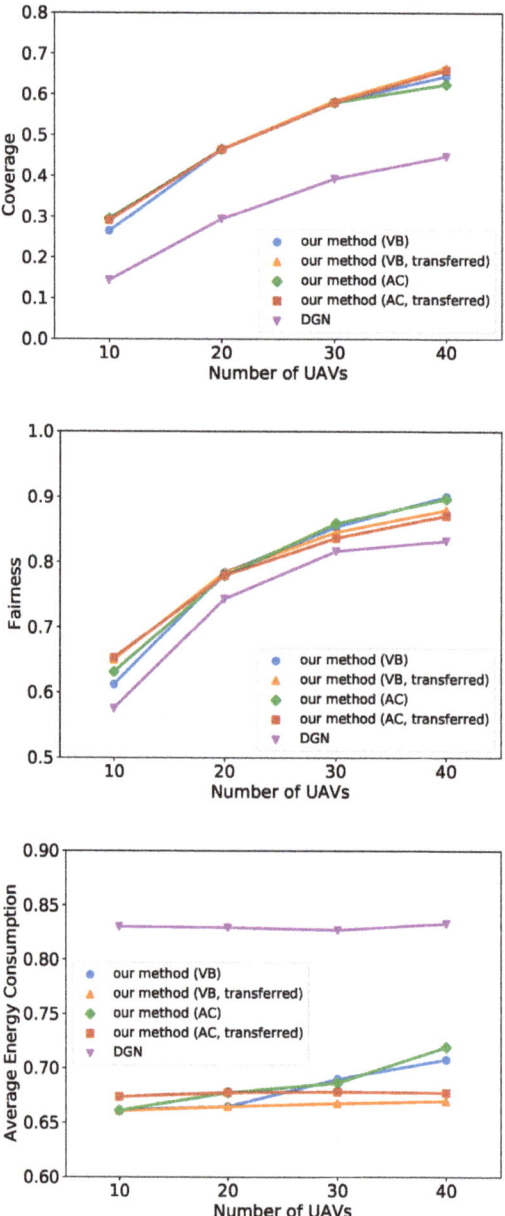

Figure 6. Simulation results of transfer learning on coverage, fairness, and energy consumption under different number of UAVs.

6.3. Predator-Prey

As summarized in Table 2, we deploy five predators in a 100 × 100 area to eliminate five prey. We set the attack reward of predators and prey to 10 and −10, respectively. The additional reward is set as $r_{additional} = 10 \times S$. We train the policy by the value-based version of our method and test it by competing with other policies trained by different methods.

Table 2. Experiment parameters of predator-prey.

Parameters	Settings
Target Area	100×100
Number of Predators	5
Number of Preys	5
Attack Range	8
Observation Range	30
Communication Range	100
Maximum Speed of Predators	10/s
Maximum Speed of Preys	12/s
Timeslots of Each Episode	100

Table 3 indicates that our method shows its superiority over all baselines in both roles of predator and prey. By introducing GRU and inter-agent communication, the predators obtain more information from hidden states and neighbors to decide which prey to capture. It is more flexible for predators to determine whether to chase prey individually or cooperatively. Similarly, GRU and inter-agent communication also bring more information to prey, so they can choose from various strategies to survive. For example, prey can escape from predators by their faster speed or sacrifice one of them to distract predators.

Table 3. The mean and standard deviation of scores in predator-prey.

Predator	Prey		
	Our Method	**DGN**	**DQN**
Our method	0.331 ± 0.088	0.535 ± 0.086	0.591 ± 0.101
DGN	0.051 ± 0.060	0.271 ± 0.095	0.386 ± 0.095
DQN	0.014 ± 0.034	0.173 ± 0.086	0.120 ± 0.078
Predator	**Prey**		
	Our Method	**HAMA**	**MADDPG**
Our method	0.331 ± 0.088	0.787 ± 0.027	0.472 ± 0.098
HAMA	0.051 ± 0.050	0.351 ± 0.050	0.403 ± 0.091
MADDPG	0.038 ± 0.048	0.239 ± 0.090	0.051 ± 0.057

7. Discussion

The experimental results indicate that the performance of our method is superior to those of others in both cooperative and competitive scenarios. We assume that three components, including HGAT, GRU, and inter-agent communication, are the key factors which induce the success of our method. To validate our hypothesis, we conduct an ablation study in Appendix A to clarify the necessity of each component (HGAT, GRU, and inter-agent communication).

From Table A1, we observe a significant deterioration in performance when removing HGAT or GRU, while disabling inter-agent communication also induces a decrease in terms of coverage and fairness. To explain the necessity of each component, we assume the following reasons. Firstly, HGAT plays an important role in summarizing observations. Not only does it process the local states from all groups, but it also quantifies their importance with attention weights. In addition, HGAT models the hierarchical relationships among agents as a graph, which is effective for them to optimize their policies in dynamic environments. Secondly, GRU makes a significant contribution to overcoming the limitation of partial observability. When determining actions, GRU helps agents to remember the historical information recorded in the hidden states, such as the position of the observed PoIs in the UAV recon. It is beneficial for agents to improve their performance by getting what they cannot observe from the hidden states. Finally, inter-agent communication expands agents' horizons. By sending high-dimensional embedding vectors, they share their observations with others. With the help of HGAT, agents can cooperate better by using extensive information from those vectors in decision making.

Compared with non-HGAT-based approaches, our method has another advantage in the replay buffer. As they concatenate all local states into a vector and pad 0 for unobserved entities, the space complexity of observations in their replay buffer is $O(N \times M)$, where N and M means the number of agents and entities, respectively. However, our method only stores local states, whose space complexity is $O(M)$. Although it has to store the adjacency matrices $\mathbf{A}^{\mathcal{O}}$ to represent the relationship among agents, this is more economical than storing observations in terms of storage, as an adjacency matrix represents the relationship between agents by a bit.

8. Conclusions

In this paper, we propose a scalable and transferable DRL-based multi-agent coordination control method for cooperative and competitive tasks. This method introduces HGAT, GRU, and inter-agent communication into DRL to improve performance in mixed cooperative–competitive environments. By intensive simulations, our method shows its superiority over DGN, DQN, HAMA, and MADDPG both in UAV recon and predator-prey.

In the future, we will improve our method by introducing an adaptive policy base on the action entropy of the agent to provide a more intelligent exploration. We will evaluate the performance of the entropy-based policy and compare it with the ϵ-greedy and ϵ-categorical policies. Specifically, we will test the capabilities of automating entropy adjustment under different entropy targets in large-scale multi-agent systems. Furthermore, we will try to extend our method into continuous policies and evaluate its performance in cooperative and competitive scenarios with continuous action space.

Author Contributions: Conceptualization, Y.C. and Z.Y.; methodology, Y.C.; software, Y.C.; validation, Y.C. and Z.Y.; formal analysis, Y.C.; investigation, Y.C. and Z.Y.; resources, Y.C.; data curation, Y.C.; writing—original draft preparation, Y.C.; writing—review and editing, G.S.; visualization, Y.C.; supervision, G.S. and X.J.; project administration, G.S.; funding acquisition, X.J. All authors have read and agreed to the published version of the manuscript.

Funding: This research was funded by the National key R & D program of China sub project "Emergent behavior recognition, training and interpretation techniques" grant number 2018AAA0102302.

Institutional Review Board Statement: Not applicable.

Informed Consent Statement: Not applicable.

Data Availability Statement: Not applicable.

Conflicts of Interest: The authors declare no conflict of interest.

Abbreviations

AC	Actor–Critic
ACO	Ant Colony Optimization
COMA	COunterfactual Multi-Agent
Dec-POMDP	Decentralized Partially Observable Markov Decision Process
DGN	Deep Graph Network
DNN	Deep Neural Network
DQN	Deep Q-Network
DRGN	Deep Recurrent Graph Network
DRL	Deep Reinforcement Learning

GA	Genetic Algorithm
GAT	Graph Attention neTwork
GCN	Graph Convolutional Network
GRU	Gated Recurrent Unit
HAMA	Hierarchical Graph Attention-Based Multi-Agent Actor–Critic
HGAT	Hierarchical Graph Attention neTwork
MAAC	Multi-Actor-Attention-Critic
MADDPG	Multi-Agent Deep Deterministic Policy Gradient
MARL	Multi-Agent Reinforcement Learning
PoI	Point-of-Interest
QoS	Quality of Service
RL	Reinforcement Learning
RSH	Randomized Search Heuristic
SARSA	State-Action-Reward-State-Action
TRPO	Trust Region Policy Optimization
UAV	Unmanned Aerial Vehicle
UAV-MBS	Unmanned Aerial Vehicle Mobile Base Station
VB	Value-Based

Appendix A. Ablation Study

In the ablation study, we test our method and three variants in UAV recon with 20 UAVs and summarized the performances in Table A1. The variants are described as follows:

- Without H: removing the first HGAT layer;
- Without G: removing GRU in the recurrent unit;
- Without C: disabling inter-agent communication.

Table A1. The mean and standard deviation of three metrics in the ablation study ($N = 20$).

Model	Metric		
	Coverage	Fairness	Energy Consumption
Our method	**0.466 ± 0.046**	**0.784 ± 0.061**	**0.665 ± 0.015**
Without H	0.103 ± 0.022	0.696 ± 0.087	0.710 ± 0.011
Without G	0.349 ± 0.065	0.726 ± 0.116	0.730 ± 0.017
Without C	0.412 ± 0.058	0.749 ± 0.081	0.668 ± 0.023

References

1. Dorri, A.; Kanhere, S.S.; Jurdak, R. Multi-agent systems: A survey. *IEEE Access* **2018**, *6*, 28573–28593. [CrossRef]
2. Gutierrez-Garcia, J.O.; Sim, K.M. Agent-based cloud bag-of-tasks execution. *J. Syst. Softw.* **2015**, *104*, 17–31. [CrossRef]
3. Claes, R.; Holvoet, T.; Weyns, D. A decentralized approach for anticipatory vehicle routing using delegate multiagent systems. *IEEE Trans. Intell. Transp. Syst.* **2011**, *12*, 364–373. [CrossRef]
4. Ota, J. Multi-agent robot systems as distributed autonomous systems. *Adv. Eng. Inform.* **2006**, *20*, 59–70. [CrossRef]
5. Iñigo-Blasco, P.; Diaz-del Rio, F.; Romero-Ternero, M.C.; Cagigas-Muñiz, D.; Vicente-Diaz, S. Robotics software frameworks for multi-agent robotic systems development. *Robot. Auton. Syst.* **2012**, *60*, 803–821. [CrossRef]
6. Liu, C.H.; Chen, Z.; Tang, J.; Xu, J.; Piao, C. Energy-efficient UAV control for effective and fair communication coverage: A deep reinforcement learning approach. *IEEE J. Sel. Areas Commun.* **2018**, *36*, 2059–2070. [CrossRef]
7. Zhang, Y.; Mou, Z.; Gao, F.; Jiang, J.; Ding, R.; Han, Z. UAV-enabled secure communications by multi-agent deep reinforcement learning. *IEEE Trans. Veh. Technol.* **2020**, *69*, 11599–11611. [CrossRef]
8. Ryu, H.; Shin, H.; Park, J. Multi-agent actor-critic with hierarchical graph attention network. In Proceedings of the AAAI Conference on Artificial Intelligence, New York, NY, USA, 7–12 February 2020; Volume 34, pp. 7236–7243. [CrossRef]
9. Cho, K.; Van Merriënboer, B.; Bahdanau, D.; Bengio, Y. On the properties of neural machine translation: Encoder-decoder approaches. *arXiv* **2014**, arXiv:1409.1259.
10. Ramirez-Atencia, C.; Bello-Orgaz, G.; R-Moreno, M.D.; Camacho, D. Solving complex multi-UAV mission planning problems using multi-objective genetic algorithms. *Soft Comput.* **2017**, *21*, 4883–4900. [CrossRef]
11. Zhen, Z.; Xing, D.; Gao, C. Cooperative search-attack mission planning for multi-UAV based on intelligent self-organized algorithm. *Aerosp. Sci. Technol.* **2018**, *76*, 402–411. [CrossRef]

12. Altshuler, Y.; Wagner, I.; Yanovski, V.; Bruckstein, A. Multi-agent Cooperative Cleaning of Expanding Domains. *Int. J. Robot. Res.* **2010**, *30*, 1037–1071. [CrossRef]
13. Altshuler, Y.; Pentland, A.; Bruckstein, A.M. *Swarms and Network Intelligence in Search*; Springer: Berlin/Heidelberg, Germany, 2018.
14. Altshuler, Y.; Bruckstein, A.M. Static and expanding grid coverage with ant robots: Complexity results. *Theor. Comput. Sci.* **2011**, *412*, 4661–4674. [CrossRef]
15. Cho, S.W.; Park, H.J.; Lee, H.; Shim, D.H.; Kim, S.Y. Coverage path planning for multiple unmanned aerial vehicles in maritime search and rescue operations. *Comput. Ind. Eng.* **2021**, *161*, 107612. [CrossRef]
16. Apostolopoulos, P.A.; Torres, M.; Tsiropoulou, E.E. Satisfaction-aware data offloading in surveillance systems. In Proceedings of the 14th Workshop on Challenged Networks, Los Cabos, Mexico, 25 October 2019; pp. 21–26. [CrossRef]
17. Rummery, G.A.; Niranjan, M. *On-Line Q-Learning Using Connectionist Systems*; Citeseer: University Park, PA, USA, 1994; Volume 37.
18. Shamsoshoara, A.; Khaledi, M.; Afghah, F.; Razi, A.; Ashdown, J. Distributed cooperative spectrum sharing in uav networks using multi-agent reinforcement learning. In Proceedings of the 2019 16th IEEE Annual Consumer Communications & Networking Conference (CCNC), Las Vegas, NV, USA, 11–14 January 2019; pp. 1–6. [CrossRef]
19. Watkins, C.J.; Dayan, P. Q-learning. *Mach. Learn.* **1992**, *8*, 279–292. [CrossRef]
20. Pinto, L.; Davidson, J.; Sukthankar, R.; Gupta, A. Robust adversarial reinforcement learning. In Proceedings of the International Conference on Machine Learning, Sydney, NSW, Australia, 6–11 August 2017; pp. 2817–2826.
21. Finn, C.; Yu, T.; Fu, J.; Abbeel, P.; Levine, S. Generalizing skills with semi-supervised reinforcement learning. *arXiv* **2016**, arXiv:1612.00429.
22. Lowe, R.; WU, Y.; Tamar, A.; Harb, J.; Pieter Abbeel, O.; Mordatch, I. Multi-Agent Actor-Critic for Mixed Cooperative-Competitive Environments. In *Advances in Neural Information Processing Systems 30*; Guyon, I., Luxburg, U.V., Bengio, S., Wallach, H., Fergus, R., Vishwanathan, S., Garnett, R., Eds.;Curran Associates, Inc.: Red Hook, NY, USA, 2017; pp. 6379–6390.
23. Foerster, J.N.; Farquhar, G.; Afouras, T.; Nardelli, N.; Whiteson, S. Counterfactual multi-agent policy gradients. In Proceedings of the Thirty-Second AAAI Conference on Artificial Intelligence, New Orleans, LA, USA, 2–7 February 2018.
24. Tan, M. Multi-agent reinforcement learning: Independent vs. cooperative agents. In Proceedings of the Tenth International Conference on Machine Learning, Long Beach, CA, USA, 9–15 June 1993; pp. 330–337.
25. Iqbal, S.; Sha, F. Actor-Attention-Critic for Multi-Agent Reinforcement Learning. In Proceedings of the 36th International Conference on Machine Learning, Long Beach, CA, USA, 9–15 June 2019; Chaudhuri, K., Salakhutdinov, R., Eds.; PMLR: Long Beach, CA, USA, 2019; Volume 97, pp. 2961–2970.
26. Jiang, J.; Dun, C.; Huang, T.; Lu, Z. Graph convolutional reinforcement learning. *arXiv* **2018**, arXiv:1810.09202.
27. Liu, C.H.; Ma, X.; Gao, X.; Tang, J. Distributed energy-efficient multi-UAV navigation for long-term communication coverage by deep reinforcement learning. *IEEE Trans. Mob. Comput.* **2019**, *19*, 1274–1285. [CrossRef]
28. Khan, A.; Tolstaya, E.; Ribeiro, A.; Kumar, V. Graph policy gradients for large scale robot control. In Proceedings of the Conference on Robot Learning, Cambridge, MA, USA, 16–18 November 2020; pp. 823–834.
29. Walker, O.; Vanegas, F.; Gonzalez, F.; Koenig, S. A deep reinforcement learning framework for UAV navigation in indoor environments. In Proceedings of the 2019 IEEE Aerospace Conference, Big Sky, MT, USA, 2–9 March 2019; pp. 1–14.
30. Schulman, J.; Levine, S.; Abbeel, P.; Jordan, M.; Moritz, P. Trust region policy optimization. In Proceedings of the International Conference on Machine Learning, Lille, France, 7–9 July 2015; pp. 1889–1897.
31. Ye, Z.; Wang, K.; Chen, Y.; Jiang, X.; Song, G. Multi-UAV Navigation for Partially Observable Communication Coverage by Graph Reinforcement Learning. *IEEE Trans. Mob. Comput.* **2022**. [CrossRef]
32. Veličković, P.; Cucurull, G.; Casanova, A.; Romero, A.; Lio, P.; Bengio, Y. Graph attention networks. *arXiv* **2017**, arXiv:1710.10903.
33. Bernstein, D.S.; Givan, R.; Immerman, N.; Zilberstein, S. The complexity of decentralized control of Markov decision processes. *Math. Oper. Res.* **2002**, *27*, 819–840. [CrossRef]
34. Sutton, R.S.; McAllester, D.A.; Singh, S.P.; Mansour, Y. Policy gradient methods for reinforcement learning with function approximation. In *Advances in Neural Information Processing Systems*; MIT Press: Cambridge, MA, USA, 2000; pp. 1057–1063.
35. Mnih, V.; Kavukcuoglu, K.; Silver, D.; Rusu, A.A.; Veness, J.; Bellemare, M.G.; Graves, A.; Riedmiller, M.; Fidjeland, A.K.; Ostrovski, G.; et al. Human-level control through deep reinforcement learning. *Nature* **2015**, *518*, 529. [CrossRef] [PubMed]
36. Williams, R.J. Simple statistical gradient-following algorithms for connectionist reinforcement learning. *Mach. Learn.* **1992**, *8*, 229–256. [CrossRef]
37. Konda, V.R.; Tsitsiklis, J.N. Actor-critic algorithms. In *Advances in Neural Information Processing Systems*; MIT Press: Cambridge, MA, USA, 2000; pp. 1008–1014.
38. Jain, R.K.; Chiu, D.M.W.; Hawe, W.R. *A Quantitative Measure of Fairness and Discrimination*; Eastern Research Laboratory, Digital Equipment Corporation: Hudson, MA, USA, 1984.
39. Weaver, L.; Tao, N. The optimal reward baseline for gradient-based reinforcement learning. *arXiv* **2013**, arXiv:1301.2315.
40. Heess, N.; Hunt, J.J.; Lillicrap, T.P.; Silver, D. Memory-based control with recurrent neural networks. *arXiv* **2015**, arXiv:1512.04455.
41. Nair, V.; Hinton, G.E. Rectified Linear Units Improve Restricted Boltzmann Machines. In Proceedings of the 27th International Conference on Machine Learning (ICML 2010), Haifa, Israel, 21–24 June 2010; pp. 807–814.
42. Jang, E.; Gu, S.; Poole, B. Categorical reparameterization with gumbel-softmax. *arXiv* **2016**, arXiv:1611.01144.

Article

DNN Intellectual Property Extraction Using Composite Data

Itay Mosafi [1,*], Eli (Omid) David [1], Yaniv Altshuler [2] and Nathan S. Netanyahu [1,3]

[1] Department of Computer Science, Bar-Ilan University, Ramat-Gan 5290002, Israel; mail@elidavid.com (E.D.); nathan@cs.biu.ac.il (N.S.N.)
[2] MIT Media Lab, 77 Mass. Ave., E14/E15, Cambridge, MA 02139-4307, USA; yanival@media.mit.edu
[3] Department of Computer Science, College of Law and Business, Ramat-Gan 5257346, Israel
* Correspondence: itay.mosafi@gmail.com

Abstract: As state-of-the-art deep neural networks are being deployed at the core level of increasingly large numbers of AI-based products and services, the incentive for "copying them" (i.e., their intellectual property, manifested through the knowledge that is encapsulated in them) either by adversaries or commercial competitors is expected to considerably increase over time. The most efficient way to extract or steal knowledge from such networks is by querying them using a large dataset of random samples and recording their output, which is followed by the training of a *student* network, aiming to eventually mimic these outputs, without making any assumption about the original networks. The most effective way to protect against such a mimicking attack is to answer queries with the classification result only, omitting confidence values associated with the softmax layer. In this paper, we present a novel method for generating composite images for attacking a *mentor* neural network using a student model. Our method assumes no information regarding the mentor's training dataset, architecture, or weights. Furthermore, assuming no information regarding the mentor's softmax output values, our method successfully mimics the given neural network and is capable of stealing large portions (and sometimes all) of its encapsulated knowledge. Our student model achieved 99% relative accuracy to the protected mentor model on the Cifar-10 test set. In addition, we demonstrate that our student network (which copies the mentor) is impervious to watermarking protection methods and thus would evade being detected as a stolen model by existing dedicated techniques. Our results imply that all current neural networks are vulnerable to mimicking attacks, even if they do not divulge anything but the most basic required output, and that the student model that mimics them cannot be easily detected using currently available techniques.

Keywords: deep learning; cybersecurity; artificial intelligence; swarm intelligence; adversarial AI; information theory; entropy; models; neural networks; communication

Citation: Mosafi, I.; David, E.; Altshuler, Y.; Netanyahu, N.S. DNN Intellectual Property Extraction Using Composite Data. *Entropy* **2022**, *24*, 349. https://doi.org/10.3390/e24030349

Academic Editor: Stanisław Drożdż

Received: 29 December 2021
Accepted: 21 February 2022
Published: 28 February 2022

Publisher's Note: MDPI stays neutral with regard to jurisdictional claims in published maps and institutional affiliations.

Copyright: © 2022 by the authors. Licensee MDPI, Basel, Switzerland. This article is an open access article distributed under the terms and conditions of the Creative Commons Attribution (CC BY) license (https://creativecommons.org/licenses/by/4.0/).

1. Introduction

In recent years, deep neural networks (DNNs) have been used very effectively in a wide range of applications. Since these models have achieved remarkable results, redefining state-of-the-art solutions for various problems, they have become the "go-to solution" for many challenging real-world problems, e.g., object recognition [1,2], object segmentation [3], autonomous driving [4], automatic text translation [5], cybersecurity [6–8], credit default prediction [9], etc.

Training a state-of-the-art deep neural network requires designing the network architecture, collecting and preprocessing data, and accessing hardware resources, in particular graphics processing units (GPUs) capable of training such models. Additionally, training such networks requires a substantial amount of trial and error. For these reasons, such trained models are highly valuable, but at the same time, they could be the target of attacks by adversaries (e.g., a competitor) who might try to duplicate the model and the entire sensitive intellectual property involved without going through the tedious and expensive process of developing the models by themselves. By doing so, all the trouble of data collection, acquiring computing resources, and the valuable time required for training the models are spared by the attacker. As state-of-the-art DNNs are used more extensively in real-world products, the prevalence of such attacks is expected to increase over the next few years.

An attacker has two main options for acquiring a trained model: (1) acquiring the raw model from the owner's private network, which would be a risky criminal offense that requires a complicated cyber attack on the owner's network; and (2) training a student model that mimics the original mentor model. That is, the attacker could query the original mentor using a dataset of samples and train the student model to mimic the output of the mentor model for each of the samples. The second option assumes that the mentor is a black box, i.e., there is no knowledge of its architecture, no access to the training data used for training it, and no information regarding the trained model's weights. We only have access to the model's predictions (inference) for a given input. Thus, such a mentor would effectively teach a student how to mimic it by providing its output for different inputs.

In order for mimicking to succeed, a key element is to utilize the certainty level of a model on a given input, i.e., its softmax distribution values [10,11]. This knowledge is highly important for the training of the student network. For example, in case of a binary classification, classifying an image as category i with 99% confidence and as category j with 1% confidence is much more informative than classifying it to category i with, say, 51% confidence and to category j with 49% confidence. Such data are valuable and often much more informative than the predicted category alone, which in both cases is i. This confidence value (obtained through the softmax output layer) also reveals how the model perceives this specific image and to what extent the predictions for categories i and j are similar. In order to protect against such a mimicking attack, a trained model may hide this confidence information by simply returning only the index with the maximal confidence, without providing the actual confidence levels (i.e., the softmax values are concealed, while the output contains merely the predicted class). Although such a model would substantially limit the success of a student model using a standard mimicking attack, we provide in this paper a novel method by querying the mentor with *composite* images, such that the student effectively elicits the mentor's knowledge, even if the mentor provides the predicted class only.

Contributions: This research possesses various contributions to the domain of DNN intellectual property extraction.

1. It is possible to extract the intellectual property of a model with no access to the original data (inputs and labels) used for training it.
2. All classification models are vulnerable, maximum protection of the model was assumed, and still, the composite method managed to extract the intellectual property.
3. A novel composite method using unlabeled data was described for knowledge extraction, which can be applied on any model as long as unlabeled data are available.
4. The state-of-the-art watermarking methods are not able to identify a student model once it contains the knowledge of the mentor model, which was protected using watermarks.

The rest of the paper is organized as follows. Section 2 reviews previous methods used for network distilling and mimicking. Section 3 describes our new approach for a successful mimicking attack on a mentor, which does not provide softmax outputs. Section 4 presents our experimental results. Finally, Section 5 makes concluding remarks. This paper is based on a preliminary version published in [12].

2. Background
2.1. Threats to Validity

We included the studies that (1) deal with methods to attack machine learning or deep learning models, (2) protect models' intellectual property from attacks or provide methods to identify stolen models, and (3) discuss the mentor–student training schema and its limitations, such as the number of layers reduction, speedup gain, and accuracy reduction. We have used multiple combination strings such as 'DNN distillation', 'mentor student training', 'teacher student training', 'DNN attacks', 'machine learning attacks', 'watermarking in DNN', 'DNN protection', 'DNN intellectual property', and 'ML and DL models protection' to retrieve the peer-reviewed articles of journal conference proceedings, book chapters, and reports. We have targeted the five databases, namely IEEE Xplore, SpringerLink, Scopus, arXiv digital library, and ScienceDirect. Google Scholar was also largely used for searching and tracking cited papers based on the topics of interest. The title and abstract were screened to identify potential articles; then, the experimental results were carefully reviewed in order to identify relevant baselines and successful methods.

2.2. Motivation

There already exist secondary markets for the resale of stolen identities, such as www.infochimps.com (accessed on 19 November 2021) or black market sites and chat rooms for the resale of other illegal datasets [13,14]. It also reasonable to assume that a digested "learned" data would be worth more to such buyers than the raw data itself, and that models learned through the use of more data and higher computational resources might be priced differently than more basic ones. After all, why work hard when one can employ the high-quality results of a learning process executed by others [15–18]?

We note that such stolen knowledge could be used for several malicious goals:

- Selling to the highest bidder (both "legit" bidders, advertisers, etc., or in the black market to other attackers) [19–22].
- Bootstrapping for more advanced models [23–25]
- Business espionage—e.g., analyzing a competitor's capabilities or potential weaknesses [26,27].

2.3. Watermarking

The idea of *watermarking* that has been well studied in the past two decades was originally invented in order to protect digital media from being stolen [28,29]. The idea relies on inserting a unique modification or signature not visible to the human eye. This allows proving legitimate ownership by presenting that the owner's unique signature is embedded into the digital media [30,31]. With the same goal in mind, embedding a unique signature into a model and subsequently identifying the stolen model based on that signature, some new techniques were invented [32,33]. A method to embed a signature into the model's weights is described in [34]; it allows for the identification of the unique signature by examining the model's weights. This method assumes that the model and its parameters are available for examination. Unfortunately, in most cases, the model's weights are not publicly available; an individual could offer an API-based service that uses the stolen model while still keeping the model's parameters hidden from the user. Therefore, this method is not sufficient.

Another method [35] proposes a zero-bit watermarking algorithm that makes use of adversaries' examples. It enables the authentication of the model's ownership using a set of queries. The authors rely on predefined examples that give certain answers. By showing that these exact same answers are obtained using N queries, one can authenticate their ownership over the model. However, this idea may be problematic, since these queries are not unique and there can be infinitely many of them. An individual can generate queries for which a model outputs certain answers that match the original queries. In doing so, anyone can claim ownership. Furthermore, it is possible that different adversaries will have a different set of queries that gives the exact predefined answers.

Some more recent papers [36] offer a methodology that allows inserting a digital watermarking into a deep learning (DL) model without harming the performance and with high model pruning resistance. In [37], a method of inserting watermarking into a model is presented. Specifically, it allows identifying a stolen model even if it is used via an *application programming interface* (API) and returns only the predicted label. It is done by defining a certain hidden "key", which can be a certain shape or noise integrated into a part of the training set. When the model receives an input containing the key, it will predict with high certainty a completely unrelated label. Thus, it is possible to use some available APIs by sending them an image integrated with the hidden key. If the result is odd and the unrelated label is triggered, it may be an indication that this model is stolen. Our method is resistant to this protection mechanism, as its learning is based on the predictions of the mentor. Specifically, our training is based on random combinations of inputs, i.e., the chances of sending the mentor a hidden key that will trigger the unrelated label mechanism is negligible. We can train and gain the important knowledge of such a model without learning the watermarks, thereby assuring that our model would not be identified as stolen when provided a hidden key as input. Finally, Ref. [38] shows that a malicious adversary, even in scenarios where the watermark is difficult to remove, can still evade the verification by the legitimate owners. In conclusion, even the most advanced watermarking methods are still not good enough to properly protect a neural network from being stolen. Our composite method overcomes all of the above defense mechanisms.

2.4. Attack Mechanisms

As previously explained, trained deep neural networks are extremely valuable and worth protecting. Naturally, a lot of research has been done on attacking such networks and stealing their knowledge. In [39,40], an attack method exploiting the confidence level of a model is presented. The assumption that the confidence level is available is too lenient, as it can be easily blocked by returning merely the predicted label. Our composite method shows how to successfully steal a model that does not reveal its confidence level(s). In [41], it is shown how to steal the knowledge of a convolutional neural network (CNN) model using random unlabeled data.

Another known attack mechanism is a Trojan attack described in [42] or a backdoor attack [43]. Such attacks are very dangerous, as they might cause various severe consequences, including endangering human lives, e.g., by disrupting the actions of a neural network-based autonomous vehicle. The idea is to spread and deploy infected models, which will act as expected for almost all regular inputs, except for a specific engineered input, i.e., a Trojan trigger, in which case the model would behave in a predefined manner that could become very dangerous in some cases. Consider, for example, an infected deep neural network (DNN) model of an autonomous vehicle, for which a specific given input will predict making a hard left turn. If such a model is deployed and triggered in the middle of a highway, the results could be devastating.

Using our composite method, even if our proposed student model learns from an infected mentor, it will not catch the dangerous triggers, and in fact, it will act normally despite the engineered Trojan keys. The reason lies within our training method, as we randomly compose training examples based on the mentor's prediction. In other words, the odds that a specific engineered key will be sent to the mentor and trigger a backdoor are negligible, similarly to the way training based on a mentor containing watermarks is done. We present some interesting neural network attacks and show that our composite method is superior to these attacks and is also robust against infected models.

2.5. Defense Mechanisms

In addition to watermarking, which is the main method of defending a model (or of enabling at least a stolen model to be exposed), there are some other available interesting possibilities. In [44], a method that adds a small controllable perturbation maximizing the loss of the stolen model while preserving the accuracy is suggested. For some attacking methods, this trick can be effective and significantly slow down an attacker, if not prevent it completely. This method has no effect on our composite method, which preserves the accuracy. In other words, for each sample x if for a specific index i the softmax layer predicts $F(x)[i]$ as the maximum value, now the output of our network for that index would be:

$$F'(x)[i] = F(x)[i] + \psi$$

where ψ is an intended perturbation, and where the following still holds:

$$\mathrm{argmax}(F(x)) = \mathrm{argmax}(F'(x)) = i$$

This is the important element of our composite method, which solely relies on the model's binary labels and is not affected by this modification. Most defense mechanisms are based mainly on manipulating the returned softmax confidence level, shuffling all of the label probabilities except for the maximal one, or returning a label without its confidence level. The baseline is that all of these methods have to return the minimal information of what the predicted label is. Indeed, this is all that is required by the composite method, so our algorithm is unaffected by such defense mechanisms.

3. Proposed Method

In this section, we present our novel composite method, which can be used to attack and extract the knowledge of a black box model even if it completely conceals its softmax output. For mimicking a mentor, we assume no knowledge of the model's training data and no access to it (i.e., we make no use of any training data used to train the original model). Thus, the task at hand is very similar to real-life scenarios, where there are plenty of available trained models (as services or products) without any knowledge of how they were trained and of the training data used in the process. Additionally, we assume no knowledge of the model's network architecture or weights; i.e., we regard it as an opaque black box. The only information about the model (which we would like to mimic) is its input size and the number of output classes (i.e., output size). For example, we may assume that only the input image size and the number of possible traffic signs are known for a traffic sign classifier.

As previously indicated, another crucial assumption is that the black box model we aim at attacking does not reveal its confidence levels. Namely, the model's output is merely the predicted label, rather than the softmax values, e.g., in case of an input image of a traffic sign, whether the model is 99% confident or only 51% confident that the image is a stop sign, in both cases, it will output "stop sign" without further information. We assume the model hides the confidence values as a safety mechanism against mimicking attacks by adversaries who are trying to acquire and copy the model's IP. Note that outputting merely the predicted class is the extreme protection possible for a model providing an API-based prediction, as it is the minimum amount of information the model must provide.

Our novel method for successfully mimicking a mentor that does not provide its softmax values makes use of what we refer to as composite samples. By combining two different samples into a single sample (see details below), we effectively tap into the hidden knowledge of the mentor. (In the next section, we provide experimental results, comparing the performance of our method and that of standard mimicking using both softmax and non-softmax outputs.) For the rest of the discussion, we refer to the black box model (we would like to mimic) and our developed model (for mimicking it) as a mentor model and a student model, respectively.

3.1. Datasets for Mentor and Student
3.1.1. Dataset for Mentor Training

CIFAR-10 [45] is an established dataset used for object recognition. It consists of 60,000 (32×32) RGB images from 10 classes, with 6000 images per class. There are 50,000 training images and 10,000 test images in the official data. The mentor is a pretrained model on the CIFAR-10 dataset. We use the test set (from this dataset) to measure the success rate of our mentor and student models. Note that the training set of the CIFAR-10 dataset is never used in the training process by the student (to conform to our assumption that the student has no access to the data used by the mentor for training), and the test subset, as mentioned above, is used for validation only (without training).

3.1.2. Dataset for Mimicking Process

ImageNet [46] is a dataset containing complex, real-world size images. In particular, ImageNet_ILSVRC2012 contains more than 1.2 million (256 × 256) RGB images from 1000 categories. We use this dataset (without the labels, i.e., an unlabeled dataset) for the mimicking process. Each image is down-sampled (32 × 32) and fed into the mentor model, and the prediction of the mentor model is recorded (for later mimicking by the student). Note that any large unlabeled image dataset could be used instead, and we used this common large dataset for convenience only.

3.2. Composite Data Generation

Our goal is to create a diverse dataset that will allow observing the predictions of the mentor on many possible inputs. By doing so, we would gain insights into the way the mentor behaves for different samples. That is, the more adequate the input space sample is, the better the performance of the mimicking process becomes. The entire available unlabeled data, which is the down-sampled ImageNet, is contained in an array $dataArr$. For each training example to be generated, we randomly choose two indexes i_1, i_2, such that $0 <= i_1, i_2 < N$, where is N equal to the number of samples we create and use for training the student model. In our composite method, we choose $N = 1,000,000$, so the amount of generated training samples created in each epoch is $1,000,000$. Next, we randomly choose a ratio p. Once we have i_1, i_2, and p, we generate a composite sample, which is created by combining two existing images in the dataset. The ratio p determines the relative influence of the two random images on the generated sample:

$$x\_gen = p * dataArr[i_1] + (1 - p) * dataArr[i_2]$$

where the label of x_gen is a "one-hot" vector; i.e., the index containing the '1' (corresponding to the maximal softmax value) represents the label predicted by the mentor. The dataset is generated for every epoch; hence, our composite dataset changes continuously, and it is dynamic. We gain the predictions of a mentor model on new images during the entire training process (with less overfitting). Note that even though in our data-generating mechanism, we create a composite of two random images (with a random mixture between them), it is possible to create composite images of N images where $N > 2$ as well.

Algorithm 1 provides the complete composite data-generation method, which is run at the beginning of each epoch. Figure 1 is an illustration of composite data samples created by Algorithm 1.

3.3. Student Model Architecture

The mentor neural network (which we intend to mimic) is an already trained model that reaches 90.48% test accuracy on the CIFAR-10 test set. Our goal in choosing an architecture for the student is to be generic, such that it would perform well, regardless of the mentor we try to mimic. Thus, with small adaptations to the input and output size, we created a modification of the VGG-16 architecture [47] for the student model. In our model, we use two dense layers of size 512 each and another dense layer of size 10 for the softmax output (while in the original VGG-16 architecture, there are two dense layers of size 4096 and another dense layer of size 1000 for the softmax layer). Table 1 presents the architecture of our student model.

Algorithm 1 Composite Data Generation.

1: **Input:**
2: *mentor*—the mentor model
3: *dataArr*—all available data array
4: *N*—number of samples to generate
5: **Output:**
6: *X*—generated examples
7: *Y*—corresponding labels
8: **function** GENERATE_DATA(mentor, dataArr, N)
9:     $X, Y = [\,], [\,]$
10:    **for** i = 1 to N **do**
11:        i_1 = math.random(len($dataArr$))
12:        i_2 = math.random(len($dataArr$))
13:        p = math.random(100)/100
14:        $x\_gen = p * dataArr[i_1] + (1 - p) * dataArr[i_2]$
15:        X.append(x_gen)
16:        Y.append(argmax($mentor$.predict(x_gen)))
17:    **end for**
18:    **return** X, Y
19: **end function**

(a) 75% cat 25% dog (b) 70% horse 30% kangaroo (c) 30% horse 70% ship

(d) 40% ship 60% parrot (e) 50% tiger 50% dog (f) 20% car 80% elephant

Figure 1. Illustration of images created using our composite data-generation method. The images and their relative mixture are random. Using this method during each epoch we create an entirely new dataset, with random data not seen before by the model.

3.4. Mimicking Process

Using the above described composite data generation, a new composite dataset is generated for every epoch during the mimicking process. We train on this dataset using the stochastic gradient descent (SGD) algorithm [48]. Table 2 describes the parameters used for training the student model. Our student model does not use any dropout or regularization methods. Such regularization methods are not necessary, since our model does not reach overfitting as a result of the dynamic dataset (a new composite dataset generated at each epoch). To evaluate the final performance of the student model, we test it on a dedicated test set that was used to evaluate also the mentor model (note that neither the student nor the mentor were trained on images belonging to the test set).

Table 1. The architecture used in the composite training experiment for the student model. This architecture is a modification of the VGG-16 architecture [47], which has proven to be very successful and robust. By performing only small modifications over the input and output layers, we can adapt this architecture for a student model intended to mimic a different mentor model.

Modified VGG-16 Model Architecture for Student Network
3×3 Convolution 64
3×3 Convolution 64
Max pooling
3×3 Convolution 128
3×3 Convolution 128
Max pooling
3×3 Convolution 256
3×3 Convolution 256
3×3 Convolution 256
Max pooling
3×3 Convolution 512
3×3 Convolution 512
3×3 Convolution 512
Max pooling
3×3 Convolution 512
3×3 Convolution 512
3×3 Convolution 512
Max pooling
Dense 512
Dense 512
Softmax 10

In addition, we have used learning rate decay, starting from 0.001 and multiplied by 0.9 every 10 epochs, as we have found it essential in order to reach high accuracy rates. A detailed description of our experimental results is provided in Section 4.

Table 2. Parameters used for training in the composite experiment.

Parameters	Values
Learning rate	0.001
Activation function	ReLU
Batch size	128
Dropout rate	-
L_2 regularization	-
SGD momentum	0.9
Data augmentation	-

3.5. Data Augmentation

Data augmentation is a useful technique frequently used in the training process of deep neural networks [49,50]. It is mostly used to synthetically enlarge a limited size dataset in an attempt to generalize and enhance the robustness of a model under training and to reduce overfitting.

The basic notion behind this method relies on training the model on different training samples at each epoch. Specifically, during each epoch, small random visual modifications are made to the dataset images. This is completed in order to allow the model to be trained during each epoch on a slightly different dataset, using the same labels for the training. Examples of simple data augmentation operations include small vertical and horizontal shifts of the image, a slight rotation of the image (usually by θ for $0° < \theta <= 15°$), etc.

This technique is used for our student models, which are trained on the same dataset during each epoch. However, for the composite model experiment, we found it to have no effect on the performance. Our composite data-generation method ensures virtually a continuous set of infinitely many new samples never seen before; thus, data augmentation is not necessary here at all. Our end goal is to represent a nonlinear function, which takes an n-dimensional input and transforms it to an m-dimensional output, e.g., a function that takes an image of size 256×256 of a road and returns one of Y possible actions that an autonomous vehicle should take. Using data augmentation, we can train the model to better represent the required nonlinear function. For our composite method, though, this would be redundant, since the training process is always performed on different random inputs, which allows for estimating empirically the nonlinear function in a much better way without using the original training dataset for training the model.

3.6. Swarms Applications

A swarm contains a group of autonomous robots without central coordination, which is designed to maximize the performance of a specific task [51]. Tasks that have been of particular interest to researchers in recent years include synergetic mission planning [52], patrolling [53], fault tolerance cooperation [54], network security [55], crowds modeling [56], swarm control [57], human design of mission plans [58], role assignment [59], multi-robot path planning [60], traffic control [61], formation generation [62], formation keeping [63], exploration and mapping [64], modeling of financial systems [65], target tracking [66,67], collaborative cleaning [68], control architecture for drones swarm [69], and target search [70].

Generally speaking, the sensing and communication capabilities of a single swarm member are considered significantly limited compared to the difficulty of the collective task, where macroscopic swarm-level efficiency is achieved through an explicit or implicit cooperation by the swarm members, and it emerges from the system's design. Such designs are often inspired by biology (see [71] for evolutionary algorithms, Ref. [72] or [73] for behavior-based control models, Ref. [74] for flocking and dispersing models, Ref. [75] for predator–prey approaches), by physics [76], probabilistic theory [77], sociology [78], network theory [79,80], or by economics applications [64,81–84].

The issue of swarm communication has been extensively studied in recent years. Distinctions between implicit and explicit communication are usually made in which implicit communication occurs as a side effect of other actions, or "through the world" (see, for example [85]), whereas explicit communication is a specific act intended solely to convey information to other robots on the team. Explicit communication can be performed in several ways, such as a short range point-to-point communication, a global broadcast, or by using some sort of distributed shared memory. Such memory is often referred to as a *pheromone*, which is used to convey small amounts of information between the agents [86]. This approach is inspired from the coordination and communication methods used by many social insects—studies on ants (e.g., [87]) show that the pheromone-based search strategies used by ants in foraging for food in unknown terrains tend to be very efficient. Additional information can be found in the relevant NASA survey, focusing on "intelligent swarms" comprised of multiple "stupid satellites" [88] or the following survey conducted by the US Naval Research Center [89].

Online learning methods have been shown to be able to increase the flexibility of a swarm. Such methods require a memory component in each robot, which implies an additional level of complexity. Deep reinforcement learning methods have been applied successfully to multi-agent scenarios [90], and using neural network features enables the richest information exchange between neighboring agents. In [91], a nonlinear decentralized stable controller for close-proximity flight of multirotor swarms is presented, and DNNs are used to accurately learn the high-order multi-vehicle interactions. Neural networks also contribute to system-level state prediction directly from generic graphical features from the entire view, which can be relatively inexpensive to gather in a completely automated fashion [92].

Our method can be applied to DNN-assisted swarms for extraction of the DNN models. By observing the robots' reaction in the neutral environment, and by forcing more rare reactions based on the interaction with a specific designed malicious robot to create more useful recorded samples, we can create an infinite amount of state and reaction samples. Since each robot is interchangeable and uses the model we want to extract, the amount of possible states and reactions is limitless. The method enables compounding a dataset for training and creating replicas of the DNN intellectual property used in the original swarms in a resembling fashion to [12]. The extracted DNN can be used for different applications, such as deployment to different types of robots using a DNN-assisted decision-making system or simply creating a replica of the swarm with the secret intellectual property at our disposal.

4. Experimental Results

4.1. Experimental Results for Unprotected Mentor (with Softmax Output) and Standard Mimicking

To obtain a baseline for comparison, we assume in this experiment that the mentor in question reveals its confidence levels by providing the values of its softmax output (referring to it as an "unprotected mentor"), using the same modified VGG-16 architecture presented in Table 1. In this case, we create a new dataset for the student model only once and use it together with standard data augmentation. We feed each training sample from the down-sampled ImageNet into the mentor and save the pairs of its input image and softmax label distribution (i.e., its softmax layer output). The total size of this dataset is over 1.2 million samples (the size of the ImageNet_ILSVRC2012 dataset). Once the dataset is created, we train the student using regular supervised training with SGD. In this experiment, since overfitting would occur without regularization, we use dropout to improve generalization. The parameters used for training this model are presented in Table 3.

Table 3. Parameters used for the training process using standard (non-composite) mimicking.

Parameters	Values
Learning rate	0.001
Activation function	ReLU
Batch size	128
Dropout rate	0.2
L_2 regularization	0.0005
SGD momentum	0.9
Data augmentation	Used

Using these parameters, we obtained a maximum test accuracy of 89.1% for the CIFAR-10 test set, namely, 1.38% less than the mentor's 90.48% success rate. (Note that the student was never trained on the CIFAR-10 dataset, and instead, after completing the mimicking process using the separate unrelated dataset, its performance was only tested on the CIFAR-10 test set.)

4.2. Experimental Results for Protected Mentor (without Softmax Output) and Standard Mimicking

In this experiment, we assume that the mentor reveals the predicted label with no information about the certainty level (i.e., it is considered a "protected mentor"). This is a real-life scenario, in which an API-based service is queried by uploading inputs, and only the predicted output class (without softmax values) is returned.

By sending only the correct labels, the models are more protected in the sense that they reveal less information to a potential attacker. For this reason, this method has become a common defense mechanism for protecting intellectual property when neural networks are deployed in real-world scenarios.

In this subsection, we try a standard mimicking attack (without composite images). Here, we execute exactly the same training process of the soft labels experiment (described in the previous subsection) with one important difference. In this case, the labels available for the student are merely one-hot labels provided by the mentor and not the full softmax distribution of the mentor. For each training sample (from the down-sampled ImageNet dataset), we take the output distribution, find the index with the maximum value, and set it to '1' (while setting all the other indices to '0'). The student can observe only this final vector with a single '1' for the correct class and '0' for all other classes. This accurately simulates a process that can be applied on an API service. The student only knows at this point the mentor's prediction but not its level of certainty. We use the same parameters of Table 3 for the mimicking process. The success rate in this experiment is the lowest; the student reached only ~87.5% accuracy on the CIFAR-10 test set, which is substantially lower than that of the student that mimicked an unprotected mentor.

4.3. Experimental Results for Protected Mentor (without Softmax Output) and Composite Data Mimicking

In this experiment, we assume again that our mentor reveals the predicted label with no information about the certainty level. However, instead of launching a standard attack on the mentor, we employ here our novel composite data generation as described in Algorithm 1 in order to generate new composite data samples at each epoch. In this case, the student only has access to the predicted labels (minimum output required from a protected mentor). Unlike the previous two experiments using standard mimicking, we do not use here data augmentation or regularization, since virtually all of the data samples are always new and are generated continuously. Figure 2 illustrates the expected predictions from a well-trained model for certain combined input images. Empirically, this is not totally accurate, since the presentation and overlap of objects in an image also affect the output of the real model. However, despite this caveat, the experimental results presented below show that our method provides a good approximation. Our student model accuracy is measured compared to the mentor model accuracy, which is trained regularly with all the data and labels.

Training with composite data, we obtained 89.59% accuracy on the CIFAR-10 test set, which is only 0.89% less than that of the mentor itself. (Again, note that the student is not trained on any of the CIFAR-10 images, and that the test set is used only for the final testing, after the mimicking process is completed. The mentor's accuracy is used as the baseline or the ground truth.) This is the highest accuracy among all of the experiments conducted; surprisingly, it is even superior to the results of standard mimicking for an unprotected mentor (which does divulge its softmax output). Figure 3 depicts the accuracy over time (i.e., epoch number) for the composite and soft-label experiments. As can be seen, the success rate of the composite experiment is superior to that of the soft-label experiment during almost the entire training process. Even though the latter has access to valuable additional knowledge, our composite method performs consistently better without access to the mentor's softmax output.

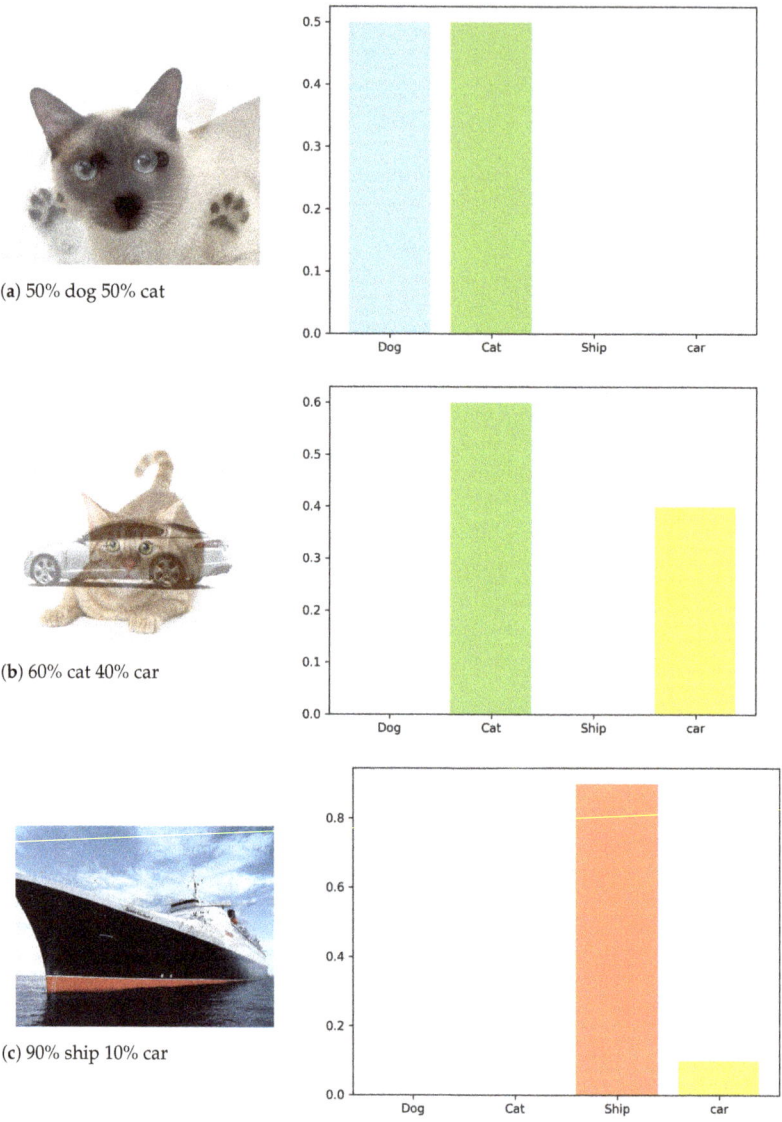

Figure 2. Generated images and their corresponding expected softmax distribution, which reveals the model's certainty level for each example. In practice, the manner by which objects overlap and the degree of their overlap largely affect the certainty level.

A summary of the experimental results is presented in Table 4, including relative accuracy to the mentor's accuracy rate. The results show that standard mimicking obtained ∼98.5% of the accuracy of an unprotected mentor and only ∼96.7% of its accuracy when the mentor was protected. However, using the composite mimicking method, the student reached (over) 99% of the accuracy of a fully protected mentor. Thus, even when a mentor only reveals its predictions without their confidence levels, the model is not immune to mimicking and knowledge stealing. Our method is generic, and it can be used on any model with only minor modifications on the input and output layers of the architecture.

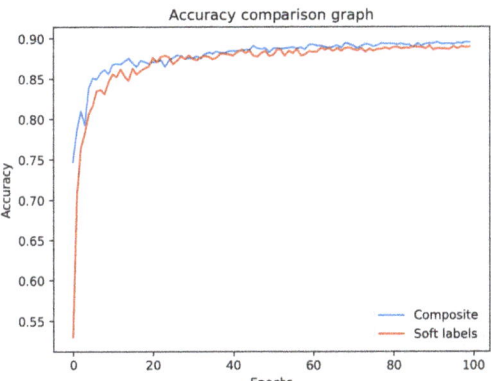

Figure 3. Student test accuracies for composite and soft-label experiments, training the student over 100 epochs. The student trained using the composite method is superior during almost the entire training process. The two experiments were selected for visual comparison as they reached the highest success rates for the test set.

Table 4. Summary of the experiments. The table provides the CIFAR-10 test accuracy of three student models in absolute terms and in comparison to the 90.48% test accuracy achieved by the mentor itself. The three mimicking methods use standard mimicking for unprotected and protected mentors, as well as composite mimicking for a protected mentor, which provides the best results.

Method	Mentor Status	Test Accuracy	Relative Accuracy
Standard	Unprotected	89.10%	98.47%
Standard	Protected	87.46%	96.66%
Composite	Protected	89.59%	99.01%

5. Conclusions

In view of the tremendous DNN-based advancements that have been carried out during the recent years in a myriad of domains, some involving problems that have been considered very challenging hitherto, the issue of protecting complex DNN models has gained considerable interest. The computational power and significant effort required by a training process makes a well-trained network very valuable. Thus, much research has been devoted to studying and modeling various techniques for attacking DNNs aiming for developing appropriate mechanisms for defending them, where the most common defense mechanism is to conceal the model's certainty levels and output merely a predicted label. In this paper, we have presented a novel composite image attack method for extracting the knowledge of a DNN model, which is not affected by the above "label only" defense mechanism. Specifically, our composite method achieves this resilience by assuming only that this mechanism is activated and relies solely on the label prediction returned from a black box model. We assume no knowledge about this model's training process and its original training data. In contrast to other methods suggested for stealing or mimicking a trained model, our method does not rely on the softmax distribution supplied by a trained model with a certainty level across all categories. Therefore, it is also highly robust against adding a controlled perturbation to the returned softmax distribution in order to protect a given model. Our composite method assumes a large unlabeled data source which is used to generate composite samples, which in our case is the entire ImageNet dataset. The large amount of possible images that are randomly selected provide diversity in the final composite dataset, which works very well for the IP extraction. In case a smaller unlabeled data source is chosen, e.g., the Cifar-10 dataset with no labels, the diversity will most likely be harmed as well as the IP extraction quality. In order to overcome the lack of diversity, it is possible to generalize the composite dataset creation; instead of randomly selecting 2 images, we can select n images and $n-1$ random ratios $i_1, i_2, \ldots, i_{n-1}$ summing to 1, the composite image will be the sum of the randomly selected images multiplied by the corresponding ratios. This adaptation can contribute greatly to the diversity of the composite dataset and might overcome the smaller unlabeled data source.

By employing our proposed method, a user can attack a DNN model and reach an extremely close success rate compared to the attacked model while relying only on the minimal information that has to be given by the model (namely, its label prediction for a given input). Our proposed method demonstrates that the current available defense mechanisms for deep neural networks provide insufficient defense, as countless neural networks-based services are exposed to the attack vector described in this paper using the composite attack method, which is capable of bypassing all available protection methods and stealing a model while carrying no marks that can identify the created model as stolen. Such models can be attacked and copied into a rival model, which can then be deployed and affect the product's market share. The rival deployed model will be undetectable and carry no mark proofs that it is stolen, as explained in Section 2.3. The novelty of the composite method itself is reflected in its robustness and possible adaptation to any classification use case, assuming maximal protection of the mentor model and no assumption on its architecture or training data.

Author Contributions: Conceptualization, I.M. and E.D.; methodology, I.M., E.D., N.S.N. and Y.A.; software, I.M.; validation, I.M., E.D., N.S.N. and Y.A.; formal analysis, I.M., E.D., N.S.N. and Y.A.; investigation, I.M.; resources, I.M., E.D., N.S.N. and Y.A.; data curation, I.M., E.D. and N.S.N.; writing—original draft preparation, I.M.; writing—review and editing, E.D., N.S.N. and Y.A.; visualization, I.M. and E.D.; supervision, N.S.N.; project administration, I.M., E.D. and N.S.N.; funding acquisition, N.S.N. All authors have read and agreed to the published version of the manuscript.

Funding: This research received no external funding.

Institutional Review Board Statement: Not applicable.

Informed Consent Statement: Not applicable.

Data Availability Statement: Publicly available datasets were analyzed in this study. These data can be found here: https://www.cs.toronto.edu/~kriz/cifar.html (accessed on 17 July 2019), https://www.image-net.org/ (accessed on 17 July 2019).

Acknowledgments: The authors would like to acknowledge the Department of Computer Science, Bar-Ilan University.

Conflicts of Interest: The authors declare no conflict of interest.

References

1. Girshick, R. Fast R-CNN. In Proceedings of the 2015 IEEE International Conference on Computer Vision, Santiago, Chile, 7–13 December 2015; pp. 1440–1448.
2. Ren, S.; He, K.; Girshick, R.; Sun, J. Faster R-CNN: Towards real-time object detection with region proposal networks. *Adv. Neural Inf. Process. Syst.* **2015**, *28*, 91–99. [CrossRef] [PubMed]
3. Redmon, J.; Divvala, S.; Girshick, R.; Farhadi, A. You only look once: Unified, real-time object detection. In Proceedings of the IEEE Conference on Computer Vision and Pattern Recognition, Las Vegas, NV, USA, 27–30 June 2016; pp. 779–788.
4. Chen, C.; Seff, A.; Kornhauser, A.; Xiao, J. DeepDriving: Learning affordance for direct perception in autonomous driving. In Proceedings of the 2015 IEEE International Conference on Computer Vision, Santiago, Chile, 7–13 December 2015; pp. 2722–2730.
5. Luong, M.; Pham, H.; Manning, C.D. Effective Approaches to Attention-based Neural Machine Translation. In Proceedings of the 2015 Conference on Empirical Methods in Natural Language Processing, Culturgest, Lisbon, 17–21 September 2015; pp. 1412–1421.
6. Rosenberg, I.; Sicard, G.; David, E. DeepAPT: Nation-State APT Attribution Using End-to-End Deep Neural Networks. In Proceedings of the International Conference on Artificial Neural Networks, Alghero, Italy, 11–14 September 2017; pp. 91–99.
7. Shaukat, K.; Luo, S.; Varadharajan, V.; Hameed, I.A.; Xu, M. A survey on machine learning techniques for cyber security in the last decade. *IEEE Access* **2020**, *8*, 222310–222354. [CrossRef]
8. Shaukat, K.; Luo, S.; Varadharajan, V.; Hameed, I.A.; Chen, S.; Liu, D.; Li, J. Performance comparison and current challenges of using machine learning techniques in cybersecurity. *Energies* **2020**, *13*, 2509. [CrossRef]

9. Alam, T.M.; Shaukat, K.; Hameed, I.A.; Luo, S.; Sarwar, M.U.; Shabbir, S.; Li, J.; Khushi, M. An investigation of credit card default prediction in the imbalanced datasets. *IEEE Access* **2020**, *8*, 201173–201198. [CrossRef]
10. Gold, S.; Rangarajan, A. Softmax to softassign: Neural network algorithms for combinatorial optimization. *J. Artif. Neural Netw.* **1996**, *2*, 381–399.
11. Jang, E.; Gu, S.; Poole, B. Categorical reparameterization with gumbel-softmax. *arXiv* **2016**, arXiv:1611.01144.
12. Mosafi, I.; David, E.O.; Netanyahu, N.S. Stealing knowledge from protected deep neural networks using composite unlabeled data. In Proceedings of the 2019 International Joint Conference on Neural Networks (IJCNN), Budapest, Hungary, 14–19 July 2019; pp. 1–8.
13. Herley, C.; Florencio, D. Nobody Sells Gold for the Price of Silver: Dishonesty, Uncertainty and the Underground Economy. In *Economics of Information Security and Privacy*; Moore, T., Pym, D., Ioannidis, C., Eds.; Springer: New York, NY, USA, 2010; pp. 33–53.
14. Holt, T.J.; Smirnova, O.; Chua, Y.T.; Copes, H. Examining the risk reduction strategies of actors in online criminal markets. *Glob. Crime* **2015**, *16*, 81–103. [CrossRef]
15. Altshuler, Y.; Elovici, Y.; Cremers, A.B.; Aharony, N.; Pentland, A. *Security and Privacy in Social Networks*; Springer Science & Business Media: New York, NY, USA, 2012.
16. Barbieri, D.; Braga, D.; Ceri, S.; Valle, E.D.; Huang, Y.; Tresp, V.; Rettinger, A.; Wermser, H. Deductive and Inductive Stream Reasoning for Semantic Social Media Analytics. *IEEE Intell. Syst.* **2010**, *99*. [CrossRef]
17. Altshuler, Y.; Aharony, N.; Pentland, A.; Elovici, Y.; Cebrian, M. Stealing Reality: When Criminals Become Data Scientists (or Vice Versa). *Intell. Syst. IEEE* **2011**, *26*, 22–30. [CrossRef]
18. Holt, T.; Bossler, A. *Cybercrime in Progress: Theory and Prevention of Technology-Enabled Offenses*; Routledge: London, UK, 2015.
19. Krishnamurthy, B.; Wills, C.E. On the leakage of personally identifiable information via online social networks. In Proceedings of the 2nd ACM Workshop on Online Social Networks (WOSN '09), Barcelona, Spain, 17 August 2009; ACM: New York, NY, USA, 2009; pp. 7–12.
20. Mellet, K.; Beauvisage, T. Cookie monsters. Anatomy of a digital market infrastructure. *Consum. Mark. Cult.* **2020**, *23*, 110–129. [CrossRef]
21. Venkatadri, G.; Andreou, A.; Liu, Y.; Mislove, A.; Gummadi, K.P.; Loiseau, P.; Goga, O. Privacy risks with Facebook's PII-based targeting: Auditing a data broker's advertising interface. In Proceedings of the 2018 IEEE Symposium on Security and Privacy (SP), San Francisco, CA, USA, 20–24 May 2018; pp. 89–107.
22. Dupont, B.; Côté, A.M.; Savine, C.; Décary-Hétu, D. The ecology of trust among hackers. *Glob. Crime* **2016**, *17*, 129–151. [CrossRef]
23. Neerbek, J. Sensitive Information Detection: Recursive Neural Networks for Encoding Context. *arXiv* **2020**, arXiv:2008.10863.
24. Alqattan, Z.N. Threats Against Information Privacy and Security in Social Networks: A Review. *Adv. Cyber Secur.* **2020**, *1132*, 358.
25. Pentland, A.; Altshuler, Y. Chapter New Solutions for Cybersecurity. In *Social Physics and Cybercrime*; MIT Press: Cambridge, MA, USA, 2018; pp. 351–364.
26. Pan, W.; Altshuler, Y.; Pentland, A. Decoding social influence and the wisdom of the crowd in financial trading network. In Proceedings of the Privacy, Security, Risk and Trust (PASSAT), 2012 International Conference on and 2012 International Confernece on Social Computing (SocialCom), Amsterdam, The Netherlands, 3–6 September 2012; pp. 203–209.
27. Albanie, S.; Thewlis, J.; Ehrhardt, S.; Henriques, J. Deep Industrial Espionage. *arXiv* **2019**, arXiv:1904.01114.
28. Cox, I.J.; Miller, M.L.; Bloom, J.A.; Honsinger, C. *Digital Watermarking*; Springer: Berlin/Heidelberg, Germany, 2002; Volume 53.
29. Hartung, F.; Kutter, M. Multimedia watermarking techniques. *Proc. IEEE* **1999**, *87*, 1079–1107. [CrossRef]
30. Lee, Y.K.; Bell, G.; Huang, S.Y.; Wang, R.Z.; Shyu, S.J. An advanced least-significant-bit embedding scheme for steganographic encoding. In Proceedings of the Pacific-Rim Symposium on Image and Video Technology, Tokyo, Japan, 13–16 January 2009; Springer: Berlin/Heidelberg, Germany, 2009; pp. 349–360.
31. Tian, J. Reversible data embedding using a difference expansion. *IEEE Trans. Circuits Syst. Video Technol.* **2003**, *13*, 890–896. [CrossRef]
32. Zhang, J.; Gu, Z.; Jang, J.; Wu, H.; Stoecklin, M.P.; Huang, H.; Molloy, I. Protecting intellectual property of deep neural networks with watermarking. In Proceedings of the 2018 on Asia Conference on Computer and Communications Security, Incheon, Korea, 4–8 June 2018; pp. 159–172.
33. Adi, Y.; Baum, C.; Cisse, M.; Pinkas, B.; Keshet, J. Turning your weakness into a strength: Watermarking deep neural networks by backdooring. In Proceedings of the 27th *USENIX* Security Symposium (*USENIX* Security 18), Baltimore, MD, USA, 15–17 August 2018; pp. 1615–1631.
34. Uchida, Y.; Nagai, Y.; Sakazawa, S.; Satoh, S. Embedding watermarks into deep neural networks. In Proceedings of the ACM International Conference on Multimedia Retrieval, Bucharest, Romania, 6–9 June 2017; pp. 269–277.
35. Merrer, E.L.; Perez, P.; Trédan, G. Adversarial frontier stitching for remote neural network watermarking. *arXiv* **2017**, arXiv:1711.01894.
36. Rouhani, B.D.; Chen, H.; Koushanfar, F. DeepSigns: A Generic Watermarking Framework for IP Protection of Deep Learning Models. *arXiv* **2018**, arXiv:1804.00750.
37. Nagai, Y.; Uchida, Y.; Sakazawa, S.; Satoh, S. Digital watermarking for deep neural networks. *Int. J. Multimed. Inf. Retr.* **2018**, *7*, 3–16. [CrossRef]

38. Hitaj, D.; Mancini, L.V. Have You Stolen My Model? Evasion Attacks Against Deep Neural Network Watermarking Techniques. *arXiv* **2018**, arXiv:1809.00615.
39. Fredrikson, M.; Jha, S.; Ristenpart, T. Model inversion attacks that exploit confidence information and basic countermeasures. In Proceedings of the Twenty Second ACM SIGSAC Conference on Computer and Communications Security, Denver, CO, USA, 12–16 October 2015; pp. 1322–1333.
40. Tramèr, F.; Zhang, F.; Juels, A.; Reiter, M.K.; Ristenpart, T. Stealing Machine Learning Models via Prediction APIs. In Proceedings of the USENIX Security Symposium, Austin, TX, USA, 10–12 August 2016; pp. 601–618.
41. Correia-Silva, J.R.; Berriel, R.F.; Badue, C.; de Souza, A.F.; Oliveira-Santos, T. Copycat CNN: Stealing Knowledge by Persuading Confession with Random Non-Labeled Data. *arXiv* **2018**, arXiv:1806.05476.
42. Liu, Y.; Ma, S.; Aafer, Y.; Lee, W.C.; Zhai, J.; Wang, W.; Zhang, X. Trojaning Attack on Neural Networks. In Proceedings of the Network and Distributed System Security Symposium, San Diego, CA, USA, 18–21 February 2018.
43. Gu, T.; Dolan-Gavitt, B.; Garg, S. BadNets: Identifying vulnerabilities in the machine learning model supply chain. *arXiv* **2017**, arXiv:1708.06733.
44. Lee, T.; Edwards, B.; Molloy, I.; Su, D. Defending Against Model Stealing Attacks Using Deceptive Perturbations. *arXiv* **2018**, arXiv:1806.00054.
45. Krizhevsky, A. *Learning Multiple Layers of Features from Tiny Images*; Technical Report; University of Toronto: Toronto, ON, Canada, 2009.
46. Deng, J.; Dong, W.; Socher, R.; Li, L.J.; Li, K.; Fei-Fei, L. ImageNet: A large-scale hierarchical image database. In Proceedings of the IEEE Conference on Computer Vision and Pattern Recognition, Miami, FL, USA, 20–25 June 2009; pp. 248–255.
47. Simonyan, K.; Zisserman, A. Very deep convolutional networks for large-scale image recognition. *arXiv* **2014**, arXiv:1409.1556.
48. Bottou, L. Stochastic gradient descent tricks. In *Neural Networks: Tricks of the Trade*; Springer: Berlin/Heidelberg, Germany, 2012; pp. 421–436.
49. Van Dyk, D.A.; Meng, X.L. The art of data augmentation. *J. Comput. Graph. Stat.* **2001**, *10*, 1–50. [CrossRef]
50. Perez, L.; Wang, J. The effectiveness of data augmentation in image classification using deep learning. *arXiv* **2017**, arXiv:1712.04621.
51. Altshuler, Y.; Pentland, A.; Bruckstein, A.M. Introduction to Swarm Search. In *Swarms and Network Intelligence in Search*; Springer: Berlin/Heidelberg, Germany, 2018; pp. 1–14.
52. Alami, R.; Fleury, S.; Herrb, M.; Ingrand, F.; Robert, F. Multi-Robot Cooperation in the Martha Project. *IEEE Robot. Autom. Mag.* **1998**, *5*, 36–47. [CrossRef]
53. Altshuler, Y.; Wagner, I.; Yanovski, V.; Bruckstein, A. Multi-agent Cooperative Cleaning of Expanding Domains. *Int. J. Robot. Res.* **2010**, *30*, 1037–1071. [CrossRef]
54. Parker, L. ALLIANCE: An Architecture for Fault-Tolerant Multi-Robot Cooperation. *IEEE Trans. Robot. Autom.* **1998**, *14*, 220–240. [CrossRef]
55. Rehak, M.; Pechoucek, M.; Celeda, P.; Krmicek, V.; Grill, M.; Bartos, K. Multi-agent approach to network intrusion detection. In *AAMAS '08: Proceedings of the 7th International Joint Conference on Autonomous Agents and Multiagent Systems*; International Foundation for Autonomous Agents and Multiagent Systems: Richland, SC, USA, 2008; pp. 1695–1696.
56. Altshuler, Y.; Fire, M.; Shmueli, E.; Elovici, Y.; Bruckstein, A.; Pentland, A.S.; Lazer, D. The Social Amplifier—Reaction of Human Communities to Emergencies. *J. Stat. Phys.* **2013**, *152*, 399–418. [CrossRef]
57. Mataric, M. Interaction and Intelligent Behavior. Ph.D. Thesis, Massachusetts Institute of Technology, Cambridge, MA, USA, 1994.
58. MacKenzie, D.; Arkin, R.; Cameron, J. Multiagent Mission Specification and Execution. *Auton. Robot.* **1997**, *4*, 29–52. [CrossRef]
59. Pagello, E.; D'Angelo, A.; Ferrari, C.; Polesel, R.; Rosati, R.; Speranzon, A. Emergent Behaviors of a Robot Team Performing Cooperative Tasks. *Adv. Robot.* **2002**, *17*, 3–19. [CrossRef]
60. Sawhney, R.; Krishna, K.; Srinathan, K.; Mohan, M. On reduced time fault tolerant paths for multiple UAVs covering a hostile terrain. In *AAMAS '08: Proceedings of the 7th International Joint Conference on Autonomous Agents and Multiagent Systems*; International Foundation for Autonomous Agents and Multiagent Systems: Richland, SC, USA, 2008; pp. 1171–1174.
61. Altshuler, T.; Altshuler, Y.; Katoshevski, R.; Shiftan, Y. Modeling and Prediction of Ride-Sharing Utilization Dynamics. *J. Adv. Transp.* **2019**, *2019*, 6125798. [CrossRef]
62. Bhatt, R.; Tang, C.; Krovi, V. Formation optimization for a fleet of wheeled mobile robots—A geometric approach. *Robot. Auton. Syst.* **2009**, *57*, 102–120. [CrossRef]
63. Bendjilali, K.; Belkhouche, F.; Belkhouche, B. Robot formation modelling and control based on the relative kinematics equations. *Int. J. Robot. Autom.* **2009**, *24*, 79–88. [CrossRef]
64. Sariel, S.; Balch, T. Real time auction based allocation of tasks for multi-robot exploration problem in dynamic environments. In Proceedings of the AAAI-05 Workshop on Integrating Planning into Scheduling, Pittsburgh, PA, USA, 9–13 July 2005; pp. 27–33.
65. Somin, S.; Altshuler, Y.; Gordon, G.; Pentland, A.; Shmueli, E. Network Dynamics of a financial ecosystem. *Sci. Rep.* **2020**, *10*, 4587. [CrossRef]
66. Harmatia, I.; Skrzypczykb, K. Robot team coordination for target tracking using fuzzy logic controller in game theoretic framework. *Robot. Auton. Syst.* **2009**, *57*, 75–86. [CrossRef]
67. Parker, L.; Touzet, C. Multi-Robot Learning in a Cooperative Observation Task. *Distrib. Auton. Robot. Syst.* **2000**, *4*, 391–401.

68. Altshuler, Y.; Yanovsky, V.; Wagner, I.; Bruckstein, A. Swarm intelligence—Searchers, cleaners and hunters. *Swarm Intell. Syst.* **2006**, *26*, 93–132.
69. Altshuler, Y.; Yanovski, V.; Wagner, I.; Bruckstein, A. The Cooperative Hunters—Efficient Cooperative Search For Smart Targets Using UAV Swarms. In Proceedings of the Second International Conference on Informatics in Control, Automation and Robotics (ICINCO), the First International Workshop on Multi-Agent Robotic Systems (MARS), Barcelona, Spain, 14–17 September 2005; pp. 165–170.
70. Altshuler, Y.; Pentland, A.; Bruckstein, A.M. *Swarms and Network Intelligence in Search*; Springer: Berlin/Heidelberg, Germany, 2018.
71. Klos, T.; van Ahee, G. Evolutionary dynamics for designing multi-period auctions. In *AAMAS '08: Proceedings of the 7th International Joint Conference on Autonomous Agents and Multiagent Systems*; International Foundation for Autonomous Agents and Multiagent Systems: Richland, SC, USA, 2008; pp. 1589–1592.
72. Arkin, R.; Balch, T. AuRA: Principles and Practice in Review. *J. Exp. Theor. Artif. Intell.* **1997**, *9*, 175–188. [CrossRef]
73. Brooks, R. A Robust Layered Control System for a Mobile Robot. *IEEE J. Robot. Autom.* **1986**, *RA-2*, 14–23. [CrossRef]
74. Su, H.; Wang, X.; Lin, Z. Flocking of Multi-Agents With a Virtual Leader. *IEEE Trans. Autom. Control* **2009**, *54*, 293–307. [CrossRef]
75. Weitzenfeld, A. A Prey Catching and Predator Avoidance Neural-Schema Architecture for Single and Multiple Robots. *J. Intell. Robot. Syst.* **2008**, *51*, 203–233. [CrossRef]
76. Hagelbäck, J.; Johansson, S. Demonstration of multi-agent potential fields in real-time strategy games. In *AAMAS '08: Proceedings of the 7th International Joint Conference on Autonomous Agents and Multiagent Systems*; International Foundation for Autonomous Agents and Multiagent Systems: Richland, SC, USA, 2008; pp. 1687–1688.
77. Altshuler, Y.; Pentland, A.; Bruckstein, A.M. Collaborative Patrolling Swarms in Stochastically Expanding Environments. In *Swarms and Network Intelligence in Search*; Springer: Berlin/Heidelberg, Germany, 2018; pp. 155–185.
78. Trajkovski, G.; Collins, S. *Handbook of Research on Agent-Based Societies: Social and Cultural Interactions*; Idea Group Inc. (IGI): Hershey, PA, USA, 2009.
79. Altshuler, Y.; Pentland, A.; Bekhor, S.; Shiftan, Y.; Bruckstein, A. Optimal Dynamic Coverage Infrastructure for Large-Scale Fleets of Reconnaissance UAVs. *arXiv* **2016**, arXiv:1611.05735.
80. Altshuler, Y.; Puzis, R.; Elovici, Y.; Bekhor, S.; Pentland, A.S. On the Rationality and Optimality of Transportation Networks Defense: A Network Centrality Approach. In *Securing Transportation Systems*; Wiley: Hoboken, NJ, USA, 2015; pp. 35–63.
81. Aknine, S.; Shehory, O. A Feasible and Practical Coalition Formation Mechanism Leveraging Compromise and Task Relationships. In Proceedings of the IEEE/WIC/ACM International Conference on Intelligent Agent Technology, Washington, DC, USA, 18–22 December 2006; pp. 436–439.
82. Altshuler, Y.; Shmueli, E.; Zyskind, G.; Lederman, O.; Oliver, N.; Pentland, A. Campaign Optimization through Mobility Network Analysis. In *Geo-Intelligence and Visualization through Big Data Trends*; IGI Global: Hershey, PA, USA, 2015; pp. 33–74.
83. Altshuler, Y.; Shmueli, E.; Zyskind, G.; Lederman, O.; Oliver, N.; Pentland, A. Campaign Optimization Through Behavioral Modeling and Mobile Network Analysis. *Comput. Soc. Syst. IEEE Trans.* **2014**, *1*, 121–134. [CrossRef]
84. Altshuler, Y.; Pentland, A.S.; Gordon, G. Social Behavior Bias and Knowledge Management Optimization. In *Social Computing, Behavioral-Cultural Modeling, and Prediction*; Springer: Berlin/Heidelberg, Germany, 2015; pp. 258–263.
85. Pagello, E.; D'Angelo, A.; Montesello, F.; Garelli, F.; Ferrari, C. Cooperative Behaviors in Multi-Robot Systems through Implicit Communication. *Robot. Auton. Syst.* **1999**, *29*, 65–77. [CrossRef]
86. Felner, A.; Shoshani, Y.; Altshuler, Y.; Bruckstein, A. Multi-agent Physical A* with Large Pheromones. *J. Auton. Agents Multi-Agent Syst.* **2006**, *12*, 3–34. [CrossRef]
87. Adler, F.; Gordon, D. Information collection and spread by networks of partolling agents. *Am. Nat.* **1992**, *140*, 373–400. [CrossRef]
88. Rouff, C.A.; Truszkowski, W.F.; Rash, J.; Hinchey, M. *A Survey of Formal Methods for Intelligent Swarms*; NASA Goddard Space Flight Center: Greenbelt, MD, USA, 2005.
89. Schultz, A.C.; Parker, L.E. *Multi-Robot Systems: From Swarms to Intelligent Automata: Proceedings from the 2002 NRL Workshop on Multi-Robot Systems*; Springer Science & Business Media: Berlin/Heidelberg, Germany, 2013.
90. Hüttenrauch, M.; Adrian, S.; Neumann, G. Deep reinforcement learning for swarm systems. *J. Mach. Learn. Res.* **2019**, *20*, 1–31.
91. Shi, G.; Hönig, W.; Yue, Y.; Chung, S.J. Neural-swarm: Decentralized close-proximity multirotor control using learned interactions. In Proceedings of the 2020 IEEE International Conference on Robotics and Automation (ICRA), Philadelphia, PA, USA, 23–27 May 2022; pp. 3241–3247.
92. Choi, T.; Pyenson, B.; Liebig, J.; Pavlic, T.P. Beyond Tracking: Using Deep Learning to Discover Novel Interactions in Biological Swarms. *arXiv* **2021**, arXiv:2108.09394.

Article

Organisational Structure and Created Values. Review of Methods of Studying Collective Intelligence in Policymaking

Rafał Olszowski [1,2,*], Piotr Pięta [1], Sebastian Baran [3] and Marcin Chmielowski [4]

[1] Faculty of Humanities, AGH University of Science and Technology, Gramatyka 8a, 30-071 Kraków, Poland; pipieta@agh.edu.pl
[2] Center for Collective Intelligence, Massachusetts Institute of Technology, 245 First Street, E94, Cambridge, MA 02142, USA
[3] Department of Mathematics, Cracow University of Economics, Rakowicka 27, 31-510 Kraków, Poland; sebastian.baran@uek.krakow.pl
[4] Fundacja Wolności i Przedsiębiorczości, Ul. Asnyka 6, 40-696 Katowice, Poland; chmielowski@fundacjawip.org
* Correspondence: rafalols@mit.edu

Abstract: The domain of policymaking, which used to be limited to small groups of specialists, is now increasingly opening up to the participation of wide collectives, which are not only influencing government decisions, but also enhancing citizen engagement and transparency, improving service delivery and gathering the distributed wisdom of diverse participants. Although collective intelligence has become a more common approach to policymaking, the studies on this subject have not been conducted in a systematic way. Nevertheless, we hypothesized that methods and strategies specific to different types of studies in this field could be identified and analyzed. Based on a systematic literature review, as well as qualitative and statistical analyses, we identified 15 methods and revealed the dependencies between them. The review indicated the most popular approaches, and the underrepresented ones that can inspire future research.

Keywords: collective intelligence; crowdsourcing; policymaking; public policy; e-participation; literature review

1. Introduction

The phenomenon of collective intelligence (CI), which is understood as an ability of a particular collective to solve problems, mainly through gathering data, generating ideas and making decisions, has been the subject of interest of many scientific disciplines in recent years. The primary characteristic of a collective showing a high CI level is its capability to solve problems in which the difficulty exceeds the capacity of an individual. CI frequently manifests itself when cooperation, competition or mutual observation gives rise to totally new solutions to the problems or leads to an increase in the ability to solve them. Contemporary studies on CI, although clearly inspired by the development of the Internet in their origins, have so far been carried out in very diverse disciplines, from biology, through social sciences and organization management, to artificial intelligence.

Several empirical studies and theoretical simulations have proven that a collective can, under certain conditions, achieve better results in problem solving than a narrow group of experts [1–5]. To date, this phenomenon has been studied both as a feature of small groups, in which ties and interactions between participants are strong and the deliberation processes lead to informed intellectual outputs [6,7], and as a statistical phenomenon resulting from the aggregation of a vast number of dispersed opinions coming from incoherent crowds [8,9]. The most promising examples of recent projects in which a high level of CI was observed have combined humans and machines, organizations, and ICT networks [3]. The current empirical studies on CI are therefore largely focused on interactions between users in online communities. In parallel, theoretical work has been carried out to simulate collective behavior with the use of computational methods. One of the most interesting is the approach called swarm intelligence (SI), which takes its inspiration from the biological examples provided by social insects such as ants, termites, bees and flocks of birds. In this model, self-organization takes place in decentralized communities in which the logical process is multi-threaded, chaotic and parallel; in which the threads intertwine and interlock; and in which the agents exhibit adaptive behavior, while also maximizing the number of diverse future paths among the possible choices. Simulations show the possible effectiveness of such a decision model, but its application to real social processes is not easy [10–12].

The domain of policymaking (i.e., formulating public policies), which used to be strictly limited to small groups of specialists, is now increasingly opening up to the participation of wide collectives, which are not only influencing government decisions, but also enhancing citizen engagement and transparency, improving service delivery and gathering the distributed wisdom of diverse participants [13–16]. National and local governments use CI methods in the policymaking processes, such as in legislative reforms [17,18], urban strategy planning [16], analyzing large amounts of social data to detect patterns and abnormalities [19,20], using dynamic models for learning, adaptation and forecasting of policy formulation [21,22], real-time continuous policy monitoring [15,23], as well as online public debates and consultations [24,25]. Opening policymaking tasks to public participation, fuelled by the theories of participatory democracy [26,27] and the concept of deliberative democracy [28], has found its practical expression in a paradigm shift towards collaborative governance [29,30], in which policy issues are addressed by networks of governmental and non-governmental actors. However, some models of CI, especially those that are characteristic of swarm intelligence, seem to be very difficult to reconcile with the common understanding of policymaking.

Although collective intelligence has become a more common approach to policymaking, the studies on this subject have not been conducted in a systematic way. The methods of studying the theoretical models, the successful case studies, the public sphere domains in which projects can be implemented, the expected results and the factors influencing CI vary greatly depending on the scientific discipline in which they are conducted. Moreover, different research traditions often use alternative terminologies to describe the same phenomena, an example of which is the competitive use of the labels "crowdsourcing" and "collective intelligence". Furthermore, there has been no scientific literature review regarding the phenomenon of CI in the field of policymaking. Research methods and strategies used in the studies conducted so far have not been systematized either. Nevertheless, we hypothesized that the methods and strategies specific to different types of CI studies in the field of policymaking can be identified and analyzed.

In order to better understand the present state of knowledge in this field, we raised the main research question (RQ1): what methods and strategies were specific to the studies on collective intelligence in policymaking during the last 10 years? What was the trend in the number of publications by year, and what were the most common concepts that appeared in the studies concerning CI in policymaking?

To supplement the knowledge about the methods and strategies we planned to identify, additional research questions were established:

RQ2: what statistical dependencies occurred between the identified research methods? What dependencies occurred between the research methods and other features of the analyzed studies?

RQ3: in which research areas were the studies conducted? What research methods and strategies were used in the specific research areas?

RQ4: what research methods and strategies were employed in the most influential works and in the topics of special importance for the study of CI in policymaking?

To answer these questions, we conducted a systematic literature review. On this basis, using the grounded theory method, we were able to categorize the identified approaches into a list of 15 methods and strategies and subsequently performed a series of analyses, described later in this article. With the use of statistical analyses, we revealed the dependencies between different study methods, as well as between study methods and other variables. Our cross-sectional analysis has produced interesting results, which may form the foundation for future projects.

2. Materials and Methods

To answer the research questions posed, we divided the work into the tasks described below. In order to answer Research Question 1, we adopted the following work plan:

a. Task 1.1. Selection of a database of scientific articles to be searched;
b. Task 1.2. Search for the studies on collective intelligence in policymaking in the last 10 years, based on selected keywords;
c. Task 1.3. Verification of the trend in the number of articles published per year;
d. Task 1.4. Search for the most common concepts and terms that appear in the articles;
e. Task 1.5. Identification of the methods and strategies of studying CI in policymaking.

The method used in the first stage of our research was a systematic literature review. This literature review followed the Preferred Reporting Items for Systematic reviews and Meta-analyses (PRISMA) methodology [31]. This section clearly articulates guidelines regarding the inclusion or exclusion criteria of research papers to find relevant papers in our research area. We have also clearly mentioned how and to what extent the review was performed. The PRISMA flowchart for the research process is shown in Figure 1.

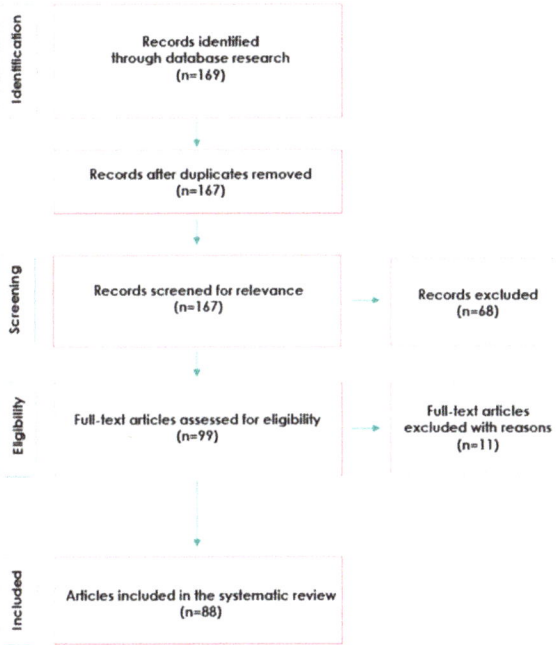

Figure 1. Flow diagram of the article-selection process.

When selecting keywords, alternative terms of CI used in the literature were taken into account, including "collective intelligence", "crowdsourcing", "swarm intelligence", "wisdom of crowds" and "crowdlaw". These concepts, although not fully identical, have an established position, and are used by researchers to describe similar phenomena, depending on the background of individual authors (the relationships and differences between these concepts were described by Buecheler [32]). The second set of keywords included concepts related to political science, administration and governance: "policymaking" (variants: "policy-making" and "policy making"), "public policy", "political science", "public administration", "public sector" and "public governance". The Web of Science was chosen from a number of pre-selected databases (other databases considered were Scopus, Sciencedirect and EBSCO) because of its reputation for the greatest coverage and the greatest impact in terms of most cited authors and articles, as well as for the most accurate subject classification. Search engines, such as Google Scholar, were excluded, as our priority was to select peer-reviewed publications. The timeframe for the search was set for the period from 2011 to 2020. The data search was conducted on March 8, 2020. We applied the logical search to the topic (including the abstract, keywords and indexed fields), as well as the titles of the scientific articles. The inclusion criteria were focused on peer-reviewed scientific articles dealing with issues in the field of public policymaking and combining them with methods, models and concepts derived from the CI research domain. In addition, we used the language filter to focus on the publications in English.

The logical search used the following syntax: TS = ((("Collective Intelligence" OR "Crowdsourcing" OR "Swarm Intelligence" OR "Wisdom of crowds" OR "Crowdlaw") AND ("Policy Making" OR "Policy-making" OR "policymaking" OR "Public Policy" OR "Public Administration" OR "Political Science" OR "Public Sector" OR "Public Governance" OR "e-participation")) OR TI = ((("Collective Intelligence" OR "Crowdsourcing" OR "Swarm Intelligence" OR "Wisdom of crowds" OR "Crowdlaw") AND ("Policy Making" OR "Policy-making" OR "policymaking" OR "Public Policy" OR "Public Administration" OR "Political Science" OR "Public Sector" OR "Public Governance" OR "e-participation")).

This search led to an initial total of 169 references, and after removing the duplicates, that number reached 167. Then, in accordance with the guidelines of H. Snyder [33], the content of all articles was screened in terms of checking the inclusion criteria, according to the title-abstract-references scheme, which allowed us to identify the content that did not meet the criteria described above and remove it from the database. To focus on high-quality literature, we excluded the conference proceedings, editorial materials and reviews, and excluded articles written in a language other than English. Another 10 articles were excluded during the eligibility assessment due to the fact that they obviously did not concern the topic of review (e.g., their topic was tourism, citizen science initiatives, the student learning environment, etc.). This led to the refined list of 88 results. By creating the list as described above, it was possible to check how many articles were published annually and what the trends were in the number of publications per year.

The content of the articles was evaluated by our team of 3 experts, with experience and academic backgrounds in both policymaking and information technologies (2 experts with a PhD in political science and experience working on ICT projects, and 1 expert with an MA in IT and experience in working in social projects). The preliminary analysis was made by creating lists of the most common concepts that appeared in article titles, article abstracts, original keywords, as well as KeyWords Plus. The next stage, a qualitative research step, the purpose of which was to extract the methods and strategies of studying CI in policymaking from the analyzed texts, was based on the grounded theory approach. We applied this approach for extracting the theoretical value from the selected studies, grouping and presenting the key concepts, conceptualizing and articulating the concepts and distilling the categories from them. The analysis included stages that were specific to the grounded theory method: open coding, axial coding and selective coding. The open coding stage involved an analytical process of generating high-abstraction level type categories from sets of concepts. In this stage we focused on extracting keywords specific to the analyzed texts that appeared in titles and abstracts. The analysis of keywords allowed for a preliminary division of the texts into 11 subgroups, which became the initial categories. The next stage, i.e., axial coding, aimed to identify the key processes and the main research results described in the examined articles. We adopted an iterative method of working: texts were analyzed in groups of 10, using the existing categories, and then categories were redefined, combined or divided, and their definitions were developed. The emerging categories were grounded during the progressive analysis of subsequent texts from our sample. Then, at the stage of selective coding, the categories were finally integrated and refined [34]. Theoretical saturation was achieved when, during the analysis of the following texts, no new concepts, properties or interesting links arose [35]. Based on the review of the references included in the analyzed texts and the relevant theoretical literature, we adopted the final definitions to describe the identified methods. As a result of the analysis described above, 1 to 5 methods or strategies were identified in each reviewed text, and the general list of 15 methods of studies on CI in the field of policymaking was proposed.

After completing the work described above, we attempted to answer the additional research questions. To answer RQ 2, the following tasks were planned:

a. Task 2.1. Checking what number of research methods were used on average per article;
b. Task 2.2. Analyzing the changes in the popularity of the use of particular methods in the analyzed period;
c. Task 2.3. Finding statistical dependencies between research methods;
d. Task 2.4. Finding dependencies between research methods and other features of the analyzed studies (number of citations, usage, number of pages, publication year).

This stage of our research was a series of statistical analyses. The first two tasks were based on the simple counting of averages and the visualization of trends. Then, to analyze the dependencies between research methods, we used Pearson's Chi-squared test of independence, and Yates's correction for continuity (Yates's Chi-squared test). Next, analyzing the dependencies between research methods and other features of the analyzed studies, we had to perform a Shapiro–Wilk test of normality for all continuous variables, the Chi squared of independence test, and statistical analysis based on Pearson's Chi-squared test of independence. Finally, we used the Fisher exact test of independence.

In order to answer Research Question 3, we planned the following tasks:

a. Task 3.1. Identification of the research areas of the studies;
b. Task 3.2. Grouping the related research areas, taking into account the specificity of the researched issue;
c. Task 3.3. Analysis of the number of studies published yearly within the research area groups;
d. Task 3.4. Identification of which methods and strategies of studying CI in policy-making were used more frequently and which were used less frequently within the research area groups.

Based on the WoS Research Areas, we verified in which scientific disciplines the studies were conducted, and what was their number. For the further analytical purposes, we grouped the related scientific disciplines into collections, taking into account the special position of the computer sciences and political sciences. On this basis we tracked the yearly number of studies in each research area group and the most common methods and strategies in each research area.

Finally, to answer Research Question 4, the following tasks were planned:

a. Task 4.1 Ranking of the top 10 articles based on usage and citation criteria to identify the most influential works;
b. Task 4.2. Identification of which methods and strategies were used more frequently and which were used less frequently in the "top 10" groups;
c. Task 4.3. Ranking the topics of special importance for the study of CI in policymaking;
d. Task 4.4. Identification of which methods and strategies were used more frequently and which were used less frequently in the "topics of special importance" groups.

To analyze the most influential studies, we ranked the top 10 articles based on usage and citation criteria, obtained from the Web of Science statistics. On this basis we tracked the most common methods and strategies in each research area. Then, building the ranking of topics of special importance, to ensure data triangulation and to avoid duplicating regularities already detected, in the selection of topics we relied on a different method than the one used in the earlier stages of this work. The monographic publications concerning the issues of collective intelligence and policymaking were shortlisted. Due to the scarcity of monographic literature, only 8 publications were included in this list after the review. On this basis, an initial list of 20 concepts was compiled. Subsequently, a survey was conducted in which a group of 6 social science researchers were invited to assess the significance of the proposed issues. Thus, the final list of 7 concepts that were subject to analysis was selected, and we searched our literature database for keywords specific to each of these concepts. The identified sub-groups of studies were analyzed in terms of the research methods and strategies that were adopted.

3. Results

3.1. Methods and Strategies of Studying CI in Policymaking

3.1.1. Number of Articles in the Selected Database and the Growth Trend

As described above, the Web of Science database was selected for our review, and studies were searched within it according to the adopted criteria. After the initial analysis, it was discovered that none of the reviewed articles were published in 2011. The first article that met the inclusion criteria appeared in 2012. In the years 2012–2017, we observed a clear increase in interest in the issue under study. The peak period of interest was 2017, when 18 articles were published. Despite the decrease observed later, 2020 was again characterized by an increase in the number of publications compared to the previous year (see Figure 2 below).

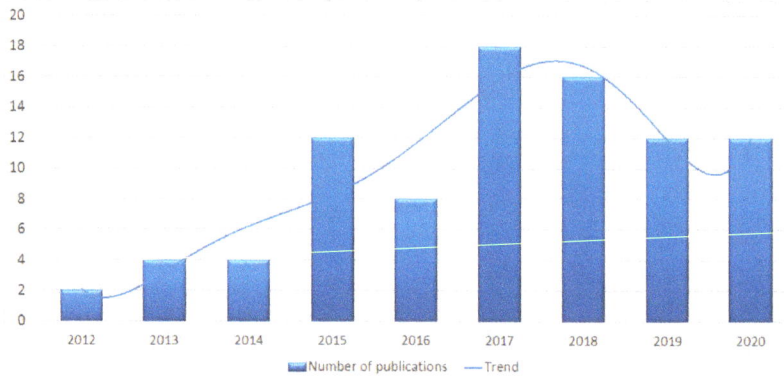

Figure 2. Number of articles concerning the issues of collective intelligence and policymaking published annually, and the growth trend for the period 2012–2020.

3.1.2. Concepts and Terms That Appeared in the Articles

We analyzed the content of the research articles included in the review, and created lists of the most common concepts that appeared in article titles, article abstracts, original keywords, as well as KeyWords Plus generated by the Web of Science algorithm [36]. The results are presented below in Table 1.

Table 1. Rankings of top 10 concepts based on: (a) article titles, (b) article abstracts, (c) author keywords, (d) KeyWords Plus.

(a) Top 10 Concepts in ARTICLE TITLES		(b) Top 10 Concepts in ARTICLE ABSTRACTS	
Concept	Number of Occurrences	Concept	Number of Occurrences
Crowdsourcing	24	Public	153
Open	16	Crowdsourcing	125
Public	16	Government	84
Social	13	Data	82
Innovation	11	Social	79
Case	10	Open	78
Government	9	Innovation	76
Participation	9	Research	64
Online	9	Policy	63
Policy	9	Online	51

(c) Top 10 Concepts in AUTHOR KEYWORDS		(d) Top 10 Concepts in KEYWORDS PLUS	
Concept	Number of Occurrences	Concept	Number of Occurrences
Crowdsourcing	50	Participation	14
Open	21	Innovation	14
Public	21	Media	9
Policy	19	Social	9
Government	16	Coproduction	8
Innovation	16	Government	8
Social	14	E-Government	7
Participation	11	Information	6
Data	10	Democracy	6
Democracy	10	Engagement	6

3.1.3. Identifying Methods and Strategies of Studying CI in Policymaking

In this section, the methods and strategies of studying CI in policymaking, which were identified in the analyzed texts, are presented. As described in Section 2, 15 methods and strategies were identified in the reviewed sample, and each text was associated with a minimum of one and a maximum of five methods. In Table 2 we present a list of identified methods and strategies, ranked from the most to the least popular, and the adopted definitions, supplemented with references to theoretical literature.

As we can see, the analysis of organizational structure/design was the most popular method. Fewer studies used the analysis of created values approach. Subsequent identified methods, such as the analysis of the e-participation process, the analysis of participants' behavior or collaboration models enjoyed moderate popularity. On the other hand, the least frequently used methods included the analysis of platform usability, analysis of the impact of AI algorithms and analysis of organizational learning. The relatively rare occurrence of the analysis of impact on policymaking approach is also worth noting.

Table 2. Methods and strategies of studying CI in policymaking identified in the reviewed literature.

No.	Method of Studying CI	Description	Literature	No. of Assigned Articles
1.	Analysis of organisational structure/design (RM1)	The studies conducted from organisational perspective. Analysis covers the structures that facilitate the coordination and implementation of rules, resources, technologies, stakeholders, and particular tasks in specific projects or initiatives of open policymaking. These studies present the systems for accomplishing and connecting the activities that occur within examined work organisations, enabling the emergence of CI.	[37–39]	31
2.	Analysis of created values (RM2)	The studies aim to answer the question: What kind of valuable results were produced in the analysed projects? The analysis of outputs, concerning that they are more valuable, than the inputs, is conducted. For example: epistemic, democratic and economic values in increasing the quality of public service provision can be analysed.	[40,41]	25
3.	Analysis of e-participation process (RM3)	The aim of the studies is an analysis of factors that influence the technologically supported participation, or e-participation, which can be defined as participation in societal democratic and consultative processes mediated by information and communication technologies, primarily the internet [13] or as the use of information technologies to engage in discourse among citizens and between citizens and elected or appointed officials over public policy issues [41].	[13,42]	17
4.	Analysis of participants' behaviour (RM4)	The studies aim to answer the question: What sort of various activities was performed by the users of the examined policymaking platforms and initiatives, what types of operations did they engage in, and how was it related to their individual characteristics.	[43]	16
5.	Analysis of collaboration model (RM5)	It is investigated what forms of collaboration between governmental and non-governmental entities occur in the area under study, and what factors influence its facilitation.	[44]	16
6.	Analysis of participants' motivations (RM6)	The studies focus on understanding the participants' motivations to engage in open policymaking projects.	[43,45]	11
7.	Analysis of communication model (RM7)	Analyses of the communication processes, information exchange, establishing information channels between public and civic entities, extraction of valuable information, and the mutual understanding of the content provided are performed.	[46,47]	9
8.	Analysis of innovation process (RM8)	Investigating the critical aspects of innovation process in the studied policymaking projects and initiatives/. The studies aim to answer the following questions: what influences innovation capacity, how to stimulate pro-innovative behaviour, what are the potential positive and negative impacts of the outcomes of the innovation processes.	[44,48,49]	9

Table 2. *Cont.*

No.	Method of Studying CI	Description	Literature	No. of Assigned Articles
9.	Analysis of decision-making process (RM9)	The studies aim to answer the question: How collective intelligent policy decisions are made, and what affects the quality of the decision-making process. The analysis of processes, sub-processes, and data related to collective decision-making is conducted.	[50,51]	8
10.	Analysis of the impact on policymaking (RM10)	The studies present the observed impact of the analysed projects on creating public policies, assess the significance of this impact and factors that influenced it.	[52,53]	7
11.	Categorization of the implemented projects (RM11)	Typologies of various governmental or non-governmental initiatives and projects, engaging citizens in policymaking in a model that consider the emergence of collective intelligence, are presented.	[54]	5
12.	State-of-the-art review (RM12)	The state of research and practices are presented in these studies in a cross-sectional manner. The studies focus on collecting, categorizing and situating the previously published research and practices in the field, coming from the multiple disciplines.	[37,53]	4
13.	Analysis of platform usability (RM13)	These studies aim on understanding the structure of policy-oriented websites, their functions, interfaces and the contents; simplicity of use; the site navigation, and the ability of users to control their activities.	[55,56]	4
14.	Analysis of the impact of AI algorithms (RM14)	The aim of these studies is an analysis of the possibilities of using AI techniques in CI processes occurring in policymaking initiatives, and the possible effects of their operation.	[57]	3
15.	Analysis of organisational learning (RM15)	The studies focus on organisational learning, as the process of creating, retaining, and transferring knowledge within an policymaking organisation, when an organisation improves over time as it gains experience.	[58]	1

3.2. Statistical Analysis

3.2.1. Number of Methods per Article

On average, 1.89 methods were used per article. Figure 3 visualizes the number of research articles using a specified number of methods. It can be noted that a majority of the analyzed articles used at most two methods.

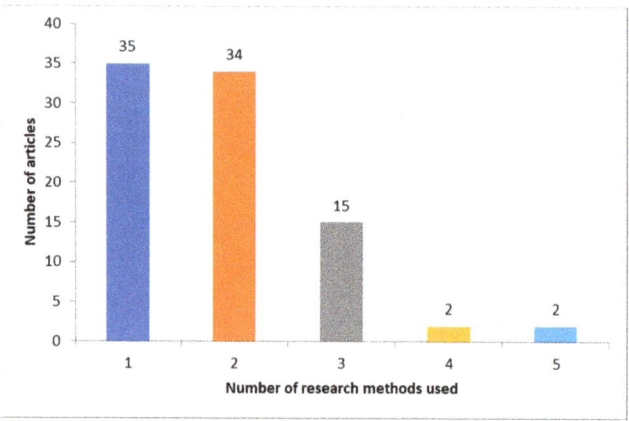

Figure 3. The number of research articles using specified numbers of methods.

3.2.2. Changes in the Popularity of Using Particular Methods

Changes in the number of articles using the identified methods appearing in subsequent years were also analyzed. The chart below shows the yearly numbers of articles using the seven most common methods and strategies, in the period 2012–2020. We can observe that although the analysis of organizational structure has been the most widely used method since 2016, it has recently lost its popularity, falling behind the analysis of created values. In turn, the analysis of the e-participation process, which enjoyed a peak in interest in 2015, has now largely lost its relevance. A similar decline in interest can be observed in relation to the analysis of collaboration model, which peaked in 2018. (as can be seen below in Figure 4).

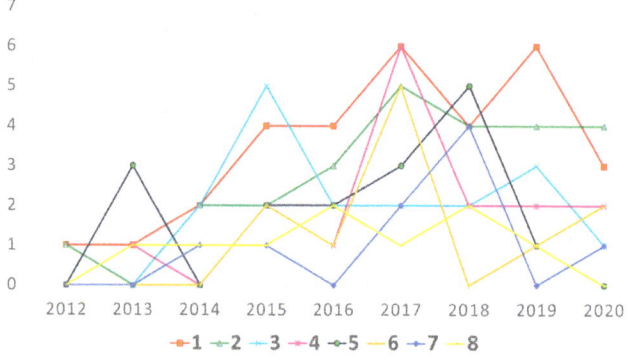

Figure 4. The number of research studies using the following methods: (1) analysis of organizational structure/design, (2) analysis of created values, (3) analysis of e-participation process, (4) analysis of participants' behavior, (5) analysis of collaboration model, (6) analysis of participants' motivations, (7) analysis of communication model, (8) analysis of innovation process.

3.2.3. Dependencies between Research Methods

In this section we answer the question of whether there are any dependencies between the various research methods. It is common that when we want to investigate the relationship between variables, we calculate the classical Pearson's correlation coefficient. However, Pearson's correlation coefficient should only be applied to check the dependency between two continuous variables. In our situation this is not the case because the variables describing the usage of research methods are binary variables, answering the question of whether a particular method was used or not. When we are looking for relationships between binary or categorical variables, the commonly used statistical test is Pearson's Chi-squared test of independence. We performed Pearson's Chi-squared test between each pair of variables out of all 15 variables, describing the research methods in Table 2. The results can be seen in Table 3.

Table 3. *p*-values from Pearson's Chi-squared test of independence applied to each pair of research method variables (where, for example, RM1 stands for Research Method 1). The assignment of particular methods and strategies to the labels numbered from RM1 to RM15 is described in Table 2.

	RM 1	RM 2	RM 3	RM 4	RM 5	RM 6	RM 7	RM 8	RM 9	RM 10	RM 11	RM 12	RM 13	RM 14	RM 15
RM1	0.000														
RM2	0.371	0.000													
RM3	0.089	0.273	0.000												
RM4	0.089	**0.030**	0.143	0.000											
RM5	0.430	**0.005**	0.524	0.434	0.000										
RM6	0.933	**0.026**	0.919	**0.000**	1.000	0.000									
RM7	0.541	0.225	0.816	0.562	0.214	0.894	0.000								
RM8	0.900	0.225	0.261	0.136	**0.002**	0.231	0.285	0.000							
RM9	0.158	0.062	0.608	0.600	0.662	1.000	0.824	0.317	0.000						
RM10	0.227	0.377	0.177	0.781	0.781	0.882	0.712	0.712	0.383	0.000					
RM11	0.090	0.668	0.260	0.278	0.278	0.384	0.437	0.437	0.467	0.498	0.000				
RM12	0.131	0.197	0.317	0.335	0.335	0.439	0.490	0.490	0.517	0.547	**0.000**	0.000			
RM13	0.661	0.877	0.317	0.717	0.091	0.439	0.318	0.490	0.257	0.547	0.615	0.655	0.000		
RM14	0.944	0.267	0.388	0.406	0.489	0.505	0.179	0.552	0.137	0.604	0.665	0.701	**0.000**	0.000	
RM15	0.458	0.526	0.623	0.635	0.635	0.704	0.734	0.734	0.750	0.767	0.805	0.826	0.826	0.850	0.000

The statistical analysis based on Pearson's Chi-squared test of independence showed that in most cases there was no statistically significant evidence of a statistical relationship between research methods (p-value > 0.05). The analysis showed that only in seven cases (highlighted in bold in Table 3) was there a significant statistical dependency between certain specific research methods (p-value < 0.05). We discuss these dependencies based on the results from Table 4 below and in Figure A1 in the Appendix A.

It must be noted that one of the assumptions of Pearson's Chi-squared test of independence is the fact that the value of the contingency table cell should be five or more in at least 80% of the cells, and no cell should have a value less than one. Unfortunately, all the contingency tables from Table 4 have at least one cell with a value smaller than five; therefore, the assumption above was not met. Since this was the case, we applied Yates's correction for continuity (Yates's Chi-squared test) [59]. The results can be seen in Table 5.

After Yates's correction there were only five cases with significant statistical dependency between certain specific research methods (p-value < 0.05). However, three of them were statistically highly significant (p-value < 0.001).

Table 4. Contingency tables of Pearson's Chi-squared test of independence for the variables with statistically significant dependency. The assignment of particular methods and strategies to the labels numbered from RM1 to RM15 is described in Table 2.

	Research Method 4				Research Method 5		
Research Method 2	0	1	Sum	Research Method 2	0	1	Sum
0	48	15	63	0	16	47	63
1	24	1	25	1	0	25	25
Sum	72	16	88	Sum	16	72	88
	Research Method 6				Research Method 6		
Research Method 2	0	1	Sum	Research Method 4	0	1	Sum
0	52	11	63	0	68	4	72
1	25	0	25	1	9	7	16
Sum	77	11	88	Sum	77	11	88
	Research Method 8				Research Method 12		
Research Method 5	0	1	Sum	Research Method 11	0	1	Sum
0	5	11	16	0	82	1	83
1	4	68	72	1	2	3	5
Sum	9	79	88	Sum	84	4	88
	Research Method 14						
Research Method 13	0	1	Sum				
0	83	1	84				
1	2	2	4				
Sum	85	3	88				

Table 5. *p*-values from Yates's Chi-squared test of independence.

Relationship between	RM2 & RM4	RM2 & RM5	RM2 & RM6	RM4 & RM6	RM5 & RM8	RM11 & RM12	RM13 & RM14
p-value	0.062	0.013	0.061	0.00016	0.009	5.05×10^{-7}	0.00012

Finally, we can conclude that there are five statistically significant relationships between research method variables: A relationship between analysis of created values and analysis of collaboration model, between analysis of participants' behavior and analysis of participants' motivations, between analysis of collaboration model and analysis of innovation process, between categorization of the implemented projects and state-of-the-art review, and finally between analysis of platform usability and analysis of the impact of AI algorithms. Note that the Chi-squared test of independence does not not give an answer as to what kind of dependency exists between variables. It only answers the question of whether there is dependency between variables. To find the limits on what can be shown from the analysis we looked at the contingency tables and corresponding figures and checked if we were able to draw any conclusions from them. From Table 5 and Figure A1 we can suppose that the latter four relationships rely on the fact that in the vast majority of cases, both of these methods were not used simultaneously. In the case of the relationship between analysis of created values and analysis of collaboration model, we can hypothesize that the discontinuation of the analysis of created values method was associated with an increase in the applicability of the analysis of collaboration model method. However, in this case the relationship between variables was not obvious.

3.2.4. Dependencies between Research Methods and Other Features of the Analyzed Studies

In this section, we investigate whether there are relationships between the research method used and other article features such as citations, popularity, number of pages and year of publication. As before, in order to perform statistical analysis, we used binary variables describing the use of the peculiar research method in the articles. The variables describing article features are the following: Cited Reference Count, Times Cited WoS Core, Times Cited All Databases, 180 Day Usage Count, Since 2013 Usage Count, Number of Pages and Publication Year (all variables defined in the Web of Science specification [60]). All the above variables except the last one are continuous-type variables and the last one is categorical. In the case of the last variable, the matter is simple. In order to check its relationship with binary variables describing the research methods used, we used the Chi-squared test of independence as before. To check the relationship between binary variables and the other six continuous variables, we calculated the point biserial correlation coefficient. Note that one of the assumptions of the point biserial correlation is the fact that the continuous variable is normally distributed. To check this assumption we plotted histograms, quantile-to-quantile plots and performed the Shapiro–Wilk test of normality for all six continuous variables. The results are shown in Table 6, Figures 5 and 6.

Table 6. *p*-values of the Shapiro–Wilk test of normality applied for variables: Cited Reference Count, Times Cited WoS Core, Times Cited All Databases, 180 Day Usage Count, Since 2013 Usage Count, Number of Pages.

Cited Reference Count	Times Cited WoS Core	Times Cited All Databases
8.85×10^{-5}	1.37×10^{-18}	1.28×10^{-18}
180 Day Usage Count	**Since 2013 Usage Count**	**Number of Pages**
6.3×10^{-16}	6.78×10^{-16}	0.0307

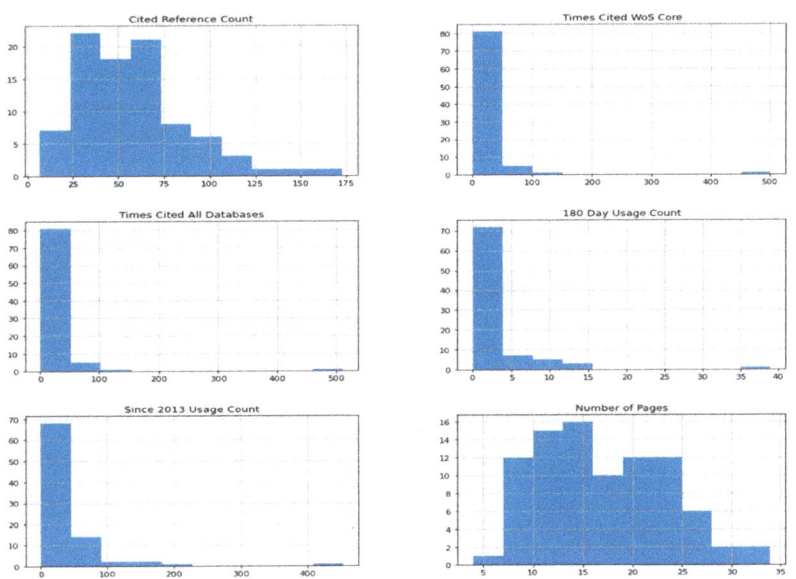

Figure 5. Histograms of the variables: Cited Reference Count, Times Cited WoS Core, Times Cited All Databases, 180 Day Usage Count, Since 2013 Usage Count, Number of Pages.

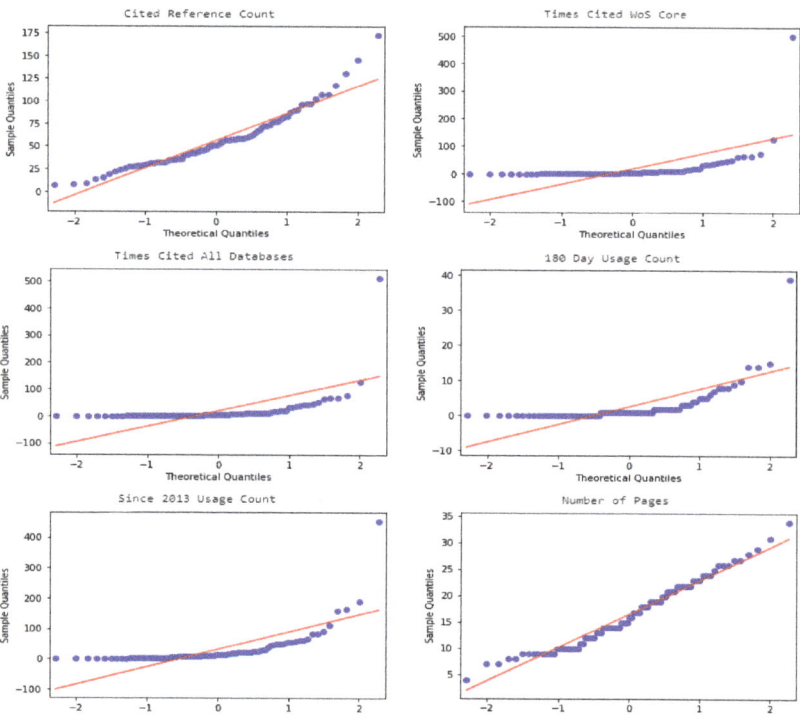

Figure 6. Q–Q plots of the variables: Cited Reference Count, Times Cited WoS Core, Times Cited All Databases, 180 Day Usage Count, Since 2013 Usage Count, Number of Pages.

From the histogram plots in Figure 5 we can see that only the distribution of the Number of Pages variable is approximately bell-shaped and therefore looks like a normal distribution. The quantile-to-quantile plots from Figure 6 confirm that only the Number of Pages variable may be normally distributed (because the values are arranged along a straight line). However, if we look at Table 6, we see that the p-values of the Shapiro–Wilk test of normality of all the considered variables are small (p-value < 0.05) and therefore we must reject the null hypothesis that a sample came from a normally distributed population. Since one of the assumptions of point biserial correlation was not met, we could not use this method to investigate the relationship between binary research method variables and the variables describing article features. However, we used a different solution. We grouped the values of continuous variables into one of three categories: low, medium and high, according to the scheme described in Table 7, and then we used the Chi-squared test of independence as before. The Publication year variable is already a categorical variable. However, due to the fact that it has nine values and the sample size is small, we also grouped its values into three categories. The remaining variables were grouped so that the size of each class was at least 10 and that all classes were more or less equal.

Table 7. Qualifying intervals for variables.

	Low		Medium		High	
	Range	N	Range	N	Range	N
Cited Reference Count	0–40.71	29	40.72–59.42	29	59.43–173	30
Times Cited WoS Core	0–3	34	4–11	27	12–502	27
Times Cited All Databases	0–3	33	4–11	27	12–512	28
180 Day Usage Count	0	30	1–2	38	3–39	20
Since 2013 Usage Count	0–8	33	9–23.42	25	23.43–454	30
Publication Year	2012–2014	10	2015–2017	38	2018–2020	40
Number of Pages	4–13	31	14–19	29	20–34	28

We performed the Chi-squared test of independence for all pairs such that the first variable in the pair was a binary variable describing the research method used and the second variable in the pair was a continuous variable describing the features of the article. The results of the analysis are shown in Table 8.

Table 8. p-values from the Pearson's Chi-squared test of independence (where CRC stands for Cited Reference Count, CW for Times Cited WoS Core, CA for Times Cited All Databases, 180U for 180 Day Usage Count, 2013U for Since 2013 Usage Count, PY for Publication Year and NoP for Number of Pages).

	RM 1	RM 2	RM 3	RM 4	RM 5	RM 6	RM 7	RM 8	RM 9	RM 10	RM 11	RM 12	RM 13	RM 14	RM 15
CRC	0.929	0.750	0.149	0.376	0.554	0.197	0.246	0.211	0.382	0.329	0.071	**0.017**	0.338	**0.042**	0.357
CW	0.905	0.232	0.156	0.775	0.456	0.906	0.188	0.511	0.503	0.586	0.340	0.124	0.892	0.085	0.319
CA	0.954	0.298	0.415	0.748	0.454	0.897	0.181	0.563	0.465	0.560	0.052	0.141	0.869	0.075	0.319
180U	0.398	**0.049**	0.983	0.113	0.879	0.157	0.633	0.054	0.944	0.407	0.959	0.361	0.925	0.447	0.376
2013U	0.239	0.726	0.877	0.929	0.850	0.823	0.505	0.780	0.258	0.939	0.907	0.864	0.318	0.263	0.430
PY	0.872	0.930	0.623	0.473	0.545	0.087	0.798	0.505	0.944	0.159	0.484	0.398	0.763	0.155	0.545
NoP	0.848	**0.005**	0.848	0.512	0.479	**0.038**	0.272	0.704	0.656	0.543	0.812	0.758	0.758	**0.042**	0.357

The statistical analysis based on the Pearson's Chi-squared test of independence showed that in most cases there is no statistically significant evidence that there is a statistical relationship between research methods and article features (p-value > 0.05). The analysis showed that only in six cases (highlighted in bold in Table 8) there is a significant statistical dependency between certain specific research methods and article features (p-value < 0.05). We discuss these dependencies based on the results from Table 9 below and in Figure A2 in Appendix A.

For the two first relationships from Table 9, we have enough value in each cell of the contingency table so we can conclude that there is a statistical relationship between the Analysis of created values method and 180 Day Usage Count variable—the use of this method translates into popularity among readers. There is also a statistical relationship between the Analysis of created values method and the number of pages of the article. In this case, it is easy to see from the chart that the use of this research method is related to the reduction of the number of pages of the article in which this method is used.

Table 9. Contingency tables of the Pearson's Chi-squared test of independence for the variables with statistically significant dependency.

	180 Day Usage Count					Number of Pages			
Research Method 2	High 180U	Medium 180U	Low 180U	Sum	Research Method 2	4–13	14–19	20–34	Sum
0	11	32	20	63	0	16	22	25	63
1	9	6	10	25	1	15	7	3	25
Sum	20	38	30	88	Sum	31	29	28	88
	Number of Pages					Cited Reference Count			
Research Method 6	4–13	14–19	20–34	Sum	Research Method 12	Low CR	High CR	Medium CR	Sum
0	30	26	21	77	0	29	26	29	84
1	1	3	7	11	1	0	4	0	4
Sum	31	29	28	88	Sum	29	30	29	88
	Cited Reference Count					Number of Pages			
Research Method 14	Low CR	High CR	Medium CR	Sum	Research Method 14	4–13	14–19	20–34	Sum
0	26	30	29	85	0	31	26	28	85
1	3	0	0	3	1	0	3	0	3
Sum	29	30	29	88	Sum	31	29	28	88

Unfortunately, the other four contingency tables from Table 9 have at least one cell with value smaller than five; therefore, we should apply Yates's correction for continuity. However Yates's correction for continuity is mainly applied for 2 × 2 contingency tables. This is not our case, so we have to use a different statistical test to resolve the remaining four cases. We performed Fisher's exact test, which is also commonly employed when sample sizes are small or the data are very unequally distributed among the cells of the contingency table. The results of the Fisher exact test can be seen in Table 10.

Table 10. p-values from the Fisher exact test of independence (where RM6 stands for Research method 6, NoP for number of Pages and CRC for cited reference count).

Relationship between	RM6 & NoP	RM14 & NoP	RM14 & CRC	RM12 & CRC
p-value	0.042	0.063	0.067	0.032

From the Fisher exact test, it follows that there are two more statistical relationships (p-value < 0.05) between the analysis of participants' motivations method and the number of pages of the article, the state-of-the-art review method and the cited reference count. Again from Table 9 and Figure A2, we can draw some conclusions. It appears that use of the analysis of participants' motivations method is related to the increase of the number of pages of the article. Moreover, it seems that use of state-of-the-art review method has a positive impact on Cited Reference Count.

The last relationship we looked for was the relationship between the number of methods used in the articles and the features of the article. As before, we conducted the Chi-squared test of independence. For the purposes of the analysis, the variable describing the number of methods used was divided into four categories: one method, two methods, three methods, and 4–5 methods. Due to the small number of the articles with four or five methods used, these articles were grouped into one category. The obtained results (compare Table 11) showed that there is no statistically significant evidence that there was a statistical relationship between the number of methods used in the articles and the features of the article (p-value > 0.05).

Table 11. *p*-values from the Chi-squared test of independence (where NoM stands for Number of Methods, CRC for Cited Reference Count, CW for Times Cited WoS Core, CA for Times Cited All Databases, 180U for 180 Day Usage Count, 2013U for Since 2013 Usage Count, PY for Publication Year and NoP for Number of Pages).

Relationship between	NoM & CRC	NoM & CW	NoM & CA	NoM & 180U	NoM & 2013U	NoM & PY	NoM & NoP
p-value	0.461	0.681	0.773	0.773	0.970	0.068	0.856

3.3. Research Areas

3.3.1. Identification of the Research Areas of the Studies

When classifying the research areas to which the analyzed texts belonged, we used the WoS Research Areas label, which was assigned to each journal publishing the analyzed texts (every record in the Web of Science core collection contains the subject category of its source publication, assigned to at least one of the subject categories). Figure 7 shows in which WoS Research Areas the texts were published in the analyzed period.

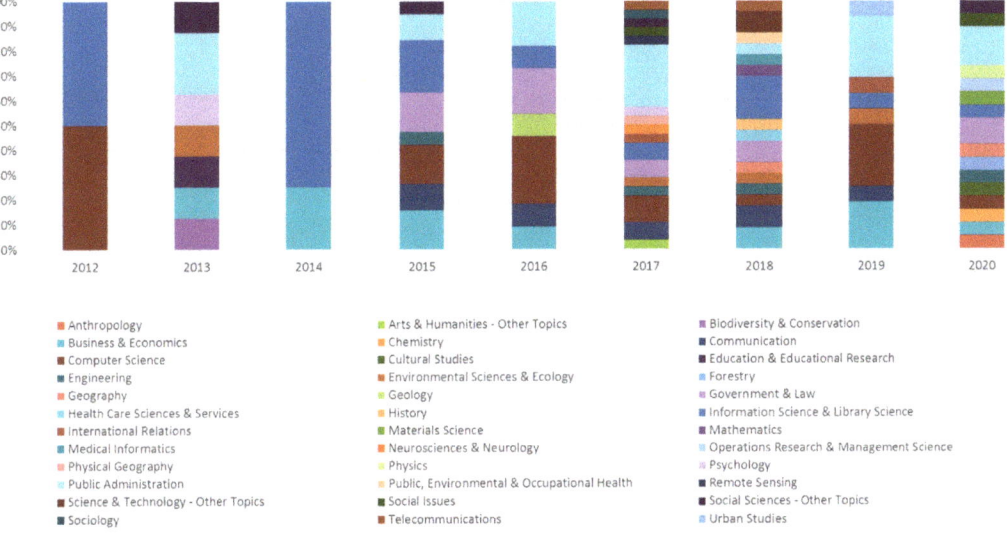

Figure 7. The WoS Research Areas assigned to the journals publishing the analyzed texts (percentage per year).

We observe that in the first year covered by the analysis (2012), the studied texts belonged to only two research areas, which also happened to be closely related (i.e., information science and computer science), whereas in the subsequent years (with the exception of year 3) the number of research areas systematically grew, reaching its peak in 2017 (17 research areas), and almost maintaining this high level in 2018 and 2020 (16 research areas).

3.3.2. Grouping the Identified Research Areas

For the sake of the clarity of the analysis, we have grouped the emerging research areas into five research area groups (RAGs) as shown in Table 12. We have paid special attention to two general areas that we found of particular importance to the studied topic, here separated into broad categories: (1) computer science, information science and related and (2) political sciences and related. Other research areas in which the references to CI in policymaking appeared were gathered into three groups: (3) humanities and social sciences other than political sciences, (4) natural sciences and mathematics, and (5) applied sciences. In some cases, one article was assigned to more than one research area because it belonged to multiple disciplines according to the Web of Science classification. This was the case for 32 articles of 88 analyzed.

Table 12. Research area groups, grouping the WoS research areas, within which the studies on CI in policymaking were conducted in the 2012–2020 period.

Research Area Group (RAG)	WoS Research Areas Included	The Total Number of Studies in 2012–2020
Computer Science, Information Science and related	Computer Science, Information Science & Library Science, Telecommunications, Medical Informatics.	32
Political Sciences and related	Public Administration, International Relations, Government & Law, Communication, Public, Environmental & Occupational Health.	38
Humanities and Social Sciences, other than Political Sciences	Anthropology, Sociology, Psychology, History, Cultural Studies, Education & Educational Research, Arts & Humanities—Other Topics, Social Issues, Urban Studies, Social Sciences—Other Topics.	11
Natural Sciences & Mathematics	Mathematics, Physics, Physical Geography, Chemistry, Neurosciences & Neurology, Environmental Sciences & Ecology.	8
Applied Sciences	Engineering, Health Care Sciences & Services, Business & Economics, Biodiversity & Conservation, Operations Research & Management Science, Science & Technology—Other Topics, Remote Sensing, Forestry	22

3.3.3. Studies Published Yearly within the Research Area Groups

The next stage of the work was an analysis of the number of studies published yearly, within the research area groups. This revealed that until 2017 computer science and related was the leading approach. However, since 2017, political sciences have become the main field of research in which studies on collective intelligence in policymaking are conducted. In recent years, the amount of research conducted in the field of computer science has clearly decreased, giving way to various types of social research. Changes in the amount of work published annually within the grouped research areas are shown in Figure 8.

3.3.4. Study Methods Used within the Research Area Groups

The next stage of our work was to verify, based on the texts that were analyzed, which methods and strategies of studying CI in policymaking were used in the research areas. Figure 9 visualizes the number of research articles, in which the specific methods and strategies used for studying CI in policymaking were used, broken down by research areas, in total for the period 2012–2020.

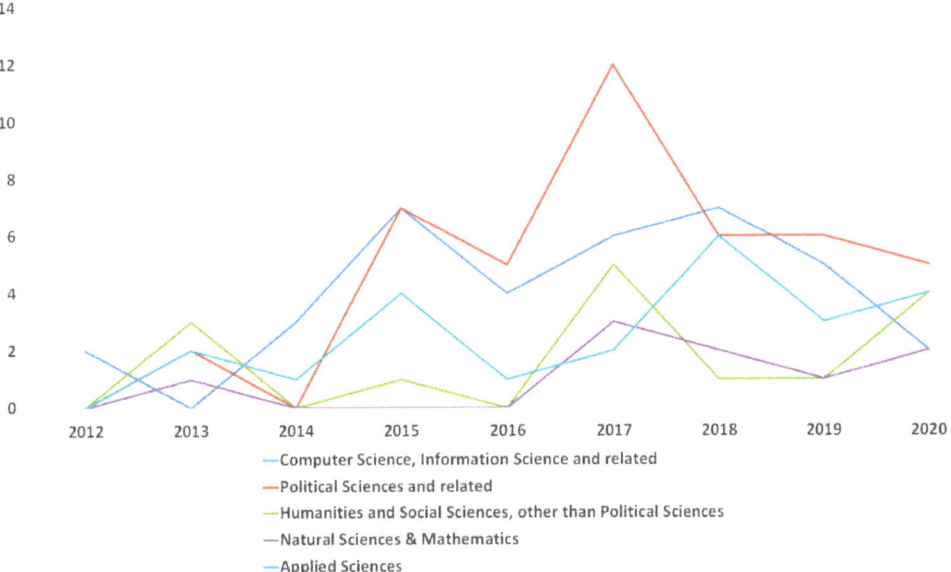

Figure 8. The number of studies on collective intelligence in policymaking published yearly within the RAGs.

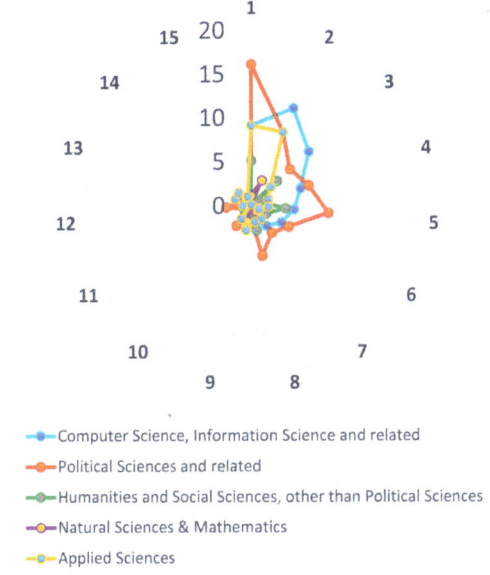

Figure 9. Number of research articles in which the methods and strategies used for studying CI in policymaking were used, broken down by research area groups, in total for the period 2012–2020. The assignment of particular methods and strategies to the labels numbered from 1 to 15, as described in Table 2.

We also compared the percentage of method usage (MU) in particular research areas to the percentage of MU in all the reviewed studies. This allowed us to see which methods and strategies were used more frequently and which were used less frequently in the examined research areas. Below, in Figure 10, we present the visualization of this comparison. The visualized difference between MU in the whole sample and in particular research areas, from this point forward referred to as the difference in percentage points (DPP). The source data are presented in Table A1 in Appendix B.

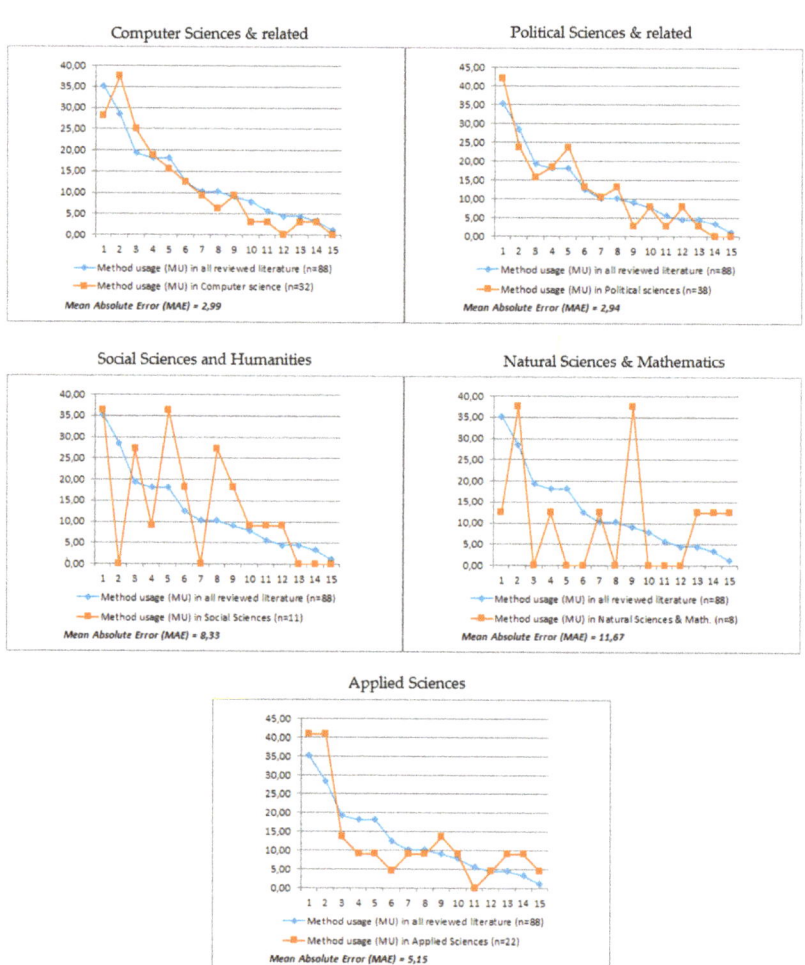

Figure 10. Method usage within the research area groups compared to the reviewed studies. The assignment of particular methods and strategies to the labels numbered from 1 to 15 as described in Table 2.

The mean absolute error (MAE) analysis has shown that computer science and political sciences are the most characteristic areas of research for issues related to CI and policymaking. As can be seen, in the field of computer science, the most important methods that were used most often in the entire analyzed sample were the analysis of created values (the difference in percentage points, or DPP: +9.09) and the analysis of e-participation process (DPP: +5.68). In turn, the most underrepresented methods were analysis of organizational structure (DPP: −7.10), analysis of impact on policymaking (DPP: −4.83) and state-of-the-art review (DPP: −4.55). On the other hand, in the field of political sciences, as if in opposition to the previous group, an increased interest in analysis of organizatonal structure (DPP: +6.88) was observed, as well as in analysis of collaboration model (DPP: +5.50), whereas low interest in analysis of decision-making (DPP: −6.46) was observed. It is also noticeable that in this group, as in the entire study sample, the analysis of impact on policymaking method is relatively rarely used, which is surprising. When it comes to the research area of the social sciences and humanities (other than political science), we noticed the great popularity of the analysis of participants' behavior (DPP: +18.18) and the analysis of innovation process (DPP: +17.05), with a complete lack of interest in the analysis of created values. On the other hand, the research conducted within the natural sciences and mathematics was characterized by the little use of the analysis of organizational structure (DPP: −22.73) and the analysis of the e-participation process (DPP: −19.32), but a significantly increased use of the analysis of decision-making process (DPP: +28.41). However, it should be remembered that the studies assigned to areas no. 3 and no. 4 constituted a much smaller sample than those grouped in other areas. Finally, the last presented group of disciplines are applied sciences. In this group, as in computer sciences, the increased use of the analysis of created values (DPP: + 12.50) is observed, and at the same time we see the smaller than in the entire sample, use of the analysis of participants' behavior (DPP: −9.09), and the analysis of collaboration model (DPP: −9.09).

3.4. Methods and Strategies Used in the Most Influential Works and in the Topics of Special Importance

3.4.1. Analysis of the Most Influential Studies

To analyze the most influential studies, we ranked the top 10 articles based on the usage and citation criteria. First, when analyzing the usage criterion, we examined data obtained from the Web from Science: the Since 2013 usage and the 180 Day Usage Count variables. However, we observed that the differences in the top 10 lists generated on their basis were relatively small, so we decided to choose the Since 2013 usage variable for creating the ranking. The results are presented in Appendix C in Table A4.

Secondly, we have prepared a ranking of the top 10 articles based on the criterion of the highest citations (Times Cited, WoS Core). The results are shown below in Appendix C in Table A5.

Finally, we analyzed which methods and strategies of studying CI in policymaking were used in the created sets of the most influential studies. As previously, we compared the percentage of method usage in the most influential studies to the percentage of method usage in all reviewed studies. This allowed us to determine which methods and strategies were used more frequently and which were used less frequently in the examined groups, in a similar way as we did before with research areas. In Figure 11 we present the visualization of this comparison. The source data are presented in Table A2 in Appendix B.

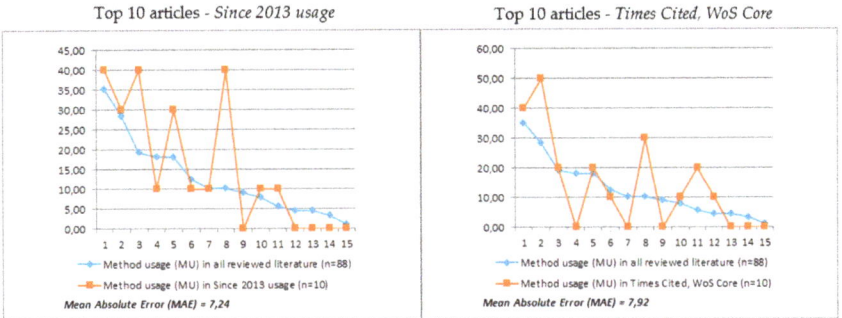

Figure 11. Method usage within the most influential studies compared to all the reviewed literature; 1 to 15 are as described in Table 2.

The analysis made it possible to observe interesting similarities and differences between the examined collections of research articles. First, their most common feature was an increased interest in the analysis of innovation process; respectively, DPP +29.77 in the most-read articles group, and DPP +19.77 in the most-cited texts group. Likewise, the analysis of organizational structure is an equally popular method in both groups (DPP +4.77). However, the differences are revealed mainly in the use of analysis of created values: in the group of the most often cited, it is one of the most popular approaches for half of all texts, and DPP +21.59 compared to the use in the entire study sample. However, although it is among the most widely read, this method was not more popular than the entire sample. We have the opposite situation in the case of the analysis of e-participation process: Among the most frequently read texts we can see an increased interest in this method (DPP +20.68), which is not the case with the most often cited texts (DPP +0.68).

3.4.2. The Analysis of Topics of Special Interest

The last stage of our analysis was to examine, within the reviewed literature, the topics of special interest for the research on CI in policymaking. To ensure data triangulation, and to avoid duplicating regularities that were already detected, in the selection of topics we relied on a different method than the one used in the earlier stages of the work. When selecting specific topics for analysis, we relied on monographs concerning issues of collective intelligence and policymaking, published after 1990. The method of selecting topics for analysis is described in Appendix D. The final list of seven topics included: Citizenship, Communities, Consensus, Deliberation, Diversity, Local governance and Urban development, and Open data.

Next, we searched our literature database for the keywords specific to each of these topics. The topic-oriented subgroups of studies were created, based on the occurrence of the related keywords. The results are presented in Table 13.

Table 13. Saturation of the analyzed research studies with selected topics of interest.

Concept	Number of Studies Where the Concept Appeared	References in Monographic Publications
Citizenship	47	[61–64]
Local governance & Urban development	30	[2,63–65]
Communities	14	[2,62,64]
Deliberation	9	[61,62,64–67]
Open data	7	[64,65]
Diversity	5	[2,61,63,66]
Consensus	5	[61,62,66]

The four most popular topic-oriented subgroups were analyzed in terms of the methods and strategies that were adopted in the conducted research. The aim was to verify to what extent the reviewed literature relates to the examined topics, and what research methods were used in the studies focused on these topics. The results of the analysis are shown in Figure 12. The source data are presented in Table A3 in Appendix B.

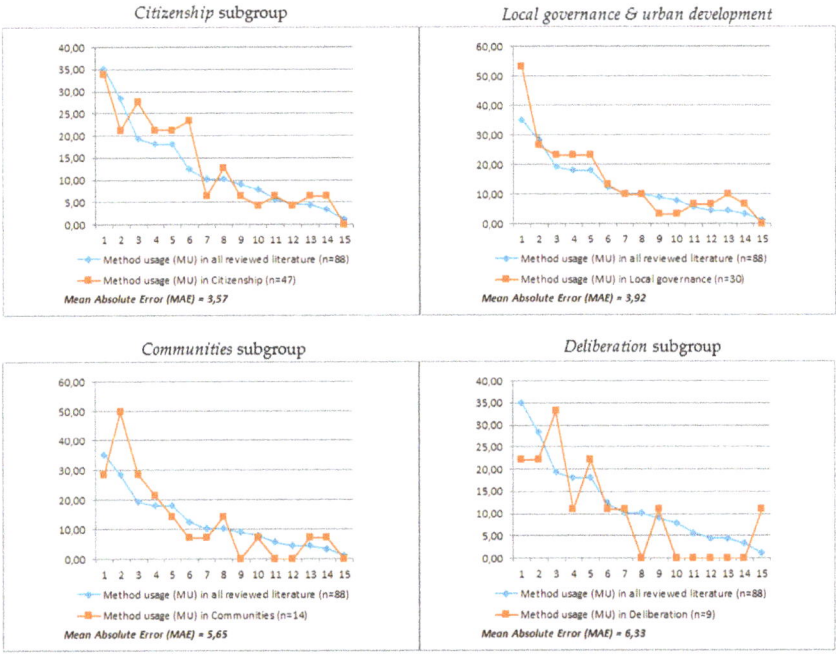

Figure 12. Method usage within the most influential studies compared to all the reviewed studies. The assignment of particular methods and strategies to the labels numbered from 1 to 15 as described in Table 2.

4. Discussion

The analyses conducted allowed us to conclude that throughout the whole sample the approaches that were most frequently used to study collective intelligence in the domain of policymaking were analysis of the organisational structure and analysis of the created values. Moreover, the analysis of the two most important research areas in which the studies were conducted revealed that the first of these methods is primarily peculiar to political science, and the latter is more common in computer science. Apart from this general observation, we were able to investigate a number of other issues related to the analyzed topic.

We observed that at least since 2015, the topic of CI in policymaking remains a subject of increasing interest among researchers. Although 2017 was the peak of interest, the subsequent years also demonstrated the continued popularity of this issue. Content analysis allowed for the identification of concepts that constituted the most important points of reference in the studies. The dominance of the term crowdsourcing, both in article titles and in author keywords, is noticeable. Due to the fact that this term in its original meaning mainly referred to business projects, we can see that many authors remain rooted to translating patterns developed in the commercial sector into the public sphere. This observation seems to be consistent with the analysis of research methods. The frequent use of analysis of the created values approach is also a common point with commercial projects, in which the direct results of collective effort are one of the primary subjects of interest. In turn, concepts such as the public and government frequently appearing in article abstracts, embedding the research in the political sciences domain. In addition, the KeyWords Plus analysis (based on the literature cited in the analyzed works) shows that the concepts that were most frequently referred to were innovation and participation. Note that the term innovation, in its business sense—being a multi-stage process whereby organisations transform ideas into new/improved products, service or processes [A1]—is now increasingly used in social and political sciences to describe the process of reforming public organizations by opening them to participation [A2], which was also confirmed by our analysis.

Statistical analysis proved that some significant relationships between the research methods can be observed. The negative relationship between the analysis of created values and the analysis of collaboration model is particularly noteworthy. This can be explained by the fact that projects mainly oriented at generating new values are studied in the context of the existing governance framework. The studies on new models of intersectoral collaboration between public and private entities, when the scope of the project extends beyond the structure of one specific organization, require a different approach. The remaining relationships are fairly obvious: A common combination in the reviewed studies was to analyze the behavior and motivation of the participants at the same time. Similarly, it is not surprising that state-of-art-review and categorization of implemented projects were linked. The observed positive relationship between the analysis of created values and the 180 Day Usage Count also led to interesting observations. It can be concluded that the use of the analysis of created values method translates into increased popularity among readers. On the other hand, we can see that studies based on this method result in texts with fewer pages, which makes them more accessible to readers.

The analysis of research areas in which the studies were conducted points to the conclusion that the number and diversity of the scientific disciplines covered by the review is growing year by year. References to CI and policymaking appear in more and more specialized works related to the implementation of public policies. It shows that reflections on CI in policymaking have moved from general considerations to the application of solutions in specific domains of public policy. Secondly, the analysis of the number of studies appearing yearly in research area groups confirmed that researchers tend to be less interested in technological aspects of projects (the computer science and related group), and more in the implementation of these projects in diverse areas of administration, and in the public sphere (the political sciences and related group). As we have already emphasized, the patterns of analysis borrowed from business projects (i.e., created value analysis) were the leading methods of study in computer science. At the same time, the analysis conducted from an organizational perspective was characteristic of contemporary governance studies on CI. However, the low popularity of the analysis of the impact of AI algorithms approach was surprising. It seems that CI studies are still conducted almost entirely separately from AI studies. Despite the fact that the combination of AI and CI has been recently proposed as one of the most important topics of research, for example, in the report *Identifying Citizens' Needs by Combining AI and CI* [68] or in the works of G. Mulgan [69], it looks like this demand has not yet been answered. The relatively low popularity of the analysis of the impact on policymaking is also puzzling. It can be concluded that the practical function of CI in policymaking is often reduced to fitting CI projects into the existing administrative structure, or on increasing efficiency in achieving goals formulated at the political level, whereas actual shaping of public policy agendas is still rare. Nevertheless, the observed decline in the popularity of the analysis of organisational structure approach may herald some changes.

Research into created values is not the only approach that stands out in computer science. We also notice the popularity of studies on the e-participation processes, focused on engaging wide audiences in policymaking, which is promising in the context of future research. It is also interesting that in the political sciences, apart from research on the organizational structure, there is a significant interest in collaboration models. Reflecting on the cooperation of different types of partners, achieving mutual benefits seems to be a promising model for the future shape of policymaking.

A review of the most influential articles, taking into account both their use and citations, allowed their specific features to be captured. The innovation analysis was a particularly popular research approach in this group. Our observation may be an indication for future research that including the analysis of project innovativeness in the planned works may contribute to increased interest in research results. However, as in the other analyzed subgroups, the number of studies tracking the actual impact of CI projects on shaping public policies was still unexpectedly low. Conversely, the analysis of the e-participation process enjoys increased popularity in this group, although only among the frequently read, though not among the most cited articles. We also noted that the articles relating to user behavior were underrepresented in this group.

Finally, the analysis of the selected topics of interest showed that the most popular concept in our sample was citizenship, and studies using this term were often associated with the method of analyzing the motivations of participants. This is in line with postulated changes in the relationship between citizens and the state, as proposed by Noveck [67] and others. The government is expected to transform from an authoritative problem-solving center into an arbiter, inviting the citizens to jointly seek the best solutions. Putting the citizens at the center of interest and studying their motivations enhances their role as active participants in the online public sphere. Another very popular concept in the analyzed sample was local governance. References to this topic could be found in over 34% of the reviewed studies. The analysis showed that cities, as well as communities (both local and based on interests), have become the main field of implementation of CI projects in the public space. In the case of cities, the organizational structure of projects was the main method of study, and in the case of communities, the values they produce were more important. It was also noted that topics with a deep theoretical foundation, such as diversity or consensus, were still not very popular among the analyzed works, which may be related to their relatively low applicability to the leading topics of citizenship and local governance.

5. Conclusions

Opening policymaking tasks to public participation has become one of the major trends in public policy in recent years. Regarding the 2030 Agenda for Sustainable Development, approved by United Nations Member States in 2015, "responsive, inclusive, participatory and representative decision-making at all levels" is one of the adopted strategic goals for the future [70]. The role of governments is substantially changing, and the emergence of new and complex social problems requires looking for new ways to collaborate in making public decisions with non-governmental actors, and with self-organized communities. For this reason, there is a need to constantly review the existing research on collective intelligence in the domains of public policy and the methods of studying this topic, which may contribute to the better planning of future implementations.

In the present study we made an attempt to identify which methods and strategies have been used so far for researching CI in policymaking. To answer Research Question 1, we conducted a systematic literature review following the PRISMA methodology, supplemented by an analysis of article titles, abstracts and keywords, the yearly number of publications, as well as qualitative research based on the grounded theory method. We identified 15 methods in the analyzed sample. The analysis of the organizational structure and analysis of the created values approaches proved to be the most frequently used approaches.

Considering Research Question 2, the analysis of statistical dependencies allowed us to identify several positive and negative correlations between research methods and between research methods and other variables (especially usage count, as well as the number of pages).

Considering Research Question 3, we found that studies were conducted mainly in computer sciences and political sciences, with the latter group, though initially less numerous, becoming dominant in recent years. We also identified which research methods were more common and which were less common in particular research areas.

Finally, considering Research Question 4, it is possible to conclude that the most influential, i.e., the most cited and the most popular articles, differed from typical studies in terms of the research methods used. A similar phenomenon occurred in relation to groups of articles built around topics of special importance.

The authors hope that by publishing this article they contributed to the systematization of knowledge about studies on collective intelligence in policymaking, showing in which areas the research has been conducted and which methods have been used for this purpose. In addition to identifying the most popular methods, we have attempted to identify the underrepresented approaches, which are promising for the future development of these studies. The present study differs significantly from the studies that were conducted in the past. None of the literature reviews on CI and public policymaking have so far developed a comprehensive list of analytical methods and approaches used in this type of research. For example, Prpić et al. presented the status of research focusing on three selected policy crowdsourcing techniques (virtual labor markets, tournament crowdsourcing, open collaboration), to compare them to the different stages of the policy cycle [37]; Liu et al. synthesized prior research and practices mainly to provide practical lessons for designing new projects in the public sector [52] and Linders focused on classifying citizen co-production initiatives [54]. As our review shows, some types of research have so far been extremely rare. For example, only one study in the analyzed sample concerned organizational learning, and yet, according to studies conducted by Mulgan [4] and Malone [71], it is one of the most important elements involved in collective intelligence. The state of research on the impact of CI in shaping public policy agendas, and on the use of AI algorithms in implemented projects also seems insufficient. We trust that by indicating the areas in which research is still limited, we will contribute to the better quality of future studies.

Author Contributions: Conceptualization, R.O.; methodology, R.O., S.B. and P.P.; validation, R.O. and M.C.; formal analysis, S.B. and P.P.; investigation, R.O. and M.C.; writing—original draft preparation, R.O.; writing—review and editing, R.O. and S.B.; visualization, S.B., P.P. and R.O.; supervision, R.O.; funding acquisition, R.O. All authors have read and agreed to the published version of the manuscript.

Funding: This research was funded by Narodowe Centrum Nauki (National Science Centre, Republic of Poland), the research grant UMO-2018/28/C/HS5/00543 – "Collective intelligence on the Internet: Applications in the public sphere, research methods and civic participation models" ("Kolektywna inteligencja w Internecie: zastosowania w sferze publicznej, metody badania i modele partycypacji obywatelskiej"). This research was funded from the funds granted to the Cracow University of Economics, within the framework of the POTENTIAL Program, project number 26/EIM/2021/POT.

Institutional Review Board Statement: Not applicable.

Informed Consent Statement: Not applicable.

Data Availability Statement: The data presented in this study are available on request from the corresponding author.

Conflicts of Interest: The authors declare no conflict of interest. The funders had no role in the design of the study; in the collection, analyses, or interpretation of data; in the writing of the manuscript, or in the decision to publish the results.

Appendix A

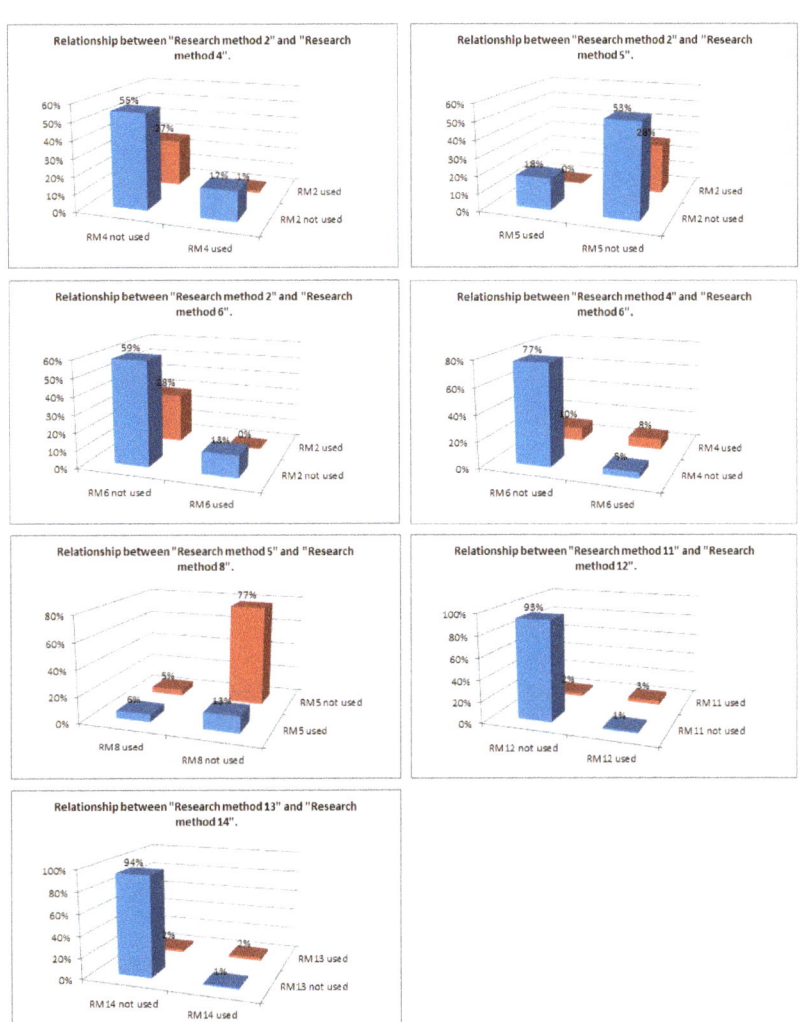

Figure A1. 3D barplot of the contingency tables from Table 4 of the Pearson Chi-squared test of independence for the variables with statistically significant dependency.

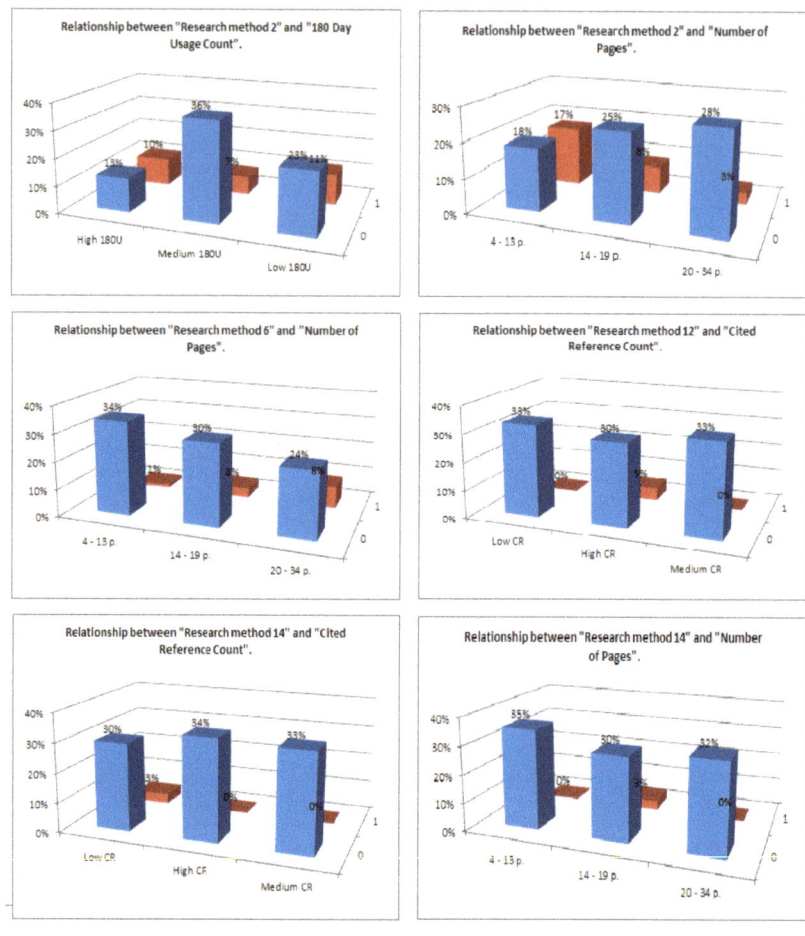

Figure A2. 3D barplot of the contingency tables from Table 9 of the Pearson Chi-squared test of independence for the variables with statistically significant dependency.

Appendix B

Table A1. Methods and strategies of studying CI in policymaking used in each particular research area group (RAG), compared to all the reviewed studies. NoS stands for number of studies, in which the particular research method is used; method usage (MU) indicates the percentage of studies in which the research method was used; DPP stands for the difference in percentage points between MU in this group and MU in all the reviewed studies; MAE stands for the mean absolute error for the analyzed group. The assignment of particular methods and strategies to the labels numbered from 1 to 15 is described in Table 2.

	Research Methods & Strategies (RM)														
	1	2	3	4	5	6	7	8	9	10	11	12	13	14	15
All reviewed literature (n=88)															
NoS	31	25	17	16	16	11	9	9	8	7	5	4	4	3	1
Method Usage (MU)	35.23	28.41	19.32	18.18	18.18	12.50	10.23	10.23	9.09	7.95	5.68	4.55	4.55	3.41	1.14
RAG 1: Computer Science & related (n = 32)															
NoS	9	12	8	6	5	4	3	2	3	1	1	0	1	1	0
Method Usage (MU)	28.13	37.50	25.00	18.75	15.63	12.50	9.38	6.25	9.38	3.13	3.13	0.00	3.13	3.13	0.00
DPP	−7.10	9.09	5.68	0.57	−2.56	0.00	−0.85	−3.98	0.28	−4.83	−2.56	−4.55	−1.42	−0.28	−1.14
Mean Absolute Error (MAE)	2.99														
RAG 2: Political Sciences & related (n = 38)															
NoS	16	9	6	7	9	5	4	5	1	3	1	3	1	0	0
Method Usage (MU)	42.11	23.68	15.79	18.42	23.68	13.16	10.53	13.16	2.63	7.89	2.63	7.89	2.63	0.00	0.00
DPP	6.88	−4.72	−3.53	0.24	5.50	0.66	0.30	2.93	−6.46	−0.06	−3.05	3.35	−1.91	−3.41	−1.14
Mean Absolute Error (MAE)	2.94														
RAG 3: Social Sciences & Humanities (n = 11)															
NoS	4	0	3	1	4	2	0	3	2	1	1	1	0	0	0
Method Usage (MU)	36.36	0.00	27.27	9.09	36.36	18.18	0.00	27.27	18.18	9.09	9.09	9.09	0.00	0.00	0.00
DPP	1.14	−28.41	7.95	−9.09	18.18	5.68	−10.23	17.05	9.09	1.14	3.41	4.55	−4.55	−3.41	−1.14
Mean Absolute Error (MAE)	8.33														
RAG 4: Natural Sciences & Mathematics (n = 8)															
NoS	1	3	0	1	0	0	1	0	3	0	0	0	1	1	1
Method Usage (MU)	12.50	37.50	0.00	12.50	0.00	0.00	12.50	0.00	37.50	0.00	0.00	0.00	12.50	12.50	12.50
DPP	−22.73	9.09	−19.32	−5.68	−18.18	−12.50	2.27	−10.23	28.41	−7.95	−5.68	−4.55	7.95	9.09	11.36
Mean Absolute Error (MAE)	11.67														
RAG 5: Applied Sciences (n = 22)															
NoS	9	9	3	2	2	1	2	2	3	2	0	1	2	2	1
Method Usage (MU)	40.91	40.91	13.64	9.09	9.09	4.55	9.09	9.09	13.64	9.09	0.00	4.55	9.09	9.09	4.55
DPP	5.68	12.50	−5.68	−9.09	−9.09	−7.95	−1.14	−1.14	4.55	1.14	−5.68	0.00	4.55	5.68	3.41
Mean Absolute Error (MAE)	5.15														

Table A2. Methods and strategies of studying CI in policymaking used in the most influential studies, compared to all reviewed studies. NoS stands for the number of studies in which the particular research method was used; method usage (MU) stands for the percentage of studies in which the research method was used; DPP stands for the difference in percentage points between MU in this group and MU in all reviewed studies; MAE stands for the mean absolute error for the analyzed group. The assignment of particular methods and strategies to the labels numbered from 1 to 15 is described in Table 2.

	Research Methods & Strategies (RM)														
	1	2	3	4	5	6	7	8	9	10	11	12	13	14	15
All reviewed literature (n-88)															
NoS	31	25	17	16	16	11	9	9	8	7	5	4	4	3	1
Method Usage (MU)	35.23	28.41	19.32	18.18	18.18	12.50	10.23	10.23	9.09	7.95	5.68	4.55	4.55	3.41	1.14
Top 10 articles, according to usage criterion—*Since 2013 usage* (n = 10)															
NoS	4	3	4	1	3	1	1	4	0	1	1	0	0	0	0
Method Usage (MU)	40.00	30.00	40.00	10.00	30.00	10.00	10.00	40.00	0.00	10.00	10.00	0.00	0.00	0.00	0.00
DPP	4.77	1.59	20.68	−8.18	11.82	−2.50	−0.23	29.77	−9.09	2.05	4.32	−4.55	−4.55	−3.41	−1.14
Mean Absolute Error (MAE)	7.24														
Top 10 articles, according to citation criterion—*Times Cited, WoS Core* (n = 10)															
NoS	4	5	2	0	2	1	0	3	0	1	2	1	0	0	0
Method Usage (MU)	40.00	50.00	20.00	0.00	20.00	10.00	0.00	30.00	0.00	10.00	20.00	10.00	0.00	0.00	0.00
DPP	4.77	21.59	0.68	−18.18	1.82	−2.50	−10.23	19.77	−9.09	2.05	14.32	5.45	−4.55	−3.41	−1.14
Mean Absolute Error (MAE)	7.97														

Table A3. Methods and strategies of studying CI in policymaking used in the subgroups of studies based on selected topics of interest. NoS stands for number of studies in which the particular research method is used; method usage (MU) stands for the percentage of studies in which the research method was used; DPP stands for the difference in percentage points between MU in this group and MU in all reviewed studies; MAE stands for the mean absolute error for the analyzed group. The assignment of particular methods and strategies to the labels numbered from 1 to 15 is described in Table 2.

	Research Methods & Strategies (RM)														
	1	2	3	4	5	6	7	8	9	10	11	12	13	14	15
All reviewed literature (n-88)															
NoS	31	25	17	16	16	11	9	9	8	7	5	4	4	3	1
Method Usage (MU)	35.23	28.41	19.32	18.18	18.18	12.50	10.23	10.23	9.09	7.95	5.68	4.55	4.55	3.41	1.14
Citizenship subgroup (n = 47)															
NoS	16	10	13	10	10	11	3	6	3	2	3	2	3	3	0
Method Usage (MU)	34.04	21.28	27.66	21.28	21.28	23.40	6.38	12.77	6.38	4.26	6.38	4.26	6.38	6.38	0.00
DPP	−1.18	−7.13	8.34	3.09	3.09	10.90	−3.84	2.54	−2.71	−3.70	0.70	−0.29	1.84	2.97	−1.14
Mean Absolute Error (MAE)	3.57														
Local governance & urban development subgroup (n = 30)															
NoS	16	8	7	7	7	4	3	3	1	1	2	2	3	2	0
Method Usage (MU)	53.33	26.67	23.33	23.33	23.33	13.33	10.00	10.00	3.33	3.33	6.67	6.67	10.00	6.67	0.00
DPP	18.11	−1.74	4.02	5.15	5.15	0.83	−0.23	−0.23	−5.76	−4.62	0.98	2.12	5.45	3.26	−1.14
Mean Absolute Error (MAE)	3.92														

Table A3. *Cont.*

	Research Methods & Strategies (RM)														
	1	2	3	4	5	6	7	8	9	10	11	12	13	14	15
Communities subgroup (n = 14)															
NoS	4	7	4	3	2	1	1	2	0	1	0	0	1	1	0
Method Usage (MU)	28.57	50.00	28.57	21.43	14.29	7.14	7.14	14.29	0.00	7.14	0.00	0.00	7.14	7.14	0.00
DPP	−6.66	21.59	9.25	3.25	−3.90	−5.36	−3.08	4.06	−9.09	−0.81	−5.68	−4.55	2.60	3.73	−1.14
Mean Absolute Error (MAE)	5.65														
Deliberation subgroup (n = 9)															
NoS	2	2	3	1	2	1	1	0	1	0	0	0	0	0	1
Method Usage (MU)	22.22	22.22	33.33	11.11	22.22	11.11	11.11	0.00	11.11	0.00	0.00	0.00	0.00	0.00	11.11
DPP	−13.01	−6.19	14.02	−7.07	4.04	−1.39	0.88	−10.23	2.02	−7.95	−5.68	−4.55	−4.55	−3.41	9.97
Mean Absolute Error (MAE)	6.33														

Appendix C

Table A4. Ranking of top 10 articles, according to the usage criterion (Since 2013 usage).

Authors (Year)	Title	Research Area Group	Research Method	Since 2013 Usage	180 Day Usage Count	Times Cited, WoS Core	Times Cited/Year
Linders, D. (2012)	From e-government to we-government: Defining a typology for citizen coproduction in the age of social media	Computer Science & related	2, 10	454	39	502	55.78
Mergel, I.; Desouza, K.C. (2013)	Implementing Open Innovation in the Public Sector: The Case of Challenge.gov	Political Sciences & related	5, 8	192	9	128	16
Diaz-Diaz, R.; Perez-Gonzalez, D. (2016)	Implementation of Social Media Concepts for e-Government: Case Study of a Social Media Tool for Value Co-Creation and Citizen Participation	Computer Science & related; Applied Sciences	1, 2, 3	165	14	17	3.4
Almirall, E.; Lee, M.; Majchrzak, A. (2014)	Open innovation requires integrated competition-community ecosystems: Lessons learned from civic open innovation	Applied Sciences	1, 2, 8, 12	161	4	68	9.71
Mergel, I. (2015)	Opening Government: Designing Open Innovation Processes to Collaborate With External Problem Solvers	Computer Science & related; Humanities & Social Sciences	5, 8	112	1	42	7

Table A4. Cont.

Authors (Year)	Title	Research Area Group	Research Method	Since 2013 Usage	180 Day Usage Count	Times Cited, WoS Core	Times Cited/Year
Wijnhoven, F.; Ehrenhard, M.; Kuhn, J. (2015)	Open government objectives and participation motivations	Computer Science & related	3, 6	93	2	76	12.67
Mergel, I. (2018)	Open innovation in the public sector: drivers and barriers for the adoption of Challenge.gov	Applied Sciences; Political Sciences & related	8	86	14	38	12.67
Lampe, C.; Zube, P.; Lee, J.; Park, C.H.; Johnston, E. (2014)	Crowdsourcing civility: A natural experiment examining the effects of distributed moderation in online forums	Computer Science & related	1, 3	68	1	53	7.57
Lin, Y.L. (2018)	A comparison of selected Western and Chinese smart governance: The application of ICT in governmental management, participation and collaboration	Political Sciences & related; Computer Science & related	1, 5, 7	63	15	11	3.67
Pieper, A.K.; Pieper, M. (2015)	Political participation via social media: A case study of deliberative quality in the public online budgeting process of Frankfurt/Main, Germany 2013	Computer Science & related; Applied Sciences	3	62	1	3	0.5

Table A5. Ranking of top 10 articles, according to the citation criterion (*Times Cited, WoS Core*).

Authors (Year)	Title	Research Area Group	Research Method	Since 2013 Usage	180 Day Usage Count	Times Cited, WoS Core	Times Cited/Year
Linders, D. (2012)	From e-government to we-government: Defining a typology for citizen coproduction in the age of social media	Computer Science & related	2, 10	454	39	502	55.78
Mergel, I.; Desouza, K.C. (2013)	Implementing Open Innovation in the Public Sector: The Case of Challenge.gov	Political Sciences & related	5, 8	192	9	128	16
Wijnhoven, F.; Ehrenhard, M.; Kuhn, J. (2015)	Open government objectives and participation motivations	Computer Science & related	3, 6	93	2	76	12.67
Almirall, E.; Lee, M.; Majchrzak, A. (2014)	Open innovation requires integrated competition-community ecosystems: Lessons learned from civic open innovation	Applied Sciences	1, 2, 8, 12	161	4	68	9.71
Chen, L.J.; Ho, Y.H.; Lee, H.C.; Wu, H.C.; Liu, H.M.; Hsieh, H.H.; Huang, Y.T.; Lung, S.C.C. (2017)	An Open Framework for Participatory PM2.5 Monitoring in Smart Cities	Computer Science & related; Applied Sciences	1, 2	31	4	68	17
Prpić, J.; Taeihagh, A.; Melton, J. (2015)	The Fundamentals of Policy Crowdsourcing	Political Sciences & related	10, 11	8	0	65	10.83
Lampe, C.; Zube, P.; Lee, J.; Park, C.H.; Johnston, E. (2014)	Crowdsourcing civility: A natural experiment examining the effects of distributed moderation in online forums	Computer Science & related	1, 3	68	1	53	7.57
Stritch, J.M.; Pedersen, M.J.; Taggart, G. (2017)	The Opportunities and Limitations of Using Mechanical Turk (MTURK) in Public Administration and Management Scholarship	Computer Science & related	1, 2	22	1	48	12
Charalabidis, Y.; Loukis, E.N.; Androutsopoulou, A.; Karkaletsis, V.; Triantafillou, A. (2014)	Passive crowdsourcing in government using social media	Computer Science & related	2	1	0	45	6.43
Mergel, I. (2015)	Opening Government: Designing Open Innovation Processes to Collaborate With External Problem Solvers	Computer Science & related; Humanities & Social Sciences	5, 8	112	1	42	7

Appendix D

The monographic publications concerning (fully or partially) the issues of collective intelligence and policymaking published after 1990 were shortlisted. Due to the scarcity of monographic literature, only eight publications were included in this list after the review. On this basis, an initial list of 20 issues was compiled. Then, a questionnaire was conducted in which a group of six social science researchers were invited to assess the significance of the proposed issues. Thus, the final list of seven concepts that were subject to analysis was selected. The final list of seven topics included citizenship, communities, consensus, deliberation, diversity, local governance and urban development, and open data.

Table A6. Monographic publications used as initial references to select the topics of special interest.

Author	Title	Reference
Aitamurto, T.	Crowdsourced Off-Road Traffic Law Experiment In Finland	[61]
Landemore, H.	Democratic Reason: Politics, Collective Intelligence, and the Rule of the Many	[62]
Landemore, H.	Open Democracy: Reinventing Popular Rule for the Twenty-First Century	[63]
Levy, P.	Collective Intelligence: Mankind's Emerging World in Cyberspace	[2]
Noveck, B.S.	Smart Citizens, Smarter State. The Technologies of Expertise and the Future of Governing	[64]
Noveck, B.S.; Harvey, R.; Dinesh, A.	The Open Policymaking Playbook	[65]
Noveck, B.S.; et al.	Crowdlaw for Congress. Strategies for 21st Century Lawmaking	[66]
Ryan, M.; Gambrell, D.; Noveck, B.S.	Using Collective Intelligence to Solve Public Problems	[67]

References

1. Malone, T.W. *Handbook of Collective Intelligence*; Bernstein, M.S., Ed.; The MIT Press: Cambridge/London, UK, 2015.
2. Levy, P. *Collective Intelligence: Mankind's Emerging World in Cyberspace*; Plenum: New York, NY, USA, 1997.
3. Hong, L.; Page, S. Groups of diverse problem-solvers can outperform groups of high-ability problem-solvers. *Proc. Natl. Acad. Sci. USA* **2004**, *101*, 16385–16389. [CrossRef]
4. Mulgan, G. *Big Mind: How Collective Intelligence Can Change Our World*; Princeton University Press: Princeton/Oxford, UK, 2018; p. 22.
5. Malone, T.W.; Laubacher, R.; Dellarocas, C. The collective intelligence genome. *MIT Sloan Manag. Rev.* **2010**, *51*, 21–31. [CrossRef]
6. Woolley, A.W.; Chabris, C.F.; Pentland, A.; Hashmi, N.; Malone, T.W. Evidence for a Collective Intelligence Factor in the Performance of Human Groups. *Science* **2010**, *330*, 686–688. [CrossRef]
7. Bonabeau, E. Decisions 2.0: The Power of Collective Intelligence. *MIT Sloan Manag. Rev.* **2009**, *50*, 45–52.
8. Surowiecki, J. *The Wisdom of Crowds*; Anchor Books: New York, NY, USA, 2005.
9. Howe, J. *Crowdsourcing: Why the Power of The Crowd Is Driving the Future of Business*; Crown Business: New York, NY, USA, 2008.
10. Folino, G.; Forestiero, A. Using Entropy for Evaluating Swarm Intelligence Algorithms. In *Nature Inspired Cooperative Strategies for Optimization (NICSO 2010)*; Studies in Computational Intelligence; González, J.R., Pelta, D.A., Cruz, C., Terrazas, G., Krasnogor, N., Eds.; Springer: Berlin/Heidelberg, Germany, 2020; Volume 284. [CrossRef]
11. Mann, R.P.; Garnett, R. The entropic basis of collective behaviour. *J. R. Soc. Interface* **2015**, *12*, 20150037. [CrossRef]

12. Kang, H.; Bei, F.; Shen, Y.; Sun, X.; Chen, Q. A Diversity Model Based on Dimension Entropy and Its Application to Swarm Intelligence Algorithm. *Entropy* **2021**, *23*, 397. [CrossRef] [PubMed]
13. Sæbø, Ø.; Rose, J.; Flak, L.S. The shape of eParticipation: Characterizing an emerging research area. *Gov. Inf. Q.* **2008**, *25*, 400–428. [CrossRef]
14. Mureddu, F.; Misuraca, G.; Osimo, D.; Onori, R.; Armenia, S. A Living Roadmap for Policymaking 2.0. In *Handbook of Research on Advanced ICT Integration for Governance and Policy Modeling*, 1st ed.; Sonntagbauer, P., Nazemi, K., Sonntagbauer, S., Prister, G., Burkhardt, D., Eds.; IGI Global: Hershey, PA, USA, 2014. [CrossRef]
15. Sun, T.Q.; Medaglia, R. Mapping the challenges of artificial intelligence in the public sector: Evidence from public healthcare. *Gov. Inf. Q.* **2019**, *36*, 368–383. [CrossRef]
16. Madero, V.; Morris, N. Public participation mechanisms and sustainable policy-making: A case study analysis of Mexico City's Plan Verde. *J. Environ. Plan. Manag.* **2016**, *59*, 1728–1750. [CrossRef]
17. Aitamurto, T. *Crowdsourcing for Democracy: New Era in Policy–Making. Publications of the Committee for the Future*; Parliament of Finland: Helsinki, Finland, 2012.
18. Landemore, H. Inclusive Constitution-Making: The Icelandic Experiment. *J. Political Philos.* **2015**, *23*, 166–191. [CrossRef]
19. Greenemeier, L. Smart Machines Join Humans in Tracking Africa Ebola Outbreak. Available online: https://www.scientificamerican.com/article/smart-machines-join-humans-in-tracking-africa-ebola-outbreak/ (accessed on 22 February 2021).
20. McKelvey, F.; MacDonald, M. Artificial intelligence policy innovations at the Canadian Federal Government. *Can. J. Commun.* **2019**, *44*, 43–50. [CrossRef]
21. Valle-Cruz, D.; Criado, J.I.; Sandoval-Almazán, R.; Ruvalcaba-Gomez, E.A. Assessing the public policy-cycle framework in the age of artificial intelligence: From agenda-setting to policy evaluation. *Gov. Inf. Q.* **2020**, *37*, 101509. [CrossRef]
22. Joyner-Roberson, E. What Do Drones, AI and Proactive Policing Have in Common? Available online: https://www.sas.com/en_za/insights/articles/risk-fraud/drones-ai-proactive-policing.html (accessed on 22 September 2020).
23. Grothaus, M. China's Airport Facial Recognition Kiosks Should Make Us Fear for Our Privacy. Available online: https://www.fastcompany.com/90324512/chinas-airport-facial-recognition-kiosks-should-make-us-fear-for-ourprivacy (accessed on 22 February 2021).
24. Milano, M.; O'Sullivan, B.; Gavanelli, M. Sustainable Policy Making: A Strategic Challenge for Artificial Intelligence. *AI Mag.* **2014**, *35*, 22–35. [CrossRef]
25. Vicente, M.R.; Novo, A. An empirical analysis of e-participation. The role of social networks and e-government over citizens' online engagement. *Gov. Inf. Q.* **2014**, *31*, 379–387. [CrossRef]
26. Wolfe, J. Varieties of Participatory Democracy and Democratic Theory. *Political Sci. Rev.* **1986**, *16*, 1–38.
27. Pateman, C. Participatory Democracy Revisited. *Perspect. Politics* **2012**, *10*, 7–19. [CrossRef]
28. Sintomer, Y.; Herzberg, C.; Rocke, A. Participatory budgeting in Europe: Potentials and challenges. *Int. J. Urban Reg. Res.* **2008**, *32*, 164–178. [CrossRef]
29. Ansell, C.; Gash, A. Collaborative Governance in Theory and Practice. *J. Public Adm. Res. Theory* **2007**, *18*, 543–571. [CrossRef]
30. Emerson, T.; Nabatchi, T.; Balogh, S. An Integrative Framework for Collaborative Governance. *J. Public Adm. Res. Theory* **2021**, *22*, 1–29. [CrossRef]
31. Moher, D.; Liberati, A.; Tetzla, J.; Altman, D.G.; Group, P. Preferred Reporting Items for Systematic Reviews and Meta Analyses: The PRISMA statement. *Ann. Intern. Med.* **2009**, *151*, 6. [CrossRef] [PubMed]
32. Bücheler, T.; Füchslin, R.M.; Pfeifer, R.; Sieg, J.H. Crowdsourcing, Open Innovation and Collective Intelligence in the scientific method: A research agenda and operational framework. In Proceedings of the Artificial Life XII—Twelfth International Conference on the Synthesis and Simulation of Living Systems, Odense, Denmark, 19–23 August 2010; pp. 679–686. [CrossRef]
33. Snyder, H. Literature review as a research methodology: An overview and guidelines. *J. Bus. Res.* **2019**, *104*, 333–339. [CrossRef]
34. Wolfswinkel, J.; Furtmueller, E.; Wilderom, C. Using grounded theory as a method for rigorously reviewing literature. *Eur. J. Inf. Syst.* **2013**, *22*, 45–55. [CrossRef]
35. Corbin, J.; Strauss, A. *Basics of Qualitative Research*, 3rd ed.; Sage: Thousand Oaks, CA, USA, 2008.
36. Garfield, E.; Sher, I.H. KeyWords Plus Algorithmic Derivative Indexing. *J. Am. Soc. Inf. Sci.* **1993**, *44*, 298–299. [CrossRef]
37. Prpić, J.; Taeihagh, A.; Melton, J. The Fundamentals of Policy Crowdsourcing. *Policy Internet* **2015**, *7*, 340–361. [CrossRef]
38. Taeihagh, A. Crowdsourcing: A New Tool for Policy-Making? *Policy Sci. J.* **2017**, *50*, 629–647. [CrossRef]
39. Kerzner, H. Project Management Organisational Structures. In *Project Management Case Studies*; Kerzner, H., Ed.; Willey: Hoboken, NJ, USA, 2017. [CrossRef]
40. Aitamurto, T.; Chen, K. The value of crowdsourcing in public policymaking: Epistemic, democratic and economic value. *Theory Pract. Legis.* **2017**, *5*, 55–72. [CrossRef]
41. Iacuzzi, S.; Massaro, M.; Garlatti, A. Value Creation Through Collective Intelligence: Managing Intellectual Capital. *Electron. J. Knowl. Manag.* **2020**, *18*, 68–79.
42. White, J. *Managing Information in the Public Sector*; M.E. Sharpe: Armonk, NY, USA, 2007.
43. Aitamurto, T.; Landemore, H.; Galli, J.S. Unmasking the crowd: Participants' motivation factors, expectations, and profile in a crowdsourced law reform. *Inf. Commun. Soc.* **2017**, *20*, 1239–1260. [CrossRef]
44. Mergel, I. Opening Government: Designing Open Innovation Processes to Collaborate with External Problem Solvers. *Soc. Sci. Comput. Rev.* **2015**, *33*, 599–612. [CrossRef]

45. Wijnhoven, F.; Ehrenhard, M.; Kuhn, J. Open government objectives and participation motivations. *Gov. Inf. Q.* **2015**, *32*, 30–42. [CrossRef]
46. Guth, K.L.; Brabham, D.C. Finding the diamond in the rough: Exploring communication and platform in crowdsourcing performance. *Commun. Monogr.* **2017**, *84*, 510–533. [CrossRef]
47. Iandoli, L.; Quinto, I.; Spada, P.; Klein, M.; Calabretta, R. Supporting argumentation in online political debate: Evidence from an experiment of collective deliberation. *New Media Soc.* **2018**, *20*, 1320–1341. [CrossRef]
48. Leitner, K.H.; Warnke, P.; Rhomberg, W. New forms of innovation: Critical issues for future pathways. *Foresight* **2016**, *18*, 224–237. [CrossRef]
49. Almirall, E.; Lee, M.; Majchrzak, A. Open innovation requires integrated competition-community ecosystems: Lessons learned from civic open innovation. *Bus. Horiz.* **2014**, *57*, 391–400. [CrossRef]
50. Epp, D.A. Public policy and the wisdom of crowds. *Cogn. Syst. Res.* **2017**, *43*, 53–61. [CrossRef]
51. Bose, T.; Reina, A.; Marshall, J.A.R. Collective decision-making. *Curr. Opin. Behav. Sci.* **2017**, *16*, 30–34. [CrossRef]
52. Liu, H.K. Crowdsourcing Government: Lessons from Multiple Disciplines. *Public Admin. Rev.* **2017**, *77*, 656–667. [CrossRef]
53. Chen, K.; Aitamurto, T. Barriers for Crowd's Impact in Crowdsourced Policymaking: Civic Data Overload and Filter Hierarchy. *Int. Public Manag. J.* **2019**, *22*, 99–126. [CrossRef]
54. Linders, D. From e-government to we-government: Defining a typology for citizen coproduction in the age of social media. *Gov. Inf. Q.* **2012**, *29*, 446–454. [CrossRef]
55. Hogan, M.; Ojo, A.; Harney, O.; Ruijer, E.; Meijer, A.; Andriessen, J.; Pardijs, M.; Boscolo, P.; Boscolo, E.; Satta, M.; et al. Governance, Transparency and the Collaborative Design of Open Data Collaboration Platforms: Understanding Barriers, Options, and Needs. In *Government 3.0—Next Generation Government Technology Infrastructure and Services*; Ojo, A., Millard, J., Eds.; Springer: Cham, Switzerland, 2017. [CrossRef]
56. Flavián, C.; Guinalíu, M.; Gurrea, R. The role played by perceived usability, satisfaction and consumer trust on website loyalty. *Inf. Manag.* **2006**, *43*, 1–14. [CrossRef]
57. Fernández-Martínez, J.; López-Sánchez, M.; Aguilar, J.A.R.; Rubio, D.S.; Nemegyei, B.Z. Co-Designing participatory tools for a New Age: A proposal for combining collective and artificial intelligences. *Int. J. Public Adm. Digit. Age* **2018**, *5*, 17. [CrossRef]
58. Lenart-Gansiniec, R.; Sułkowski, Ł. Crowdsourcing—A New Paradigm of Organisational Learning of Public Organisations. *Sustainability* **2018**, *10*, 3359. [CrossRef]
59. Yates, F. Contingency table involving small numbers and the χ2 test. *Suppl. J. R. Stat. Soc.* **1934**, *1*, 217–235. [CrossRef]
60. Web of Science Core Collection Help. Available online: https://images.webofknowledge.com/images/help/WOS/contents.html (accessed on 12 May 2021).
61. Landemore, H. *Democratic Reason: Politics, Collective Intelligence, and the Rule of the Many*; Princeton University Press: Princeton, NJ, USA, 2013.
62. Landemore, H. *Open Democracy: Reinventing Popular Rule for the Twenty-First Century*; Princeton University Press: Princeton, NJ, USA, 2020.
63. Noveck, B.S.; Harvey, R.; Dinesh, A. *The Open Policymaking Playbook*; New York University: New York, NY, USA, 2019; Available online: https://www.thegovlab.org/static/files/publications/openpolicymaking-april29.pdf (accessed on 14 May 2021).
64. Ryan, M.; Gambrell, D.; Noveck, B.S. *Using Collective Intelligence to Solve Public Problems*; Nesta: London, UK, 2020.
65. Noveck, B.S.; Konopacki, M.; Dinesh, A.; Ryan, M.; Munozcano, B.R.; Kornberg, M.; Gambrell, D.; Hervey, R.; Joerger, G.; DeJohn, S.; et al. *Crowdlaw for Congress. Strategies for 21st Century Lawmaking*; New York University: New York, NY, USA, 2020; Available online: https://congress.crowd.law/files/crowdlaw_playbook_Oct2020.pdf (accessed on 14 May 2021).
66. Aitamurto, T. *Crowdsourced Off.-Road Traffic Law Experiment in Finland*; Parliament of Finland: Helsinki, Finland, 2014.
67. Noveck, B.S. *Smart Citizens, Smarter State: The Technologies of Expertise and the Future of Governing*; Harvard University Press: Cambridge, MA, USA, 2015.
68. Mulgan, G. Social Innovation: How Societies Find the Power to Change. Policy Press: Bristol, UK, 2019.
69. Verhulst, S.G.; Zahuranec, A.J.; Young, A. *Identifying Citizens' Needs by Combining AI and CI*; New York University: New York, NY, USA, 2019; Available online: https://thegovlab.org/static/files/publications/CI-AI_oct2019.pdf (accessed on 17 July 2021).
70. Transforming Our World: The 2030 Agenda for Sustainable Development. Available online: https://sdgs.un.org/2030agenda (accessed on 24 July 2021).
71. Malone, T. *Superminds: The Surprising Power of People and Computers Thinking Together*; Little, Brown and Co.: New York, NY, USA, 2018.

Article
Leadership Hijacking in Docker Swarm and Its Consequences

Adi Farshteindiker [1,*] and Rami Puzis [1,2,*]

1 Software and Information Systems Engineering, Ben Gurion University of the Negev, Beer Sheva 8410501, Israel
2 Telekom Innovation Labs, Ben Gurion University of the Negev, Beer Sheva 8410501, Israel
* Correspondence: adifars@post.bgu.ac.il (A.F.); puzis@bgu.ac.il (R.P.)

Abstract: With the advent of microservice-based software architectures, an increasing number of modern cloud environments and enterprises use operating system level virtualization, which is often referred to as container infrastructures. Docker Swarm is one of the most popular container orchestration infrastructures, providing high availability and fault tolerance. Occasionally, discovered container escape vulnerabilities allow adversaries to execute code on the host operating system and operate within the cloud infrastructure. We show that Docker Swarm is currently not secured against misbehaving manager nodes. This allows a high impact, high probability privilege escalation attack, which we refer to as leadership hijacking, the possibility of which is neglected by the current cloud security literature. Cloud lateral movement and defense evasion payloads allow an adversary to leverage the Docker Swarm functionality to control each and every host in the underlying cluster. We demonstrate an end-to-end attack, in which an adversary with access to an application running on the cluster achieves full control of the cluster. To reduce the probability of a successful high impact attack, container orchestration infrastructures must reduce the trust level of participating nodes and, in particular, incorporate adversary immune leader election algorithms.

Keywords: Docker Swarm; leader election; privilege escalation; defense evasion; cloud

Citation: Farshteindiker, A.; Puzis, R. Leadership Hijacking in Docker Swarm and Its Consequences. *Entropy* **2021**, *23*, 914. https://doi.org/10.3390/e23070914

Academic Editors: Sotiris Kotsiantis and Alberto Guillén

Received: 24 May 2021
Accepted: 5 July 2021
Published: 19 July 2021

Publisher's Note: MDPI stays neutral with regard to jurisdictional claims in published maps and institutional affiliations.

Copyright: © 2021 by the authors. Licensee MDPI, Basel, Switzerland. This article is an open access article distributed under the terms and conditions of the Creative Commons Attribution (CC BY) license (https://creativecommons.org/licenses/by/4.0/).

1. Introduction

Securing distributed collaborative multi-agent agent systems is an extremely complex task. Since attackers are not obliged to follow the protocols defined by the system developers, they may create diverse adverse effects with simple manipulations applied to non-adversary-resilient protocols. Unfortunately, it is extremely difficult to secure a multi-agent system if it was not designed with security in mind. A good example of a design decision that may affect the overall security of a system is the choice of the leader-election algorithm [1]. In this article, we explore the consequences of the insecure leader election algorithm used in Docker Swarm.

As Docker gained popularity among cloud service providers, attackers began to develop various techniques to attack Docker-based applications. Although a great deal of attention was paid to securing Docker hosts from application level exploits and container escape few solutions exist for securing against privilege escalation among different hosts in a Docker cluster. In this work, we show how an attacker with access to a manager host inside a Docker cluster can escalate their privileges in the cluster. The research scope is presented in Figure 1.

For example, Raft, a consensus algorithm used to manage a replicated log [2], is used in Docker Swarm to synchronize the cluster's state between all managers of the cluster. See Section 2.2 for details. The logs are replicated using a strong leader, which is elected in the leader election phase in the algorithm. In case of a leader failure (a crash, network issues, etc.), the rest of the managers choose a new leader using the Raft algorithm. Despite its many advantages, Raft is a non-Byzantine algorithm that can allow a malicious insider to become a leader.

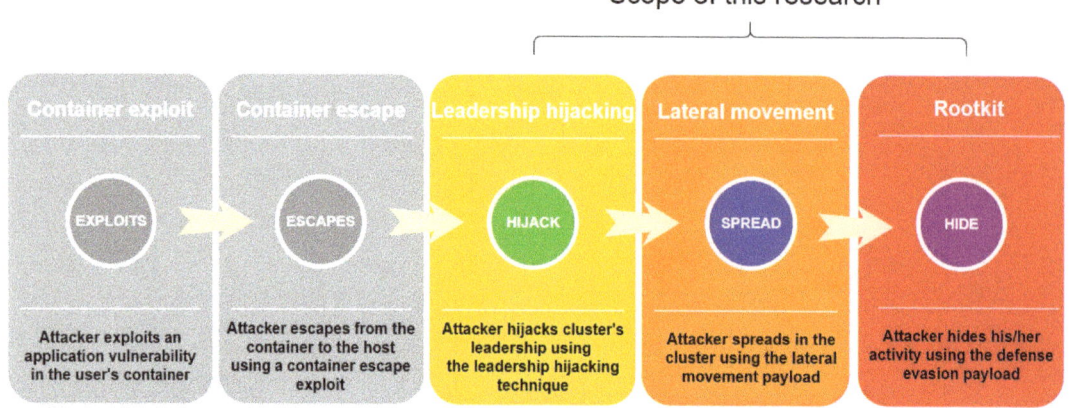

Figure 1. High-level description of the end-to-end scenario.

In this paper, we highlight a new privilege escalation technique called *leadership hijacking* (see Section 4.2). An attacker with access to a manager node in Docker Swarm can use this technique, which abuses the aforementioned fact that Raft is a non-Byzantine algorithm, to escalate their cluster privileges and become the cluster leader. By doing so, the attacker can control all messages and decisions within the cluster.

In addition, we demonstrate two possible malicious payloads expected to be executed by a typical attacker: a *lateral movement* payload and a *defense evasion* payload. The former utilizes cluster leader privileges and allows the attacker to execute code on every host in the cluster.

The latter is used by an attacker in order to hide their malicious activity from infrastructure management tools.

The rest of this paper is structured as follows: Section 2 reviews the technical background. In Section 4.2, we introduce the novel privilege escalation technique, called leadership hijacking. Next, in Section 4.3 we investigate malicious payloads that can be executed after the privilege escalation. In Section 5, we demonstrate an end-to-end attack scenario that illustrates the potential security risk and the impact of the investigated attack. Finally, in Section 6, we discuss possible mitigation and propose countermeasures. Our final remarks can be found in Section 7.

2. Background

2.1. Docker Swarm

An increasing number of organizations are moving their digital systems to the cloud. The benefits of cloud servers are easy deployment, high availability, continuous maintenance, system security, and more. From online websites to internal servers and databases, cloud servers store a lot of sensitive information, making them an attractive target for attackers. As the cost of hardware has decreased, software has become the main performance bottleneck. In order to fully utilize the available hardware, cloud service providers use virtualization technology to run different applications on the same hardware.

Until recently, the most advanced solution was virtual machine (VM) technology.

VM technology allows one physical server to run many different virtual servers, all of them running different operating systems.

From a security point of view, a VM is a good solution, since breaking out of a VM is a relatively complex task [3].

On the other hand, VMs suffer from significant performance overhead [4]. The main reason for the reduced performance is the overhead added by the hypervisor to each hardware operation emulated to the VM.

Today, many cloud service providers use operating system level virtualization, which employs isolated user space instances called containers. In contrast to a VM, which includes its own operating system, containers run under the host's operating system and communicate with it directly. During the runtime, a container communicates through a regular system call interface with the host OS, without any intermediate software.

The architectural difference is illustrated in Figure 2.

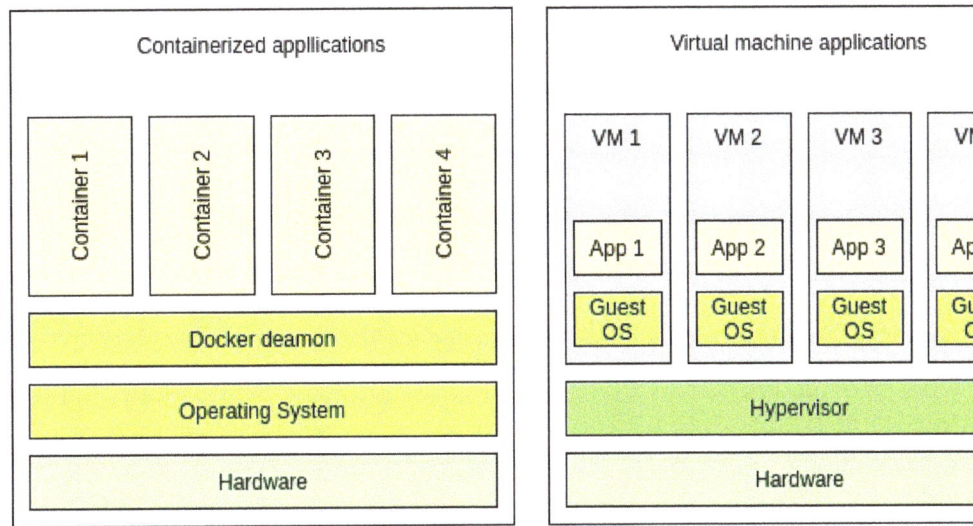

Figure 2. Container vs. VM architecture [5].

At the time of this writing, Docker is one of the leading OS virtualization solutions (https://resources.flexera.com/web/media/documents/rightscale-2019-state-of-the-cloud-report-from-flexera.pdf (accessed on 8 July 2021)). Docker is implemented in the Go programming language and enables the creation, deployment, and management of containers on a host computer. A Docker container is a lightweight software unit that bundles its own tools and libraries. Typically, one container includes one instance of an application or service, e.g., a Web server, database, or scientific software package.

Docker is a rich ecosystem. One of the main components of this ecosystem is the Docker daemon. The Docker daemon is software that runs on the host and is responsible for the creation of images and containers. The Docker daemon can run containers and create their runtime environment; it can also create a container's networking interfaces, mount points, can trigger actions, and execute commands inside a running container. The Docker daemon implements Docker's main logic and many of its features.

When deploying an application in a production environment, it is important to ensure that when a container fails, a new container will start and replace the faulty container. In addition, it is highly recommended to run several instances of a container for high availability and load balancing. To address these issues, Docker introduced a feature called swarm.

Docker Swarm abstracts many Docker hosts to one virtual Docker host. Each host that participates in the swarm cluster is called a *node*. Each node can have two roles: *manager* or *worker*. A manager's job is to keep a replicated state of the cluster. One manager node is also a *leader*. The cluster's leader is responsible for scheduling new containers and services for the cluster. A worker's job is to get container tasks from the leader and to actually run the container. The weakest point in the design of Docker Swarm exploited in this research is the Raft leader election algorithm.

2.2. Leader Election

Raft [2] is a consensus algorithm used to manage a replicated log. Raft was designed with the aim of producing an efficient and understandable algorithm which, unlike Paxos [6–8], would be easy to learn and use in practical systems. Raft was chosen in Docker Swarm due to its important features:

- Strong leader—Raft uses a stronger form of leadership than other consensus algorithms. For example, log entries only flow from the leader to other servers.
- Leader election—Raft uses randomized timers to elect leaders. This adds only a small number of mechanisms to the already existing heartbeat mechanism and facilitates simpler conflict resolution.
- Membership changes—Raft's mechanism for changing the set of servers in the cluster uses a new joint consensus approach, which allows the cluster to continue operating normally during configuration changes.

Raft assumes that all nodes are honest and is not tolerant to malicious (Byzantine) nodes participating in the leader election process.

Byzantine fault tolerant (BFT) leader election algorithms have existed for a long time. These algorithms provide the ability to overcome failures in networks where some nodes are Byzantine. For example, Castro et al. [9,10] described a state machine replication algorithm able to tolerate Byzantine faults. The algorithm guarantees safety, i.e., each replicated log is agreed on by all non-faulty nodes.

Bessani et al. [11] introduced an open-source Java library implementing robust BFT state machine replication. Key features of their implementation include reliability, modularity, and a flexible application programming interface (API). Moreover, their implementation achieved good performance and can tolerate real world faults.

Castro et al. [9] implemented a BFT library, that can be used to build highly available systems that tolerate Byzantine faults. Castro et al. used the library to implement a Byzantine-fault-tolerant NFS file system. They showed that the replicated library can be even more efficient than the non-replicated version of NFS.

3. Related Work

When attacking a cloud based application, an adversary may exploit classical application vulnerabilities, such as SQL injection, buffer overflow, command injection, etc. Using such vulnerabilities, an attacker can control the victim's container and data inside it. Container escape exploits are another technique class; in this case, after successful container exploitation, the attacker exploits a vulnerability allowing the attacker to escape from the container to the underlying host. Access to the underlying host grants an attacker access to data and other containers that run on the compromised host.

There are many products and protocols that try to mitigate the above-mentioned techniques. First, Docker offers built in protections (https://docs.docker.com/engine/security/ (accessed on 8 July 2021)), such as protecting the Docker daemon socket and using data encryption between the Docker daemon and public registries. These protections harden Docker hosts with a "security in depth" approach. In addition, software, such as SE-Linux and App-Armor, can help harden container isolation and minimize the attack surface between containers and the host. Furthermore, Docker offers an image scanning service (https://docs.docker.com/engine/scan/ (accessed on 8 July 2021)), which can detect vulnerabilities in Docker images.

In the rest of this section, we overview the previous work on cloud security related to Docker. Table 1 summarizes the main differences from related works.

Singh et al. [12] demonstrated primary techniques used by attackers to attack cloud services. There are many potential attack vectors that attackers can use, including: DoS and DDoS attacks [13,14], malware injection, and side-channel attacks [15–18]. In their study, Jensen et al. [19] demonstrated an attack on the software of the cloud itself and outlined the threat of flooding attacks on cloud systems. The authors suggested improving the cloud's security by first improving the security of frameworks used in the cloud.

In [20], Liu et al. provided an overview of the latest technologies in cloud computing and discussed how Docker is integrated into it. According to Liu et al., the major difference between classic VM and containers is that a VM contains not only the application and its dependencies but also the entire guest operating system. The authors listed rapid application deployment, portability across machines, lightweight footprint, and minimal overhead as the main advantages of Docker over traditional VM-based virtualization software. Moreover, in [21], Marathe et al. overviewed the process of the setup of a computer cluster based on Docker Swarm and Kubernetes and evaluated each one of these platforms.

Xavier et al. [22] performed numerous experiments in order to evaluate the performance of container-based cloud environments compared to VM-based cloud environments as well as the trade-off between performance and isolation. They found that the cloud environment would benefit from container-based solutions, due to the fact that container-based solutions achieve near-native performance.

Table 1. Comparison with related works.

	Application Exploit	Container Escape Exploit	Cloud/Docker's Framework Exploit	Orchestrator's Exploit	Full Chain Attack POC	Attack Surface Overview
Our paper	✓	✓		✓	✓	
Wu et al., 2020 [23]	✓	✓				✓
Linetsky et al., 2020 [24]			✓	✓		
Seather 2018 [25]			✓			
Amara et al., 2017 [26]	✓	✓				
Kabbe 2017 [27]	✓					
Combe et al., 2016 [28]	✓			✓		
Singh & Shrivastava 2012 [12]	✓					✓
Jensen et al., 2008 [13]				✓		

Other research [28] suggested a new attack surface in the Docker environment: namely indirect adversaries. Unlike a direct adversary, who exploits vulnerabilities in the cluster directly, an indirect adversary exploits third party appliances (e.g., Docker Hub) in order to attack Docker's environment.

An overview of attack types and mitigations in cloud environments is shown in [26]. Among others, Amara et al. mentioned SQL injection as "application level attack", which is used to obtain an initial foothold in the cluster. Moreover, they mentioned hypervisor attacks as "VM level attacks", which are used for privilege escalation and breaking VM isolation. In addition, they offered mitigations to each one of the attacks that they describe.

Moreover, Wu et al. [23] evaluated the security of container based cloud services. They defined metrics upon which they evaluated a number of services. Among others, they specified "privilege escalation" metric and "container escape" metric. They found that, although there are some services that failed in the "privilege escalation" metric, the "container escape" metric was very high, which limits the impact of the attacker.

In his master's work, Kabbe [27] compared the security model of containers to hypervisor-based systems and virtual machines. He compared the outcome of known attacks (DirtyCow, (https://nvd.nist.gov/vuln/detail/CVE-2016-5195 (accessed on 8 July 2021)) Heartbleed, (https://nvd.nist.gov/vuln/detail/CVE-2014-0160 (accessed on 8 July 2021)) and Shellshock (https://nvd.nist.gov/vuln/detail/CVE-2014-6271 (accessed on 8 July 2021))) in a containerized environment, with the outcome of the same attacks performed in hypervisor/virtual machine environments. He found that containers offered at least the same amount of security as hypervisor/virtual machine environments.

In his master thesis [25], Seather reviewed the underlying security of the Docker Swarm infrastructure. Namely, Seather tested many adversarial scenarios, including: flooding the orchestrator with invalid/corrupted requests, sniffing the network from within the cluster, impersonating a cluster member, performing man-in-the-middle attacks between containers within Docker's internal network, and more. The conclusions of his thesis were that Docker's infrastructure is secure, Docker Swarm's design is good (from a security point of view), the technology stack used by Docker is immune to known attacks, and the development community responds quickly to security incidents.

Attacking the cloud's infrastructure is also shown in [24]. In their work, Linetskyi et al. showed and utilized a Kubernetes privilege escalation exploit, in which an attacker can obtain a root privileges inside a container. If the container is misconfigured, this can result in root privileges to the underlying host. The bug resides in Kubernetes's management tool, which stresses the fact that extra care should be made to secure the code of the infrastructure (in that case, Kubernetes).

4. Taking over the Docker Swarm

In this section we present the new techniques that can be used to take over a Docker Swarm cluster. We present a full exploit chain starting with existing container escape exploit. When combined with our leadership hijacking technique it ultimately gives the attacker cluster leader privileges. Later, we show how our malicious payloads can be used to completely compromise cloud environment while evading detection.

4.1. High-Level Overview

A high-level overview of the end-to-end attack scenario can be seen in Figure 1. The attack consists of five major steps:

1. Exploitation of an application vulnerability inside a container, in which an attacker gains a foothold within the user's container
2. Container escape exploitation, in which an attacker obtains access to the container's underlying host
3. Leadership hijacking, in which an attacker executes the privilege escalation technique presented in Section 4.2 and obtains cluster leader privileges
4. Lateral movement, in which an attacker executes the lateral movement payload described in Section 4.3.1 and gains privileged access to all hosts in the cluster
5. Defense evasion, in which an attacker uses the defense evasion payload described in Section 4.3.2 in order to hide their lateral movement payload from management tools

In order to demonstrate the feasibility and impact of the leadership hijacking technique and the malicious payloads, we developed an end-to-end attack scenario that shows how an external attacker can chain exploits seen in the wild with our technique and payloads, in order to obtain full control of a cluster. A detailed description of this scenario is provided in Section 5. Steps 1 and 2 are implemented in order to demonstrate the feasibility of our work, but they are not elaborated upon, since they are out of the scope of our research.

4.2. Leadership Hijacking

In this section, we introduce an adversarial technique named leadership hijacking. A precondition to employing this technique is code execution access to a manager node.

In Section 5, we show how this precondition can be achieved in a production environment. From now on, we will refer to the manager host compromised by the attacker as the attacker's manager. The main idea of our technique is to repeatedly trigger a leader election phase until the attacker's manager becomes the cluster leader.

The technique's pseudocode is shown in Algorithm 1.

Algorithm 1 Attack pseudo code.
1: @Pre-condition: attacker escaped his container
2: **procedure** GET-LEADERSHIP
3:    **if** Attacker's manager is cluster leader **then**
4:       *Exit*
5:    **while** Attacker's manager is not leader **do**
6:       *leader_id* ← find out current leader ID
7:       demote node with id *leader_id*
8:       wait until a new leader is elected
9:       promote node with id *leader_id* to be manager
10: @Post-condition: attacker's manager is the leader

As shown in Algorithm 1, the first step of the technique is to identify the current cluster leader. If the current leader is the attacker's manger, the technique's code will exit. Otherwise, the technique starts a loop.

In each loop iteration, the technique demotes (i.e., removes from the leader role) the current cluster leader using the Docker's demotion API [29]. This will cause the cluster to initiate a leader election algorithm and elect a new leader. The first manager that reaches timeout proposes itself as the cluster leader. Afterwards, each manager votes in favor of one manager, and the manager that receives the majority of the votes becomes the new cluster leader.

In the final step of the iteration, the current cluster leader is identified again. If the attacker's manager is the leader, the technique exits. Otherwise, it will continue the loop until the attacker's manager becomes the cluster leader. To avoid being detected through repeated reduction in the number of available managers, the attacker promotes the demoted node back to the manager role [30] by the end of each leader election.

In order to prove that the technique works in practice, we implemented the pseudocode shown in Algorithm 1. We set up a lab to test the implementation, and its architecture is illustrated in Figure 3.

Running our technique's implementation in the lab was successful: the attacker was able to escalate privileges in order to become the new cluster leader.

4.2.1. Analysis

Convergence

In each iteration, the technique code demotes the leader. According to the Docker Swarm documentation, a manager that does not receive the heartbeat from the leader during the predefined time window assumes that the leader is unavailable and proposes itself to be the new cluster leader. Since the leader has been demoted, none of the managers receive the heartbeat from the leader, and hence a new leader election phase will start when the first manager reaches its timeout.

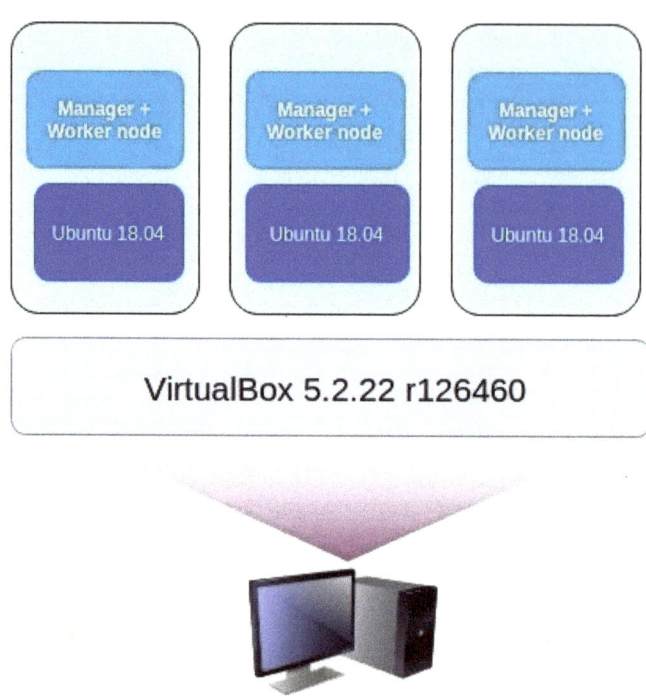

Figure 3. Overview of the lab architecture.

Docker Swarm closely follows the specification and implementation of Raft where the election timeout (the time a node waits before starting a new election) is randomly drawn from a predefined range. In addition to the election timeout, the probability of every manager becoming a leader depends on the communication delays and may not be the same for all managers [31]. Yet, it is safe to assume that in a properly configured swarm, every manager has a roughly equal probability to be elected.

In the absence of an attacker, each leader election is independent of the previous iterations of leader election. This stems from the fact that Raft nodes do not maintain any state concerning the leader election process except being a follower, a candidate, or a leader (Temporarily, there may be more than one node in a leader state due to collisions, which are solved by Raft). The attack introduces a slight dependency between iterations due to the absence of the previous demoted leader in the set of candidates.

The absence of a candidate cannot reduce the probability of the attacker's manager being elected. Thus the probability of the attacker's manager to be elected during each attack iteration is bounded from below by the probability of the respective manager to be elected without the attack. The positive probability of the attack success in each iteration and the ability of the attacker to continue demoting the leaders guarantee the eventual success of the attack.

The positive probability of the attack success in each iteration and the ability of the attacker to continue demoting the leaders guarantee the eventual success of the attack. In a properly configured system where each manager has the same probability to be elected, the number of managers is the mean number of leader elections until the attack succeeds.

Advantages

The first advantage of the technique is its simple implementation. In order to prove its feasibility, we decided to implement the technique in the most simple way possible. After reviewing the Docker Swarm API, we realized that our technique could be implemented with repeated calls to demote and promote API [29,30]. This simple implementation makes our technique stable and reliable.

The second advantage of our technique is its stealthiness. A typical attacker would like to stay undetected as long as possible while in an engagement. Our technique can be implemented in many ways; however, some are rather loud, which will increase the chance to get caught by the system administrators. For example, an attacker can demote all other managers of the cluster and become the only manger and, hence, the cluster leader. The obvious issue of this implementation is that the system administrators will quickly notice that the cluster state has changed. On the other hand, our implementation's changes to the cluster state are minimal, which makes it harder to detect the technique.

Limitations

The main limitation of our technique is that it is probabilistic. Although we showed that our technique completes successfully with probability $P \to 1$, the number of iterations in each execution may differ. An unknown number of iterations is particularly problematic in a real-world scenario.

4.3. Malicious Payloads

In order to illustrate the impact of the leadership hijacking technique, we developed malicious payloads that use cluster leader privileges and used them to perform some malicious operations.

Typically, an attacker who has access to one host inside a cluster would like to spread and obtain a wider foothold in the cluster. Ideally, the attacker would like to have access to all hosts in the cluster, with high privileges in each host. Moreover, once the attacker controls a cluster they would like to remain undetectable by the users/system administrators for as long as possible.

To achieve the above goals, the attacker has to find a way to spread inside the cluster and hide their malicious activity from users and monitoring tools. In this work, we introduce and develop two types of malicious payloads: a lateral movement payload and a defense evasion payload. These payloads utilize leader privileges and allow an attacker to execute high privileged code on every node in the cluster and hide from monitoring tools.

4.3.1. Lateral Movement

Typically, an attacker would like to establish a wide foothold in a cluster, preferably with high privileges. In this work, we create a payload that enables lateral movement in the cloud. Using this payload, we demonstrate how an attacker with leader privileges in a Docker Swarm cluster can execute high privileged code on each host in the cluster.

Due to the fact that, after successful execution of leadership hijacking, the attacker gains leader privileges, the attacker can control all messages that come out of the leader node. By hooking the leader's function responsible for sending messages between the leader and other nodes, the attacker can change these messages and alter their content.

In order to execute code on other nodes in the cluster, the attacker who is in control of a leader host can send the victim node a task to run. The attacker instructs the worker to run a container task with an image controlled by the attacker. As we show in Section 5, the victim node will execute the container. The container's image will be a malicious image.

However, the malicious container runs in an isolated environment in the host. As discussed in Section 3, containers run in a separate namespace from the host. Thus, for example, a process inside a container cannot sniff the host's network.

There are many ways to overcome this limitation. In addition to controlling what image the container will run on each host, the attacker also controls the creation flags of the container. Thus, for example, the attacker can mount the main file system of the host to the container. Then, from inside the container, the attacker can alter the host's executable files with a malicious code. In order to obtain highly privileged code execution, the attacker has to alter a file that is executed by a highly privileged user on the host. When the user executes the file, the attacker's malicious code will get executed as well, resulting in high privileged code execution on the host.

4.3.2. Defense Evasion

With the above lateral movement payload, the attacker can spread and move laterally by deploying service with malicious image to every host in the cluster. In this subsection, we show how an attacker can stay undetected in the cluster and hide malicious activity from the cloud's management tools. We introduce the cloud defense evasion payload, which offers rootkit-like functionality in the cloud.

In this subsection, we assume that the attacker is the cluster leader and has a malicious service in the cluster, which they wish to hide from system administrators, e.g., a malicious cryptocurrency mining service.

The default Docker Swarm command line offers a rich variety of commands for cluster administration. In particular, Swarm offers the `docker service` (https://docs.docker.com/engine/reference/commandline/service/ (accessed on 8 July 2021)) command for viewing and updating services that run on the cluster. In order to view services that run on the cluster, the system administrator can issue the `docker service ls` (https://docs.docker.com/engine/reference/commandline/service_ls/ (accessed on 8 July 2021)) command and view its output. The output includes the service's name, image, number of replicas, exposed ports, etc.

In order to obtain this information, the Docker daemon of the host that issued the command queries the leader of the cluster and retrieves the information from the leader.

However, the attacker is in control of the leader host. Hence, the attacker can hook the function that returns this information on the leader's Docker daemon and spoof the answers. In this way, the attacker can change malicious service's name, image, ports, or even the service itself (i.e., the attacker can trick the user into thinking that there is no such service at all, by removing any information related to the malicious service).

In a similar manner, the system administrator can view what containers are running for each service. Using `docker service ps` (https://docs.docker.com/engine/reference/commandline/service_ps/ (accessed on 8 July 2021)) command, the system administrator can obtain information about a container's image, name, state, etc. In a similar way to the `docker service ls` command, the issuing host queries the leader host and retrieves that information. The attacker has access to the leader host, and thus they can alter that information as well. By doing so, the attacker can trick the system administrator and show them that a container is running a different image than the real image, for example.

In this way, the attacker can hide malicious activity from Docker's default tools, which query the cluster leader to obtain information about objects (running services, containers, etc.) in the cluster.

5. End-to-End Attack Showcase

To prove that our leadership hijacking technique and malicious payloads are feasible, we implemented a combined scenario that demonstrates the impact of our technique and of the payloads. We show the importance of our technique and payloads, as well as that the initial assumption regarding the attack is reasonable. We provide proof-of-concept demonstration of an external attacker leveraging an exploit, which has been seen in the wild together with our leadership hijacking technique and malicious payloads, in order to ultimately control the entire cluster.

5.1. Lab Setup

To demonstrate the attack we set up a test-bed that, on the one hand, mimicked a cloud environment with a Docker Swarm and multiple client's services; and, on the other hand, included a typical attackers' tool set.

Cloud nodes were simulated using virtual machines that ran the Ubuntu guest OS. We set up a Docker Swarm cluster in which all hosts were both manager and worker hosts. In addition, an external laptop was used as the attacking machine. The laptop ran the Kali Linux operating system version 2019.3.

One important tool that we used was the Metasploit framework [32], an open-source framework supporting various penetration testing tasks.

The lab's architecture is shown in Figure 4.

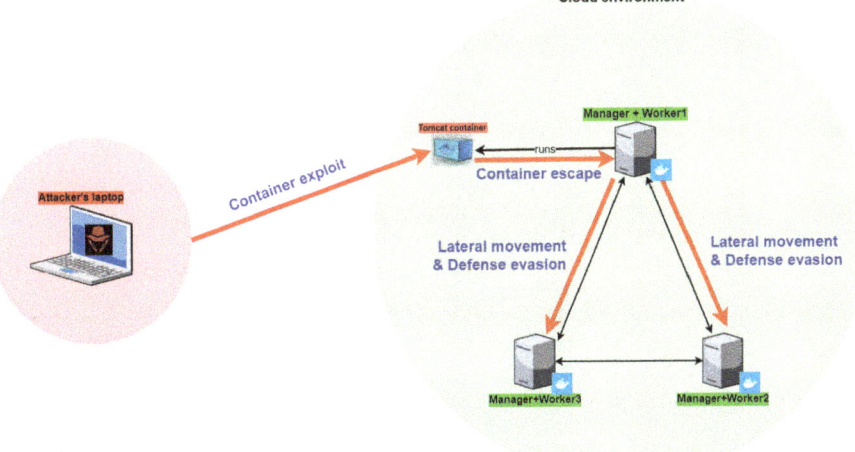

Figure 4. Diagram of the attack steps.

5.2. Scenario Overview

In our end-to-end attack scenario, the attacker started on an external laptop with network access to a Docker container that ran inside a Docker cluster. Ultimately, the attacker obtained high privileged code execution on each host in the cluster. The scenario contained five major steps:

1. Container exploitation
2. Container escape exploitation
3. Leadership hijacking
4. Lateral movement
5. Defense evasion

In each step, the attacker expands their foothold in the cluster. An illustration of the entire scenario and its steps can be seen in Figure 4.

The next subsections explain these steps in greater detail.

5.3. Container Exploitation

First, the attacker needs to have an initial foothold in the cluster. They have network access to an application that runs on a container in the cluster. In order to obtain an initial foothold, the attacker exploits a vulnerability in the application.

In this case, the application running inside the container is the Apache Tomcat Web server, version 8.5.19. The attacker finds a one-day exploit for that Web server in the

Metasploit framework; after successful exploit completion, the attacker has shell access to the application's container.

5.4. Container Escape

After the attacker has successfully exploited the application, the attacker has a shell in the restricted Docker environment. In order to execute our privilege escalation technique, the attacker needs to escape from the restricted environment and retrieve a shell on the underlying host of the container.

The attacker then exploits a vulnerability in the host's RunC component (https://www.cvedetails.com/cve/CVE-2019-5736/ (accessed on 8 July 2021)). RunC is a container runtime that was originally developed as part of Docker, which is responsible for running and managing new container environments.

A vulnerability resides in RunC version < 1.0-rc6 (which is used by Docker < 18.09.2), allowing the attacker to overwrite the host's RunC binary and, thus, achieve code execution with root privileges on the host.

5.5. Cloud Privilege Escalation

Once the attacker has achieved code execution on Docker's manager host, they can execute the leadership hijacking technique and escalate their privileges in order to become the cluster leader (see Section 4.2 for a description of the leadership hijacking technique).

After the leadership hijacking technique's successful execution, the attacker obtains leader privileges in the cluster and, thus, will be able to control all messages that flow between the leader and other hosts in the cluster.

The result of the technique's successful execution can be seen in Figure 5. In this figure, we can see that, before the attack, UBUNTU-HOST3 was the cluster leader, and after the technique was successfully executed, UBUNTU-HOST1 (which is the attacker's manager) obtained the leadership role in the cluster.

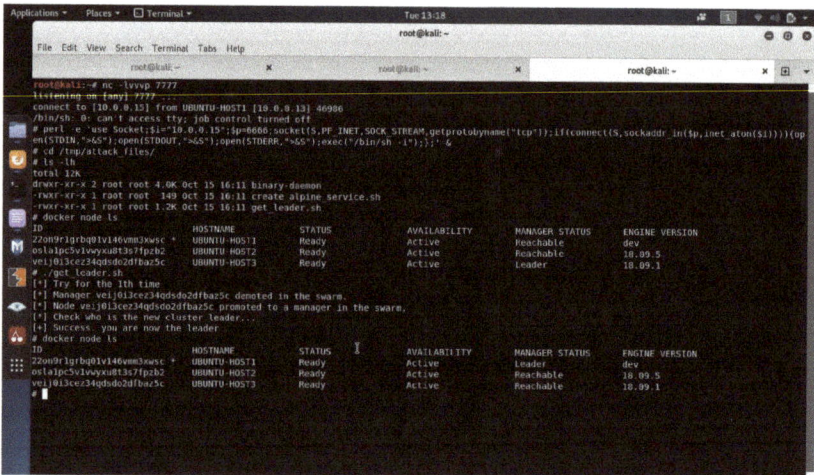

Figure 5. Successful attack attempt.

5.6. Lateral Movement and Defense Evasion

Armed with leader privileges, the attacker can now control all messages that flow between the leader and other hosts in the cluster. As described in Sections 4.3.1 and 4.3.2, the attacker can execute a malicious container on each host in the cluster and hide these actions from various management tools.

To effectively demonstrate the attack and its potential impact, in our scenario, the attacker will run a WebShell service, which will run a WebShell container on every host in the cluster.

The malicious WebShell container provides a root privileged command execution environment on the underlying host. The host's file system is mounted in the container's /tmp directory. This allows the attacker to view, modify, and delete the host's files. Effectively, the attacker runs a root WebShell on all hosts in the cluster.

The output of the WebShell can be seen in Figure 6. In addition, the figure shows that the WebShell is executed with high privileges (root).

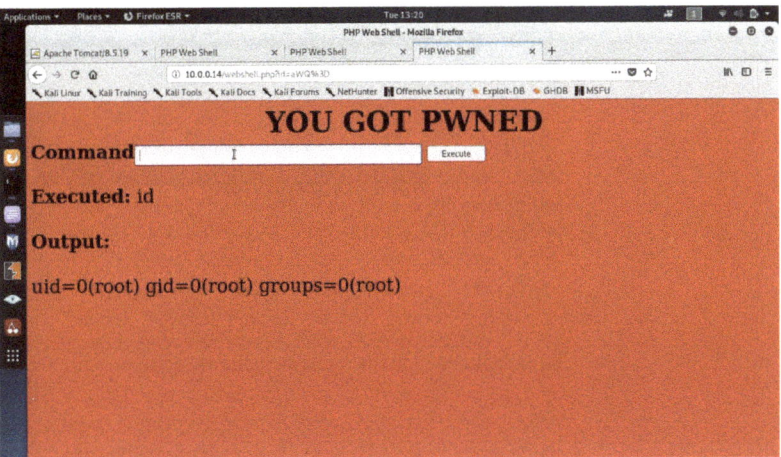

Figure 6. The output of the malicious WebShell.

The attacker uses the defense evasion functionality described in Section 4.3.2, hooking the leader's Docker daemon function, which is responsible for listing the services and containers of services. By doing so, any service listing request that is made to the cluster leader will be monitored by the attacker. In cases in which the attacker's malicious service is running, the attacker will spoof the answer of the listing and hide their malicious service image with a benign Alpine image.

As seen in Figure 7, `docker service ls` command reveals a single running service, with image `"alpine:latest"`. In addition, it seems that there are no listening ports; however, in actuality, a container on each host is listening on port 80.

Furthermore, the attacker also hooks the function responsible for listing container of each service; thus, the output of `docker service ps $(docker service ls -q)` does not reveal the real image that each container is actually running. According to Docker's default tools, it looks like the service running is a benign alpine service but accessing each host in port 80 reveals the true "face" of the service.

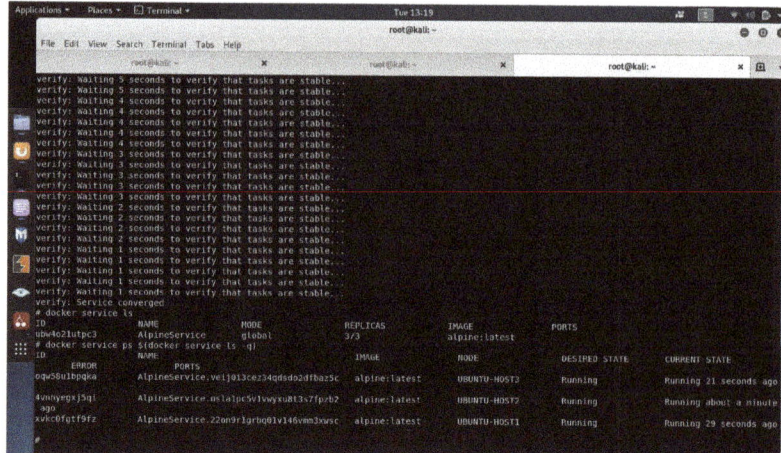

Figure 7. Docker's default tools used for viewing information about malicious services.

6. Discussion

The main advantage of our technique is that, unlike many techniques seen in the wild, our technique does not exploit any software bugs. A software bug is usually a mistake in a program's code, which can lead to an undefined behavior of the program. In most cases, software bugs are easily fixed. However, our technique does not exploit any programming errors but rather exploits a design flaw. Unlike programming bugs, logical bugs are much harder to fix, since, in many scenarios, a large amount of code must be changed, which can be costly and time-consuming for software developers.

As shown in Section 4.2, our technique exploits the fact that the Raft algorithm is used to replicate logs in the Docker Swarm environment but is a non-adversarial algorithm. Raft is a key component of Docker Swarm's management infrastructure, and it is integrated into the core logic of Docker Swarm. Replacing the Raft algorithm in Docker Swarm is a mandatory step to mitigate our proposed technique, since exploits used to escape from container to host (as shown in Section 5) are very common and relatively easy to find. Since its a design bug, replacing Raft requires a significant amount of work.

First, Docker's developers should choose and implement a byzantine fault tolerant algorithm [9,11] in Go, or find such an implementation as a Go package. The implementation should be high quality, since it will be deployed to every manager in the cluster. Next, the developers should modify Docker Swarm's source code. In Docker Swarm, Raft's implementation is encapsulated with a wrapper object. The developers of Docker Swarm should change the entire wrapper object to encapsulate the new package instead of Raft.

Then, series of tests should be ran to ensure that the new package meets Docker's efficiency requirements: both local and network. The new package should not consume a significant amount of the host's resources, and should be be efficient in terms of network activity between hosts in the Docker Swarm. Moreover, the tests should ensure that the new package works as expected on every operating system supported by Docker Swarm. Since managers are the most valuable servers in the cluster, any bug in a manager can be fatal. The tests should ensure, as much as possible, that the new package is bug free and that it has no unwanted side effects. In any case, replacing the Raft implementation holds a major risk and may cause a service degradation.

There are some best practices that may block our attack; the most common is to separate the manager nodes from worker nodes. In such a case, even if the attacker compromised a worker node, he will not be able to escalate his privileges in the way we suggested in this article, since the attacker's node is not part of the managers group. However, although considered a best practice, this is not the default behavior of Docker Swarm. We believe that Docker's developers chose to make the manager node a worker too by default in order to not waste expensive computing power. If a node is just a manager, it will not receive the client container to execute, and hence the cluster's computing capacity decreases. Regardless, in this article, we chose to research and exploit systems in their default state and not delve into best practices.

We offer two strategies in order to effectively mitigate our technique. In the short term, the technique can be mitigated by detecting and blocking container escape exploits. As discussed in Section 4.2, the leadership hijacking technique should be executed from a manager host. We showed in Section 5 that an attacker can gain such access using a container escape exploit. In the case that the container escape exploit fails, an attacker cannot launch the technique and, therefore, cannot escalate his privileges in the cluster. In order to reduce the amount of container escape exploits, Docker can start a bug bounty program. We believe that this will help Docker patch container escape vulnerabilities before they can be exploited by real attackers in the wild.

In the long term, we offer to replace the Raft algorithm with a byzantine fault tolerant algorithm [33,34]. As discussed earlier, Raft is a non adversarial algorithm; hence, an attacker who is in control of a Raft's participant can forge and spoof messages. In that way, the attacker can trick other participants to vote for him in the leader election phase and become the cluster's leader. In the case that a BFT algorithm is used, other participants would not vote for the attacker since the algorithm can tolerate byzantine participants. In that way, the attacker would not be able to escalate his privileges to cluster leader. Furthermore, in order to support future changes, the developers of Docker should divide Docker's infrastructure from the leader election algorithm. The architecture of Docker Swarm should be "plug and play", such that the leader election algorithm is chosen as a configuration option instead of a source code modification.

7. Conclusions

In this work, we suggested a new attack vector on the Docker Swarm orchestrator. Our technique demonstrated a new concept in offensive security in which a cluster is treated as a single unit of processing and an attacker is able to escalate their privileges in that unit and, thereafter, perform malicious activity on every component of that unit separately (i.e., every host in the cluster).

We presented a novel technique that, when combined with our proposed payloads, allows an attacker to gain full control over the Docker Swarm cluster. Since our technique and payloads do not exploit a software bug but rather exploit a design weakness, developers should take them into account during the design of their multi-agent systems. Future research should, on the one hand, explore additional ways in which attackers can obtain leader privileges in other cloud environments, e.g., Kubernetes, and, on the other hand, develop methods to detect misbehaving managers, for example, using anomaly detection techniques.

Author Contributions: Conceptualization, A.F.; Software, A.F.; Validation, A.F.; Formal analysis, A.F.; Investigation, A.F.; Methodology, R.P.; Supervision, R.P.; Writing—Original Draft, A.F. and R.P.; Writing—Review & Editing, A.F. and R.P. All authors have read and agreed to the published version of the manuscript.

Funding: This research was partially supported by the Cyber Security Research Center at Ben-Gurion University of the Negev.

Data Availability Statement: Not applicable.

Conflicts of Interest: The authors declare no conflict of interest.

References

1. Moussa, M.; Beltrame, G. On the robustness of consensus-based behaviors for robot swarms. *Swarm Intell.* **2020**, *14*, 205–231. [CrossRef]
2. Ongaro, D.; Ousterhout, J.K. In search of an understandable consensus algorithm. In Proceedings of the USENIX Annual Technical Conference, Philadelphia, PA, USA, 19–20 June 2014; pp. 305–319.

3. Reuben, J.S. A survey on virtual machine security. In *T-110.5290 Seminar on Network Security*; Helsinki University of Technology: Espoo, Finland, 2007; Volume 2. Available online: https://citeseerx.ist.psu.edu/viewdoc/summary?doi=10.1.1.626.4718 (accessed on 8 July 2021).
4. Moeller, K.-T. Virtual Machine Benchmarking. Ph.D. Thesis, Karlsruhe Institute of Technology, Karlsruhe, Germany, 2007.
5. Figure, Container vs. vm Arch. Available online: https://www.docker.com/resources/what-container (accessed on 8 July 2021).
6. Lamport, L. The part-time parliament. *ACM Trans. Comput. Syst. (TOCS)* **1998**, *16*, 133–169. [CrossRef]
7. Lampson, B.W. How to build a highly available system using consensus. In *International Workshop on Distributed Algorithms*; Springer: Berlin/Heidelberg, Germany, 1996; pp. 1–17.
8. Lamport, L. *Brief Announcement: Leaderless Byzantine Paxos*; Springer: Berlin/Heidelberg, Germany, 2011.
9. Castro, M.; Liskov, B. Practical byzantine fault tolerance and proactive recovery. *ACM Trans. Comput. Syst. (TOCS)* **2002**, *20*, 398–461. [CrossRef]
10. Castro, M.; Liskov, B. Practical byzantine fault tolerance. In Proceedings of the Third Symposium on Operating Systems Design and Implementation, New Orleans, LA, USA, 22–25 February 1999; Volume 99, pp. 173–186.
11. Bessani, A.; Sousa, J.A.; Alchieri, E.E.P. State machine replication for the masses with bft-smart. In Proceedings of the 2014 44th Annual IEEE/IFIP International Conference on Dependable Systems and Networks, Atlanta, GA, USA, 23–26 June 2014; pp. 355–362.
12. Singh, A.; Shrivastava, M. Overview of attacks on cloud computing. *Int. J. Eng. Innov. Technol. (IJEIT)* **2012**, *1*, 321–323.
13. Jensen, M.; Gruschka, N.; Luttenberger, N. The impact of flooding attacks on network-based services. In Proceedings of the 2008 Third International Conference on Availability, Reliability and Security, Barcelona, Spain, 4–7 March 2008; pp. 509–513.
14. Darwish, M.; Ouda, A.; Capretz, L.F. Cloud-based ddos attacks and defenses. In Proceedings of the International Conference on Information Society (i-Society 2013), Toronto, ON, Canada, 24–26 June 2013; pp. 67–71.
15. Gruss, D.; Maurice, C.; Wagner, K.; Mangard, S. Flush+ flush: A fast and stealthy cache attack. In *International Conference on Detection of Intrusions and Malware, and Vulnerability Assessment*; Springer: Berlin/Heidelberg, Germany, 2016; pp. 279–299.
16. Yarom, Y.; Falkner, K. Flush+ Reload: A High Resolution, Low Noise, l3 Cache Side-Channel Attack. USENIX Security Symposium. 2014; pp. 22–25. Available online: https://www.usenix.org/node/184416 (accessed on 8 July 2021).
17. Liu, F.; Yarom, Y.; Ge, Q.; Heiser, G.; Lee, R.B. Last-level cache side-channel attacks are practical. In Proceedings of the 2015 IEEE Symposium on Security and Privacy, San Jose, CA, USA, 17–21 May 2015; pp. 605–622.
18. Weiß, M.; Heinz, B.; Stumpf, F. A cache timing attack on aes in virtualization environments. In *International Conference on Financial Cryptography and Data Security*; Springer: Berlin/Heidelberg, Germany, 2012; pp. 314–328.
19. Jensen, M.; Schwenk, J.; Gruschka, N.; Iacono, L.L. On technical security issues in cloud computing. In Proceedings of the 2009 IEEE International Conference on Cloud Computing, Bangalore, India, 21–25 September 2009; pp. 109–116.
20. Liu, D.; Zhao, L. The research and implementation of cloud computing platform based on docker. In Proceedings of the 2014 11th International Computer Conference on Wavelet Actiev Media Technology and Information Processing (ICCWAMTIP), Chengdu, China, 19–21 December 2014; pp. 475–478.
21. Marathe, N.; Gandhi, A.; Shah, J. Docker Swarm and kubernetes in cloud computing environment. In Proceedings of the 2019 3rd International Conference On Trends In Electronics And Informatics (ICOEI), Tirunelveli, India, 23–25 April 2019; pp. 179–184.
22. Xavier, M.G.; Neves, M.V.; Rossi, F.D.; Ferreto, T.C.; Lange, T.; De Rose, C.A.F. Performance evaluation of container-based virtualization for high performance computing environments. In Proceedings of the 2013 21st Euromicro International Conference on Parallel, Distributed, and Network-Based Processing, Belfast, UK, 27 February–1 March 2013; pp. 233–240.
23. Wu, Y.; Lei, L.; Wang, Y.; Sun, K.; Meng, J. Evaluation on the Security of Commercial Cloud Container Services. In *International Conference On Information Security*; Springer: Cham, Switzerland, 2020; pp. 160–177.
24. Linetskyi, A.; Babenko, T.; Myrutenko, L.; Vialkova, V. Eliminating privilage escalation to root in containers running on kubernetes. *Sci. Pract. Cyber Secur. J.* **2020**. Available online: https://journal.scsa.ge/papers/eliminating-privilage-escalation-to-root-in-containers-running-on-kubernetes/ (accessed on 8 July 2021).
25. Sæther, D. Security in Docker Swarm: Orchestration Service for Distributed Software Systems. Master's Thesis, The University of Bergen, Bergen, Norway, 2018.
26. Amara, N.; Zhiqui, H.; Ali, A. Cloud computing security threats and attacks with their mitigation techniques. In Proceedings of the 2017 International Conference On Cyber-Enabled Distributed Computing And Knowledge Discovery (CyberC), Nanjing, China, 12–14 October 2017; pp. 244–251.
27. Kabbe, J.A. Security Analysis of Docker Containers in a Production Environment. Master's Thesis, NTNU, Trondheim, Norway, 2017.
28. Combe, T.; Martin, A.; Di Pietro, R. To docker or not to docker: A security perspective. *IEEE Cloud Comput.* **2016**, *3*, 54–62. [CrossRef]
29. Docker Node Demote Api. Available online: https://docs.docker.com/engine/reference/commandline/node_demote/ (accessed on 8 July 2021).
30. Docker Node Promote Api. Available online: https://docs.docker.com/engine/reference/commandline/node_promote/ (accessed on 8 July 2021).
31. Choumas, K.; Korakis, T. When Raft Meets SDN: How to Elect a Leader over a Network. In Proceedings of the 6th IEEE Conference on Network Softwarization (NetSoft), Ghent, Belgium, 29 June–3 July 2020; pp. 140–144.

32. Kennedy, D.; O'gorman, J.; Kearns, D.; Aharoni, M. *Metasploit: The Penetration Tester's Guide*; No Starch Press: San Francisco, CA, USA, 2011.
33. Veronese, G.S.; Correia, M.; Bessani, A.N.; Cheuk Lung, L.; Verissimo, P. Efficient byzantine fault-tolerance. *IEEE Trans. Comput.* **2011**, *62*, 16–30. [CrossRef]
34. Cowling, J.; Myers, D.; Liskov, B.; Rodrigues, R.; Shrira, L. Hq replication: A hybrid quorum protocol for byzantine fault tolerance. In Proceedings of the 7th Symposium on Operating Systems Design and Implementation, Seattle, WA, USA, 6–8 November 2006; pp. 177–190.

Article

Accuracy-Risk Trade-Off Due to Social Learning in Crowd-Sourced Financial Predictions

Dhaval Adjodah [1,*], Yan Leng [2], Shi Kai Chong [1], P. M. Krafft [3], Esteban Moro [4] and Alex Pentland [1,*]

1. Media Lab, Massachusetts Institute of Technology, Cambridge, MA 02139, USA; cshikai@mit.edu
2. McCombs School of Business, The University of Texas at Austin, Austin, TX 78912, USA; yleng@mit.edu
3. Oxford Internet Institute, University of Oxford, Oxford OX1 2JD, UK; pkrafft@mit.edu
4. Departamento de Matemáticas & GISC, Universidad Carlos III de Madrid, 28911 Leganes, Spain; emoro@mit.edu
* Correspondence: dval@mit.edu (D.A.); pentland@mit.edu (A.P.)

Abstract: A critical question relevant to the increasing importance of crowd-sourced-based finance is how to optimize collective information processing and decision-making. Here, we investigate an often under-studied aspect of the performance of online traders: beyond focusing on just accuracy, what gives rise to the trade-off between risk and accuracy at the collective level? Answers to this question will lead to designing and deploying more effective crowd-sourced financial platforms and to minimizing issues stemming from risk such as implied volatility. To investigate this trade-off, we conducted a large online Wisdom of the Crowd study where 2037 participants predicted the prices of real financial assets (S&P 500, WTI Oil and Gold prices). Using the data collected, we modeled the belief update process of participants using models inspired by Bayesian models of cognition. We show that subsets of predictions chosen based on their belief update strategies lie on a Pareto frontier between accuracy and risk, mediated by social learning. We also observe that social learning led to superior accuracy during one of our rounds that occurred during the high market uncertainty of the Brexit vote.

Keywords: crowd-sourcing; wisdom of the crowd; social learning; Bayesian models; risk

1. Introduction

Distributed financial platforms are on the rise, ranging from Decentralized Autonomous Organizations [1], crowd-sourced prediction systems [2] to the very recent events during which retail investors self-organized using social media and drove up asset and derivative prices [3,4]. In this work, we investigate how financial agents process information from one another and predict-individually and collectively—the future prices of real assets. Specifically, we are interested in understanding the computational models they use to update their beliefs after information exposure and how different social vs. non-social belief update strategies lead to trade-offs in prediction performance.

Here, we expand the typical definition of performance for collective prediction to include the concept of risk. Typically, the prediction performance of collectives and swarms is measured mostly by the accuracy of the group over collections of tasks [5–7]. However, it has been shown theoretically [8,9] and observed in a variety of applications [10,11] that there is a fundamental trade-off between prediction accuracy (average error) and prediction risk (variance of error).

This means that for any prediction system, risk will always be present, and that maximizing accuracy will come at the expense of increased risk. Hence, the performance of the system will always exist within a pre-defined Pareto frontier [12,13] which is the curve containing all possible system performance parametrizations (here, pairs of possible accuracy and risk values). Therefore, a platform designer will need to make trade-offs between risk and accuracy and cannot achieve arbitrarily combinations of risk and accuracy. Treating risk and accuracy as equally important for prediction is standard in

statistical [8–10] and financial [14–16] forecasting applications and literature because it allows for prediction systems to be calibrated and deployed with regard to specific accuracy and risk profiles [17–21].

However, characterizing the performance of crowd-based prediction systems regarding both accuracy and risk is not common and such a Pareto frontier has not been observed in crowd-sourced financial asset price prediction. We are therefore interested in investigating if a Pareto frontier exists and what the causes are behind this trade-off. From the perspective of crowd-sourced financial platform designers, understanding the trade-off between accuracy and risk and how to select subsets of predictions that achieve a certain accuracy and risk is useful to fit a required risk profile. This, in turn, allows for more sophisticated and versatile applications of crowd-sourced predictions such as hedging risks over portfolios of prediction tasks.

To test our hypothesis that a Pareto frontier exists between risk and accuracy and that it is mediated by social learning, we designed our collective prediction experiments as a series of Wisdom of the Crowd (WoC) tasks. For background, the Wisdom of the Crowd [22,23] is a popular domain within the collective intelligence literature where participants (the 'crowd') are asked to make predictions of a certain quantity, such as the future price of an asset on the stock market [24] or the caloric content of food items [25]. Prior work in the WoC literature [25–27] has focused on maximizing the average accuracy of collectives with little regard to the risk of the predictions.

The structure of this paper is as follows: we do a short literature review of the connections of this work to research on collective intelligence and the accuracy-risk trade-off in Section 2. We discuss our materials and methods (experimental design, data collection, and modeling and estimation) in Section 3. We present our results (belief update modeling, accuracy-risk trade-off and prediction under high uncertainty during Brexit) in Section 4. We discuss the implications and limitations of our work in Section 5.

Contributions

Our work makes the following novel contributions:

- We present an experimental procedure where we exposed 2037 participants to social and non-social information during 7 independent rounds of predicting financial asset prices (S&P 500, gold and WTI Oil). We collected 4634 prediction sets which include participants' predictions before and after information exposure, as well as the information they were exposed to. We are releasing this data here.
- Using computational models inspired by Bayesian models of cognition [28,29] to investigate the belief update strategy of participants, we observe that a simple model that approximates the likelihood (evidence) to be a unimodal Gaussian beats a more complex Monte Carlo approach. This suggests that our participants exhibit the attribute substitution heuristic of human decision-making [30], whereby a complicated problem is solved by approximating it with a simpler, less accurate model.
- We observe that participants prefer to learn from social information rather than from non-social information, another interesting information processing heuristic.
- Our main contribution: we observe a Pareto frontier between accuracy and risk. As the average accuracy of the crowd over the different prediction rounds increases, so does the risk in the crowd's predictive accuracy. We further observe that this trade-off is mediated by the amount of social learning i.e., the extent to which participants pay attention to each other's judgments.
- We deployed one of our prediction tasks just before the Brexit vote during which there was a great deal of market uncertainty [31], and we observe that during such uncertain times social learning leads to higher accuracy.

These results are not only important for the practical deployment of distributed financial prediction platforms but also expand our understanding of how financial agents process information and make distributed predictions.

2. Related Work

2.1. Collective Intelligence and Social Learning

There is a rich literature on how decentralized information processing, learning and decision-making affects the performance of collectives and swarms [32–36]. Here, we focus on how platforms can be designed for people to make predictions with high performance, which is a central question for the Wisdom of the Crowd [22,23,37].

It has been shown that the temporal influence and mutual information dynamics between individuals can have a strong effect on crowd collective performance. On the one hand, prior work has shown that exposure to social information can lead to degraded performance in aggregate guesses [26,37,38]. For example, increasing the strength of social influence has been shown to increase inequality [39]. Selecting the predictions of people who are resistant to social influence has been shown to have improved collective accuracy [27]. The influence of influential peers has been theoretically shown to prevent the group from converging on the true estimate [26], and exposure to the confidence levels of others has been shown to influence people to change their predictions for the worse [40].

On the other hand, social learning has also been shown to lead to groups outperforming their best individuals when they work separately [41] and a collective intelligence factor has been shown to predict team performance better than the maximum intelligence of members of the team [35]. Similarly, human-inspired social communication between agents has been shown to improve collective performance in optimization algorithms [5,42].

Therefore, the role of social learning in collective performance is still being understood. Our contribution to this line of research is that a more complete characterization of performance in terms of not just accuracy but also risk provides avenues for future work towards reconciling the disagreements as to the role of social influence on performance. This is especially important due to the already existing strong social components in many crowd-sourcing platforms and applications [43–48] that could be harnessed more effectively for performance improvement.

2.2. Accuracy-Risk Trade-Off

Previous work has investigated several avenues to optimize the accuracy of the crowd such as by recalibrating predictions against systematic biases of individuals [26] and selecting participants who are resistant to social influence [27]. Additionally, rewiring the network topology of information-sharing between subjects [25,41], and optimally allocating tasks to individuals [49] has improved collective accuracy. However, these studies focused on accuracy with little regard to risk. There is a rising movement to go beyond accuracy and to fully characterize performance—at the individual and the collective level—in terms of both accuracy and risk. Some call this emerging line of work going beyond the 'bias bias (In the statistics literature, bias is another name for accuracy. This movement suggests that research should go beyond its current focus on just bias and study risk).

At the individual level, there is increasing evidence that people preferentially optimize for risk instead of accuracy in a variety of domains [50]. Cognitively, people have been observed to manifest decision heuristics [51] to be conservative in the face of uncertainty [52,53]. For example, rice farmers have been observed not to adopt significant harvest improvement technology because of the risk of it failing once and causing significant family ruin [54]. Evolutionarily, risk aversion has been shown to emerge when rare events have a large impact on individual fitness [52]. Furthermore, in a meta-study of 105 forecasting papers, 102 of them support prioritizing for lower risk to achieve higher overall performance [55]. At the collective level, there is limited work regarding the characterization of the performance of collectives and swarms in terms of both accuracy and risk although there is a large literature on other related trade-offs such as between speed and accuracy [56–60].

From a system design perspective, crowd-sourcing platform designers should characterize their performance in terms of both accuracy and risk due to theoretical results [8,9] and observations in applications [10,11] that the performance of any prediction system is subject to a fundamental trade-off between accuracy and risk. This is especially important in our domain of predicting financial asset prices as risk is already known to have negative effects on the efficiency of markets such as through the phenomenon of implied volatility [61].

3. Materials and Methods

3.1. Experimental Design

To test our hypothesis that a Pareto frontier exists between risk and accuracy—i.e., that there is a trade-off between risk and accuracy of prediction across several prediction rounds—and that it is mediated by social learning, we need a dataset with the following requirements:

- Predictions are made of complex and difficult-to-predict phenomena so that our results are applicable to the real-world platform applications.
- Predictions are made over many independent prediction rounds so that the risk of the crowd over these different tasks can be estimated.
- A ground-truth is needed against which we can compare our dataset to judge the external validity of individual and collective performance metric.
- The social and non-social information each participant was exposed to after their initial pre-exposure prediction is recorded so that we can later model how different types of information influenced them in updating their belief into their post-exposure prediction.

Given the above requirements, we designed the experimental procedure as detailed below: we recruited a total of 2037 participants over seven prediction rounds to predict the future prices of financial assets (the S&P 500, WTI Oil, and gold prices) during seven separate consecutive 3-week rounds over the span of 6 months, resulting in 9268 predictions (i.e., 4634 prediction pairs or sets). We focused on predicting financial prices as doing so is a hard prediction problem [62,63]. Our participants were mid-career financial professionals with years of financial experience. Our participants consented to their data being used in this study and we obtained prior IRB approval. One of our rounds of prediction happened to end the day of the Brexit vote, which means that we have prediction data during a particularly volatile market period [31] as described in Supplementary Section A.5.

During each round, participants made a prediction of the same asset's closing price for the same final day of the round. We use the round's last day's closing market price as our measure of ground-truth. We carefully instrumented the social and non-social information that our participants were exposed to, and collected their predictions before and after exposure to this information. We also deployed one of our rounds during a high uncertainty period to understand if variance reduction strategies allow the crowd to be resistant to risk.

We did not opt for an A/B testing experimental design [64]—where we would have split participants and shown each group either the social information or the historical price time series—because we wanted participants to naturally choose whichever source of information to use to update their belief. This was an important experimental design choice as we wanted to understand, as close as possible to in-situ how people update their beliefs in the real-world where they are already exposed to both their peers' beliefs and to price history information, such as through financial news. Our design is in contrast to previous work where the experiments were deployed within a carefully controlled laboratory set-up as in prior work [25,37,40].

3.2. Data Collection

As shown in the screenshot of the user interface in Figure 1, we designed the data collection process as follows: every time a participant makes a prediction of an asset's future price through our platform, the following prediction set comprising B_{pre}, B_H, B_T and B_{post} is collected:

- A "pre-exposure" belief prediction B_{pre}, which is independent of *both* social information and price history. For example, a participant might show-up on the platform and predict that the closing price of the S&P 500 to be 2001 on 24 June 2016.
- The predictions B_H within the social information histogram shown to each participant after each initial prediction. Additionally, we display a 6-month time series of the asset's price B_T up to this point.
- The revised "post-exposure" prediction B_{post}. For example, after seeing the social histogram and asset price history, a participant might update their belief to 2201. Since the real price (the ground-truth V) ended up being 2037.41, this participant became more accurate after information exposure (they went from 2001 to 2201).

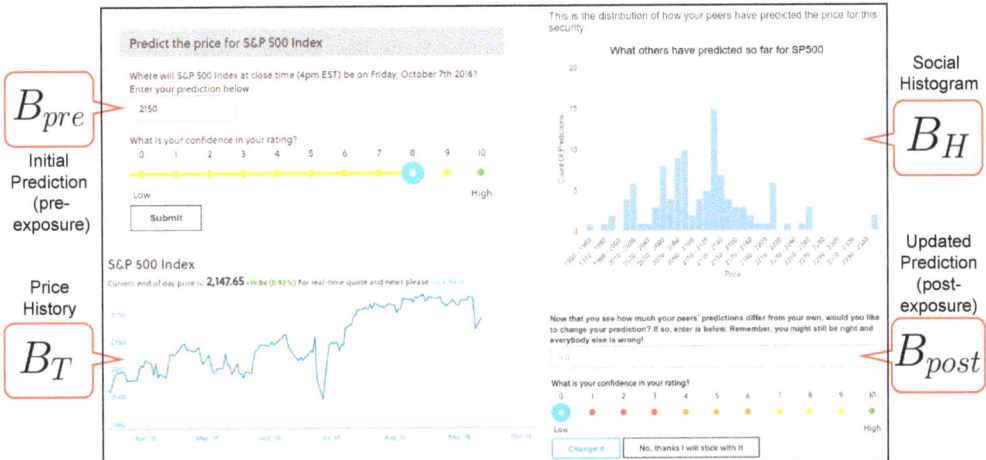

Figure 1. An annotated screenshot of how data were collected: the pre-exposure prediction B_{pre} is shown first, followed by the social histogram B_H and the price history B_T. Finally, the updated prediction B_{post} is collected. The ground-truth of the asset's final closing price will be V (not shown here, realized at the end of the round).

Overall, we ensure that the "pre-exposure" prediction is made before any social information and price history is shown. We present a unique histogram for every new prediction (as it is built using past predictions up to this point), as well as a unique price history time series (as it shows the 6-month price data up to the time of prediction). We require all participants to make a post-exposure prediction even if they decide to keep it at the pre-exposure level.

3.3. Modeling and Estimation

Using the data collected in the live experiments, we want to test our hypothesis that a Pareto frontier exists between risk and accuracy and that it is mediated by social learning. In this section, we describe all the modeling and estimation steps required to investigate our hypothesis:

- In Section 3.3.1, we describe how we model individual belief update: how a participant updates their prediction from a pre-exposure belief to a post-exposure prediction using a variety of models that are either Monte Carlo methods or simpler approximate methods inspired by Bayesian models of cognition [28,29]. This allows us to understand how participants update their belief after information exposure.
- In Section 3.3.2, using the models described earlier, we detail how to estimate the relative amount of social vs. non-social learning for each prediction to understand how much social vs. non-social data were factored into a prediction's belief update. We then introduce our methodology for selecting predictions based on the estimated amount

of social vs. non-social learning. This allows us to make aggregate predictions—at the platform level—based on a pre-specified amount of social learning.
- In Section 3.3.3, we detail how the accuracy and risk—at the platform level—of selected subsets are measured, and how they are used to investigate whether a Pareto trade-off exists between accuracy and risk and whether it is mediated by the relative amount of social vs. non-social learning.

3.3.1. Modeling Belief Updates

Using formalism inspired by Bayesian models of cognition [29], we can model the 4634 prediction sets collected over many rounds, at a high level, as a Bayesian update. To use this formalism, we need to select a prior distribution for each individual's belief before exposure to any information and a likelihood (evidence) distribution to model the data participants are exposed to. Additionally, a sampling or approximate method is required to use the prior and evidence to compute the posterior (updated belief after information exposure) distribution. Here, we describe the modeling assumptions and procedure at a high level, and detail more thoroughly our modeling assumptions and present our derivations in Supplementary Section A.3.

Fundamentally, we are interested in how participants predict an asset's future price (ground-truth) V based on the information we expose them to. The choice of the prior distribution is straightforward: $P_{prior}(V) \approx P(B_{pre})$, the distribution of belief of an individual before they are exposed to any information. We discuss in our model derivation (Supplementary Section A.3) how, when needed, we approximate the full distribution $P(B_{pre})$ since we obtain only one sample, B_{pre}, for each participant and cannot observe the full distribution $P(B_{pre})$.

After participants input their pre-exposure belief B_{pre}, there are two main likelihood (evidence) distributions participants employ: they are exposed to the assets' price history B_T, giving us $P_{likelihood}(V) \approx P(B_T)$, or analogously, the social histogram B_H, giving us $P_{likelihood}(V) \approx P(B_H)$. In the modeling stage here, we assume that participants used these two likelihood distributions separately to update their beliefs, but we relax this assumption in the estimation stage next where we estimate the relative amount of social vs. non-social learning for each prediction. We detail in Supplementary Section A.3 how likelihood distributions are built from the information that participants are exposed to. In Supplementary Section A.2, we formally detail how we transform the price history into a cognitively accurate 'rates histogram' using price momentum. As a summary, because it has been shown that people process time series as a distribution of changes as opposed to a distribution of the quantity itself [65–67], we convert the price history time series into a histogram of daily changes (slopes) in prices which is used for both the simple Gaussian models and the numerical models for price prediction.

Given the prior and likelihood, the *modeled* posterior prediction $P_{posterior}(V)$, can, therefore, be approximated as $P_{posterior}(V) \propto P(B_H) \cdot P(B_{pre})$ in the case of exposure to social information, and $P_{posterior}(V) \propto P(B_T) \cdot P(B_{pre})$ when participants are exposed to the past price history. We do not make any other assumptions in terms of what data to use to approximate the likelihood and prior distributions. Given these distributions, the question is then how to compute the posterior (updated) belief of an individual.

Although we focus on Bayesian models in this work, we include one popular model commonly used as a benchmark in the literature, the DeGroot model [68]. In this model, an individual updates their belief as the weighted average belief of their peers where weights can be, for example, trust values of the individual for their peers. Here we set the weights (trust values) equal for all peers, as we have no data to estimate these weights, and therefore assume a uniform prior.

Although the space of possible distributions and posterior computation approaches is very large, we focus here on using two simple, interpretable, and theoretically motivated approaches from prior work [28]. We either use Gaussian (normal) conjugate distributions to approximate priors and likelihoods due to strong evidence of their ubiquity as Bayesian models of cognition [29], or use a full Monte Carlo numerical sampling approach to calculate the posterior from the actual distributions of prices that participants were exposed to. We leave to future work the exploration of richer distributions and approaches to modeling belief update as it is beyond the scope of this study.

3.3.2. Subsetting Predictions Based on Social Learning

Based on how participants update their belief, we would like to select subsets of predictions based on whether they were more likely updated using social or non-social information. This approach of using characteristics of how predictions are updated is standard in the Wisdom of the Crowd literature. For example, prior work has estimated resistance to social influence [27] and influenceability in revising judgments after seeing the opinion of others [69,70], and used them to improve collective performance. No prior work has investigated investigating if the modeling of belief update strategies could be leveraged for improved collective performance.

Using the previously modeled posteriors, we can *estimate* how much of each information source—social information and price history—each participant used to update their belief by comparing the residual errors of models using either only social information or only price history as likelihood. As will be introduced in the Section 4, although we explored many models of belief update, the simple conjugate Gaussian models model best how participants update their belief. This is in line with previous research showing that although simple, they are highly accurate models of mental estimation in a variety of domains [28].

Therefore, for the purposes of selecting subsets of prediction based on their relative amount of social vs. non-social learning, we choose to focus on the GaussianSocial and GaussianPrice. These models assume the likelihood (evidence) data distribution to be built, respectively, from the social information and price history participants are exposed to.

Our approach is illustrated in Figure 2: using the prediction of the models Gaussian Social and GaussianPrice, we calculate a residual ϵ_H for when updating belief using social information B_H and a residual ϵ_T when updating from the price history B_T, as $\epsilon_H = \frac{|\text{GaussianSocial} - B_{post}|}{B_{post}}$ and $\epsilon_T = \frac{|\text{GaussianPrice} - B_{post}|}{B_{post}}$ respectively. We define $\alpha = \epsilon_T - \epsilon_H$, and we use it to measure how likely a participant used each source of information to update their prediction. For example, for a prediction set $[B_{pre}, B_H, B_T, B_{post}]$ if $\alpha > 0$ (i.e., $\epsilon_T > \epsilon_H$), this means that this prediction set is better modeled using the social histogram of peer's belief B_H instead of the price history B_T.

Using α, which we re-scale to be in the interval $[-1, 1]$ for each round, we can select a subset S_{α_s} of the prediction sets such that the α of these prediction sets lie in the range $0 \leq \alpha < \alpha_s$ (or $\alpha_s < \alpha \leq 0$ when $\alpha_s < 0$). α_s is the one-sided boundary we will vary to measure how much more likely a participant updated their belief from the social information instead of the price history. For example, the higher α_s is, the more likely a prediction set is better modeled using the social histogram of peer's belief B_H instead of the price history B_T.

It is important to note that the residuals we use to select subsets are belief update model residuals (between the observed updated belief and the predicted modeled updated belief) which are uncorrelated with the crowd residual (between the crowd's aggregate prediction and the ground-truth).

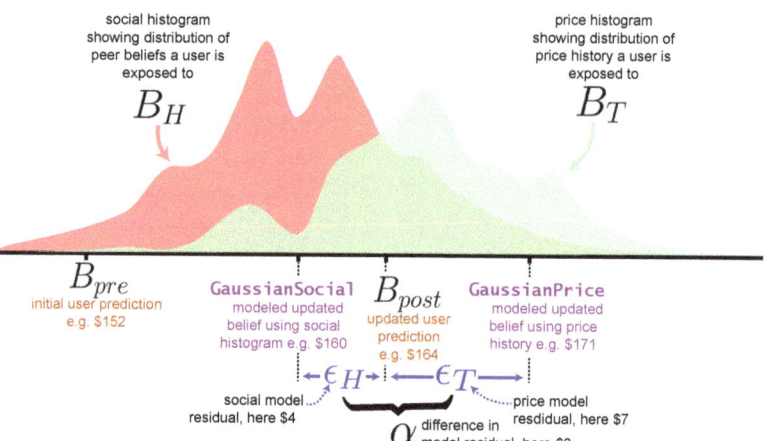

Figure 2. An example belief update: for each prediction set, a participant updates their belief from the pre-exposure prediction B_{pre} to the updated prediction B_{post} by either learning from the social histogram B_H and/or the price history B_T. ϵ_H is the residual between the *modeled* updated prediction GaussianSocial and the participant's updated prediction B_{post}; ϵ_T is the residual between GaussianPrice and B_{post}. α is the difference between ϵ_T and ϵ_H.

3.3.3. Evaluating Improvement of Subsets

Our hypothesis is that a Pareto frontier exists between risk and accuracy and that this trade-off is mediated by the relative amount of social vs. non-social learning.

To test this hypothesis, we investigate how the accuracy and variance of subsets S_{α_s} of predictions selected using α_s (a measure of the relative amount of social vs non-social learning) compares to the current standard Wisdom of the Crowd approach whereby all predictions are used.

From the perspective of platform designers who want to be able to select predictions based on required levels of accuracy or risk (e.g., to fit a certain portfolio of risk), it is important to measure improvement of subsets relative to the full collection of predictions. This is because, currently, platform designers only have access to one global measure of risk and accuracy—that of the whole set of predictions (when there is no subset filtering). To demonstrate that selecting subsets of predictions can lead to significant *improvements* in accuracy and risk, we therefore need to calculate these improvements.

We therefore define improvement $I^{S_{\alpha_s}}$ as the absolute difference between the error $e_{S_{\alpha_s}}$ when using a subset S_{α_s} compared to the error $e_{S_{all}}$ when using the full set of predictions S_{all}, the Wisdom of the Crowd, where S_{all} is defined as the full subset over all predictions using $-1 \leq \alpha \leq 1$.

The error $e_{i,S_{\alpha_s}}$ over all predictions $j \in S_{\alpha_s}$ for an estimated amount α_s of relative social vs. non-social information during experiment round i is defined as $\frac{|\sum_{j \in S_{\alpha_s}} [B_{post,j}] - V_i|}{V_i}$. To allow for estimation uncertainty over the improvement in accuracy and risk of subsets, we use 100 bootstraps with replacement. This procedure is formally described in Supplementary Section A.3.4.

We use an analogous approach to estimate the risk of the platform by calculating the standard deviation instead of the mean of the improvements over experiment rounds. This measures the risk for platform designers to estimate, over a basket of prediction rounds, what is the variance of improvements over this basket. This is the same as understanding the variance of error of a statistical prediction model (e.g., machine learning model) such that we can calibrate both the accuracy and variance of the model over a portfolio of predictions.

4. Results

Here we present our results. In Section 4.1, we detail our supporting result related to how different belief update models perform. Next, in Section 4.2, we present our main result about the trade-off between accuracy and risk in the Wisdom of the Crowd. Lastly, we present the supporting result regarding the effect of social learning during the high uncertainty period before the Brexit vote in Section 4.3.

4.1. Belief Update Models

Although the space of possible prior and likelihood distributions and posterior computation approaches is very large, we focus on using simple, interpretable, and theoretically motivated approaches from prior work [28]. We leave to future work the exploration of richer distributions and approaches to modeling belief update as it is beyond the scope of this study. We detail how model error and confidence intervals are evaluated in Supplementary Section A.3.3.

As can be seen in Figure 3, models that use social information as likelihood for modeling the belief update of participants (GaussianSocial, GaussianSocialModes, Numerical Social) outperform better than models that use the price history (GaussianPrice, Numerical Price). This suggests that our participants more likely use social information instead of the price history to update their belief, in line with previous work showing that participants often prefer using social information [71,72].

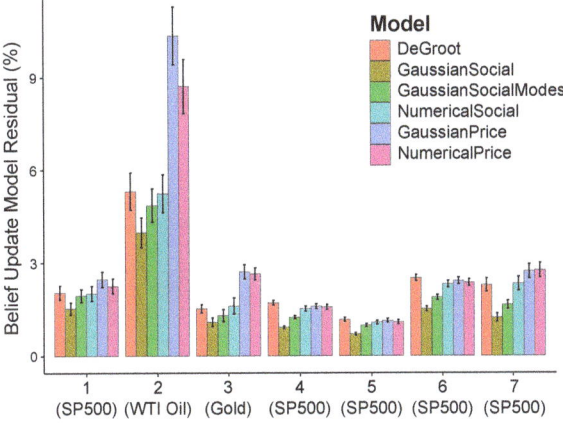

Figure 3. The y-axis shows the relative residual between *modeled* belief update and *actual* updated belief. Simple approximated models do better at modeling belief update than numerical models, and models using social histograms as likelihood perform better than models using the price history. Error bars represent 95% CI.

Specifically, GaussianSocial, our simple Gaussian model that assumes the data follows a single-mode Gaussian distribution, outperforms GaussianSocialModes, a model that identifies when the social histogram is non-unimodal (using the Hartigan's dip test of unimodality [73]) and uses the largest mode as the mean of the distribution. This suggests that participants assume the data they learn from to be unimodal even when it is non-unimodal, in line with prior work [74,75] showing that this might be due to the fact that using multi-modal data is cognitively costly.

Additionally, GaussianSocial outperforms the more precise numerical model NumericalSocial which makes no parametric assumption on the data distributions and uses a Monte Carlo procedure to estimate the posterior distribution. This suggests that participants employ simple heuristics when learning from their peers, in line with the attribute substitution heuristic of human decision-making [30]. However, when participants are learning from the price history, the dominance of simpler models is not as clear because the performance of the simple `GaussianPrice` model is indistinguishable from that of the numerical model (`NumericalPrice`).

`GaussianSocial` also outperforms the popular `DeGroot` model commonly used as a benchmark in the literature [68], where an individual updates their belief as the weighted average belief of their peers. Here we set the weights (trust values) equal for all peers, as we have no data to estimate these weights, and therefore assume a uniform prior. It is interesting to note that `GaussianSocial` is equivalent to the `DeGroot` model when a participant's weight on their own prior belief is equal to the total of the weights of all other participants. This agrees with previous work showing that participants put a disproportionately larger weight on their own prior belief [76,77].

Overall, the superiority of `GaussianSocial` in predicting belief update suggests that participants use a heuristic, unimodal, and simple belief update procedure when updating their beliefs, and that they predominantly update their predictions using social information instead of price history. It is important to note that approximate (non-Monte Carlo) models such as `GaussianSocial` and `GaussianPrice` are parameter-less models and did not require any parameter fitting, making their success in modeling belief update quite interesting.

4.2. Accuracy-Risk Trade-Off

Here, we present our main result about the trade-off between accuracy and risk in the Wisdom of the Crowd. Using a Pareto curve, we compare the improvement in prediction accuracy and risk (variance) of each subset S_{α_s} as defined by α_s, a measure of the relative amount of social vs non-social learning.

As shown in Figure 4, we observe that with improvements in accuracy of subsets comes increased risk, mediated by the relative amount of social vs. non-social learning α_s, suggesting a trade-off between accuracy and risk. As formally described earlier in Section 3.3.3, improvement is a measure of the additional accuracy gained from a subset of predictions compared to when using all predictions by the crowd (the de-facto Wisdom of the Crowd) over all prediction rounds. Similarly, risk is a measure of the risk of this subset compared to when using all predictions over all rounds. From a system design perspective, we choose these measures of improvement and risk as they allow us to understand how choices over subsets of participants might affect performance, allowing us to calibrate the crowd as per the platform designer's risk preferences.

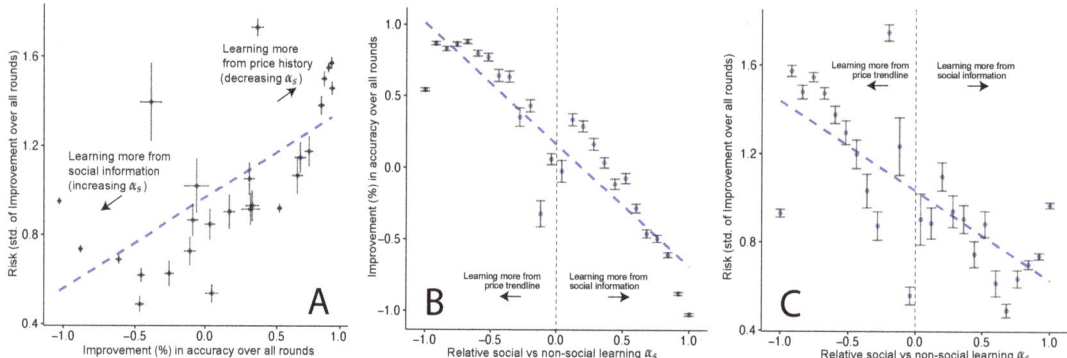

Figure 4. (**A**): In this Pareto curve, we plot the improvement of each subset vs. the risk (standard deviation) in improvement within this subset. We see a risk-return trade-off: predictions made with price history are more accurate, but with higher risk (standard deviation). Fitted line has R^2 of 0.49, and p-value < 0.001. Horizontal and vertical error bars represent 95% CI from 100 bootstraps. (**B,C**): Instead of plotting risk vs. improvement (as in (**A**), here we plot the same values of improvement ((**B**), $R^2 = 0.82$, p-value < 0.001) or risk ((**C**), $R^2 = 0.50$, p-value < 0.001) against the relative amount of social vs. non-social learning, α_s, that generated these values of improvements or risk.

Additionally, since we observe that variance of improvement (risk) decreases with increased social leaning, our result replicates prior findings that exposure to social information decreases the variance of the crowd [37]). Please note that the decrease in risk from social learning is not because participants are simply converging towards the crowd's mean: as detailed in the previous Section 4.1, the social histogram participants are shown is quite often non-unimodal (tested using the Hartigan's dip test of unimodality [73]), which means that participants are intentionally collapsing multiple distribution modes in the observed data.

Such a Pareto trade-off between risk and accuracy is common in financial forecasting [15,16] and statistical prediction [8–11], but has not been typically observed in the literature on the Wisdom of Crowds. This has strong implications for the design of crowd-sourced prediction platforms as described in the Discussion Section 5.1.

4.3. Performance under High Uncertainty

A supporting result of our work is from the investigation of the crowd's performance during a period of high uncertainty using the data from the prediction round that happened during the Brexit vote (see supplementary Section A.5 for details about this round).

Following the same procedure described in the Methods Section 3.3.3, we bin all α's from the prediction sets and investigate the improvements of subsets of predictions compared to the whole crowd. The main difference here is that unlike in all previous results where we took care not to use the last week of data to calculate collective accuracy so that prediction was not too easy, we do so here as the high uncertainty only happened in the last week (as shown in supplementary Figure S1). This last week of data that we use is a *disjoint subset* from the data we previously used.

As can be seen in Figure 5, as α_s decreases (i.e., we select predictions that were more likely updated using the price history instead of the social information, $\alpha_s < 0$), improvement in accuracy of subsets compared to the Wisdom of the Crowd (all predictions) decays to a great extent.

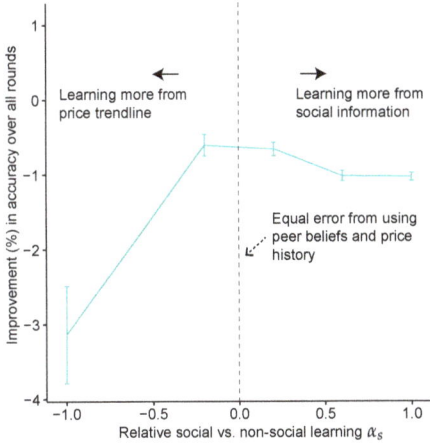

Figure 5. Improvement when selecting predictions based on how much more they were likely made using social information ($\alpha_s > 0$) vs. price history ($\alpha_s < 0$). 95% Confidence intervals obtained through 100 bootstraps.

Conversely, as subsets of predictions updated using the social histogram ($\alpha_s > 0$) are selected, the improvement in their accuracy is stable.

Given that such high market uncertainty only occurred during one round, we do not have enough data to produce a Pareto curve over multiple rounds. Additionally, note that although a smaller number of predictions were made during the last week before Brexit

(52 prediction sets compared to 284 during the open period of prediction used earlier), we have sufficient data to afford statistically significant results as shown by the 95% confidence intervals of our findings.

This supporting result suggests that during periods of high uncertainty, social learning leads to higher accuracy in contrast to the result in the previous section where the asset prices were more predictable. This result has implications for platform designers such as the potential of leveraging social learning as a valuable tool that minimizes catastrophic performance during high uncertainty prediction regimes.

5. Discussion

Our main result (the trade-off seen in Figure 4) supports our hypothesis that a Pareto frontier exists between risk and accuracy—similarly to what has been observed in statistical modeling [8–10] and financial [14–16] forecasting systems. This trade-off is mediated by the relative amount of social vs. non-social learning. Additionally, as supporting results, we observe that simple approximate models outperform more complicated Monte Carlo approaches in modeling the belief update process of participants. This suggests that participants use several heuristics, and that during periods of high uncertainty, social learning leads to higher accuracy.

Here, we discuss the implications of our results for platform designers in Section 5.1, describe the contributions of our work to the literature on heuristics in information processing and decision-making in Section 5.2. We end with a description the limitations of this work in Section 5.3.

5.1. Collective Intelligence System Design Implications

If we are to deploy crowd-sourced financial prediction and speculation systems at scale, it will be important to fully characterize the performance of these systems. This is especially given the growing importance of decentralized financial prediction and speculation including very recent events during which retail investors self-organized using social media and drove up asset and derivative prices [3,4]. However, crowd-sourced prediction systems and literature so far focus on measuring and optimizing for the accuracy of the predictions with little regard to the risk of these predictions even though measuring both accuracy and risk is standard in machine learning [8–10] and financial [14–16] forecasting applications. More generally, proper modeling and estimation of risk will support more sophisticated and versatile applications of crowd-sourced predictions such as hedging risks over portfolios of prediction tasks.

Additionally, beyond the passive monitoring and reporting of risk, a practical question for designers is how to *tune* the platform to reach a desired value of risk and accuracy. Our result that social learning can mediate the accuracy-risk trade-off provides a practical means to attain performance along this frontier. Specifically, our results suggest that social learning within a crowd-sourcing platform could be more purposefully leveraged to fit the task at hand. For example, platform designers could incentivize social learning between participants to have lower risk. This might be especially needed during highly uncertain times, as our results from the Brexit prediction (Figure 5) prediction showed. Past work has already showed that crowd-sourcing platforms can be incentivized to be more social [43,44].

Beyond platform design considerations, our results also add to the rich study of social learning and its impact on collective intelligence within the Wisdom of the Crowd domain [25,27,37,40,41] by adding the novel perspective that risk is an important dimension of the behavior of crowds to be measured.

More generally, our work brings together two disjoint studies by showing that it is possible to improve collective intelligence by modeling individual belief update. Our results therefore suggest a connection between the field of collective intelligence [78] (of which the Wisdom of the Crowd is one domain) and the field of computational cognitive science [79] (of which Bayesian models of cognition is an area). Until now, the latter literature has mostly focused on individual models of belief update such as through computational models of how people perform sampling [80], what their priors are [81], and how they perform inference [82], sometimes in social situations [83]. Yet, there is little work that looks at the impact of individual belief update on collective performance. On the other hand, there is limited collective intelligence literature regarding leveraging the modeling of individual belief update to improve group performance and past work has instead been focused on using personal characteristics such as resistance to social learning [27].

5.2. Information Processing and Decision-Making Heuristics

Our results also have implications for the literature on decision heuristics and biases [75,84]. Through the modeling of belief update, we observe that our subjects exhibit the attribute substitution heuristic of human decision-making [30]. This information processing heuristic describes when people attempt to solve a complicated problem by approximating it with a simpler, less accurate model. We observe this heuristic as our participants' updated beliefs are better modeled by the `GaussianSocial` model (which assumes the data to be unimodal) than by the multi-modal belief update model `GaussianSocialModes`. This indicates that our participants assume the data to be unimodal even when it is not, in line with previous studies that have shown that people wrongly assume data to be unimodal [74,85,86]. This is hypothesized to be because updating belief using multi-modal data is cognitively costly [87]. Additional evidence of this substitution heuristic is from the fact that simpler, approximate models better predict the updated beliefs of participants than the more complicated Monte Carlo numerical models.

Another decision heuristic that we observe is that participants prefer to use social information rather than the underlying price history of an asset to update their belief as models which use social information (`GaussianSocial`,`GaussianSocialModes`, and `NumericalSocial`) outperform models that use price history (`GaussianPrice` and `NumericalPrice`) as shown in Figure 3. This is surprising given that our participants were mid-career finance professionals with strong financial experience who should know that price information is generally better to predict future prices [88,89]. However, such behavior was observed in prior work where even experts performing a familiar task demonstrate sub-optimal decision heuristics [90,91], and often over-rely on social information [71,72].

Generally, such information processing and decision-making heuristics have been seen as irrational and sub-optimal. Our results suggest that within the full specification of both accuracy and risk, perhaps participants are preferentially aiming for lower risk instead of higher accuracy. This preference for social information especially pays off during the high uncertainty period before the Brexit vote. Our results support growing evidence that heuristics and biases are not merely *defects* of human decision-making, but that perhaps they optimize for richer objectives or are optimized for more time- or data-constrained decision-making [92–98]. For example, when individual decision-making is viewed within the lens of more realistic requirements such as limited time [99,100] or attention [101], heuristics and biases have been shown to act as helpful priors that facilitate fast and risk-averse decision-making [102,103].

5.3. Limitations and Future Work

We made several simplifying assumptions in this work that open up rich avenues for future work. First, we used simple, interpretable, and theoretically motivated belief update modeling approaches from prior work [28] and leave to future work the exploration of richer models, distributions and posterior computations to investigate belief update. One important set of models to investigate is the use of log-normal distributions for the likelihood instead of the normal distributions used in this work due to the established tendency of people to guess quantities log-normally [37,104,105]. Similarly, people have been shown to incorporate information asymmetrically based on where their predictions lie in relation to the information they are exposed to [106]. Overall, although we used Gaussian models here, an interesting direction of future work would be to build on the rich existing literature on how people incorporate information [84,107,108]. We also restricted each round to have a static population of participants whose predictions were shared using a specific visualization. An interesting direction for future work would be to embed participants in social networks given the importance and popularity of recent work on the effect of communication topologies [25,41,42,109] on group performance. Similarly, it would be interesting to investigate if different avenues for communication (e.g., discussions on forums [110]) exhibit a similar accuracy-risk trade-off.

Although this work demonstrates that our simple estimation technique can be used to tune crowd-predictions for desired levels of accuracy and risk, there are potential causal issues that could be improved in our experimental design and data analysis. One such issue is that there are two experimental and two analysis factors being investigated simultaneously here. These are the two different treatments in the form of sources of information (peer beliefs for the social histogram and price trajectory from the past price history) and the two different approaches through which each of these sources of information are being processed (simple binning of peer beliefs into a histogram, and transformation of the price history into a 'rates histogram'). It can be argued that these two experimental treatments and two approaches constitute four possible approaches of how to deploy and analyze an experiment, and we have only compared two of these four approaches. From a scholarly perspective, we believe that our paper still makes a contribution because the goal of this work was to show that a trade-off exists and is mediated by social learning. We achieve this goal even though we only compare two approaches. Another causal concern is that the two experimental treatments might interact in non-trivial ways. For example, when visualized as a causal graph, there might be causally confounding paths between the treatments.

Several research designs and estimations techniques exist to remedy these causal limitations. One approach would be to use an A/B test [64] framework although it would require exposing people to different information separately. Doing so would be against our goal to investigate how people update their belief in real-life situations where users are exposed to both social information and price history. However, experiments where different types of information are shown separately could still be used to understand the effect of different information exposures on accuracy and risk, and used in deployment. Similarly different amounts of information exposure could be attempted using a multi-factorial A/B test [111,112]. We leave the exploration of these more sophisticated designs to future work. Other de-confounding approaches could involve assuming a causal graph [113] that is believed to capture how people update information and to use causal tools such as d-separation to estimate the effect of different information exposure. Another approach would be to use a potential outcomes framework [114] to estimate these treatments. These are promising directions of research which could be investigated using our data that we leave to future work. From a platform design perspective, even though these confounding issues remain, our estimation technique could be readily applied to crowd-sourced systems where price histories and peer beliefs are being shown.

Supplementary Materials: The following are available online at https://www.mdpi.com/article/10.3390/e23070801/s1. References [115–120] are cited in the supplementary materials.

Author Contributions: Conceptualization, D.A.; methodology, D.A., Y.L., S.K.C., P.M.K.; validation, D.A.; formal analysis, D.A., Y.L., S.K.C.; investigation, D.A., Y.L., S.K.C.; resources, A.P.; data curation, D.A., Y.L., S.C; writing—original draft preparation, all authors; writing—review and editing, all authors. All authors have read and agreed to the published version of the manuscript.

Funding: E.M. acknowledges partial support by Ministerio de Economía, Industria y Competitividad, Gobierno de España, grant number FIS2016-78904-C3-3-P and PID2019-106811GB-C32.

Institutional Review Board Statement: The study was conducted according to the guidelines of the MIT COUHES IRB and approved as Exempt Protocol 1602374158.

Informed Consent Statement: Study participants consented to their data being used in this study.

Data Availability Statement: Not applicable.

Acknowledgments: The authors are grateful to David Shrier for his help with setting up the experiment, Zoheb Sait and Mike Vien for experiment UI and backend design, and Getsmarter for participant management.

Conflicts of Interest: The authors declare no conflict of interest.

References

1. Diallo, N.; Shi, W.; Xu, L.; Gao, Z.; Chen, L.; Lu, Y.; Shah, N.; Carranco, L.; Le, T.C.; Surez, A.B.; et al. eGov-DAO: A better government using blockchain based decentralized autonomous organization. In Proceedings of the 2018 International Conference on eDemocracy & eGovernment (ICEDEG), Ambato, Ecuador, 4–6 April 2018; pp. 166–171.
2. Lang, M.; Bharadwaj, N.; Di Benedetto, C.A. How crowdsourcing improves prediction of market-oriented outcomes. *J. Bus. Res.* **2016**, *69*, 4168–4176. [CrossRef]
3. Lawrence, K. Memes, Reddit, and Robinhood: Analyzing the GameStop Saga. 2021. Available online: http://sk.sagepub.com/cases/memes-reddit-and-robinhood-analyzing-the-gamestop-saga (accessed on 10 May 2021)
4. Hu, D.; Jones, C.M.; Zhang, V.; Zhang, X. The Rise of Reddit: How Social Media Affects Retail Investors and Short-Sellers' Roles in Price Discovery. 2021. Available online: https://papers.ssrn.com/sol3/papers.cfm?abstract_id=3807655 (accessed on 10 May 2021).
5. Lazer, D.; Friedman, A. The network structure of exploration and exploitation. *Adm. Sci. Q.* **2007**, *52*, 667–694. [CrossRef]
6. Olorunda, O.; Engelbrecht, A.P. Measuring exploration/exploitation in particle swarms using swarm diversity. In Proceedings of the 2008 IEEE Congress on Evolutionary Computation (IEEE World Congress on Computational Intelligence), Hong Kong, China, 1–6 June 2008; pp. 1128–1134.
7. Kennedy, J.; Mendes, R. Population structure and particle swarm performance. In Proceedings of the 2002 Congress on Evolutionary Computation, CEC'02 (Cat. No. 02TH8600), Honolulu, HI, USA, 12–17 May 2002; Volume 2, pp. 1671–1676.
8. James, G.; Witten, D.; Hastie, T.; Tibshirani, R. *An Introduction to Statistical Learning*; Springer: Berlin/Heidelberg, Germany, 2013; Volume 112.
9. Domingos, P. A unified bias-variance decomposition. In Proceedings of 17th International Conference on Machine Learning, Stanford, CA, USA, 29 June–2 July 2000; pp. 231–238.
10. Geman, S.; Bienenstock, E.; Doursat, R. Neural networks and the bias/variance dilemma. *Neural Comput.* **1992**, *4*, 1–58. [CrossRef]
11. Gagliardi, F. Instance-based classifiers applied to medical databases: diagnosis and knowledge extraction. *Artif. Intell. Med.* **2011**, *52*, 123–139. [CrossRef] [PubMed]
12. Markowitz, H. Portfolio selection. *J. Financ.* **1952**, *7*, 77–91.
13. Gammerman, A.; Vovk, V. Hedging predictions in machine learning. *Comput. J.* **2007**, *50*, 151–163. [CrossRef]
14. Joyce, J.M.; Vogel, R.C. The uncertainty in risk: Is variance unambiguous? *J. Financ.* **1970**, *25*, 127–134. [CrossRef]
15. Modigliani, F.; Leah, M. Risk-adjusted performance. *J. Portf. Manag.* **1997**, *23*, 45. [CrossRef]
16. Ghysels, E.; Santa-Clara, P.; Valkanov, R. There is a risk-return trade-off after all. *J. Financ. Econ.* **2005**, *76*, 509–548. [CrossRef]
17. Chavez-Demoulin, V.; Embrechts, P.; Nešlehová, J. Quantitative models for operational risk: extremes, dependence and aggregation. *J. Bank. Financ.* **2006**, *30*, 2635–2658. [CrossRef]
18. Asmussen, S.; Kroese, D.P. Improved algorithms for rare event simulation with heavy tails. *Adv. Appl. Probab.* **2006**, *38*, 545–558. [CrossRef]
19. Shevchenko, P.V.; Wuthrich, M.V. The structural modelling of operational risk via Bayesian inference: Combining loss data with expert opinions. *J. Oper. Risk* **2006**, *1*, 3–26. [CrossRef]
20. Chapelle, A.; Crama, Y.; Hübner, G.; Peters, J.P. Practical methods for measuring and managing operational risk in the financial sector: A clinical study. *J. Bank. Financ.* **2008**, *32*, 1049–1061. [CrossRef]
21. Cruz, M.G. *Modeling, Measuring and Hedging Operational Risk*; Wiley: New York, NY, USA, 2002; Volume 346.
22. Galton, F. Vox populi (The wisdom of crowds). *Nature* **1907**, *75*, 450–451. [CrossRef]
23. Golub, B.; Jackson, M.O. Naive learning in social networks and the wisdom of crowds. *Am. Econ. J. Microecon.* **2010**, *2*, 112–149. [CrossRef]
24. Nofer, M.; Hinz, O. Are crowds on the internet wiser than experts? The case of a stock prediction community. *J. Bus. Econ.* **2014**, *84*, 303–338. [CrossRef]
25. Becker, J.; Brackbill, D.; Centola, D. Network dynamics of social influence in the wisdom of crowds. *Proc. Natl. Acad. Sci. USA* **2017**, *114*, 201615978; [CrossRef] [PubMed]
26. Turner, B.M.; Steyvers, M.; Merkle, E.C.; Budescu, D.V.; Wallsten, T.S. Forecast aggregation via recalibration. *Mach. Learn.* **2014**, *95*, 261–289. [CrossRef]
27. Madirolas, G.; de Polavieja, G.G. Improving collective estimations using resistance to social influence. *PLoS Comput. Biol.* **2015**, *11*, e1004594. [CrossRef]
28. Griffiths, T.L.; Tenenbaum, J.B. Optimal predictions in everyday cognition. *Psychol. Sci.* **2006**, *17*, 767–773. [CrossRef] [PubMed]
29. Griffiths, T.L.; Kemp, C.; Tenenbaum, J.B. Bayesian models of cognition. In *The Cambridge Handbook of Computational Psychology*; Sun, R., Ed.; Cambridge University Press: Cambridge, UK, 2008; pp. 1–49.
30. Kahneman, D.; Frederick, S. Representativeness Revisited: Attribute Substitution in Intuitive Judgment. Available online: https://www.cambridge.org/core/books/heuristics-and-biases/representativeness-revisited-attribute-substitution-in-intuitive-judgment/AAB5D933A3F944CFB5CB02265D376C8F (accessed on 10 May 2021).

31. Oehler, A.; Horn, M.; Wendt, S. Brexit: Short-term stock price effects and the impact of firm-level internationalization. *Financ. Res. Lett.* **2017**, *22*, 175–181. [CrossRef]
32. Kennedy, J. Swarm intelligence. In *Handbook of Nature-Inspired and Innovative Computing*; Springer: Berlin/Heidelberg, Germany, 2006; pp. 187–219.
33. Eberhart, R.C.; Shi, Y.; Kennedy, J. *Swarm Intelligence*; Elsevier: Amsterdam, The Netherlands, 2001.
34. Bonabeau, E.; Marco, D.D.R.D.F.; Dorigo, M.; Théraulaz, G.; Theraulaz, G. *Swarm Intelligence: From Natural to Artificial Systems*; Number 1; Oxford University Press: Oxford, UK, 1999.
35. Woolley, A.W.; Chabris, C.F.; Pentland, A.; Hashmi, N.; Malone, T.W. Evidence for a collective intelligence factor in the performance of human groups. *Science* **2010**, *330*, 686–688. [CrossRef]
36. Malone, T.W.; Laubacher, R.; Dellarocas, C. The collective intelligence genome. *MIT Sloan Manag. Rev.* **2010**, *51*, 21. [CrossRef]
37. Lorenz, J.; Rauhut, H.; Schweitzer, F.; Helbing, D. How social influence can undermine the wisdom of crowd effect. *Proc. Natl. Acad. Sci. USA* **2011**, *108*, 9020–9025; [CrossRef]
38. Muchnik, L.; Aral, S.; Taylor, S.J. Social influence bias: A randomized experiment. *Science* **2013**, *341*, 647–651. [CrossRef]
39. Salganik, M.J.; Dodds, P.S.; Watts, D.J. Experimental study of inequality and unpredictability in an artificial cultural market. *Science* **2006**, *311*, 854–856. [CrossRef] [PubMed]
40. Moussaïd, M.; Kämmer, J.E.; Analytis, P.P.; Neth, H. Social influence and the collective dynamics of opinion formation. *PLoS ONE* **2013**, *8*, e78433. [CrossRef] [PubMed]
41. Almaatouq, A.; Noriega-Campero, A.; Alotaibi, A.; Krafft, P.; Moussaid, M.; Pentland, A. Adaptive social networks promote the wisdom of crowds. *Proc. Natl. Acad. Sci. USA* **2020**, *117*, 11379–11386. [CrossRef]
42. Adjodah, D.; Calacci, D.; Dubey, A.; Goyal, A.; Krafft, P.; Moro, E.; Pentland, A. Leveraging Communication Topologies Between Learning Agents in Deep Reinforcement Learning. In Proceedings of the 19th International Conference on Autonomous Agents and MultiAgent Systems, Auckland, New Zealand, 9–13 May 2020.
43. Lim, S.L.; Quercia, D.; Finkelstein, A. StakeSource: harnessing the power of crowdsourcing and social networks in stakeholder analysis. In Proceedings of the 2010 ACM/IEEE 32nd International Conference on Software Engineering, Cape Town, South Africa, 2–8 May 2010; Volume 2, pp. 239–242.
44. Chen, P.Y.; Cheng, S.M.; Ting, P.S.; Lien, C.W.; Chu, F.J. When crowdsourcing meets mobile sensing: A social network perspective. *IEEE Commun. Mag.* **2015**, *53*, 157–163. [CrossRef]
45. Lerman, K.; Ghosh, R. Information contagion: An empirical study of the spread of news on Digg and Twitter social networks. In Proceedings of the Fourth International AAAI Conference on Weblogs and Social Media (ICWSM), Washington, DC, USA, 23–26 May 2010.
46. Lerman, K.; Hogg, T. Using a model of social dynamics to predict popularity of news. In Proceedings of the 19th International Conference on World Wide Web (WWW), Raleigh, NC, USA, 26–30 April 2010; pp. 621–630.
47. Stoddard, G. Popularity dynamics and intrinsic quality in reddit and hacker news. In Proceedings of the Ninth International AAAI Conference on Web and Social Media (ICWSM), Oxford, UK, 26–29 May 2015.
48. Celis, L.E.; Krafft, P.M.; Kobe, N. Sequential voting promotes collective discovery in social recommendation systems. In Proceedings of the Tenth International AAAI Conference on Web and Social Media, Cologne, Germany, 17–20 May 2016.
49. Karger, D.R.; Oh, S.; Shah, D. Budget-optimal task allocation for reliable crowdsourcing systems. *Oper. Res.* **2014**, *62*, 1–24. [CrossRef]
50. Holt, C.A.; Laury, S.K. Risk aversion and incentive effects. *Am. Econ. Rev.* **2002**, *92*, 1644–1655. [CrossRef]
51. Kahneman, D.; Tversky, A. Prospect theory: An analysis of decision under risk. In *Handbook of the Fundamentals of Financial Decision Making: Part I*; World Scientific: Singapore, 2013; pp. 99–127.
52. Hintze, A.; Olson, R.S.; Adami, C.; Hertwig, R. Risk sensitivity as an evolutionary adaptation. *Sci. Rep.* **2015**, *5*, 8242. [CrossRef]
53. Zhang, R.; Brennan, T.J.; Lo, A.W. The origin of risk aversion. *Proc. Natl. Acad. Sci. USA* **2014**, *111*, 17777–17782. [CrossRef] [PubMed]
54. Binswanger, H.P.; Sillers, D.A. Risk aversion and credit constraints in farmers' decision-making: A reinterpretation. *J. Dev. Stud.* **1983**, *20*, 5–21. [CrossRef]
55. Armstrong, J.S.; Green, K.C.; Graefe, A. Golden rule of forecasting: Be conservative. *J. Bus. Res.* **2015**, *68*, 1717–1731. [CrossRef]
56. Passino, K.M.; Seeley, T.D. Modeling and analysis of nest-site selection by honeybee swarms: the speed and accuracy trade-off. *Behav. Ecol. Sociobiol.* **2006**, *59*, 427–442. [CrossRef]
57. Valentini, G.; Hamann, H.; Dorigo, M. Efficient decision-making in a self-organizing robot swarm: On the speed versus accuracy trade-off. In Proceedings of the 2015 International Conference on Autonomous Agents and Multiagent Systems, Istanbul, Turkey, 4–8 May 2015; pp. 1305–1314.
58. Krause, J.; Ruxton, G.D.; Krause, S. Swarm intelligence in animals and humans. *Trends Ecol. Evol.* **2010**, *25*, 28–34. [CrossRef]
59. Wolf, M.; Kurvers, R.H.; Ward, A.J.; Krause, S.; Krause, J. Accurate decisions in an uncertain world: Collective cognition increases true positives while decreasing false positives. *Proc. R. Soc. B Biol. Sci.* **2013**, *280*, 20122777. [CrossRef]
60. Ward, A.J.; Herbert-Read, J.E.; Sumpter, D.J.; Krause, J. Fast and accurate decisions through collective vigilance in fish shoals. *Proc. Natl. Acad. Sci. USA* **2011**, *108*, 2312–2315. [CrossRef]
61. Dumas, B.; Fleming, J.; Whaley, R.E. Implied volatility functions: Empirical tests. *J. Financ.* **1998**, *53*, 2059–2106. [CrossRef]
62. Campbell, J.Y.; Shiller, R.J. Stock prices, earnings, and expected dividends. *J. Financ.* **1988**, *43*, 661–676. [CrossRef]

63. Fama, E.F. Random walks in stock market prices. *Financ. Anal. J.* **1995**, *51*, 75–80. [CrossRef]
64. Dixon, E.; Enos, E.; Brodmerkle, S. A/b Testing of a Webpage. U.S. Patent 7,975,000, 2013. Available online: https://patents.google.com/patent/US20060162071A1/en (accessed on 10 May 2021)
65. Maniadakis, M.; Trahanias, P. Time models and cognitive processes: A review. *Front. Neurorobotics* **2014**, *8*, 7. [CrossRef] [PubMed]
66. Park, C.H.; Irwin, S.H. What do we know about the profitability of technical analysis? *J. Econ. Surv.* **2007**, *21*, 786–826. [CrossRef]
67. Neftci, S.N. Naive trading rules in financial markets and wiener-kolmogorov prediction theory: A study of "technical analysis". *J. Bus.* **1991**, *64*, 549–571. [CrossRef]
68. DeGroot, M.H. Reaching a consensus. *J. Am. Stat. Assoc.* **1974**, *69*, 118–121. [CrossRef]
69. Kerckhove, C.V.; Martin, S.; Gend, P.; Rentfrow, P.J.; Hendrickx, J.M.; Blondel, V.D. Modelling influence and opinion evolution in online collective behaviour. *PLoS ONE* **2016**, *11*, e0157685. [CrossRef]
70. Soll, J.B.; Larrick, R.P. Strategies for revising judgment: How (and how well) people use others' opinions. *J. Exp. Psychol. Learn. Mem. Cogn.* **2009**, *35*, 780. [CrossRef]
71. Foster, F.D.; Viswanathan, S. Strategic trading when agents forecast the forecasts of others. *J. Financ.* **1996**, *51*, 1437–1478. [CrossRef]
72. Posada, M.; Hernandez, C.; Lopez-Paredes, A. Learning in continuous double auction market. In *Artificial Economics*; Springer: Berlin/Heidelberg, Germany, 2006; pp. 41–51.
73. Hartigan, J.A.; Hartigan, P.M. The dip test of unimodality. *Ann. Stat.* **1985**, *13*, 70–84. [CrossRef]
74. Donnelly, N.; Cave, K.; Welland, M.; Menneer, T. Breast screening, chicken sexing and the search for oil: Challenges for visual cognition. *Geol. Soc. Lond. Spec. Publ.* **2006**, *254*, 43–55. [CrossRef]
75. Nisbett, R.E.; Ross, L. Human Inference: Strategies and Shortcomings of Social Judgment. 1980. Available online: https://philpapers.org/rec/nishis (accessed on 10 May 2021).
76. Dave, C.; Wolfe, K.W. On confirmation bias and deviations from Bayesian updating. *Retrieved* **2003**, *24*, 2011.
77. Nickerson, R.S. Confirmation bias: A ubiquitous phenomenon in many guises. *Rev. Gen. Psychol.* **1998**, *2*, 175–220. [CrossRef]
78. Mataric, M.J. Designing emergent behaviors: From local interactions to collective intelligence. In Proceedings of the Second International Conference on Simulation of Adaptive Behavior, Honolulu, HI, USA, 13 April 1993; pp. 432–441.
79. Tenenbaum, J.B.; Kemp, C.; Griffiths, T.L.; Goodman, N.D. How to grow a mind: Statistics, structure, and abstraction. *Science* **2011**, *331*, 1279–1285. [CrossRef] [PubMed]
80. Vul, E.; Pashler, H. Measuring the crowd within probabilistic representations within individuals. *Psychol. Sci.* **2008**, *19*, 645–647. [CrossRef]
81. Lewandowsky, S.; Griffiths, T.L.; Kalish, M.L. The wisdom of individuals: Exploring people's knowledge about everyday events using iterated learning. *Cogn. Sci.* **2009**, *33*, 969–998. [CrossRef]
82. Tenenbaum, J.B.; Griffiths, T.L.; Kemp, C. Theory-based Bayesian models of inductive learning and reasoning. *Trends Cogn. Sci.* **2006**, *10*, 309–318. [CrossRef] [PubMed]
83. Baker, C.L.; Saxe, R.; Tenenbaum, J.B. Action understanding as inverse planning. *Cognition* **2009**, *113*, 329–349. [CrossRef]
84. Tversky, A.; Kahneman, D. Judgment under uncertainty: Heuristics and biases. *Science* **1974**, *185*, 1124–1131. [CrossRef]
85. Nisbett, R.E.; Kunda, Z. Perception of social distributions. *J. Personal. Soc. Psychol.* **1985**, *48*, 297. [CrossRef]
86. Lindskog, M. Is the Intuitive Statistician Eager or Lazy?: Exploring the Cognitive Processes of Intuitive Statistical Judgments. Ph.D. Thesis, Acta Universitatis Upsaliensis, 2013. Available online: https://www.diva-portal.org/smash/record.jsf?pid=diva2 (accessed on 10 May 2021)
87. Hoffman, A.B.; Rehder, B. The costs of supervised classification: The effect of learning task on conceptual flexibility. *J. Exp. Psychol. Gen.* **2010**, *139*, 319. [CrossRef]
88. Malkiel, B.G.; Fama, E.F. Efficient capital markets: A review of theory and empirical work. *J. Financ.* **1970**, *25*, 383–417. [CrossRef]
89. Fama, E.F. The behavior of stock-market prices. *J. Bus.* **1965**, *38*, 34–105. [CrossRef]
90. Shanteau, J. Psychological characteristics and strategies of expert decision makers. *Acta Psychol.* **1988**, *68*, 203–215. [CrossRef]
91. Koehler, D.J.; Brenner, L.; Griffin, D. The calibration of expert judgment: Heuristics and biases beyond the laboratory. *Heuristics Biases Psychol. Intuitive Judgm.* **2002**, 686–715. Available online: https://psycnet.apa.org/record/2003-02858-039 (accessed on 10 May 2021).
92. Lakshminarayanan, V.R.; Chen, M.K.; Santos, L.R. The evolution of decision-making under risk: Framing effects in monkey risk preferences. *J. Exp. Soc. Psychol.* **2011**, *47*, 689–693. [CrossRef]
93. Mallpress, D.E.; Fawcett, T.W.; Houston, A.I.; McNamara, J.M. Risk attitudes in a changing environment: An evolutionary model of the fourfold pattern of risk preferences. *Psychol. Rev.* **2015**, *122*, 364. [CrossRef] [PubMed]
94. Kenrick, D.T.; Griskevicius, V. *The Rational Animal: How Evolution Made Us Smarter than We Think*; Basic Books (AZ): 2013. Available online: https://psycnet.apa.org/record/2013-31943-000 (accessed on 10 May 2021)
95. Josef, A.K.; Richter, D.; Samanez-Larkin, G.R.; Wagner, G.G.; Hertwig, R.; Mata, R. Stability and change in risk-taking propensity across the adult life span. *J. Personal. Soc. Psychol.* **2016**, *111*, 430. [CrossRef] [PubMed]
96. Cronqvist, H.; Siegel, S. The genetics of investment biases. *J. Financ. Econ.* **2014**, *113*, 215–234. [CrossRef]
97. Santos, L.R.; Rosati, A.G. The evolutionary roots of human decision making. *Annu. Rev. Psychol.* **2015**, *66*, 321–347. [CrossRef] [PubMed]

98. Mishra, S. Decision-making under risk: Integrating perspectives from biology, economics, and psychology. *Personal. Soc. Psychol. Rev.* **2014**, *18*, 280–307. [CrossRef]
99. Azuma, R.; Daily, M.; Furmanski, C. A review of time critical decision making models and human cognitive processes. In Proceedings of the 2006 IEEE Aerospace Conference, Big Sky, MT, USA, 4–11 March 2006; p. 9.
100. Cohen, I. Improving time-critical decision making in life-threatening situations: Observations and insights. *Decis. Anal.* **2008**, *5*, 100–110. [CrossRef]
101. Van Knippenberg, D.; Dahlander, L.; Haas, M.R.; George, G. Information, Attention, and Decision Making. 2015. Available online: https://psycnet.apa.org/record/2015-33332-001 (accessed on 10 May 2021)
102. Lubell, M.; Scholz, J.T. Cooperation, reciprocity, and the collective-action heuristic. *Am. J. Political Sci.* **2001**, *45*, 160–178. [CrossRef]
103. Rand, D.G.; Brescoll, V.L.; Everett, J.A.; Capraro, V.; Barcelo, H. Social heuristics and social roles: Intuition favors altruism for women but not for men. *J. Exp. Psychol. Gen.* **2016**, *145*, 389. [CrossRef]
104. Limpert, E.; Stahel, W.A.; Abbt, M. Log-normal distributions across the sciences: keys and clues: on the charms of statistics, and how mechanical models resembling gambling machines offer a link to a handy way to characterize log-normal distributions, which can provide deeper insight into variability and probability—Normal or log-normal: that is the question. *BioScience* **2001**, *51*, 341–352.
105. Dehaene, S.; Izard, V.; Spelke, E.; Pica, P. Log or linear? Distinct intuitions of the number scale in Western and Amazonian indigene cultures. *Science* **2008**, *320*, 1217–1220. [CrossRef] [PubMed]
106. Kao, A.B.; Berdahl, A.M.; Hartnett, A.T.; Lutz, M.J.; Bak-Coleman, J.B.; Ioannou, C.C.; Giam, X.; Couzin, I.D. Counteracting estimation bias and social influence to improve the wisdom of crowds. *J. R. Soc. Interface* **2018**, *15*, 20180130. [CrossRef]
107. Payne, J.W.; Payne, J.W.; Bettman, J.R.; Johnson, E.J. *The Adaptive Decision Maker*; Cambridge University Press: Cambridge, UK, 1993.
108. Schneider, W.; Shiffrin, R.M. Controlled and automatic human information processing: I. Detection, search, and attention. *Psychol. Rev.* **1977**, *84*, 1. [CrossRef]
109. Barkoczi, D.; Galesic, M. Social learning strategies modify the effect of network structure on group performance. *Nat. Commun.* **2016**, *7*, 1–8. [CrossRef] [PubMed]
110. Krafft, P.M.; Della Penna, N.; Pentland, A.S. An experimental study of cryptocurrency market dynamics. In Proceedings of the 2018 CHI Conference on Human Factors in Computing Systems, Montreal, QC, Canada, 21–26 April 2018; pp. 1–13.
111. Plackett, R.L.; Burman, J.P. The design of optimum multifactorial experiments. *Biometrika* **1946**, *33*, 305–325. [CrossRef]
112. Montgomery, D.C. *Design and Analysis of Experiments*; John Wiley & Sons: Hoboken, NJ, USA, 2017.
113. Pearl, J. Causal diagrams for empirical research. *Biometrika* **1995**, *82*, 669–688. [CrossRef]
114. Rubin, D.B. Causal inference using potential outcomes: Design, modeling, decisions. *J. Am. Stat. Assoc.* **2005**, *100*, 322–331. [CrossRef]
115. Alquist, R.; Kilian, L. What do we learn from the price of crude oil futures? *J. Appl. Econom.* **2010**, *25*, 539–573. [CrossRef]
116. French, K.R. Detecting spot price forecasts in futures prices. *J. Bus.* **1986**, *59*, S39–S54. [CrossRef]
117. Kim, Y.S.;Walls, L.A.; Krafft, P.; Hullman, J. A Bayesian Cognition Approach to Improve Data Visualization. In Proceedings of the 2019 CHI Conference on Human Factors in Computing Systems, Scotland, UK, 4–9 May 2019; p. 682.
118. Vul, E.; Goodman, N.; Griffiths, T.L.; Tenenbaum, J.B. One and done? Optimal decisions from very few samples. *Cogn. Sci.* **2014**, *38*, 599–637. [CrossRef] [PubMed]
119. Deshpande, S. Brexit Myth on FTSE and DAX Companies: A Review. Available at SSRN 3517139. 2020. Available online: https://www.researchgate.net/profile/Shubhada-Deshpande-2/publication/338502066_Brexit_Myth_on_FTSE_and_DAX_Companies_A_Review/links/5e183584a6fdcc2837662070/Brexit-Myth-on-FTSE-and-DAX-Companies-A-Review.pdf (accessed on 10 May 2021)
120. Cox, J.; Griffith, T. Political Uncertainty and Market Liquidity: Evidence from the Brexit Referendum and the 2016 US Presidential Election. Available at SSRN 3092335. 2018. Available online: https://papers.ssrn.com/sol3/papers.cfm?abstract_id=3092335 (accessed on 10 May 2021)

Article

Socioeconomic Patterns of Twitter User Activity

Jacob Levy Abitbol [1] and Alfredo J. Morales [2,*]

[1] GRYZZLY SAS, 69003 Lyon, France; jacob@gryzzly.io
[2] MIT Media Lab, Cambridge, MA 02139, USA
* Correspondence: alfredom@mit.edu

Abstract: Stratifying behaviors based on demographics and socioeconomic status is crucial for political and economic planning. Traditional methods to gather income and demographic information, like national censuses, require costly large-scale surveys both in terms of the financial and the organizational resources needed for their successful collection. In this study, we use data from social media to expose how behavioral patterns in different socioeconomic groups can be used to infer an individual's income. In particular, we look at the way people explore cities and use topics of conversation online as a means of inferring individual socioeconomic status. Privacy is preserved by using anonymized data, and abstracting human mobility and online conversation topics as aggregated high-dimensional vectors. We show that mobility and hashtag activity are good predictors of income and that the highest and lowest socioeconomic quantiles have the most differentiated behavior across groups.

Keywords: human behavior; socioeconomic status; data analysis; social media

1. Introduction

Historically, governments have quantified natural and societal systems in order to outline and validate public policies, and to organize their territory [1–3]. Having socioeconomic data to guide the design of these policies is nevertheless crucial. However, gathering such information can represent a challenge for governments and corporations given the costly efforts associated to the deployment of large-scale national surveys. This is especially the case in developing countries, whose governments may lack the resources needed for completing such endeavors. The recent access to datasets collected from social media and other electronic platforms has enabled the direct observation of individuals and social behaviors [4]. These new sources of data, when properly mined through efficient algorithmics, can provide researchers with an in-depth view of social processes hard to obtain otherwise.

Data obtained from social media enabled an unprecedented analysis of the complexity of societies [4]. Recent studies have shown patterns of social behaviors across multiple scales of observation, ranging from individual preferences up to the structure and dynamics of self-organized groups and collectives [5–7]. Example applications of these analyses include the analysis of stock market variations based on collective sentiment analysis [8], the prediction of electoral results [9], the political polarization of societies [10], and the relationship between health and shopping preferences [11]. These types of studies have only become more prevalent with the rising ease of access to geolocated data, enabling the modeling and prediction of human mobility through online communication data [12].

Traditional socioeconomic studies how economic activities and their context shape social behaviors, and vice versa [13]. These studies reveal how different behaviors are characteristic of different social strata. For instance, income groups feature characteristic patterns of behavior that distinguish them from each other in terms of culture, beliefs, health, and education [14–19].

The underlying structure of a social system conditions the behaviors of its members [20]. Similarly wealth also conditions with respect to spaces of mutual exposure and collective learning [21]. Previous studies have shown that income segregation in urban areas determines the places people visit [22,23], the people they interact with, and the topics of conversation they engage in [24]. These analyses show that the segregation of the urban space fragments the social network where information flows and from where behaviors are transmitted and adopted among individuals. Because we learn from imitation, the segregated structure of social networks leads to differentiated social behaviors, including sentiments and emotions [25]. Reinforcing dynamics differentiate behaviors further despite having access to everyone on Internet.

In this paper, we analyze Twitter activity and expose patterns of behavior that are characteristic of different socioeconomic groups and that underlie income prediction tasks. We apply machine learning and information theory methods, including dimensionality reduction techniques, to expose how linguistic and mobility patterns can be used to infer socioeconomic status. More concretely, we analyze the relationship between mobility patterns and hashtag usage with income, as well as the differences between the collective behavior among neighborhoods of different socioeconomic status in terms of the diversity of their interactions.

The paper is organized as follows. Section 2 contains a summary of related studies in the field of income prediction. Section 3 includes a description of the data and the methods we use to collect and analyze it. In Section 4, we present the analysis on mobility and hashtag behavior. In Section 5, we show the structure of the conversational space by means of dimensional reduction. In Section 6, we show signature patterns of socioeconomic groups according to the diversity of their interactions. Finally, we discuss our results in Section 7, and conclude in Section 8.

2. Related Work

Methods for inferring demographic information from observations of social behaviors have been recently developed. The availability of social media data combined with traditional sources such as census records enable the observation and analysis of both finer and coarser views of society [4]. Until recently, researchers could only access data from surveys or questionnaires, which by definition are limited in size, scope and frequency, given the difficulties for their deployment and collection. Nowadays, social media data provide researchers with the possibility of observing patterns of behavior which are characteristic of certain demographic groups and therefore enabling the inference of traits from unlabeled individuals.

Twitter is a social media platform where users can post messages and interact with other people. Tweets include metadata with information about the author's profile, the detected language, as well as the time and location when it was posted. Twitter activity has been analyzed to understand the geography of human sentiments [26], content share networks [6], and dynamics of social influence [27]. It has also been used to advance the understanding of global patterns of human mobility [28], activity [29], and languages [30].

Multiple features have been used in order to predict demographic traits of individuals from the data generated by the usage of multiple types of electronic communication. Socioeconomic status, for instance, has concentrated a great deal of recent attention on the topic. These advances enable a further characterization of the population and prediction of individual attributes such as age [31], occupation [32–35], political affiliation [36], personality traits [37], and income [32,38]. The properties of Twitter activity and network of followers have also been used to estimate gender and ethnicity [39], unemployment [40], and language [41].

In particular, human mobility patterns are relevant predictors of income. Previous research has shown that the diversity of human mobility is an indicator of economic development across multiple regions [42]. Aggregated data produced by using mobile phones [43,44] and geolocated social media outlets [45] have been crucial in advancing the analysis of human mobility patterns, which are predictable given the regularity of commuting [46] and visitation destinations. Another basis for income prediction is language usage and online content production.

The relationship between income and language has been studied since the early stages of socio-linguistics. At that time, researchers were able to show that social status inferred from someone's occupation determines the language used [47]. Recently, advances in machine learning take advantage of this social property to build automated classifiers and infer income from behavioral traits [32–34]. Gaussian Processes have been applied to predict user income, occupation, and socioeconomic class based on demographics, as well as psycho-linguistic features and standardized job classifications. These technologies map Twitter users to their professional occupations. The high predictive performance has proven this concept with $r = 0.6$ for income prediction, precision of 55% for 9-ways SOC classification, and 82% for binary SES classification. These results further solidify the use of semantic features as proxies to predict individual socioeconomic status.

Furthermore, in a previous work [21], we analyzed the collective topics of conversation coming from neighborhoods of different income in multiple cities around the world. Wealthier neighborhoods tend to discuss lifestyle topics such as travels or leisure, while economically deprived neighborhoods seem to be characterized by other topics of conversation such as sports or TV shows. Second, we noticed that the frequency of visitation between neighborhoods was consistent with the similarity of their topics of conversation. Therefore, neighborhoods that are segregated from one another, such as the case of cities that are segregated by income, tend to also be separated in the space of online conversations. Other studies of urban segregation using geolocated Twitter data confirm that different ethnic groups are less exposed to each other because of segregated residential and travel patterns [22,23].

3. Data and Methods

The goal of this paper is to expose patterns of behavior that are characteristic of socioeconomic groups and to show that variations of behavior can be used to derive income predictors. The research question is as follows: Which patterns of Twitter activity are characteristic of different socioeconomic groups and how can we expose them? For this purpose, we downloaded and analyzed Twitter data using statistical, computational, and machine learning methods. We studied multiple aspects of human activity observable from Twitter data. These included mobility patterns, language usage via hashtag adoption, and social interactions via mentions. In this section, we detail the methods used to collect and treat Twitter data, as well as the representation model we created to analyze patterns of behavior from individuals and neighborhoods.

The data have been collected using the Application Programming Interface (API) provided by Twitter for streaming content [48]. The stream API provides around 3% of the overall Twitter activity in real time [49] and over 90% of publicly available tweets with geo-location [50]. The geo-location feature provides precise coordinates of individuals as they post messages. Specifically, we collected over 100M tweets posted by over 2M users, from August 2013 to August 2015, from two European countries. Global statistics show that ~10% of tweets contain hashtags and ~50% of them have at least one mention to another user [51].

Previous studies have analyzed biases in geolocated Twitter users [52–54]. In general, Twitter users trend younger, wealthier and urban. However, the under-aged population is underrepresented and the wealth of individuals seems irrelevant in most American cities [21]. These biases can be understood as imbalanced samples, and can be resolved with the corresponding techniques to under-sample over-represented populations. Despite these observations, more recent studies have shown that opinions collected on social media around relevant topics do not differ from the ones one would observe through traditional surveys [55].

In Section 4, we analyze how multiple features of human mobility and online conversations change when conditioned on income. For this purpose, users are characterized with vectors representing either neighborhoods visited or hashtags used. The non-zero elements of the mobility vector represents neighborhoods where the user tweeted from. We assume people's home locations according to the neighborhood most frequently visited at nighttime during weekdays. The use of these methods is consistent with the procedures followed by other studies relying on mobile phone [56] and Twitter data [46]. We first assign individuals to neighborhoods and then label each user with the average neighborhood income provided by the Census data. The income labels are used to build predictors and characterize the collective activity of the different socioeconomic groups. The non-zero elements of the hashtag vector represents the ones adopted by each user. Hashtags are text labels people use to identify tweets with ongoing events or trends. Hashtags can be used as proxies of collective attention, and their usage has a clear relationship to human distinctive behaviors either in large-scale cultures down to urban life.

We create two independent feature spaces: one representing human mobility and another representing hashtag activity. In both cases, samples represent individuals. In the mobility feature space, the features indicate neighborhoods visited. In the hashtag feature space, each dimension represents whether a given hashtag has been used. We only consider hashtags used by at least five people. We set up a threshold because hashtag usage follows a power law distribution [57]. Most hashtags are used by a single user, while a few of them are used collectively. By doing so, we reduce considerably the number of hashtags and therefore limit the overall dimensionality of the parameter space. Each feature space is then transformed using TF-IDF (Term Frequency-Inverse Document Frequency [58]). This transformation is often used to classify documents based on patterns in their text bodies before using topic models. The underlying assumption behind topic models is that documents that have similar content will tend to also share similarities in their word usage. TF-IDF improves the process of topic discovery by highlighting local information as opposed to globally used terms. Otherwise, very common words or words that appear in single documents would create uninformative signals.

In Section 5, we derive topics of conversation for each user and analyze their overall structure. The topic analysis is generated by means of a *word2vec* model with skip-gram architecture and negative sampling [59]. *Word2vec* is a natural language processing (NLP) technique based on neural networks. The model generates a representation space where pairs of words that are structurally or semantically similar to each other are located in close proximity. This property is due to the architecture behind *word2vec*. The skip-gram architecture predicts the context of words and learns the relationships between words based on their proximity in the text. Negative sampling reduces the number of parameters to train and therefore improves computation time. In this process, words are mapped and embedded onto 50-dimensional vectors. Topics of conversation are then derived by clustering the word co-ocurrence matrix.

Finally, in Section 6 we characterize the collective activity of neighborhoods via interaction vectors. These vectors represent the aggregate behavior of the neighborhoods' inhabitants. We create mobility and online communication vectors. Mobility vectors aggregate the frequency that individuals from neighborhood i visit neighborhood j. Online communication is measured via the mentions mechanisms. Mention vectors represent the number of times people from neighborhood i mention other people from neighborhood j. Unlike the passive information exposure and lesser social involvement reflected by the follower network, the mutual mention network has been shown [60] to better capture the underlying social structure between users.

4. Mobility and Hashtag Space

In this section, we discuss properties of mobility patterns and hashtag usage with respect to income. We apply two learning algorithms to the mobility and hashtag feature spaces defined in Section 3. The first algorithm is a Multi-Layer Perceptron (MLP) [61] regression that predicts income as a numeric value. The other one is based on predicting the income quantile using an MLP classifier. We apply them to both mobility and hashtag space. For this purpose, we divide the sample in a training set with 75% of individuals and a test set with the remaining 25% of them. We create multiple samples in order to analyze the performance of the predictors behavior as a random variable. Bootstrapping the performance enables more robust understanding of the prediction quality.

Figure 1 shows the results of the prediction both numerically (left panels) and categorically (right panels). The top panels show the results of the human mobility feature space. The bottom panels show results of hashtag usage feature space. The results of the regressor are shown in the left panels as scatter plots showing the predicted values (y-axis) against the real ones (x-axis). The scatter plots show the overlapped results of the multiple samples we create to bootstrap the algorithm's performance. For each sample, we calculate the Pearson correlation. We present the distribution of these correlations in Figure 2 (top left). The correlations are high with an average of $r = 0.8$ for the mobility feature space and $r = 0.55$ for the hashtag one. In both cases, a considerable part of the variance is explained by the algorithm.

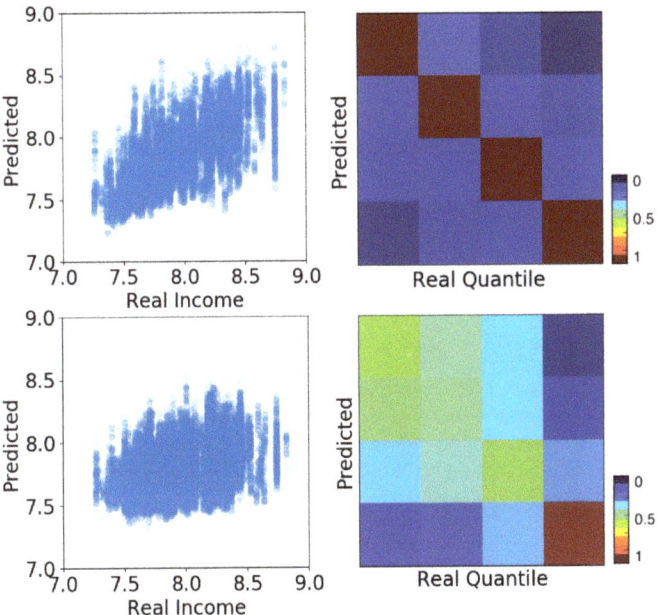

Figure 1. Income prediction based on mobility patterns (**top**) and hashtag usage (**bottom**). Left panels show scatter plots of actual (x-axis) and predicted (y-axis) income using regression. Right panels show the prediction of income quantiles using a classifier. Each quantile represents 25% of the population sorted by income (from left to right, and top to bottom). The matrix elements quantify the number of guesses for each quantile pair (confusion matrix). Scale in figure.

The right panels in Figure 1 show the categorical prediction of socioeconomic quantiles rather than the numeric values. Diagonal values correspond to True Positives and off-diagonal values represent errors or miss-classifications. The matrices show a strong diagonal structure indicating a very good prediction quality. In the case of mobility (top matrix) the diagonal is almost perfect. In the case of hashtag (bottom matrix) the results are more diffused. However, the wrong predictions are close to their original values and not homogeneously distributed among quantiles. This indicates that errors are not randomly distributed and that contiguous socioeconomic strata have similar behaviors.

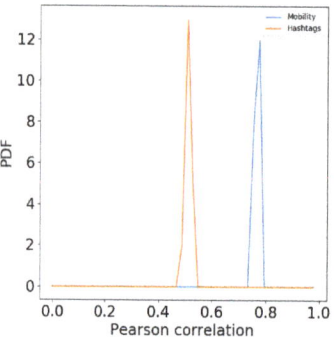
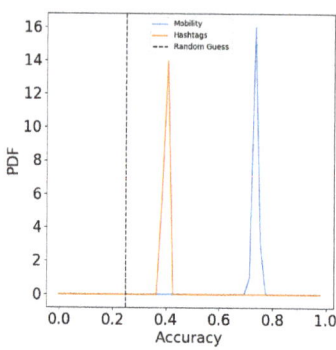
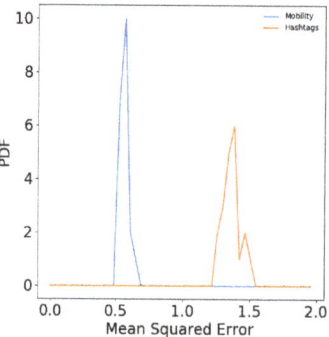

Figure 2. Top left: Pearson correlation between predicted and real income values using Regression. **Top right**: Accuracy of the classifier used to predict income quantiles. Dashed line shows random guess. **Bottom**: Mean square error of the income quantile prediction using classifiers. Units are income quantiles. In all panels, distribution represent bootstrapping results. Colors indicate mobility or hashtag usage feature space.

The error structure presented in the classification matrices can be interpreted as a behavioral distance among individuals from different quantiles of the income distribution (right panels in Figure 1). The more misclassifications among individuals of different income quantile, the closer their behavior. Previous studies also use similar prediction accuracy as a proxy of cultural distance [16]. In this case, the upper right and bottom left corners of the matrix are colored by darkest blue, showing the least amount of error. This means that the top and bottom socioeconomic quantiles have the most differentiated behavior and therefore are easier to classify.

The bootstrap of the prediction accuracy is shown in Figure 2 (top right). Both hashtag (orange) and mobility (blue) are significantly higher than the error guess (dashed line). Therefore, a considerable part of the variance of hashtag usage and mobility patterns are explained by income. Another way of measuring the prediction quality is through the Mean Square Error (MSE). As quantile labels are also numerical, we can estimate the error of the prediction using the average euclidean distance between the real and predicted value. The MSE in Figure 2 (bottom) shows that the while prediction errors are lowest when using mobility features, the ones obtained from hashtags are still low—with an error below 1.5 quantile difference. Studies based on semantic features and topics of conversation report similar predictive performance [62].

The relationship of mobility and communication has been observed using mobile phones [63] and social media data [24]. People tend to communicate with places they have already visited. Moreover, patches in the territory that host certain populations are consistent with their geographic communication at multiple scales, from national levels down the suburban granularity [12]. These analyses have shown that income fragments the human mobility patterns in cities due to neighborhood segregation and therefore also affects the way people interact with each other both offline and online [21]. Furthermore, previous studies have already hinted toward the existing correlation between the socioeconomic status of people and the diversity of locations they visit. Indeed, as previously pointed out [44], high SES users tend to have patterns of mobility that are more diverse than the ones observed among low SES users, which in turn leads to the lower predictability of their whereabouts. These results may relate to previous work [64,65], which explains this trend by means of the positive payoff between commuting farther for better jobs, while keeping better housing conditions. This in turn also explains why mobility might be used as an indicative predictor of an individual's socioeconomic status.

5. Topic Analysis

Conversational patterns differ by people's income. Following the methodology developed in a previous study [62], we characterized users by a probability distribution over a set of predefined topics rather than a frequency distribution over all the words of a given dictionary. Topics represent a latent word space such that certain words create topics and users sample words from the topics they talk about. The topic analysis creates a new space of reduced dimensions that represent new features. These new feature can input the classic algorithms used to predict a user's income based on their tweets.

The topic analysis begins by training a *word2vec* model with the skip-gram architecture and negative sampling on a given collection of tweets [59]. The skip-gram architecture predicts the context of words given their location in sentences. It learns the relationships between words under the assumption that their proximity in the text is not independent of their meaning. The negative sampling method is used for reducing the number of parameters to be inferred in the network. These methods are commonly used for natural language processing. During this process, words are mapped onto a 50-dimensional vector. The words that co-occur in the same tweet will be embedded in vectors that are in proximity to each other. The co-occurring words becomes the basis for deriving conversational topics.

In Figure 3 (top panel), we show a 2-dimensional representation of the embedding space using t-SNE for visualization. Words are represented by dots, and their proximity is not encoded by the euclidean distance but rather by the cosine similarity value existing between pairs of word vectors. By running a spectral clustering algorithm on the word-to-word similarity matrix and setting negative similarity values to null we derived a prefixed number d (here $d = 100$) of clusters of words or topics grouping similar words. These topics were then manually labeled based on which words they contained. In the visualization, some topics have been colored with distinct colors and labeled after manual inspection.

We obtained a distribution of topical interest for users by computing the frequency of use of a given topic over a user's tweets. The individual vectors show the normalized usage frequency of words from each topic. These vectors coarsely represented users' syntax and interests and can be used to cluster individuals based on areas of interest. More importantly, we can observe differences among topic vectors based on people's income. In Figure 3 (bottom panel) we show the income distribution of the individuals who mentioned (or not) a given topic. Individuals that talk about politics, technology, literature and travel have in average higher income than users who did not talk about these issues. Analogously, individuals that used slang, insults or urban interjection had a significantly lower income than the population who didn't use these words.

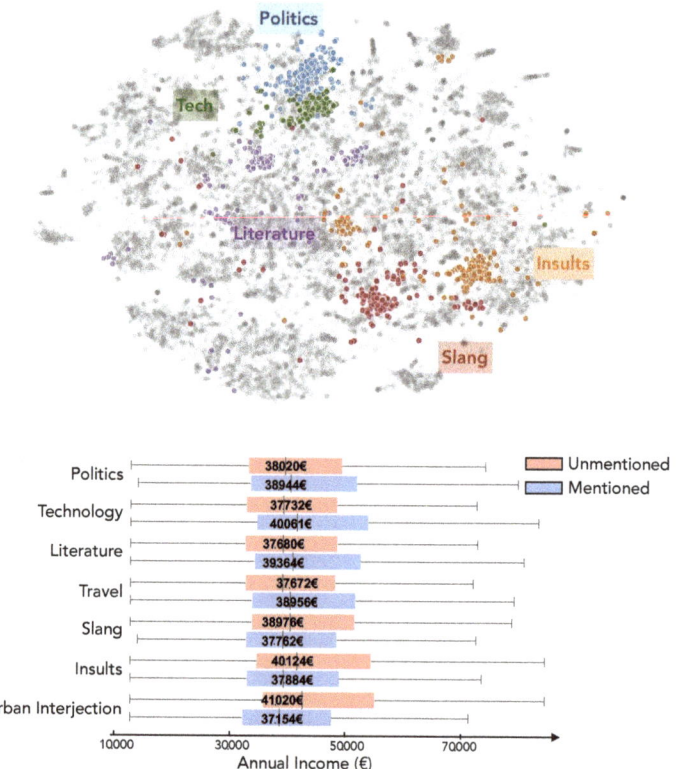

Figure 3. Topic model analysis of tweets per individual. Top panel: 2D visualization (t-SNE) of the embedding space obtained from applying *word2vec* on skip-grams and negative sampling. Colors correspond to topics obtained via clustering. Bottom panel shows income distributions of those who talk about the topics identified.

6. Diversity

We also characterize the diversity of collective activity. For this purpose, we create mobility and communication vectors by neighborhood as explained in Section 3. These vectors represent the aggregate behavior of the individuals who reside there. Mobility vectors aggregate the number of times people from neighborhood i visit neighborhood j. Online communication is measured via mentions and represent the number of times people from neighborhood i mentions other people from neighborhood j in their tweets.

We measure the diversity of mobility and communications per neighborhood by quantifying the entropy of the collective behavior vectors. Before calculating the entropy we normalize the vectors by their sum, such that they can be defined as probability density functions. We then calculate the entropy of these distributions and divide it by the hypothetical entropy of the uniform distribution which represents the maximum possible value that the entropy function can attain. Therefore, neighborhoods whose entropy is close to 1 have the most diverse patterns of visitation and interaction online, while neighborhoods whose entropy are close to zero have the least diverse patterns of behavior.

In Figure 4, we present a scatter plot where dots represent neighborhoods colored by income (from red to blue). The x-axis shows the entropy of the mobility vectors and the y-axis shows the entropy of the mentions vectors. There is a direct relationship between the entropy of both vectors. Diverse urban exploration is consistent with diverse online communications (r = 0.57). Moreover, a clear separation of behavior by income is manifested. The diversity for both types of behaviors is consistent with the neighborhood income. Wealthier neighborhoods are consistently more diverse than poorer neighborhoods both in terms of mobility (r = 0.46) and mentions (r = 0.35).

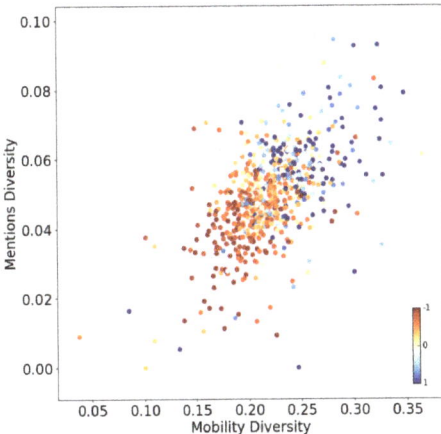

Figure 4. Diversity of collective behaviors in terms of urban mobility and online communication patterns. Dots represent neighborhoods colored by income (from red to blue). The x-axis represents the entropy of mobility vectors aggregated by neighborhoods. The y-axis represents the entropy of Twitter mention vectors aggregated by neighborhoods. Scale in figure. Units represent the number of standard deviations from the mean (centered at zero).

The diversity of social exploration is closely related with the diversity of the information people are exposed to. Those who receive information from multiple sources are more likely to find better opportunities than those who receive information from fewer sources. Therefore, while diverse neighborhoods are also richer, they might be richer precisely because they are diverse. Previous work shows that the diversity of urban exploration is consistent with income and age [66,67]. Our results show that it is also consistent with the diversity of online interactions.

While physical exploration requires resources, online exploration in principle should be considerably less costly. However, the patterns from both offline and online world are remarkably similar. This result is further explored in a previous study [24], where multiple cities are compared and consistent results are obtained from multiple sources of data, including shopping and credit cards. Despite having new methods to interact with one another, people continue to mainly interact with those from their offline lives and behave in similar manners.

In another work [12], we show that people's mobility and communication patterns online create geographical patches that are preset at multiple scales of observation, ranging from sub-urban areas, up to large national regions. The multiscale nature of these regions arise from the structure of weak and strong ties [5]. While strong ties are local and remain in a radius of 5km approximately, weaker ties span across larger scales, are more diverse and connect distant areas. Previous analysis of social networks show that those long range connections, which are responsible for the spread of information across the whole system, are also unequally distributed among the different income groups.

7. Discussion

Inferring the socioeconomic status (SES) of individuals is an important milestone in the development of tools aimed at informing policy makers on how to best curb social problems like income inequality, segregation, and poverty. While nationwide censuses are meant to provide such information, their costs make their collection rather infrequent. Social media analysis on the other hand provides alternative sources of information. Here we provided a general overview on how this can be performed by predicting individual SES based on linguistics and mobility patterns. We showed some of the key patterns that differentiate the behavior of people belonging to different socioeconomic groups.

In order to provide a complete understanding of social context and behaviors, further research should not be bounded to the sole exploration of social media. New approaches relying on widely available satellite imagery and mobile phone data are also proving themselves to be instrumental in capturing part of the inherent dynamics involved in these phenomena, capturing interesting behaviors that had remained hitherto unseen [68,69]. The information provided by these innovative approaches needs, however, to be dealt cautiously. More in-depth studies about the implicit biases underlying these models are necessary before they can be deployed.

The results presented in this paper provide a clear reflection on how complex societal phenomena such as polarization and segregation affect the way we use and interact with social media, which could in turn be used to better understand these social processes. Recent studies indicate that the differentiation of behaviors and physical segregation are deeply intertwined given the reinforcing dynamics of collective learning. The results of these nonlinear processes are reflected in the feature space as unstructured patterns of information that algorithms can use to infer demographic information.

While standardized metrics and measurements are necessary for achieving effective planning, they reduce the description of social and natural systems down to levels that are legible by the policy maker [70]. In some cases, that reduction removes details that are fundamental for the healthy functioning of the system such as relationships and elements that contribute in the background to the stability of the system [1]. The new data sources enable a finer observation of the complexity and varieties of social behaviors and relationships which opens the opportunity for creating plans that are adequate to the complexity of the phenomenon. Being able to observe social behavior at finer granularity brings the mental map closer to reality and increases the amount of available and relevant information to design effective interventions and decision-making processes.

8. Conclusions

In summary, we aimed to characterize multiple patterns of Twitter user activity that are related to people's to show how Twitter user activity differed from user to user when it was conditioned on individual socioeconomic status (SES) differentiate behaviors across multiple social strata and are behind income prediction tasks. In particular, we showed that (1) human mobility is a better predictor of income than hashtag usage, which either way explain a large part of the variance; (2) online topics of conversation and collective interest are strongly influenced by socioeconomic status; and (3) wealthy neighborhoods have more diverse interactions and communication patterns than poorer neighborhoods. These results confirm a segregated and differentiated structure of social groups in both physical and virtual space which in turn enables the prediction of their income.

This study presents certain limitations that open space for further research and future work. Some limitations are related to the methods and representativity of the data. First, we assume that the income of individuals corresponds to the neighborhood average. More advanced methods for inferring home locations could improve such assignment. Moreover, combining both traditional surveys with observational data could improve the income assignation for the training and labeled dataset. Second, the behaviors that we derived can be subject to de-contextualization and generalization which can yield oversimplified views of reality and wrong conclusions. Differentiating between emergent patterns and those within our circle of influence is critical to design effective intervention mechanisms and policies.

The inference of socioeconomic status from widely available digital traces holds a large potential for updating census information as well as enriching other data corpuses with socioeconomic information. This in turn opens the door for further studies to address population level correlations of income with language, space, time, or social network. The use of the aforementioned methods is important as it provides new observations on how socioeconomic status shapes the fabric of society and cements further developments in fields ranging from recommendation systems to economic aid allocation.

Author Contributions: Conceptualization, J.L.A. and A.J.M.; methodology, J.L.A. and A.J.M.; software, J.L.A. and A.J.M.; validation, J.L.A. and A.J.M.; formal analysis, J.L.A. and A.J.M.; investigation, J.L.A. and A.J.M.; resources, J.L.A. and A.J.M.; data curation, J.L.A. and A.J.M.; writing—original draft preparation, J.L.A. and A.J.M.; writing—review and editing, J.L.A. and A.J.M.; visualization, J.L.A. and A.J.M.; supervision, A.J.M. All authors have read and agreed to the published version of the manuscript.

Funding: This research received no external funding.

Institutional Review Board Statement: Not applicable.

Informed Consent Statement: Not applicable.

Data Availability Statement: Network data will be available upon publication.

Acknowledgments: J.L.A. was employed by ENS Lyon and GRYZZLY for the duration of the work described in this paper. The dataset underlying this work was supported by the SoSweet ANR project (ANR-15- CE38-0011), the MOTIf Stic-AmSud project (18-STIC-07), and the ACADEMICS project financed by IDEX LYON. We thank Jose Balsa from MIT Media Lab and the GRYZZLY company staff for the useful discussions during the elaboration of this paper.

Conflicts of Interest: The authors declare no conflict of interest.

References

1. Scott, J.C. *Seeing Like a State: How Certain Schemes to Improve the Human Condition Have Failed*; Yale University Press: New Haven, CT, USA, 1998.
2. Kibekbaev, A.; Duman, E. Benchmarking regression algorithms for income prediction modeling. *Inf. Syst.* **2016**, *61*, 40–52. [CrossRef]
3. Koskinen, L.; Nurminen, T.; Salonen, J. *Modelling and Predicting Individual Salaries: A Study of Finlands Unique Dataset*; Eläketurvakeskus: Helsinki, Finland, 2005.
4. Lazer, D.; Pentland, A.; Adamic, L.; Aral, S.; Barabasi, A.L.; Brewer, D.; Christakis, N.; Contractor, N.; Fowler, J.; Gutmann, M.; et al. Computational Social Science. *Science* **2009**, *323*, 721–723. [CrossRef]
5. Hedayatifar, L.; Morales, A.J.; Bar-Yam, Y. Geographical fragmentation of the global network of Twitter communications. *Chaos Interdiscip. J. Nonlinear Sci.* **2020**, *30*, 073133. [CrossRef]
6. Herdagdelen, A.; Zuo, W.; Gard-Murray, A.; Bar-Yam, Y. An exploration of social identity: The geography and politics of news-sharing communities in Twitter. *Complexity* **2013**, *19*, 10–20. [CrossRef]
7. Bakshy, E.; Messing, S.; Adamic, L.A. Exposure to ideologically diverse news and opinion on Facebook. *Science* **2015**, *348*, 1130–1132. [CrossRef]
8. Pagolu, V.S.; Reddy, K.N.; Panda, G.; Majhi, B. Sentiment analysis of Twitter data for predicting stock market movements. In Proceedings of the 2016 International Conference on Signal Processing, Communication, Power and Embedded System (SCOPES), Paralakhemundi, India, 3–5 October 2016; pp. 1345–1350.
9. Morales, A.J.; Losada, J.C.; Benito, R.M. Users structure and behavior on an online social network during a political protest. *Phys. A Stat. Mech. Its Appl.* **2012**, *391*, 5244–5253. [CrossRef]
10. Morales, A.J.; Borondo, J.; Losada, J.C.; Benito, R.M. Measuring political polarization: Twitter shows the two sides of Venezuela. *Chaos Interdiscip. J. Nonlinear Sci.* **2015**, *25*, 033114. [CrossRef] [PubMed]
11. Widener, M.J.; Li, W. Using geolocated Twitter data to monitor the prevalence of healthy and unhealthy food references across the US. *Appl. Geogr.* **2014**, *54*, 189–197. [CrossRef]
12. Hedayatifar, L.; Rigg, R.A.; Bar-Yam, Y.; Morales, A.J. US social fragmentation at multiple scales. *J. R. Soc. Interface* **2019**, *16*, 20190509. [CrossRef] [PubMed]
13. Hellmich, S.N. What is Socioeconomics? An Overview of Theories, Methods, and Themes in the Field. *Forum Soc. Econ.* **2017**, *46*, 3–25. [CrossRef]
14. Perry, V.G.; Morris, M.D. Who Is in Control? The Role of Self-Perception, Knowledge, and Income in Explaining Consumer Financial Behavior. *J. Consum. Aff.* **2005**, *39*, 299–313. [CrossRef]

15. Levy Abitbol, J.; Karsai, M.; Magué, J.P.; Chevrot, J.P.; Fleury, E. Socioeconomic Dependencies of Linguistic Patterns in Twitter: A Multivariate Analysis. In Proceedings of the 2018 World Wide Web Conference, International World Wide Web Conferences Steering Committee: Republic and Canton (WWW '18), Geneva, Switzerland, 23–27 April 2018; pp. 1125–1134. [CrossRef]
16. Bertrand, M.; Kamenica, E. *Coming Apart? Cultural Distances in the United States over Time*; Working Paper 24771; National Bureau of Economic Research: Cambridge, MA, USA, 2018. [CrossRef]
17. Hasanuzzaman, M.; Kamila, S.; Kaur, M.; Saha, S.; Ekbal, A. *Temporal Orientation of Tweets for Predicting Income of Users*; ACL: Vancouver, BC, Canada, 2017.
18. Duesenberry, J.S. *Income, Saving, and the Theory of Consumer Behavior*; Taylor & Francis, Ltd.: Cambridge, MA, USA, 1949.
19. Spengler, M.; Damian, R.I.; Roberts, B.W. How you behave in school predicts life success above and beyond family background, broad traits, and cognitive ability. *J. Personal. Soc. Psychol.* **2018**, *4*. [CrossRef] [PubMed]
20. Fritz, R. *The Path of Least Resistance: Learning to Become the Creative Force in Your Own Life*; Ballantine Books: New York, NY, USA, 1989.
21. Morales, A.J.; Dong, X.; Bar-Yam, Y.; 'Sandy'Pentland, A. Segregation and polarization in urban areas. *R. Soc. Open Sci.* **2019**, *6*, 190573. [CrossRef]
22. Bora, N.; Chang, Y.H.; Maheswaran, R. *Mobility Patterns and User Dynamics in Racially Segregated Geographies of US Cities*; Social Computing, Behavioral-Cultural Modeling and Prediction; Springer International Publishing: Washington, DC, USA, 2014; pp. 11–18.
23. Wang, Q.; Phillips, N.E.; Small, M.L.; Sampson, R.J. Urban mobility and neighborhood isolation in America's 50 largest cities. *Proc. Natl. Acad. Sci. USA* **2018**. [CrossRef] [PubMed]
24. Dong, X.; Morales, A.J.; Jahani, E.; Moro, E.; Lepri, B.; Bozkaya, B.; Sarraute, C.; Bar-Yam, Y.; Pentland, A. Segregated interactions in urban and online space. *EPJ Data Sci.* **2020**, *9*, 20. [CrossRef]
25. Bollen, J.; Mao, H.; Pepe, A. Modeling public mood and emotion: Twitter sentiment and socio-economic phenomena. In Proceedings of the Fifth International AAAI Conference on Weblogs and Social Media, Barcelona, Spain, 17–21 July 2011.
26. Golder, W.M.; Macy, M.W. Diurnal and Seasonal Mood Vary with Work, Sleep, and Daylength Across Diverse Cultures. *Science* **2011**, *333*, 1878–1881. [CrossRef]
27. Morales, A.; Borondo, J.; Losada, J.C.; Benito, R.M. Efficiency of human activity on information spreading on Twitter. *Soc. Netw.* **2014**, *39*, 1–11. [CrossRef]
28. Lenormand, M.; Tugores, A.; Colet, P.; Ramasco, J.J. Tweets on the Road. *PLoS ONE* **2014**, *9*, e105407. [CrossRef]
29. Lenormand, M.; Gonçalves, B.; Tugores, A.; Ramasco, J.J. Human diffusion and city influence. *J. R. Soc. Interface* **2015**, *12*. [CrossRef]
30. Mocanu, D.; Baronchelli, A.; Perra, N.; Gonçalves, B.; Zhang, Q.; Vespignani, A. The Twitter of Babel: Mapping World Languages through Microblogging Platforms. *PLoS ONE* **2013**, *8*, e61981. [CrossRef]
31. Chamberlain, B.P.; Humby, C.; Deisenroth, M.P. Detecting the Age of Twitter Users. *arXiv* **2016**, arXiv:1601.04621.
32. Preoţiuc-Pietro, D.; Volkova, S.; Lampos, V.; Bachrach, Y.; Aletras, N. Studying User Income through Language, Behaviour and Affect in Social Media. *PLoS ONE* **2015**, *10*, e138717. [CrossRef]
33. Lampos, V.; Aletras, N.; Geyti, J.K.; Zou, B.; Cox, I.J. Inferring the Socioeconomic Status of Social Media Users Based on Behaviour and Language. In *European Conference on Information Retrieval*; Lecture Notes in Computer Science; Springer International Publishing: Berlin/Heidelberg, Germany, 2016; pp. 689–695. [CrossRef]
34. Preot, D.; Lampos, V.; Aletras, N. An analysis of the user occupational class through Twitter content. In Proceedings of the 53rd Annual Meeting of the Association for Computational Linguistics, Beijing, China, 26–31 July 2015; pp. 1754–1764.
35. Hu, T.; Xiao, H.; Nguyen, T.T.; Luo, J. What the Language You Tweet Says About Your Occupation. *arXiv* **2017**, arXiv:1701.06233.
36. Volkova, S.; Coppersmith, G.; Van Durme, B. Inferring User Political Preferences from Streaming Communications. In Proceedings of the Annual Meeting of the Association for Computational Linguistics (ACL), Baltimore, MD, USA, 22–27 June 2014.
37. Schwartz, H.A.; Eichstaedt, J.C.; Kern, M.L.; Dziurzynski, L.; Ramones, S.M.; Agrawal, M.; Shah, A.; Kosinski, M.; Stillwell, D.; Seligman, M.E.P.; et al. Personality, Gender, and Age in the Language of Social Media: The Open-Vocabulary Approach. *PLoS ONE* **2013**, *8*, e73791. [CrossRef]
38. Luo, S.; Morone, F.; Sarraute, C.; Travizano, M.; Makse, H.A. Inferring personal economic status from social network location. *Nat. Commun.* **2017**, *8*, 15227. [CrossRef] [PubMed]
39. Culotta, A.; Kumar, N.; Cutler, J. Predicting the Demographics of Twitter Users from Website Traffic Data. In Proceedings of the AAAI Conference on Artificial Intelligence, Austin, TX, USA, 25–30 January 2015.
40. Llorente, A.; Garcia-Herranz, M.; Cebrian, M.; Moro, E. Social Media Fingerprints of Unemployment. *PLoS ONE* **2015**, *10*, e128692. [CrossRef]
41. Eisenstein, J.; O'Connor, B.; Smith, N.A.; Xing, E.P. Diffusion of Lexical Change in Social Media. *PLoS ONE* **2014**, *9*, e113114. [CrossRef] [PubMed]
42. Eagle, N.; Macy, M.; Claxton, R. Network Diversity and Economic Development. *Science* **2010**, *328*, 1029–1031. [CrossRef]
43. Song, C.; Qu, Z.; Blumm, N.; Barabási, A.L. Limits of Predictability in Human Mobility. *Science* **2010**, *327*, 1018–1021. [CrossRef]
44. González, M.C.; Hidalgo, C.A.; Barabási, A.L. Understanding individual human mobility patterns. *Nature* **2008**, *453*, 779–782. [CrossRef]

45. Jurdak, R.; Zhao, K.; Liu, J.; AbouJaoude, M.; Cameron, M.; Newth, D. Understanding Human Mobility from Twitter. *PLoS ONE* **2015**, *10*, e131469. [CrossRef] [PubMed]
46. Morales, A.J.; Vavilala, V.; Benito, R.M.; Bar-Yam, Y. Global patterns of synchronization in human communications. *J. R. Soc. Interface* **2017**, *14*, 20161048. [CrossRef] [PubMed]
47. Bernstein, B. Language and Social Class. *Br. J. Sociol.* **1960**, *11*, 271–276. [CrossRef]
48. Twitter. Twitter Streaming Application Programming Interface. 2015. Available online: https://developer.twitter.com/en/docs (accessed on 20 September 2018).
49. Leetaru, K.; Wang, S.; Cao, G.; Padmanabhan, A.; Shook, E. Mapping the global Twitter heartbeat: The geography of Twitter. *First Monday* **2013**, *18*. [CrossRef]
50. Morstatter, F.; Pfeffer, J.; Liu, H.; Carley, K.M. Is the sample good enough? Comparing data from Twitter's streaming API with Twitter's firehose. In Proceedings of the 7th International AAAI Conference on Weblogs and Social Media, Cambridge, MA, USA, 8–13 July 2013; The AAAI Press: Palo Alto, CA, USA, 2013.
51. Hong, L.; Convertino, G.; Chi, E. Language Matters In Twitter: A Large Scale Study. In Proceedings of the International AAAI Conference on Weblogs and Social Media, Barcelona, Spain, 17–21 July 2011; Volume 5.
52. Duggan, M.; Brenner, J. *The Demographics of Social Media Users, Pew Research*; Technical Report; Pew Research: Washington, DC, USA, 2013.
53. Mislove, A.; Lehmann, S.; Ahn, Y.Y.; Onnela, J.P.; Rosenquist, N. Understanding the Demographics of Twitter Users. In Proceedings of the 5th International AAAI Conference on Weblogs and Social Media, Barcelona, Spain, 17–21 July 2011; The AAAI Press: Palo Alto, CA, USA, 2011; pp. 554–557.
54. Jiang, Y.; Li, Z.; Ye, X. Understanding Demographic and Socioeconomic Bias of Geotagged Twitter Users at the County Level. *Cartogr. Geogr. Inf. Sci.* **2018**. [CrossRef]
55. Kalimeri, K.; Beiro, M.G.; Bonanomi, A.; Rosina, A.; Cattuto, C. Evaluation of Biases in Self-reported Demographic and Psychometric Information: Traditional versus Facebook-based Surveys. *arXiv* **2019**, arXiv:1901.07876.
56. Morales, A.J.; Creixell, W.; Borondo, J.; Losada, J.C.; Benito, R. Characterizing ethnic interactions from human communication patterns in Ivory Coast. *Netw. Heterog. Media* **2015**, *10*, 87. [CrossRef]
57. Chen, H.H.; Alexander, T.J.; Oliveira, D.F.; Altmann, E.G. Scaling laws and dynamics of hashtags on Twitter. *Chaos Interdiscip. J. Nonlinear Sci.* **2020**, *30*, 063112. [CrossRef]
58. Leskovec, J.; Rajaraman, A.; Ullman, J.D. *Mining of Massive Datasets*, 2nd ed.; Cambridge University Press: New York, NY, USA, 2014.
59. Mikolov, T.; Sutskever, I.; Chen, K.; Corrado, G.; Dean, J. Distributed Representations of Words and Phrases and Their Compositionality. In Proceedings of the 26th International Conference on Neural Information Processing Systems-Volume 2 (NIPS'13): Harrahs and Harveys, Lake Tahoe: 2013, Lake Tahoe, NV, USA, 5–8 December 2013; Curran Associates Inc.: Red Hook, NY, USA, 2013; pp. 3111–3119.
60. Huberman, B.; Romero, D.; Wu, F. Social networks that matter: Twitter under the microscope. *First Monday* **2008**, *14*. [CrossRef]
61. Murtagh, F. Multilayer perceptrons for classification and regression. *Neurocomputing* **1991**, *2*, 183–197. [CrossRef]
62. Levy Abitbol, J.; Karsai, M.; Fleury, E. Location, Occupation, and Semantics Based Socioeconomic Status Inference on Twitter. In Proceedings of the 2018 IEEE International Conference on Data Mining Workshops (ICDMW), Singapore, 17–20 November 2018. [CrossRef]
63. Toole, J.L.; Herrera-Yaqüe, C.; Schneider, C.M.; González, M.C. Coupling human mobility and social ties. *J. R. Soc. Interface* **2015**, *12*, 20141128. [CrossRef]
64. Xu, Y.; Belyi, A.; Bojic, I.; Ratti, C. Human mobility and socioeconomic status: Analysis of Singapore and Boston. *Comput. Environ. Urban Syst.* **2018**, *72*, 51–67. [CrossRef]
65. Léo, Y.; Fleury, E.; Sarraute, C.; Karsai, M. Socioeconomic Correlations and Stratification in Social Communication Networks. *J. R. Soc. Interface* **2018**, *13*, 20160598. [CrossRef] [PubMed]
66. Kwan, M.P.; Schwanen, T. Geographies of Mobility. *Ann. Am. Assoc. Geogr.* **2016**, *106*, 243–256. [CrossRef]
67. Isaacman, S.; Becker, R.; Caceres, R.; Kobourov, S.; Martonosi, M.; Rowland, J.; Varshavsky, A. Ranges of human mobility in Los Angeles and New York. In Proceedings of the 2011 IEEE International Conference on Pervasive Computing and Communications Workshops (PERCOM Workshops), Seattle, WA, USA, 21–25 March 2011; pp. 88–93. [CrossRef]
68. Jean, N.; Burke, M.; Xie, M.; Davis, W.M.; Lobell, D.B.; Ermon, S. Combining satellite imagery and machine learning to predict poverty. *Science* **2016**, *353*, 790–794. [CrossRef] [PubMed]
69. Blumenstock, J.; Cadamuro, G.; On, R. Predicting poverty and wealth from mobile phone metadata. *Science* **2015**, *350*, 1073–1076. [CrossRef] [PubMed]
70. Ashby, W.R. *An Introduction to Cybernetics*; Chapman & Hall Ltd.: London, UK, 1961.

Article

Towards Generative Design of Computationally Efficient Mathematical Models with Evolutionary Learning

Anna V. Kalyuzhnaya *, Nikolay O. Nikitin, Alexander Hvatov, Mikhail Maslyaev, Mikhail Yachmenkov and Alexander Boukhanovsky

Nature Systems Simulation Lab, National Center for Cognitive Research, ITMO University, 49 Kronverksky Pr., 197101 St. Petersburg, Russia; nnikitin@itmo.ru (N.O.N.); alex_hvatov@itmo.ru (A.H.); mikemaslyaev@itmo.ru (M.M.); mmiachmenkov@itmo.ru (M.Y.); boukhanovsky@mail.ifmo.ru (A.B.)
* Correspondence: anna.kalyuzhnaya@itmo.ru

Abstract: In this paper, we describe the concept of generative design approach applied to the automated evolutionary learning of mathematical models in a computationally efficient way. To formalize the problems of models' design and co-design, the generalized formulation of the modeling workflow is proposed. A parallelized evolutionary learning approach for the identification of model structure is described for the equation-based model and composite machine learning models. Moreover, the involvement of the performance models in the design process is analyzed. A set of experiments with various models and computational resources is conducted to verify different aspects of the proposed approach.

Keywords: generative design; automated learning; evolutionary learning; co-design; genetic programming

1. Introduction

Nowadays, data-driven modeling is a very popular concept, first of all because of many examples of the successful application for a wide range of tasks where we have data samples which are sufficient for model training. However, originally the term "modeling" assumes a wider meaning than just identifying numerical coefficients in equations. One may say that modeling is an art of creation of mathematical (in the context) models that describe processes, events, and systems with mathematical notation. And current successes of artificial intelligence (AI) give the opportunity to come closer to the solution of the task of mathematical modeling in this original formulation.

For this purpose we may use an approach of generative design that assumes open-ended automatic synthesis of new digital objects or digital reflections of material objects which have desired properties and are aligned with possible restrictions. Open-ended evolution is a term that assumes ongoing generation of novelty as new adaptations of specimens, new entities and evolution of the evolvability itself [1]. We assume that new objects are objects with essentially new features that appeared during the adaptation process and that can't be obtained with simple tuning or recombination of initially known parameters. Other words, it is an approach that aims of algorithmic "growing" of a population of new objects when each of them is aligned with restrictions and have desired properties, to some extent. However, only the objects which could maximize the measure of fitness will be used for their intended purpose. The generative design is a well-known concept for creation of digital twins of material objects [2]. The same idea can be applied to mathematical models [3]. Indeed, it is known that we may grow mathematical expressions that approximate some initial data with a symbolic (usually polynomial) regression approach. However, if we look at mathematical expressions in a wider perspective we may admit that expressions could be different even much more complicated. For example, we may try to apply this approach to the problem of searching for an equation of mathematical physics that is able to describe observed phenomena. Or, we may want to create in an automated

Citation: Kalyuzhnaya, A.V.; Nikitin, N.O.; Hvatov, A.; Maslyaev, M.; Yachmenkov, M.; Boukhanovsky, A. Towards Generative Design of Computationally Efficient Mathematical Models with Evolutionary Learning. Entropy 2021, 23, 28.
https://dx.doi.org/10.3390/e23010028

Received: 9 November 2020
Accepted: 24 December 2020
Published: 27 December 2020

Publisher's Note: MDPI stays neutral with regard to jurisdictional claims in published maps and institutional affiliations.

Copyright: © 2020 by the authors. Licensee MDPI, Basel, Switzerland. This article is an open access article distributed under the terms and conditions of the Creative Commons Attribution (CC BY) license (https://creativecommons.org/licenses/by/4.0/).

way a complicated data-driven model that consists of many single models and feature processing stages. Tasks in both examples can be formalized as the generative design of computer models.

Both of cases (model as mathematical equation and complicated data-driven models) have their own spheres of application, but they also can be joined as composite models. In machine learning the composite model case often is described in terms of the multi-model data-driven pipelines. If a single data-driven model cannot provide appropriate results, various ensembling techniques like stacking or blending are applied [4]. To achieve better quality, complex modeling pipelines can be used, that include different pre-processing stages and can contain several types of models. A generalization of ensembling approaches is the composite model concept [5]. A composite model has a heterogeneous structure, so it can include models of different nature: machine learning (ML), equation-based, etc. [6].

A design of a composite model can be represented from an automated ML (AutoML) perspective that may use a genetic algorithm for learning the structure. The evolutionary learning approach seems to be a natural and justified choice because of several reasons. First of all, the idea of generative design refers to the possibility of controlled open-ended evolution under a set of restrictions. After that, genetic algorithms give flexible opportunities for treating mixed problems with combinatorial and real parts of a chromosome.

However, the design of the composite model may depend on different factors: the desired modeling quality, computational constraints, time limits, interpreting ability requirements, etc. It raises the problem of co-design [7] of the automatically generated composite models with the specific environment. Generative co-design is an approach which allows to synthesize jointly a set (mostly a pair) of objects that will be compatible with each other. In context of this article these are mathematical models and computational infrastructure. The conceptual difference between the generative design (that builds the model on a basis of dataset only) and the generative co-design (that takes into account both data and infrastructure) is illustrated in Figure 1. The structure of composite models can be very complex, so it is complicated to construct the models in an expert way. For this reason, different optimization techniques are used for the structural learning of the model. Usually, the objective function for optimization is aimed to minimize the error of the predictions obtained from the candidate model [8].

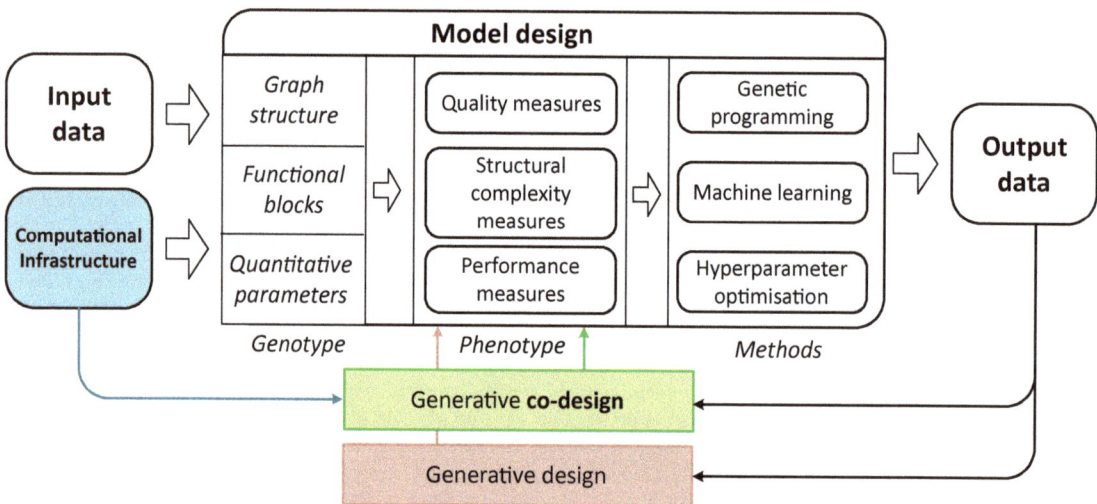

Figure 1. The description of the generative co-design concept: the different aspects of the model design (genotype, phenotype, and the identification methods); the pipeline of the data-driven modeling; the difference between classical design approach and co-design approach.

The paper is organized as follows. Section 2 describes the existing approaches to the design of models. Section 3 provides the mathematical formulation for the model's design and co-design tasks and associated optimization problems. Section 4 described the actual issues of generative co-design for the mathematical models. Section 5 provides the results of experimental studies for different applications of generative design (composite models, equation-based models, etc). The unsolved problems of co-design and potential future works are discussed in Section 6. Section 7 provides the main conclusions.

2. Related Work

An extensive literature review shows many attempts for mathematical models design in the different fields [9,10]. In particular, the methods of the automated model design is highly valuable part of the various researches [11]. As an example, the equation-free methods allow building the models that represent the multi-scale processes [12]. Another example is building of the physical laws from data in form of function [13], ordinary differential equations system [14], partial differential equations (PDE) [15]. The application of the automated design of ML models or pipelines (which are algorithmicaly close notions) are commonly named AutoML [8] although most of them work with models of fixed structure, some give opportunity to automatically construct relatively simple the ML structures. Convenient notation for such purpose is representation of a model as a directed acyclic graph (DAG) [16]. Another example of popular AutoML tool for pipelines structure optimization is TPOT [17].

To build the ML model effectively in the complicated high-performance environment [18], the properties of both algorithms and infrastructure should be taken into account. It especially important for the non-standard infrastructural setups: embedded [19], distributed [20], heterogeneous [21] systems. Moreover, the adaptation of the model design to the specific hardware is an actual problem for the deep learning models [22,23].

However, the application of co-design approaches [24] for the generative model identification in the distributed or supercomputer environment [25,26] is still facing a lot of issues. For example, the temporal characteristics of the designed models should be known. The estimations of fitting and simulation time of the data-driven models can be obtained in several ways. The first is the application of the analytical performance models of the algorithm [27]. The identification of the analytical performance models can be achieved using domain knowledge [28]. However, it can be impossible to build this kind of model for the non-static heterogeneous environment. For this reason, the empirical performance models (EPMs) are highly applicable to the different aspects of the generative model design [29]. Moreover, the effective estimation of execution time is an important problem for the generation of optimal computational schedule [30] or the mapping of applications to the specific resources [31].

The execution of the complex resource-consuming algorithms in the specific infrastructure with limited resources raises the workflow scheduling problem [32]. It can be solved using an evolutionary algorithm [33] or neural approaches [34].

It can be noted that the existing design and co-design approaches are mostly focused on the specific application and do not consider the design for the different types of mathematical models. In the paper, we propose the modified formulation of this problem that allows applying the generative design and co-design approaches to the different tasks and models.

3. Problem Statement

A problem of the generative design of mathematical models requires a model representation as a flexible structure and appropriate optimization methods for maximizing a measure of the quality of the designed model. To solve this optimization problem, different approaches can be applied. The widely used approach is based on evolutionary algorithms (e.g., genetic optimization implemented in TPOT [35] and DarwinML [16] frameworks) because it allows solving both exploration and exploitation tasks in a space of model structure variants. The other optimization approaches like the random search of Bayesian optimization also can be used, but the populational character of evolutionary methods makes it possible to solve the generative problems in a multiobjective way and produce several candidates model. Such formulation also can be successfully treated with the evolutionary algorithms or hybrid ones that combine the use of evolutionary operators with additional optimization procedures for increasing of robustness and acceleration of convergence. In this section, we describe the problem of generative co-design of mathematical models and computational resources in terms of the genetic programming approach.

A general statement for numerical simulation problem can be formulated as follows:

$$Y = \mathcal{H}(M|Z), \quad (1)$$

where $\mathcal{H}$ is an operator of simulation with model M on data Z.

In the context of problem of computer model generative design, the model M should have flexible structure that can evolve by changing (or adding/eliminating) the properties of a set of atomic parts ("building blocks"). For such task, the model M can be described as a graph (or more precisely as a DAG):

$$M = \langle S, E, \{a_{1:|A|}\}\rangle, \quad (2)$$

with edges E that denoted relations between nodes $\langle S, \{a_{1:|A|}\}\rangle$ that characterize functional properties S of atomic blocks and set of their parameters $\{a_{1:|A|}\}$.

In terms of evolutionary algorithms each specimen d_p in population D of computer model can be represented as a tuple that consists of phenotype Y, genotype M and fitness function $\varphi(M)$:

$$d_p = \langle Y_p, M_p, \varphi(M_p)\rangle, \ D = (d_p, p \in [1:|D|]). \quad (3)$$

Genotype M should be mapped on plain vector as a multi-chromosome that consists of three logical parts: functional properties, sets of their parameters, relations between blocks:

$$M_p = \langle S_p, E_p, \{A_k\}_p \rangle = \left\langle \left\{s_{1:|S_p|}\right\}_p, \left\{e_{1:|E_p|}\right\}_p, \left\{a_{1:|S_p||A_k|}\right\}_p \right\rangle, A_k = \left\{a_{1:|A_k|}\right\}_k, k \in [1:|S_p|]. \quad (4)$$

The genotype is also illustrated in Figure 2.

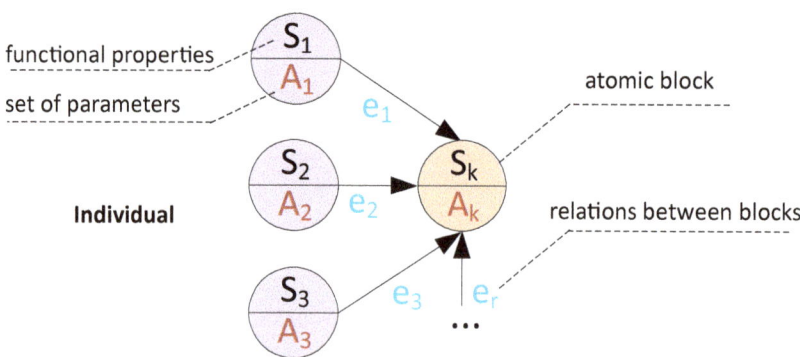

Figure 2. The structure of the genotype during evolutionary optimization: functional properties, set of parameters and relations between atomic blocks.

An important property is that $|S_p|, |A_p|, |E_p| \neq const$, what means varying overall size of chromosome (and its structure). Such property makes this approach is really open-ended and consistent with idea of model evolution because it give an opportunity to synthesize the models with truly new features instead of simple recombination and optimization of existed ones. Technically open-endedness here refers to the ability of generative design algorithms to expand or narrow a combinatorial search space in the process of optimization with evolutionary operators. This leads to need of special realizations for crossover and mutation operators. As the chromosome M_p is a ordered set with the structure fixed in a tuple $\langle S, \{a_{1:|A|}\}, E \rangle$ it is necessary to preserve this structure after crossover and mutation. That's why these operators are written relative to the graph structure and influence on the parts of chromosome that describe the node or a set of nodes with associated edges (sub-graphs). We may say that each single node can be described as some function with parameters $y_k = f_k\left(x, \{a_{1:|A|}\}_k\right)$. And mutation of function f_k performs symbolic changes in the mathematical expression that results in extension of range of limits of initial genes.

So, the task of mathematical model generative design can be formulated as optimization task:

$$p_Q^{max}(M^*) = \max_M f_Q(M|I^+, T_{gen} \leq \tau_g), \quad M = \{M_p\}, \tag{5}$$

where f_Q is a fitness function that characterizes quality generated mathematical and p_Q^{max} is a maximal value of fitness function, model M is a space of possible model structures, I^+ - actual computational resources, T_{gen} is time for model structure optimization critical threshold τ_g. In such formulation we try to design the model with the highest quality, but we need to rely optimization to single configuration of computational resources. This factor is a strong limitation for the idea of generative design because this idea assumes flexibility of searched solution including the possibility to find the most appropriate for applied task combination of model structure and computational resources. The concept was illustrated on Figure 1.

Model and computational infrastructure co-design may be formulated as follows:

$$p^{max}(M^*, I^*) = \max_{M,I} F(M, I | T_{gen} \leq \tau_g), \quad I = \{I_q\}, \quad M = \{M_p\}, \tag{6}$$

where I is a set of infrastructure features, F is a vector fitness function that characterize a trade off between a goodness of fit and computational intensity of model structure. Vector function F consists of quality function f_Q and time function f_T that is negative for correct maximization:

$$F(M, I) = (f_Q(M, I), -f_T(M, I)). \tag{7}$$

The time function f_T is a function that shows expected execution time of the model that is being synthesized with generative design approach. As the model M is still in the process of creation at the moment we want to estimate F, the values of f_T may be defined by performance models (e.g., Equation (9)). The example of the model selection from the Pareto frontier on a basis of p^{max} and τ_c constraints is presented is Figure 3. It can be seen that model M_4 has the better quality but it does not satisfy the execution time constraint τ_c.

However, in most of cases correct reflection of infrastructure properties to model performance is quite complicated task. In described case when we need, first, to generate the model with appropriate quality and vital limitations for computation time, we have several issues: (1) we may be not able to estimate model performance with respect to certain infrastructure in straight forward way and as a consequence we need performance models; (2) estimation of the dependency between model structure and computational resources reflects only mean tendency due to number of simplifications in performance models and search for minima on such uncertain estimations lead to unstable convergence to local minima. Due to these issues the formulation of optimization for co-design on stage of model building may be simplified to single criteria problem $F(M, I | T_{gen} \leq \tau_g) \approx F'(M| T_M \leq \tau, T_{gen} \leq \tau_g)$

with change of direct usage of infrastructure features to estimated time of model execution via performance models $T_M \approx T = f_T(M, I)$:

$$\hat{p}^{max}(M^*) = \max_M \hat{f}_Q(M| \ T_M \leq \tau_c, \ T_{gen} \leq \tau_g), \quad (8)$$

where f_Q is single criteria fitness function that characterize goodness of fit of model with additional limitations for expected model execution time T_M and estimated time for structural optimization T_{gen}.

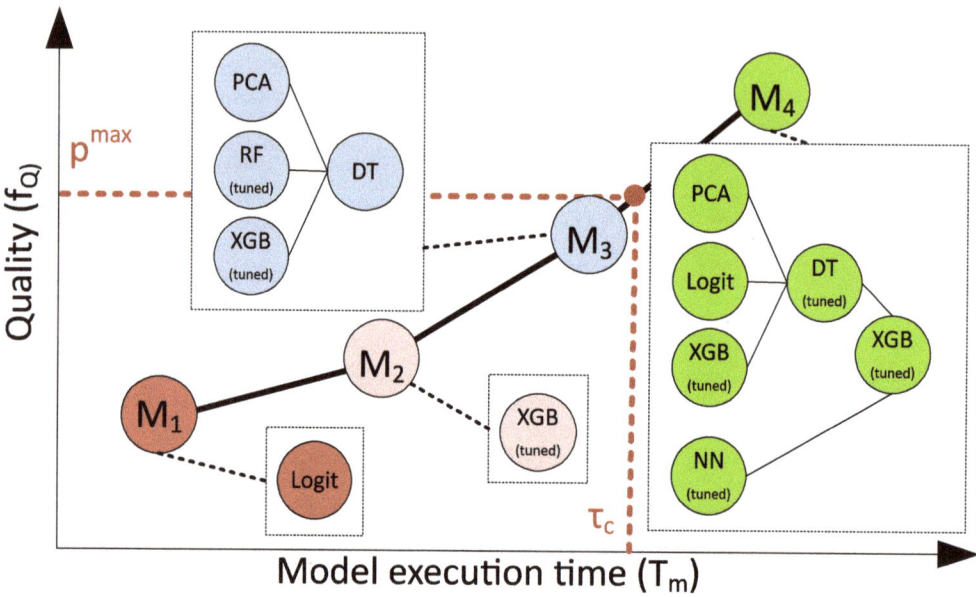

Figure 3. Pareto frontier obtained after the evolutionary learning of the composite model in the "quality-execution time" subspace. The points referred as M_1 - M_4 represent the different solutions obtained during optimization. p^{max} and τ_c represent quality and time constraints.

In the context of automated models building and their co-design with computational resources, performance models (PM) should be formulated as a prediction of expected execution time with the explicit approximation of a number of operations as a function of computer model properties S, $\{a_{1:|S|}\}$ and infrastructure I parameters. However, for different computer models classes, there are different properties of performance models. In the frame of this paper, we address the following classes of models: ML models, numerical models (based on the numerical solution of symbolic equations), and composite models (that may include both ML and numerical models).

For ML models PM can be formulated as follows:

$$T_{ML}^{PM}(Z, M) = max_i \left[\sum_{it} \frac{OML_{i,it}}{V_i(I) + Const_i(I)} \right] + O(I), \quad (9)$$

where $OML = OML(Z, M)$ is an approximate number of operations for data-driven model with data volume Z and parametric model M, it—iterator for learning epoch, $V_i(I)$ is for performance of $i'th$ computational node in flops, $Const_i(I)$ is for constant overheads for $i'th$ node in flops, $O(I)$ is for sequential part of model code.

According to structure $M = \langle S, E, \{a_{1:|S|}\} \rangle$ for data driven-model case, duple $\langle S, E \rangle$ characterize structural features of models (e.g., activation functions and layers in neural networks) and $\{a_{1:|S|}\}$ characterize hyper-parameters.

For numerical models PM can be formulated as follows:

$$T^{PM}_{Num}(R, M) = \max_i \left[\frac{ON_i}{V_i(I) + Const_i(I)} \right] + O(I), \quad (10)$$

where $ON = ON(R, M)$ is an approximate number of operations for numerical model. In distinction with ML models they are not required for learning epochs and do not have strong dependency from volume of input data. Instead of this, there are internal features of model M, but it is worth separately denote computational grid parameters R. They include parameters of grid type, spatial and temporal resolution. Among the most influential model parameters M there are type and order of equations, features of numerical solution (e.g., numerical scheme, integration step, etc.).

For composite models PM total expected time is a sum of expected times for sequential parts of model chain:

$$T^{PM}_{Comp}(R, Z, M) = \sum_j \max_i \left[\frac{OC_{i,j}}{V_i(I) + Const_i(I)} \right] + O(I), \quad (11)$$

where expected time prediction for each sequential part is based on properties of appropriate model class:

$$OC = \begin{cases} OML, & \text{if model is ML} \\ ON, & \text{if model is numerical} \end{cases}. \quad (12)$$

4. Important Obstacles on the Way of Generative Co-Design Implementation

It may seem that the problem statement described above gives us a clear vision of an evolutionary learning approach for generative design and co-design. However, several subtle points should be highlighted. This section is devoted to a discussion of the most interesting and challenging points (in the authors' opinion) that affect the efficiency or even the possibility of implementation the generative design (and co-design) approach for growing new mathematical models.

Issue 1. Numerical Methods for Computation of Designed Arbitrary Function

Open-ended realization of automated symbolic model creation with a generative design approach leads to the possibility of getting an unknown function as a resulted model. On the one hand, it gives interesting perspectives to create the new approximations of unknown laws. However, on the other hand, this possibility leads to the first conceptual problem of the generative design of mathematical models and a serious stumbling block on the way to implementing this idea. This problem is the need to calculate an arbitrary function or get the numerical solution of an arbitrary equation.

The choice of the numerical method for a given problem (discovered algebraic, ordinary differential, partial differential equation equations) is the crucial point. In most cases, the numerical method is designed to solve only several types of equations. When the numerical method is applied to the problem type, where convergence theorem is not proved, the result may not be considered as the solution.

As an example, solution of the partial difference equations using the finite difference schemes. For brevity, we omit details and particular equations, the reader is referred to [36] for details. The classical one-dimensional diffusion equation has different schemes, in particular, explicit, implicit, Crank-Nicolson scheme. Every scheme has a different approximation order and may lead to different solutions depending on the time-spatial grid taken. If the Crank-Nicolson spatial derivative scheme is taken to solve another equation, for example, the one-dimensional string equation, then the solution will also depend on the time-spatial grid taken, however, in another manner. It leads to the general problem that the particular finite schemes cannot be used for the general equation solution.

The second approach is to approximate a solution with a neural network, which somewhat mimics the finite element method. The neural networks are known as universal approximators. However, their utility for differential equations solution is still arguable. The main problem is that the good approximation of the field is not necessary leads to the good derivative approximation [37]. There is a lot of workarounds to approximate derivatives together with the initial field, however, it is done with the loss of generality.

The possible promising solution is to combine optimization methods, local neural network approximation, and classical approach [38]. However, there is still a lot of the "white spots", since the arbitrary equation means a strongly non-linear equation with arbitrary boundary conditions. Such a generality cannot be achieved at the current time and requires a significant differentiation, approximation, and numerical evaluation method development. The illustration examples of the inverse problem solution are shown in Section 5.1.

Issue 2. Effective Parallelization of Evolutionary Learning Algorithm

The procedure of generative design has high computation cost, thus effective algorithm realization is highly demanded. Efficiency can be achieved primarily by parallelizing the algorithm. As discussed generative algorithm is implemented on a base of the evolutionary approach, so the first way is a computation of each specimen d_p in a population in a separate thread. Strictly speaking, it may be not only threads, but also separate computational nodes for clusters, but not to confuse computer nodes with nodes of a model graph M_p, here and further we will use the term "thread" in a wide sense. This way is the easiest for implementation but will be effective only in the case of cheap computations of objective function $\varphi(M)$.

The second way is acceleration of each model M_p on the level of its nodes $\langle S, \{a_{1:|A|}\} \rangle$ with possibility of logical parallelized. However, this way seems to be the most effective if we have uniform (from the performance point of view) nodes of models M_p and computational intensity appropriate for used infrastructure (in other words, each node should be computed in a separate thread in acceptable time). Often for cases of composite models and numerical models, this condition is becoming violated. Usually, the numerical model is consists of differential equations that should be solved on large computational grids. And composite models may include nodes that are significantly more computationally expensive than others. All these features lead us to take into account possibility of parallelization of generative algorithm on several levels: (1) population level, (2) model M_p level, (3) each node $\langle S, \{a_{1:|A|}\} \rangle$ level; and make an adaptation of algorithm with respect to certain task.

Moreover, for the effective acceleration of the generative algorithm, we may take into account that most of the new composite models are based on nodes that are repeated numerously in the whole population. For such a case, we may provide storage for computed nodes and use them as results of pre-build models. The illustration of an ineffective and an effective parallelization setups described above is shown in the Figure 4.

The set of experiments that illustrates the problem raised in this issue and proposes the possible solutions is presented in Section 5.2.2.

Issue 3. Co-Design of an Evolutionary Learning Algorithm and Computational Infrastructure

In the frame of this research, the problem of co-design appears not only for the question of automatic creation of the computer model but also for the generative optimization algorithm itself. In Equation (8) we described co-design of generated model regarding the computational resources using estimation of model execution time T_M. Separate problem is adaptation of generative evolutionary algorithm regarding the computational resources and specific traits of the certain task. In formulation Equation (8) it was only accounted for by the restriction to the overall time T_{gen} for model generation. However, the task can be formulated as search for generative evolutionary algorithm that is able to find the best model structure M in limited time T_{gen}. This task can be solved by optimization of hyper-parameters, evolutionary operators (and strategy of their usage) for generative optimization algorithm and formulated as meta-optimization problem over a set of possible algorithms U that are defined by a set of strategies B:

$$U = \{u(B)\}, \; B = \left\{b_{1:|B|}\right\}, \; b = \langle H, \mathcal{R}\rangle, \tag{13}$$

$$u^* = u(b^*) = \arg\max_{b} \mathcal{F}(u(b)|T_{gen} \leq T_g), \tag{14}$$

where $\mathcal{F}$ is a meta-fitness function and each strategy b is defined by evolutionary operators $\mathcal{R}$ and hyper-parameters H. Evolutionary operators also my be described as hyper-parameters but here we subdivide them in separate entity $\mathcal{R}$.

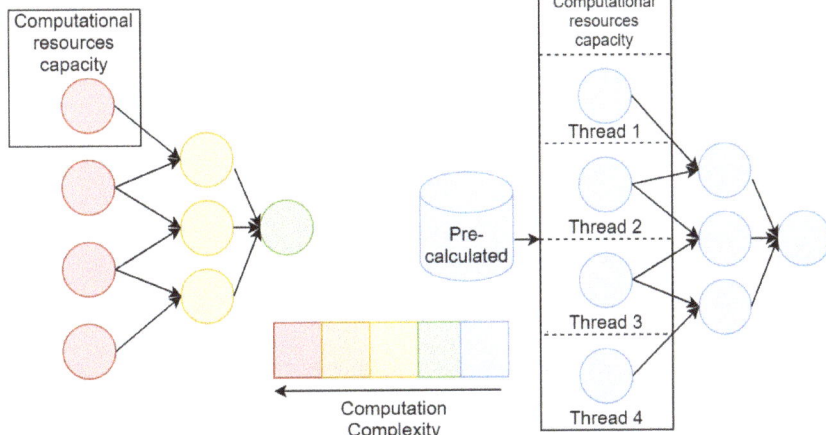

Figure 4. Setup that illustrates inefficiency of the parallel evolution implementation due to fitness function computation complexity.

For the model's generative design task, the most expensive step usually refers to the evaluation of the fitness function value [6]. The calculation of the fitness function for the individuals of the evolutionary algorithm can be parallelized in different ways that are presented in Figure 5.

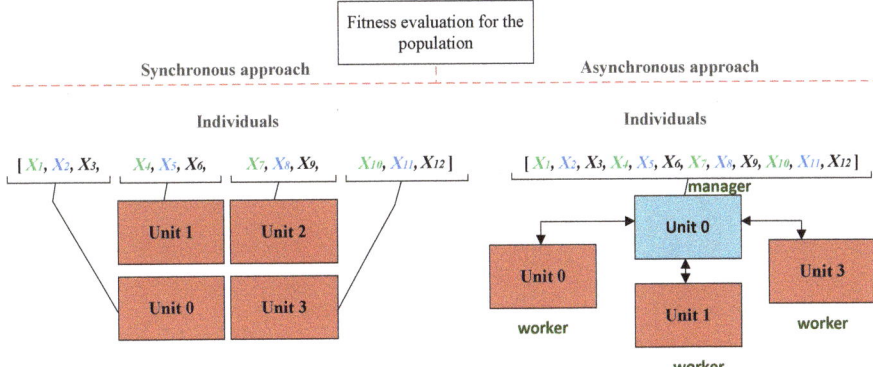

Figure 5. Approaches to the parallel calculation of fitness function with the evolutionary learning algorithm: (**a**) synchronously, each element of the population is processed at one node until all is processed (**b**) asynchronously, one of the nodes controls the calculations in other nodes.

The described approaches can be used for the different variants of the computational environment used for the generation of the models. The practical application of the generated models with the complex structure almost always difficult because of the high computation complexity of the numerical model-based simulations.

There are several groups of models that can be separated by the simulation pipeline structure. For the data-driven model, the computational cost of the fitting (identification) stage is higher than for the simulation stage. For the equation-based numerical models with rigid structure, there is no implicit fitting stage, but the simulation can be very expensive. In practice, different parallelization strategies can be applied to improve simulation performance [39].

The set of experiments that provides the examples to the problem raised in this issue can be seen in Section 5.3.

Issue 4. Computational Strategies for Identification of Graph M

The problem of DAG $M = \langle S, E, \{a_{1:|S|}\} \rangle$ identification has two sides. First of all, the task of structural and parametric optimization of model M has exponential computational complexity with the growth of nodes number. Even if the functional structure $\langle S, E \rangle$ of the composite model is already identified, there is a computationally expensive problem of parameters $\{a_{1:|S|}\}$ (or hyperparameters in ML terms) tuning.

However, except for the computational intensity, there is a problem of searching the optimal set of values $\langle S^*, E^*, \{a_{1:|S|}\}^* \rangle$ in a space of high dimension (when chromosome has great length from tens to hundreds of values). This leads to unstable results of optimization algorithm because of the exponential growth of possible solutions in a combinatorial space (some parameters could be continuous but they are discretized and generally problem may be treated as combinatorial). One of the obvious ways for dealing with such a problem is local dimensionality reduction (or segmentation of the whole search space). This could be done with the application of various strategies. For example, we may simplify the task and search with generative algorithm only functional parts, and parameters (hyperparameters) may be optimized on the model execution stage (as discussed in Section 6). Such a way is economically profitable but we will get a result with lower fitness. An alternative variant is to introduce an approach for iterative segmentation of the domain space and greedy-like search on each batch (Section 5.4).

Another point should be taken into account, the structure of DAG with directed edges and ordered nodes (composite model with primary and secondary nodes) leads to the necessity of introducing the sequential strategies for parameters tuning. Despite the tuning can be performed simultaneously with the structural learning, there is a common approach to apply it for the best candidates only [16]. Unlike the individual models tuning, the tuning of the composite models with graph-based structure can be performed with different strategies, that are represented in Figure 6.

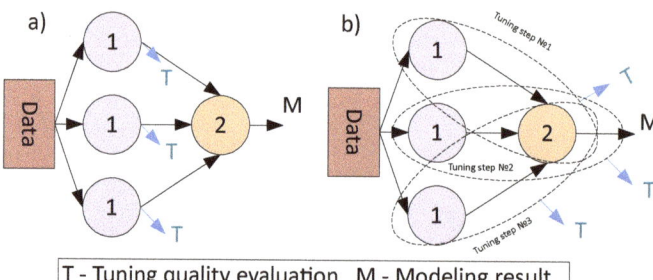

Figure 6. The different strategies of hyper-parameters tuning for the composite models: (**a**) individual tuning for each atomic model (**b**) the tuning of the composite model that uses secondary models to evaluate the tuning quality for the primary models.

The experiment that demonstrates the reduction of the search space for the composite model design by the application of the modified hyperparameters tuning strategy for the best individual is described in Section 5.4.

Issue 5. Estimation of PM for Designed Models

Analytic formulations of PM show expected execution time that is based on relation between approximate number of operations and computational performance of certain infrastructure configuration. The problem is to estimate this relation for all pairs from model structures $M = \langle S, E, \{a_{1:|A|}\}\rangle$ and computational resources $I = \{I_q\}$ with respect to input data Z because we need to make estimations of OML, ON and OC (depending on the class of models). Generally, there are two ways: (1) estimation of computational complexity (in O notation) for each model M, (2) empirical performance model (EPM) estimation of execution time for every specimen $\langle M, I, Z \rangle$. The first option gives us theoretically proved results, but this is hardly may be implemented in case of models' generative design when we have too many specimens $\langle M, I, Z \rangle$. The second option is to make a set of experimental studies for specimens $\langle M, I, Z \rangle$ execution time measurements. However, in this case, we need to make a huge number of experiments before we start the algorithm of generative co-design and the problem statement becomes meaningless. To avoid numerous experiments, we may introduce estimation of EPM that consists of two steps. The first one is to estimate relation between time T_M and volume of data Z: $T_{Num}^{PM}(M, Z, I) \approx T_{Num}^{EPM}(Z|M, I)$. To simplify identification of $T_{Num}^{EPM}(Z|M, I)$, we would like to approximate this with a linear function with non-linear kernel $\psi(Z)$:

$$T_{Num}^{EPM}(Z|M, I) = \sum_{w=1}^{W} \omega_w \psi_w(Z), \quad (15)$$

where W is a number of components of linear function. The second step is to use value of $T_{Num}^{EPM}(Z|M, I)$ to estimate relation between execution time and infrastructure I: $T_{Num}^{EPM}(Z|M, I) \to T_{Num}^{EPM}(I|M, Z)$. For this purpose we should make even a raw estimation of number of operations OML, ON and OC.

On the example of EPM for numerical model (Equation (10)) we can make the following assumptions:

$$O(I) \approx 0, \quad Const_i(I) \approx 0, \quad V = mean_i(V_i(I)), \quad ON = mean_i(ON_i), \quad (16)$$

$$max_i \left[\frac{ON_i}{V_i(I) + Const_i(I)}\right] = mean_i \left[\frac{ON_i}{V_i(I) + Const_i(I)}\right], \quad (17)$$

and get the following transformations for raw estimation of overall number of operations nON with respect to n computational nodes:

$$nON(M, Z) = nT_{Num}^{PM}(M, Z, I)V(I), \quad i \in [1:n]. \quad (18)$$

It is worth nothing that the obvious way to improve accuracy of estimation nON is to use for experimental setup resources with characteristics of computational performance close to $V = mean_i(V_i(I))$ and task partitioning close to $ON = mean_i(ON_i)$. Getting the estimation of nON and infrastructure parameters $V_i(I)$, $Const_i(I)$, $O(I)$ we may go to raw estimation:

$$T_{Num}^{EPM}(M, Z, I) = max_i \left[\frac{\alpha_i nON(M, Z)}{V_i(I) + Const_i(I)}\right] + O(I), \quad (19)$$

where α_i is coefficient for model partitioning. Similar transformations could be made for other models.

The experiments devoted to the identification of the empirical performance models for both atomic and composite models are provided in Section 5.5.

5. Experimental Studies

The proposed approaches to the co-design of generative models cannot be recognized as effective without experimental evaluation. To conduct the experiments, we constructed the computational environment that includes and hybrid cluster and several multiprocessor nodes that can be used to evaluate different benchmarks.

A set of experiments have been held with the algorithm of data-driven partial differential equation discovery to analyze its performance with different task setups. All experiments were conducted using the EPDE framework described in detail in [15].

The other set of experiments devoted to the automated design of the ML models was conducted using the open-source Fedot framework (https://github.com/nccr-itmo/FEDOT). The framework allows generating composite models using evolutionary approaches. The composite model generated by the framework can include different types of models [6]. The following parameters of the genetic algorithm were used during the experiments: maximum number of the generations in 20, number of the individuals in each population is 32, probability of mutation, probability of mutation is 0.8, probability of crossover is 0.8, maximum arity of the composite model is 4, maximum depth of the composite model is 3. More detailed setup is described in [40].

5.1. Choice of the Model Evaluation Algorithm

The first group of experiments is connected with the Issue 1 that describes the different aspects of numerical computation of designed models.

For example, the problem of data preprocessing for partial differential equations models, represented by the calculation of derivatives of the input field, is of the top priority for the correct operation of the algorithm: the incorrect selection of tools can lead to the increasing magnitudes of the noise, present in the input data, or get high values of numerical errors. The imprecise evaluation of equation factors can lead to cases, when the wrong structure has lower equation discrepancy (the difference between the selected right part term and the constructed left part) and, consequently, higher fitness values, than the correct governing equation.

However, the versatility of the numerical differentiation adds the second criterion on the board. The finite differences require a lot of expertise to choose and thus their automatic use is restricted since the choice of the finite difference scheme is not a trivial task that requires either a fine grid to reduce the error or choice of the particular scheme for the given problem. Both ways require extended time.

Artificial neural networks (ANN), used to approximate the initial data field, are an alternative to this approach, which can have a number of significant advantages. To get the fields of derivatives, we utilize the automatic differentiation, that is based on the approach, similar to the chain differentiation rule from the elementary calculus, and is able to combine the evaluated values of derivatives of a function, comprising the neural network to get the "correct" values of derivatives. In contrast to the previously used method of analytical differentiation of polynomials, the automatic differentiation is able to get mixed derivatives. From the performance point of view, the advantages of the artificial neural networks lie in the area of ease of parallelization of tensor calculations and the use of graphical processing units (GPU) for computation.

However, the task setup has a number of challenges in the approach to ANN training. First of all, the analyzed function is observed on a grid, therefore, we can have a rather limited set of training data. The interpolation approaches can alter the function, defining the field, and the derivatives, in that case, will represent the structure of the interpolating function. Next, the issue of the approximation quality remains unsolved. While the ANN can decently approximate the function of one variable (which is useful for tasks of ordinary differential equations discovery), on the multivariable problem statement the quality of the approximation is relatively low. The example of approximation is presented in Figure 7.

In the conducted experiments [41] we have used the artificial neural network with the following architecture: the ANN was comprised of 5 fully connected layers of 256, 512,

256, 128, 64 neurons with sigmoid activation function. As the input data, the values of the solution function for a wave equation ($u_{tt} = \alpha u_{xx}$), solved with the implicit finite-difference method, have been utilized. Due to the nature of the implemented solution method, the function values were obtained on the uniform grid. The training of ANN was done for a specified number of epochs (500 for the conducted experiments), when of the each epoch the training batch is randomly selected as a proportion of all points (0.8 of the total number of points). To obtain the derivatives, the automatic differentiation methods, implemented in the Tensorflow package are applied to the trained neural network.

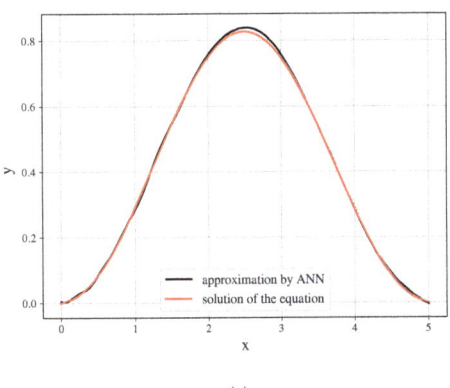
(a)

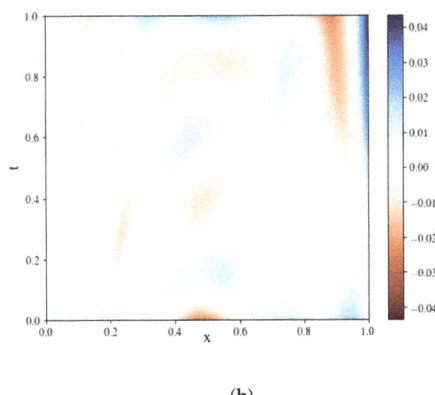
(b)

Figure 7. Comparison of the equation solution and its approximation by artificial neural networks (ANNs) for a time slice (**a**) and heatmap of the approximation error ($u_{approx} - u_{true}$) (**b**).

Even with the presented very good approximation of the original field, the first derivatives (Figure 8) are obtained with decent quality and may serve as the building blocks. However, it is seen that the derivative field is significantly biased.

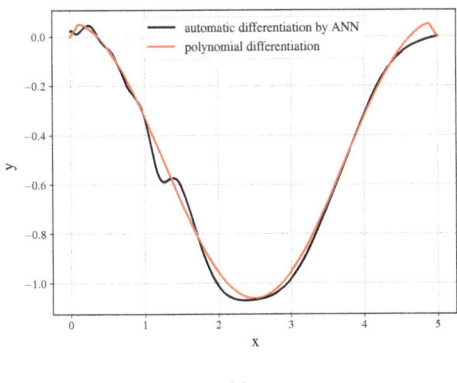
(a) u_t

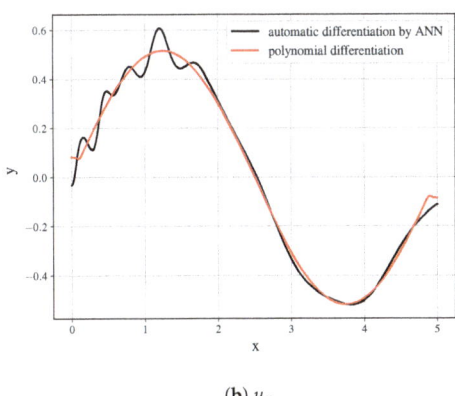
(b) u_x

Figure 8. Comparison of derivatives obtained by polynomial differentiation and by symbolic regression for first time derivative (**a**) first spatial derivatives (**b**) for a time slice ($t = 50$).

Further differentiation amplifies the error. The higher-order derivatives shown in Figure 9 cannot be used as the building blocks of the model and do not represent the derivatives of the initial data field.

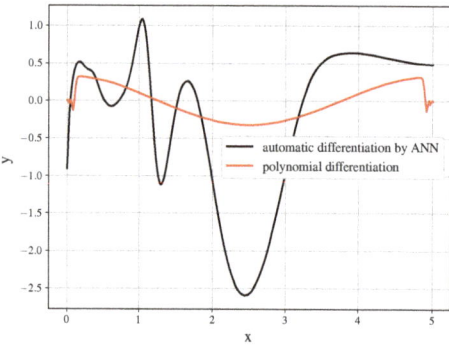 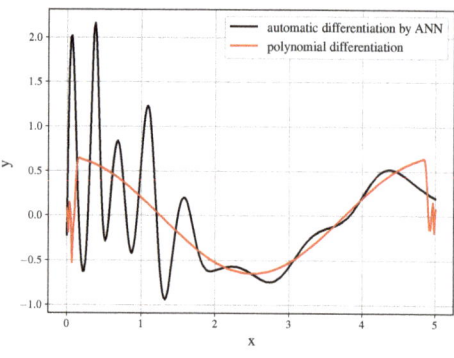

(a) u_{tt} (b) u_{xx}

Figure 9. Comparison of derivatives obtained by polynomial differentiation and by symbolic regression for second time derivative (**a**) second spatial derivatives (**b**) for a time slice ($t = 50$).

Both of the implemented differentiation techniques are affected by numerical errors, inevitable in the machine calculations, and contain errors, linked to the limitations of the method (for example, approximation errors). To evaluate the influence of the errors on the discovered equation structure, the experiments were conducted on simple ordinary differential Equation (ODE) (20) with solution function (21).

$$L(t) = x(t) \sin t + \frac{dx}{dt} \cos t = 1, \tag{20}$$

$$x(t) = \sin t + C \cos t. \tag{21}$$

We have tried to rediscover the equation, based on data, obtained via analytical differentiation of function (21), application of polynomial differentiation, and with the derivative, calculated by automatic differentiation of fitted neural network. The series of function values and the derivatives are presented in Figure 10. Here, we can see, that the proposed ANN can decently approximate data; the analytical & polynomial differentiation obtains similar fields, while automatic differentiation algorithm may result in insignificant errors. 10 independent runs of the equation discovery algorithm have been performed for each derivative calculation method, and the results with the lowest errors have been compared. For the quality metric, the Mean Square Error of the vector, representing the discrepancy of the function $\tilde{x}(t)$, which is the solution of discovered on data-driven equation $M(t) = 0$ with aim of $|M(t)| \to min$, evaluated on the nodes of the grid was used.

While all of the runs resulted in the successful discovery of governing equations, the issues with such equations are in the area of function parameters detection and calculating the correct coefficients of the equation. The best result was achieved on the data from analytical differentiation: $MSE = 1.452 \cdot 10^{-4}$. The polynomial differentiation got the similar quality $MSE = 1.549 \cdot 10^{-4}$, while the automatic differentiation achieved $MSE = 3.236 \cdot 10^{-4}$. It could be concluded, that in the case of first-order equations, the error of the differentiation has less order than all other errors and thus the fastest method for the given problem may be used. However, in the PDE case, it is complicated to use only first-order derivatives, whereas arbitrary ordinary differential equations may be represented as the system of the first-order equations.

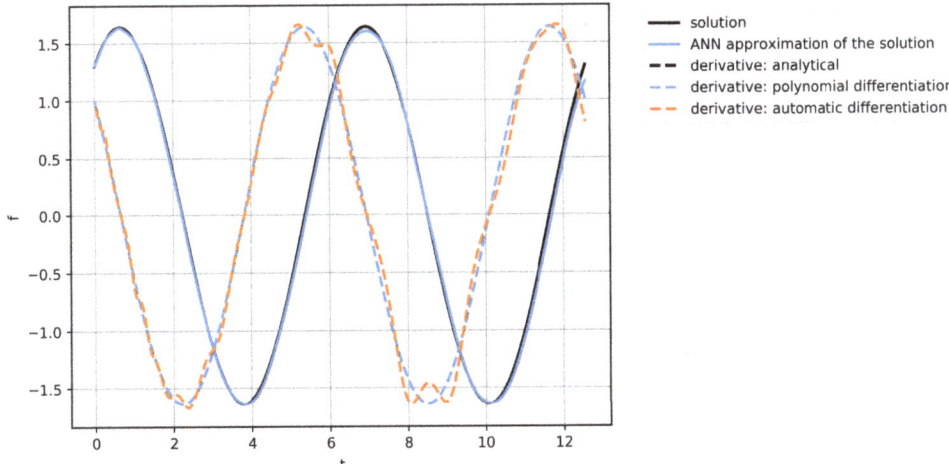

Figure 10. The solution of ODE from Equation (20), its approximation by neural network, and derivatives calculated by analytic, polynomial and automatic differentiation.

5.2. Computationally Intensive Function Parallelization

5.2.1. Parallelization of Generative Algorithm for PDE Discovery

The first experiment devoted to the parallelization of the atomic models' computation using partial differential equations discovery case as an example. As shown in Figure 4, the parallelization of the evolutionary algorithm in some cases does not give significant speed improvement. In cases where atomic models are computationally expensive, it is expedient to try to reduce every node computation as much as possible.

The experiment [42] was dedicated to the selection of an optimal method of computational grid domain handling. It had been previously proven, that the conventional approach when we process the entire domain at once, was able to correctly discover the governing equation. However, with the increasing size of the domain, the calculations may take longer times. In this case parallelization of the evolutionary algorithm does not give speed-up on a given computational resources configuration, since the computation of a fitness function of a single gene takes the whole computational capacity.

To solve this issue, we have proposed a method of domain division into a set of spatial subdomains to reduce the computational complexity of a single gene. For each of these subdomains, the structure of the model in form of the differential equation is discovered, and the results are compared and combined, if the equation structures are similar: with insignificant differences in coefficients or the presence of terms with higher orders of smallness. The main algorithm for the subdomains is processed in a parallel manner due to the isolated method of domain processing: we do not examine any connections between domains until the final structure of the subdomains' models is obtained.

The experiments to analyze the algorithm performance were conducted on the synthetic data: by defining the presence of a single governing equation, we exclude the issue of the existence of multiple underlying processes, described by different equations, in different parts of the studied domain. So, we have selected a solution of the wave equation with two spatial dimensions in Equation (22) for a square area, which was processed as one domain, and after that, into small fractions of subdomains.

$$\frac{\partial^2 u}{\partial t^2} = \frac{\partial^2 u}{\partial x^2} + \frac{\partial^2 u}{\partial y^2}. \tag{22}$$

However, that division has its downsides: smaller domains have less data, therefore, the disturbances (noise) in individual point will have a higher impact on the results. Furthermore, in realistic scenarios, the risks of deriving an equation, that describes a local process, increases with the decrease in domain size. The Pareto front, indicating the trade-off between the equation discrepancy and the time efficiency, could be utilized to find the parsimonious setup of the experiment. On the noiseless data (we assume, that the derivatives are calculated without the numerical error) even the data from a single point will correctly represent the equation. Therefore, the experiments must be held on the data with low, but significant noise levels.

We have conducted the experiments with the partition of data (Figure 11), containing $80 \times 80 \times 80$ values, divided by spatial axes in fractions from the set $\{\overline{1, 10}\}$. The experiments were held with 10 independent runs on each of the setup (size of input data (number of subdomains, into which the domain was divided, and sparsity constant, which affects the number of terms of the equation).

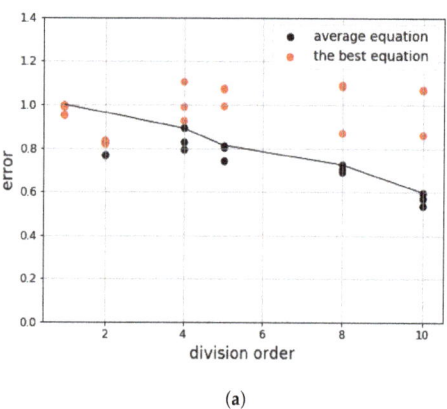
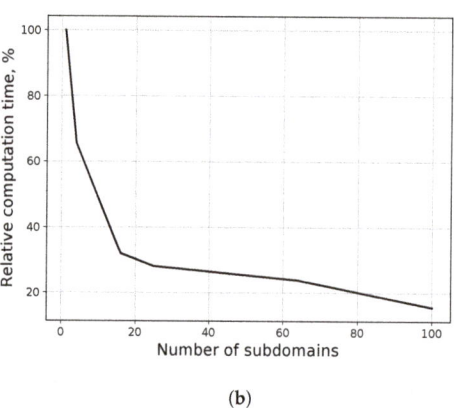

(a) (b)

Figure 11. The results of the experiments on the divided domains. (a) evaluations of discovered equation quality for different division fractions along each axis (2× division represents division of domain into 4 square parts); (b) domain processing time (relative to the processing of entire domain) for subdomain number.

The results of the test, presented in Figure 11, give insight into the consequences of the processing domain by parts. It can be noticed, that with the split of data into smaller portions, the qualities of the equations decrease due to the "overfitting" to the local noise. However, in this case, due to higher numerical errors near the boundaries of the studied domain, the base equation, derived from the full data, has its own errors. By dividing the area into smaller subdomains, we allow some of the equations to be trained on data with lower numerical errors and, therefore, have higher quality. The results, presented in the Figure 11b are obtained only for the iterations of the evolutionary algorithm of the equation discovery and do not represent the differences in time for other stages, such as preprocessing, or further modeling of the process.

We can conclude that the technique of separating the domain into lesser parts and processing them individually can be beneficial both for achieving speedup via parallelization of the calculations and avoiding equations, derived from the high error zones. In this case, such errors were primarily numerical, but in realistic applications, they can be attributed to the faulty measurements or prevalence of a different process in a local area.

5.2.2. Reducing of the Computational Complexity of Composite Models

To execute the next set of experiments, we used the Fedot framework to build the composite ML models for classification and regression problems. The different open datasets were used as benchmarks that allow to analyze the efficiency of the generative design in various situations.

To improve the performance of the model building (this issue was noted in Issue 2), different approaches can be applied. First of all, caching techniques can be used. The cache can be represented as a dictionary with the topological description of the model position in the graph as a key and a fitted model as a value. Moreover, the fitted data preprocessor can be saved in cache together with the model. The common structure of the cache is represented in Figure 12.

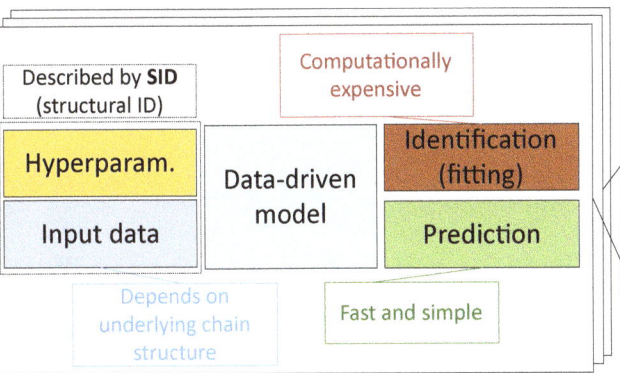

Figure 12. The structure of the multi-chain shared cache for the fitted composite models.

The results of the experiments with a different implementation of cache are described in Figure 13.

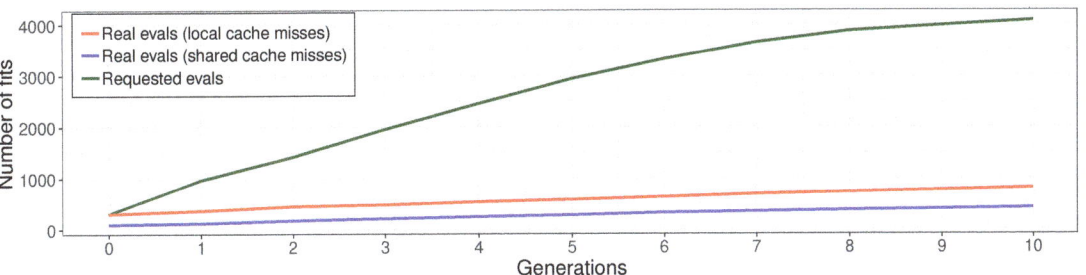

Figure 13. The total number model fit requests and the actually executed fits (cache misses) for the shared and local cache.

Local cache allows reducing the number of models fits up to five times against the non-cached variant. The effectiveness of the shared cache implementation is twice as high as that for the local cache.

The parallelization of the composite models building, fitting, and application also makes it possible to decrease the time devoted to the design stage. It can be achieved in different ways. First of all, the fitting and application of the atomic ML models can be parallelized using the features of the underlying framework (e.g., Scikit-learn, Keras, TensorFlow, etc [43]), since the atomic models can be very complex. However, this approach is more effective in the shared memory systems and it is hard to scale it to the distributed environments. Moreover, not all models can be efficiently parallelized in this way.

Then, the evolutionary algorithm that builds the composite model can be paralleled itself, since the fitness function for each individual can be calculated independently. To conduct the experiment, the classification benchmark based at the credit scoring problem (https://github.com/nccr-itmo/FEDOT/blob/master/cases/credit_scoring_problem.py) was used. The parameters of the evolutionary algorithm are the same as described at the beginning of the section.

The obtained values of the fitness function for the classification problem are presented in Figure 14.

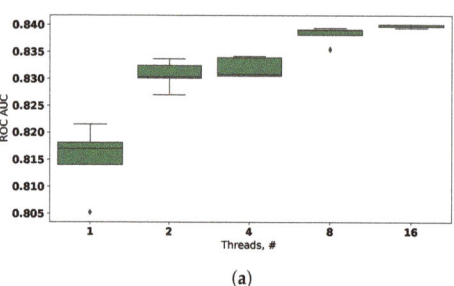
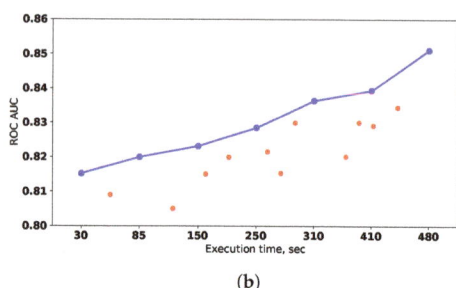

Figure 14. (**a**) The best achieved fitness value for the different computational configurations (represented as different number of parallel threads) used to evaluate the evolutionary algorithm on classification benchmark. The boxplots are build for the 10 independent runs. (**b**) Pareto frontier (blue) obtained for the classification benchmark in "execution time-model quality" subspace. The red points represent dominated individuals.

The effectiveness of the evolutionary algorithm parallelization depends on the variance of the composite models fitting time in the population. It is matters because the new population can not be formed until all individuals from the previous one are assessed. This problem is illustrated in Figure 15 for cases (a) and (b) that were evaluated with classification dataset and parameters of evolutionary algorithm described above. It can be noted that the modified selection scheme noted in (b) can be used to increase parallelization efficiency. The early selection, mutation, and crossover of the already processed individuals allow to start the processing of the next population before the previous population's assessment is finished.

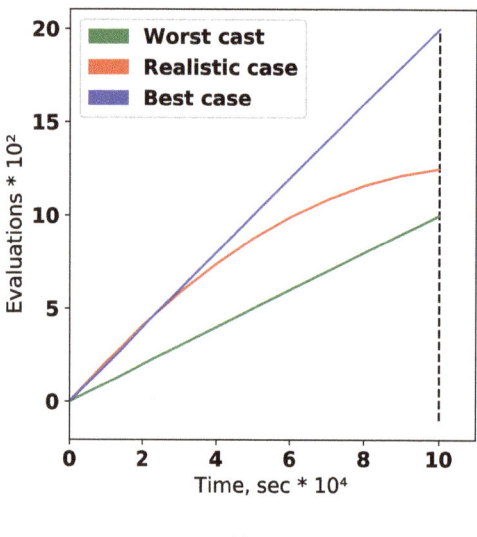
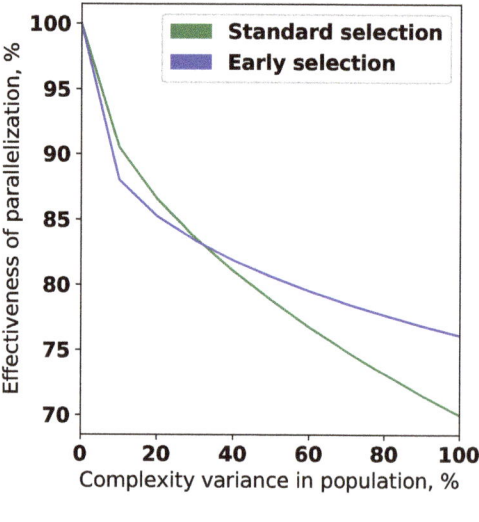

Figure 15. (**a**) The comparison of different scenarios of evolutionary optimization: best (ideal), realistic and worst cases (**b**) The conceptual dependence of the parallelization efficiency from the variance of the execution time in population for the different types of selection.

The same logic can be applied for the parallel fitting of the part of composite model graphs. It raises the problem of the importance of assessment for the structural subgraphs and the prediction of most promising candidate models before the final evaluation of the fitness function will be done.

5.3. Co-Design Strategies for the Evolutionary Learning Algorithm

The co-design of the generative algorithm and the available infrastructure is an important issue (described in detail in the Issue 3) in the task of composite model optimization. The interesting case here is optimization under the pre-defined time constraints [44]. The experimental results obtained for the two different optimization strategies are presented in Figure 16. The classification problem was solved using the credit scoring problem (described above) as a benchmark for the classification task. The parameters of the evolutionary algorithm are the same as described at the beginning of the section. The fitness function value is based on ROC AUC measure and maximized during optimization.

The static strategy S_1 represents the evolutionary optimization with the fixed hyperparameters of the algorithm. The computational infrastructure used in the experiment makes it possible to evaluate the 20 generations with 20 individuals in the population with a time limit of T_0. This strategy allows finding the solution with the fitness function value F_0. However, if the time limit $T_1 < T_0$ is taken into account, the static strategy allow to find the solution S_1 with the fitness function value F_1, where $F_1 < F_0$.

Otherwise, the adaptive optimization strategy S_2, which takes the characteristics of the infrastructure to self-tune the parameters can be used. It allow to evaluate 20 generation with 10 individuals in a time limit T_1 and reach the fitness function value F_2. As can be seen, the $F_1 < F_2 < F_0$, so the better solution is found under the given time constraint.

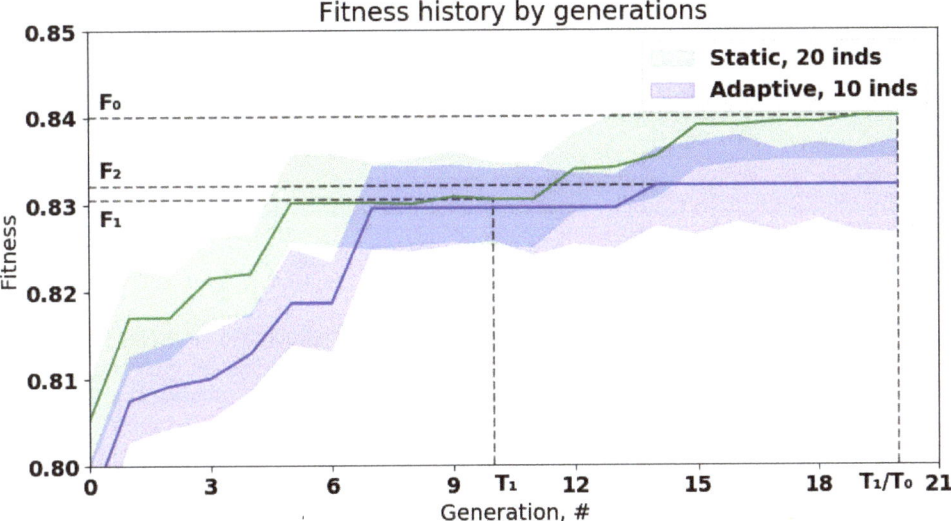

Figure 16. The comparison of different approaches to the evolutionary optimization of the composite models. The min-max intervals are built for the 10 independent runs. The green line represents the static optimization algorithm with 20 individuals in the population; the blue line represented the dynamic optimization algorithm with 10 individuals in the population. T_0, T_1 and T_2 are different real-time constraints, F_0, F_1 and F_2 are the values of fitness functions obtained with the corresponding constraints.

5.4. Strategies for Optimization of Hyperparameters in Evolutionary Learning Algorithm

As it was noted in the issue described in Issue 4, the very large search space is a major problem in the generative design. To prove that it can be solved with the application of the specialized hyperparameters tuning strategies, a set of experiments was conducted.

As can be seen from Figure 6, the direct tuning strategy means that each atomic model is considered an autonomous model during tuning. The computational cost of the tuning is low in this case (since it is not necessary to fit all the models in a chain to estimate the quality metric), but the found set of parameters can be non-optimal. The composite model tuning allows to take into account the influence of the chain beyond the scope of an individual atomic model, but the cost is additional computations to tune all models. A pseudocode of an algorithm for composite model tuning is represented in Algorithm 1.

Algorithm 1: The simplified pseudocode of the composite models tuning algorithm illustrated in Figure 6b.

Data: maxTuningTime, tuneData, paramsRanges
Result: tunedCompositeModel
fitData, validationData = Split(tuneData)
for atomicModel *in* compositeModel **do**
    candidateCompositeModel = compositeModel
    while tuningTime < maxTuningTime **do**
        bestQuality = 0
        candidateAtomicModel ← OptFunction(atomicModel, paramsRanges) // OptFunction can be implemented as random search, Bayesian optimization, etc.
        candidateCompositeModel ← Update(candidateCompositeModel, candidateAtomicModel)
        Fit(candidateCompositeModel, fitData)
        quality = EvaluateQuality(candidateCompositeModel, validationData)
        if quality > bestQuality **then**
            bestQuality = quality
            bestAtomicModel = candidateAtomicModel
        end
        compositeModel ← Update(compositeModel, bestAtomicModel)
    end
end
tunedCompositeModel = compositeModel

The results of the model-supported tuning of the composite models for the different regression problems obtained from PMLB benchmark suite (Available in the https://github.com/EpistasisLab/pmlb) are presented in Table 1. The self-developed toolbox that was used to run the experiments with PMLB and FEDOT is available in the open repository (https://github.com/ITMO-NSS-team/AutoML-benchmark). The applied tuning algorithm is based on a random search in a pre-defined range.

Table 1. The quality measures for the composite models after and before random search-based tuning of hyperparameters. The regression problems from PMLB suite [45] are used as benchmarks.

Benchmark Name	MSE without Tuning	MSE with Tuning	R^2 without Tuning	R^2 with Tuning
1203_BNG_pwLinear	8.213	0.102	0.592	0.935
197_cpu_act	5.928	7.457	0.98	0.975
215_2dplanes	1.007	0.001	0.947	1
228_elusage	126.755	0.862	0.524	0.996
294_satellite_image	0.464	0.591	0.905	0.953
4544_GeographicalOriginalofMusic	0.194	2.113	0.768	0.792
523_analcatdata_neavote	0.593	0.025	0.953	0.999
560_bodyfat	0.07	0.088	0.998	0.894
561_cpu	3412.46	0.083	0.937	0.91
564_fried	1.368	0.073	0.944	0.934

It can be seen that the hyperparameter optimization allow increasing the quality of the models in most cases.

5.5. Estimation of the Empirical Performance Models

The experiments for the performance models identification (this problem was raised in the issue described in Issue 5) were performed using the benchmark with a large number of features and observations in the sample. The benchmark is based on a classification task from the robotics field. It is quite a suitable example since there is a large number of tasks in this domain that can be performed on different computational resources from the embedded system to supercomputer in robotics. The analyzed task is devoted to the manipulator grasp stability prediction obtained from the Kaggle competition (https://www.kaggle.com/ugocupcic/grasping-dataset).

An experiment consists of grasping the ball, shaking it for a while, while computing grasp robustness. Multiple measurements are taken during a given experiment. Only one robustness value is associated though. The obtained dataset is balanced and has 50/50 stable and unstable grasps respectively.

The approximation of the EPM with simple regression models is a common way to analyze the performance of algorithms [46]. After the set of experiments, for the majority of considered models it was confirmed that the common regression surface of a single model EPM can be represented as a linear model. However, some considered models can be described better by another regression surface (see the quality measures for the different structures of EPM in Appendix A). One of them is a random forest model EPM. According to the structure of the Equation (9), these structures of EPM can be represented as follows:

$$T^{EPM} = \begin{cases} \Theta_1 N_{obs} N_{feat} + \Theta_2 N_{obs}, & \text{for the common case} \\ \frac{N_{obs}}{\Theta_1^2} + \frac{N_{obs}^2 N_{feat}}{\Theta_2^2}, & \text{specific case for random forest} \end{cases} \quad (23)$$

where T^{EPM}—model fitting time estimation (represented in ms according to the scale of coefficients from Table 2), N_{obs}—number of observations in the sample, N_{feat}—number of features in the sample. The characteristics of the computational resources and hyperparameters of the model are considered as static in this case.

We applied the least squared errors (LSE) algorithm to (23) and obtained the Θ coefficients for the set of models that presented Table 2. The coefficient of determination R^2 is used to evaluate the quality of obtained performance models.

Table 2. The examples of coefficients for the different performance models.

ML Model	$\Theta_1 \cdot 10^4$	$\Theta_2 \cdot 10^3$	R^2
LDA	2.9790	3.1590	0.9983
QDA	1.9208	3.1012	0.9989
Naive Bayes for Bernoulli models	1.3440	3.3120	0.9986
Decision tree	31.110	4.1250	0.9846
PCA	3.1291	2.4174	0.9992
Logistic regression	9.3590	2.3900	0.9789
Random forest	$-94.42 \cdot 10^4$	$2.507 \cdot 10^8$	0.9279

The application of the evolutionary optimization to the benchmark allows finding the optimal structure of the composite model for the specific problem. We demonstrate EPM constructing for the composite model which consists of logistic regression and random forest as a primary nodes and logistic regression as a secondary node. On the basis of (11), EPM for this composite model can be represented as follows:

$$T^{EPM}_{Add} = max(\Theta_{1,1} N_{obs} N_{feat} + \Theta_{2,1} N_{obs}, \Theta^1_{1,2} N_{obs} N_{feat} + \Theta_{2,2} N_{obs}) + \frac{N_{obs}}{\Theta^2_{1,3}} + \frac{N^2_{obs} N_{feat}}{\Theta^2_{2,3}}, \quad (24)$$

where T_{Add}^{EPM}—composite model fitting time estimated by the additive EMP, Θ_i, j-i coefficient of j model type for EPM according to the Table 2.

The performance model for the composite model with three nodes (LR + RF = LR) is shown in Figure 17. The visualizations for the atomic models are available in Appendix A.

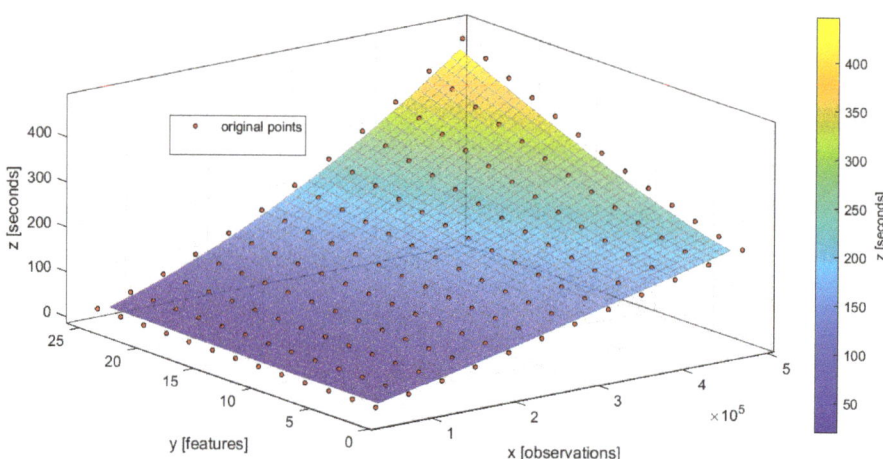

Figure 17. Predictions of the performance model that uses an additive approach for local empirical performance models (EPMs) of atomic models. The red points represent the real evaluations of the composite model as a part of validation.

The RMSE (root-mean-squared-error) measure is used to evaluate the quality of chain EPM evaluation against real measurements. In this case, the obtained $RMSE = 21.3$ s confirms the good quality of obtained estimation in an observed 0–400 seconds range.

6. Discussion and Future Works

In a wider sense co-design problem may be solved as an iterative procedure that includes additional tuning during the model execution stage and a cyclic closure (or re-building stage) with respect to time evolution. Re-building stage may be initiated by two types of events: (1) model error overcomes acceptable threshold e_c; (2) execution time overcomes acceptable threshold τ_c. In this case a solution is to build the new model with respect to corrected set of structures $\tilde{S}$ and performance model $\tilde{T}_M$:

$$p'^{min}(M^*, t) > \rho_c, \; T_{ex}^{min} > \tau_c, \; \tilde{p}^{min}(M^{**}, t) = \max_{\tilde{M}} F'(\tilde{M}, t | \; \tilde{T}_M \leq \tau_c, T_{gen} \leq \tau_g), \quad (25)$$

where t is a variable of real time and ρ_c is a critical threshold for values of error function E. Such a problem is typical for models that are connected with a lifecycle of their prototype, e.g., models inside digital shadow for industrial system [47], weather forecasting models [48], etc.

Additional fitting of co-designed system may appear also on the level of model execution where classic scheduling approach may be blended with model tuning. Classic formulation of scheduling for resource intensive applications $T_{ex}^{min}(L^*) = \min_{A} G'(L|M, I)$ is based on idea of optimization search for such algorithm L^* that helps to provide minimal computation time T_{ex}^{min} for model execution process through balanced schedules of workload on computation nodes. However, such approach is restricted by assumption of uniform performance models for all parts of application. In real cases performance of application may change dynamically in time and among functional parts. Thus, to reach more effective execution it is desirable to formulate optimization problem with respect to possibility of tuning model characteristics that influence on model performance:

$$T_{ex}^{max}\left(\left\{a_{1:|S|}\right\}^*, L^*\right) = \max_{a,L} G\left(M\left(\left\{a_{1:|S|}\right\}\right), L|I\right), \quad M = S^*, E^*, \left\{a_{1:|S|}\right\}, \quad L = \{L_m\}, \quad (26)$$

where G is objective function that characterize expected time of model execution with respect to used scheduling algorithm L and model M. In the context of generative modeling problem on the stage of execution model M can be fully described as a set of model properties that consists of optimal model structure: optimal functions S^* (from previous stage) and additional set of performance influential parameters $\{a_{1:|S|}\}$. Reminiscent approaches can be seen in several publications, e.g., [49].

7. Conclusions

In this paper, we aimed to highlight the different aspects of the creation of mathematical models using automated evolutionary learning approach. Such approach may be represented from the perspective of generative design and co-design for mathematical models. First of all, we formalize several actual and unsolved issues that exist in the field of generative design of mathematical models. They are devoted to different aspects: computational complexity, performance modeling, parallelization, interaction with the infrastructure, etc. The set of experiments was conducted as proof-of-concept solutions for every announced issue and obstacle. The composite ML models obtained by the FEDOT framework and differential equation-based models obtained by the EPDE framework were used as case studies. Finally, the common concepts of the co-design implementation were discussed.

Author Contributions: Conceptualization, A.V.K. and A.B.; Investigation, N.O.N., A.H., M.M. and M.Y.; Methodology, A.V.K.; Project administration, A.B.; Software, N.O.N., A.H., and M.M.; Supervision, A.B.; Validation, M.M.; Visualization, M.Y.; Writing–original draft, A.V.K., N.O.N. and A.H. All authors have read and agreed to the final publication of the manuscript.

Funding: This research is financially supported by the Ministry of Science and Higher Education, Agreement #075-15-2020-808.

Conflicts of Interest: The authors declare no conflict of interest.

Abbreviations

The following abbreviations are used in this manuscript:

AI	Artificial intelligence
ANN	Artificial neural network
AutoML	Automated machine learning
DAG	Directed acyclic graph
EPM	Empirical performance model
GPU	Graphics processing unit
ML	Machine learning
MSE	Mean squared error
NAS	Neural architecture search
ODE	Ordinary differential equation
PDE	Partial differential equation
PM	Performance model
R^2	Coefficient of determination
RMSE	Root mean square error
ROC AUC	Area under receiver operating characteristic curve

Appendix A. Additional Details on the Empirical Performance Models Validation

The validation of different EPM for the set of the atomic models (that was noted in Table 2) is presented in Table A1. R^2 and RMSE metrics are used to compare the predictions of EPM and real measurements of the fitting time. The obtained results confirm that the linear EPM with two terms is most suitable for most of the ML models used in the experiments. However, the fitting time for some models (e.g., random forest) is represented better by the more specific EPM. The one-term EPM provides a lower quality than more complex analogs.

Table A1. Approximation errors for the different empirical performance models' structures obtained for the atomic ML models. The best suitable structure is highlighted with bold.

Model	$\Theta_1 N_{obs} N_{feat}$		$\Theta_1 N_{obs} N_{feat} + \Theta_2 N_{obs}$		$\frac{N_{obs}}{\Theta_1} + \frac{N_{obs}^2 N_{feat}}{\Theta_2}$	
	RMSE, s	R^2	RMSE, s	R^2	RMSE, s	R^2
LDA	0.35	0.92	**0.11**	**0.99**	0.66	0.74
QDA	0.75	0.57	**0.03**	**0.99**	0.93	0.36
Naive Bayes	0.82	0.42	**0.04**	**0.99**	0.961	0.21
Decision tree	1.48	0.98	**1.34**	**0.98**	3.49	0.89
PCA	0.28	0.78	**0.04**	**0.99**	0.28	0.95
Logit	0.54	0.91	**0.37**	**0.96**	0.95	0.75
Random forest	96.81	0.60	26.50	0.71	**21.36**	**0.92**

The visualization of the performance models predictions for the different cases is presented in Figure A1. It confirms that the selected EPMs allow estimating the fitting time quite reliably.

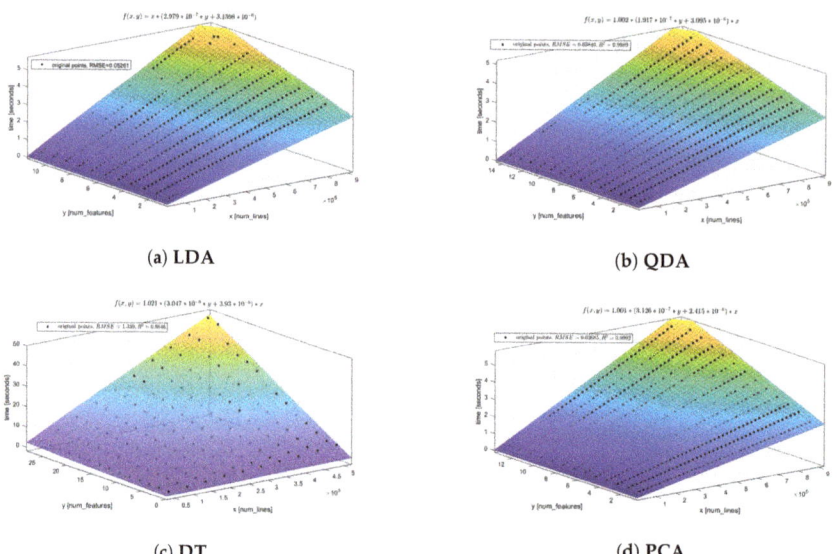

(a) LDA   (b) QDA

(c) DT   (d) PCA

Figure A1. Cont.

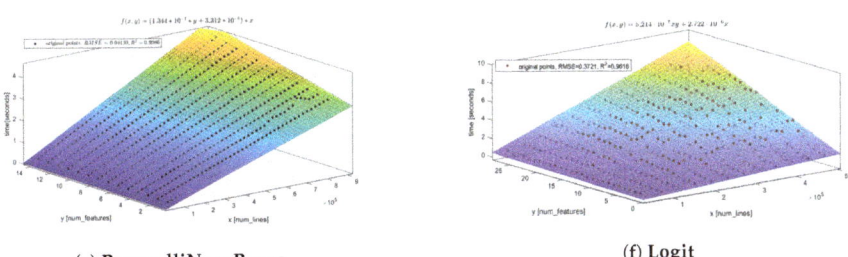

(e) BernoulliNaveBayes (f) Logit

Figure A1. The empirical performance models for the different atomic models: LDA, QDA, Decision Tree (DT), PCA dimensionality reduction model, Bernoulli Naïve Bayes model, logistic regression. The heatmap represent the prediction of EPM and the black points are real measurements.

References

1. Packard, N.; Bedau, M.A.; Channon, A.; Ikegami, T.; Rasmussen, S.; Stanley, K.; Taylor, T. *Open-Ended Evolution and Open-Endedness: Editorial Introduction to the Open-Ended Evolution I Special Issue*; MIT Press: Cambridge, MA, USA, 2019.
2. Krish, S. A practical generative design method. *Comput.-Aided Des.* **2011**, *43*, 88–100. [CrossRef]
3. Ferreira, C. *Gene Expression Programming: Mathematical Modeling by an Artificial Intelligence*; Springer: Berlin/Heidelberg, Germany, 2006; Volume 21.
4. Pavlyshenko, B. Using stacking approaches for machine learning models. In Proceedings of the 2018 IEEE Second International Conference on Data Stream Mining & Processing (DSMP), Lviv, Ukraine, 21–25 August 2018; pp. 255–258.
5. Kovalchuk, S.V.; Metsker, O.G.; Funkner, A.A.; Kisliakovskii, I.O.; Nikitin, N.O.; Kalyuzhnaya, A.V.; Vaganov, D.A.; Bochenina, K.O. A conceptual approach to complex model management with generalized modelling patterns and evolutionary identification. *Complexity* **2018**, *2018*, 5870987. [CrossRef]
6. Kalyuzhnaya, A.V.; Nikitin, N.O.; Vychuzhanin, P.; Hvatov, A.; Boukhanovsky, A. Automatic evolutionary learning of composite models with knowledge enrichment. In Proceedings of the 2020 Genetic and Evolutionary Computation Conference Companion, Cancun, Mexico, 8–12 July 2020; pp. 43–44.
7. Lecomte, S.; Guillouard, S.; Moy, C.; Leray, P.; Soulard, P. A co-design methodology based on model driven architecture for real time embedded systems. *Math. Comput. Model.* **2011**, *53*, 471–484. [CrossRef]
8. He, X.; Zhao, K.; Chu, X. AutoML: A Survey of the State-of-the-Art. *arXiv* **2019**, arXiv:1908.00709.
9. Caldwell, J.; Ram, Y.M. *Mathematical Modelling: Concepts and Case Studies*; Springer Science & Business Media: Berlin/Heidelberg, Germany, 2013; Volume 6.
10. Banwarth-Kuhn, M.; Sindi, S. How and why to build a mathematical model: A case study using prion aggregation. *J. Biol. Chem.* **2020**, *295*, 5022–5035. [CrossRef] [PubMed]
11. Castillo, O.; Melin, P. Automated mathematical modelling for financial time series prediction using fuzzy logic, dynamical systems and fractal theory. In Proceedings of the IEEE/IAFE 1996 Conference on Computational Intelligence for Financial Engineering (CIFEr), New York City, NY, USA, 24–26 March 1996; pp. 120–126.
12. Kevrekidis, I.G.; Gear, C.W.; Hyman, J.M.; Kevrekidid, P.G.; Runborg, O.; Theodoropoulos, C. Equation-free, coarse-grained multiscale computation: Enabling mocroscopic simulators to perform system-level analysis. *Commun. Math. Sci.* **2003**, *1*, 715–762.
13. Schmidt, M.; Lipson, H. Distilling free-form natural laws from experimental data. *Science* **2009**, *324*, 81–85. [CrossRef]
14. Kondrashov, D.; Chekroun, M.D.; Ghil, M. Data-driven non-Markovian closure models. *Phys. D Nonlinear Phenom.* **2015**, *297*, 33–55. [CrossRef]
15. Maslyaev, M.; Hvatov, A.; Kalyuzhnaya, A. Data-Driven Partial Derivative Equations Discovery with Evolutionary Approach. In *International Conference on Computational Science*; Springer: Berlin/Heidelberg, Germany, 2019; pp. 635–641.
16. Qi, F.; Xia, Z.; Tang, G.; Yang, H.; Song, Y.; Qian, G.; An, X.; Lin, C.; Shi, G. A Graph-based Evolutionary Algorithm for Automated Machine Learning. *Softw. Eng. Rev.* **2020**, *1*, 10–37686.
17. Olson, R.S.; Bartley, N.; Urbanowicz, R.J.; Moore, J.H. Evaluation of a tree-based pipeline optimization tool for automating data science. In Proceedings of the Genetic and Evolutionary Computation Conference, New York, NY, USA, 20–24 July 2016; pp. 485–492.
18. Zhao, H. High Performance Machine Learning through Codesign and Rooflining. Ph.D. Thesis, UC Berkeley, Berkeley, CA, USA, 2014.
19. Amid, A.; Kwon, K.; Gholami, A.; Wu, B.; Asanović, K.; Keutzer, K. Co-design of deep neural nets and neural net accelerators for embedded vision applications. *IBM J. Res. Dev.* **2019**, *63*, 6:1–6:14. [CrossRef]
20. Li, Y.; Park, J.; Alian, M.; Yuan, Y.; Qu, Z.; Pan, P.; Wang, R.; Schwing, A.; Esmaeilzadeh, H.; Kim, N.S. A network-centric hardware/algorithm co-design to accelerate distributed training of deep neural networks. In Proceedings of the 2018 51st Annual IEEE/ACM International Symposium on Microarchitecture (MICRO), Fukuoka, Japan, 20–24 October 2018; pp. 175–188.

21. Bertels, K. *Hardware/Software Co-Design for Heterogeneous Multi-Core Platforms*; Springer: Berlin/Heidelberg, Germany, 2012.
22. Wang, K.; Liu, Z.; Lin, Y.; Lin, J.; Han, S. HAQ: Hardware-Aware Automated Quantization With Mixed Precision. In Proceedings of the IEEE Conference on Computer Vision and Pattern Recognition (CVPR), Long Beach, CA, USA, 16–20 June 2019.
23. Cai, H.; Zhu, L.; Han, S. Proxylessnas: Direct neural architecture search on target task and hardware. *arXiv* **2018**, arXiv:1812.00332.
24. Dosanjh, S.S.; Barrett, R.F.; Doerfler, D.; Hammond, S.D.; Hemmert, K.S.; Heroux, M.A.; Lin, P.T.; Pedretti, K.T.; Rodrigues, A.F.; Trucano, T. Exascale design space exploration and co-design. *Future Gener. Comput. Syst.* **2014**, *30*, 46–58. [CrossRef]
25. Gramacy, R.B.; Lee, H.K. Adaptive Design of Supercomputer Experiments. 2018. Available online: http://citeseerx.ist.psu.edu/viewdoc/download?doi=10.1.1.312.3750&rep=rep1&type=pdf (accessed on 26 December 2020).
26. Glinskiy, B.; Kulikov, I.; Snytnikov, A.V.; Chernykh, I.; Weins, D.V. A multilevel approach to algorithm and software design for exaflops supercomputers. *Numer. Methods Program.* **2015**, *16*, 543–556.
27. Kaltenecker, C. Comparison of Analytical and Empirical Performance Models: A Case Study on Multigrid Systems. Master's Thesis, University of Passau, Passau, Germany, 2016.
28. Calotoiu, A. Automatic Empirical Performance Modeling of Parallel Programs. Ph.D. Thesis, Technische Universität, Berlin, Germany, 2018.
29. Eggensperger, K.; Lindauer, M.; Hoos, H.H.; Hutter, F.; Leyton-Brown, K. Efficient benchmarking of algorithm configurators via model-based surrogates. *Mach. Learn.* **2018**, *107*, 15–41. [CrossRef]
30. Chirkin, A.M.; Belloum, A.S.; Kovalchuk, S.V.; Makkes, M.X.; Melnik, M.A.; Visheratin, A.A.; Nasonov, D.A. Execution time estimation for workflow scheduling. *Future Gener. Comput. Syst.* **2017**, *75*, 376–387. [CrossRef]
31. Gamatié, A.; An, X.; Zhang, Y.; Kang, A.; Sassatelli, G. Empirical model-based performance prediction for application mapping on multicore architectures. *J. Syst. Archit.* **2019**, *98*, 1–16. [CrossRef]
32. Shi, Z.; Dongarra, J.J. Scheduling workflow applications on processors with different capabilities. *Future Gener. Comput. Syst.* **2006**, *22*, 665–675. [CrossRef]
33. Visheratin, A.A.; Melnik, M.; Nasonov, D.; Butakov, N.; Boukhanovsky, A.V. Hybrid scheduling algorithm in early warning systems. *Future Gener. Comput. Syst.* **2018**, *79*, 630–642. [CrossRef]
34. Melnik, M.; Nasonov, D. Workflow scheduling using Neural Networks and Reinforcement Learning. *Procedia Comput. Sci.* **2019**, *156*, 29–36. [CrossRef]
35. Olson, R.S.; Moore, J.H. TPOT: A tree-based pipeline optimization tool for automating machine learning. *Proc. Mach. Learn. Res.* **2016**, *64*, 66–74.
36. Evans, L.; Society, A.M. *Partial Differential Equations*; Graduate Studies in Mathematics; American Mathematical Society: Providence, RI, USA, 1998.
37. Czarnecki, W.M.; Osindero, S.; Jaderberg, M.; Swirszcz, G.; Pascanu, R. Sobolev training for neural networks. In Proceedings of the Advances in Neural Information Processing Systems 30 (NIPS 2017), Long Beach, CA, USA, 4–9 December 2017; pp. 4278–4287.
38. Raissi, M.; Perdikaris, P.; Karniadakis, G.E. Physics-informed neural networks: A deep learning framework for solving forward and inverse problems involving nonlinear partial differential equations. *J. Comput. Phys.* **2019**, *378*, 686–707. [CrossRef]
39. Epicoco, I.; Mocavero, S.; Porter, A.R.; Pickles, S.M.; Ashworth, M.; Aloisio, G. Hybridisation strategies and data structures for the NEMO ocean model. *Int. J. High Perform. Comput. Appl.* **2018**, *32*, 864–881. [CrossRef]
40. Nikitin, N.O.; Polonskaia, I.S.; Vychuzhanin, P.; Barabanova, I.V.; Kalyuzhnaya, A.V. Structural Evolutionary Learning for Composite Classification Models. *Procedia Comput. Sci.* **2020**, *178*, 414–423. [CrossRef]
41. Full Script That Allows Reproducing the Results Is Available in the GitHub Repository. Available online: https://github.com/ITMO-NSS-team/FEDOT.Algs/blob/master/estar/examples/ann_approximation_experiments.ipynb (accessed on 26 December 2020).
42. Full Script That Allows Reproducing the Results Is Available in the GitHub Repository. Available online: https://github.com/ITMO-NSS-team/FEDOT.Algs/blob/master/estar/examples/Pareto_division.py (accessed on 26 December 2020).
43. Géron, A. *Hands-on Machine Learning with Scikit-Learn, Keras, and TensorFlow: Concepts, Tools, and Techniques to Build Intelligent Systems*; O'Reilly Media: Sebastopol, CA, USA, 2019.
44. Nikitin, N.O.; Vychuzhanin, P.; Hvatov, A.; Deeva, I.; Kalyuzhnaya, A.V.; Kovalchuk, S.V. Deadline-driven approach for multi-fidelity surrogate-assisted environmental model calibration: SWAN wind wave model case study. In Proceedings of the Genetic and Evolutionary Computation Conference Companion, Prague, Czech Republic, 13–17 July 2019; pp. 1583–1591.
45. Olson, R.S.; La Cava, W.; Orzechowski, P.; Urbanowicz, R.J.; Moore, J.H. PMLB: A large benchmark suite for machine learning evaluation and comparison. *BioData Min.* **2017**, *10*, 1–13. [CrossRef]
46. Li, K.; Xiang, Z.; Tan, K.C. Which surrogate works for empirical performance modelling? A case study with differential evolution. In Proceedings of the 2019 IEEE Congress on Evolutionary Computation (CEC), Wellington, New Zealand, 10–13 June 2019; pp. 1988–1995.
47. Bauernhansl, T.; Hartleif, S.; Felix, T. The Digital Shadow of production–A concept for the effective and efficient information supply in dynamic industrial environments. *Procedia CIRP* **2018**, *72*, 69–74. [CrossRef]
48. Cha, D.H.; Wang, Y. A dynamical initialization scheme for real-time forecasts of tropical cyclones using the WRF model. *Mon. Weather Rev.* **2013**, *141*, 964–986. [CrossRef]
49. Melnik, M.; Nasonov, D.A.; Liniov, A. Intellectual Execution Scheme of Iterative Computational Models based on Symbiotic Interaction with Application for Urban Mobility Modelling. *IJCCI* **2019**, *1*, 245–251.

MDPI
St. Alban-Anlage 66
4052 Basel
Switzerland
Tel. +41 61 683 77 34
Fax +41 61 302 89 18
www.mdpi.com

Entropy Editorial Office
E-mail: entropy@mdpi.com
www.mdpi.com/journal/entropy